Secrecy, National Security and the Vindication of Constitutional Law

Edited by

David Cole

Georgetown University Law Center, USA

Federico Fabbrini

Tilburg Law School, The Netherlands

Arianna Vedaschi

Bocconi University, Italy

Edward Elgar

Cheltenham, UK • Northampton, MA, USA

Published by
Edward Elgar Publishing Limited
The Lypiatts
15 Lansdown Road
Cheltenham
Glos GL50 2JA
UK

Edward Elgar Publishing, Inc.
William Pratt House
9 Dewey Court
Northampton
Massachusetts 01060
USA

A catalogue record for this book
is available from the British Library

Library of Congress Control Number: 2012954989

This book is available electronically in the ElgarOnline.com Law Subject Collection, E-ISBN 978 1 78195 386 0

FSC
www.fsc.org
MIX
Paper from
responsible sources
FSC® C018575

ISBN 978 1 78195 385 3

Typeset by Columns Design XML Ltd, Reading
Printed by MPG PRINTGROUP, UK

Contents

Contributors

Ori Aronson is Assistant Professor at Bar-Ilan University Faculty of Law

Kathleen Clark is John S. Lehmann Research Professor of Law at Washington University in St. Louis

David Cole is Professor of Law at Georgetown University Law Center

Deirdre Curtin is Professor of European Law at the University of Amsterdam

Federico Fabbrini holds a Ph.D. in Law from the European University Institute and is Assistant Professor of European & Comparative Constitutional Law at Tilburg Law School

Tobias Fischer is a J.D. candidate at Brooklyn Law School

Lech Garlicki is Professor of Constitutional Law and Justice (retired) at the European Court of Human Rights in Strasbourg

Shiri Krebs is a J.S.D. candidate at Stanford Law School and Teaching Scholar at Santa Clara University

Nino Lomjaria is an LL.M. candidate at Washington University in St. Louis

Andrew Lynch is Professor of Law and Director, Gilbert + Tobin Centre of Public Law at the University of New South Wales

Jason Mazzone is Professor of Law and Lynn H. Murray Faculty Scholar in Law at the University of Illinois

Cian C. Murphy is a Lecturer at King's College London

Tuomas Ojanen is Professor of Constitutional Law at the University of Helsinki and Member of the Centre of Excellence (CoE) in Research in the Foundations of European Law and Polity, funded by the Academy of Finland

Kent Roach is Professor of Law and Prichard Wilson Chair in Law and Public Policy at the University of Toronto. He is a former member of the research advisory committee of Canada's Arar Inquiry and former Director of Research (Legal Studies) of its Air India Inquiry

Martin Scheinin is Professor of Public International Law at the European University Institute and President of the International Association of Constitutional Law. He is the former UN Special Rapporteur on the promotion and protection of human rights and fundamental freedoms while countering terrorism

Stephen Schulhofer is Robert B. McKay Professor of Law at NYU

Stephen Sedley is Lord Justice (retired) of the Court of Appeals for England and Wales

Sudha Setty is Professor of Law at Western New England University School of Law

Tamara Tulich is a Ph.D. candidate at the University of New South Wales

Mindia Vashakmadze, Dr. Iur., is Senior Research Fellow at the Max Planck Foundation for International Peace and the Rule of Law

Arianna Vedaschi is Associate Professor of Constitutional Law at Bocconi University

Stephen I. Vladeck is Professor of Law at the American University Washington College of Law

Clive Walker is Professor of Law at the Centre for Criminal Justice Studies, University of Leeds School of Law

Rebecca Welsh is a Ph.D. candidate at the University of New South Wales

Foreword

Martin Scheinin

It gives me much pleasure to be in a position to recommend this collection of essays to anyone interested in constitutional law, counter-terrorism measures, national security or questions of secrecy and accountability. The various chapters included provide a multifaceted, balanced and highly rewarding analysis of the issues and their intersections.

The semi-autonomous research group on 'Constitutional Responses to Terrorism', acting under the auspices of the International Association of Constitutional Law (IACL) has become a great success, particularly thanks to its chair, Professor David Cole, and coordinator, Federico Fabbrini, PhD. This volume of excellent studies is a direct consequence of the operation of the research group and the level of scholarly networking created through it.

The question of secrecy, usually on grounds related to national security, in the context of countering terrorism is one of the most intriguing legal issues that have gained unprecedented importance in our post-9/11 world of global terrorism and global counter-terrorism cooperation. While no constitutional lawyer can deny that the threat of terrorism is real, or that there are situations where it is legitimate to accompany counter-terrorism measures with a degree of secrecy, it is nevertheless the task of this group of professionals to guard constitutionalism against the threat of erosion posed by various deviations from principles of rule of law, transparency and accountability. Therefore, it is also their task to propose solutions that do provide effective responses to terrorism while not sacrificing constitutionalism.

Both in my capacity as an academic scholar[1] and as former United Nations Special Rapporteur on human rights and counter-

[1] See Lisa Ginsborg and Martin Scheinin, 'You Can't Always Get What You Want: The Kadi II Conundrum and the Security Council 1267 Terrorist Sanctions Regime', Essex Human Rights Review, vol. 8 (2011) 7–19, and Martin Scheinin, 'Is the ECJ Ruling in Kadi Incompatible with International Law?' in Yearbook of European Law, vol. 28 (2009) 637–53.

terrorism,[2] I have addressed some major problems in the current international regime of terrorist listings. Through its so-called 1267 Committee, the Security Council continues to list individuals and entities as terrorists associated with Al-Qaida, and to utilize its powers under Chapter VII of the UN Charter to impose upon all states the obligation to implement sanctions against those on the list, including a travel ban and the freezing of assets.[3] Secrecy is one of the fundamental problems in that listing regime. The listing is decided behind closed doors by 15 diplomatic representatives of those states that constitute the Security Council. There are no hearings and no access to judicial review. The threshold for listing is consensus within a political body and therefore not a question of evidence. By and large, the information used by individual states, when forming their own position about the listing of an individual or entity, would be gathered through intelligence and be classified in nature. What is worse is that the actual information is not necessarily shared even within the Security Council, as the mere composition of that body will always cause limits upon the free flow of information between the involved states. Hence, access by national or regional courts to the 'evidence' used by the Security Council cannot be the solution to the various problems related to the terrorist listings. While the creation of the office of a Delisting Ombudsperson[4] and the subsequent extension of the powers of the Ombudsperson[5] are certainly positive steps that subject the terrorist listings to a degree of independent review, these measures will remain insufficient as long as the member states of the Security Council retain the possibility to overrule the delisting proposal by the Ombudsperson.[6]

Let me also refer to those reports where the Special Rapporteur has addressed the role of intelligence agencies and their oversight mechanisms in counter-terrorism measures. Following a 2009 report to the

---

[2] See, in particular, the 2006 and 2010 reports by the Special Rapporteur to the UN General Assembly, UN documents A/61/267 and A/65/258, respectively. See, also, the 2011 report to the Human Rights Council, A/HRC/16/51.

[3] The terrorist listing regime was originally created through Security Council Resolution 1267 (1999) to enable sanctions against the Taleban regime of Afghanistan. Through Resolution 1390 (2002) it was expanded into a global list of Al-Qaida and Taleban terrorists. After Resolution 1989 (2011) the original 1267 regime only applies to persons or entities associated with Al-Qaida.

[4] See, Resolution 1904 (2009).

[5] Resolution 1989 (2011).

[6] See, Resolution 1989 (2011), paras. 21 and 23.

Human Rights Council in the issue,[7] the Special Rapporteur was requested to produce a compilation of good practice in the area of intelligence and intelligence oversight. The resulting 2010 report, 'Compilation of good practices on legal and institutional frameworks and measures that ensure respect for human rights by intelligence agencies while countering terrorism'[8] dismisses the approach of secret regulations in the field of intelligence, identifying as good practice that the operation of intelligence agencies must be based on publicly available laws.[9] While the need for confidentiality of classified information is acknowledged,[10] the report proposes that intelligence agencies are subject to a combination of multiple oversight mechanisms[11] that have, inter alia, full access to information.[12] A set of good practices was identified specifically in the area of data protection, addressing also the question of limiting access by the concerned individual to data related to himself or herself, and what complementary mechanisms may be put in place to secure the rule of law and accountability.[13]

The authors and editors of this volume are to be congratulated for taking the discussion further. The answer to the dilemma between transparency and the protection of information vital to national security is not in bypassing constitutional standards or international human rights. Rather, the answer is in more attention to constitutional law, and in making the law better so that it will provide effective tools against terrorism without compromising the principles of constitutionalism.

Florence, 12 July 2012

---

7 UN document A/HRC/10/3.

8 UN document A/HRC/14/46.

9 Practice 4. All intelligence services are constituted through, and operate under, publicly available laws that comply with the Constitution and international human rights law. Intelligence services can only undertake or be instructed to undertake activities that are prescribed by and in accordance with national law. The use of subsidiary regulations that are not publicly available is strictly limited, and such regulations are both authorized by and remain within the parameters of publicly available laws. Regulations that are not made public do not serve as the basis for any activities that restrict human rights.

10 See Practice 8.

11 See Practice 6.

12 See Practices 7 and 10.

13 See Practices 23–6.

1. Introduction

David Cole, Federico Fabbrini and Arianna Vedaschi

No issue more profoundly challenges the commitments of constitutional democracy than secrecy in government. Representative democracy and the rule of law both require transparency and accountability, and secrecy strikes at the heart of both values. When government officials engage in secret actions on behalf of the state, they generally cannot be held accountable to the people for whom they purportedly act. What does it mean to have a government under law if it can act in ways that are effectively immune from legal regulation? Moreover, when the government's actions affect the life, liberty, or property interests of individuals, secret actions – or public actions justified on the basis of secret evidence – threaten to undermine basic protections of procedural fairness. How can one defend oneself against a case that is not disclosed?

At the same time, secrecy is essential to effective governance, nowhere more so than in the arena of national security. Even where national security is not at issue, much of the work government does occurs behind closed doors – including, for example, the deliberations of courts. If governance had to be conducted entirely in the open, it would be impossible to get candid advice, and thus most legal systems recognize the validity of privileges that keep confidential many of the internal discussions that inform government actions. Where the police are investigating crime, secrecy is also often essential, so as not to tip off those who may be under suspicion. When the crimes being investigated are not just any crimes, but crimes that seek to spread terror through the civilian population so as to undermine the government itself, the need for secrecy is still higher. When matters rise to the level of an armed conflict, as they did in Afghanistan and the border regions of Pakistan after the terrorist attacks of September 11, 2001, the demands of secrecy reach their highest intensity.

In short, constitutional democracies cannot live with secrecy, but cannot live without it either. Secrecy is a necessary part of governance, and in particular of the state's efforts to keep its citizens secure from threats posed by others. At the same time, secrecy directly undermines the representative validity of the government to the extent that it impedes citizens' ability to know what their government is doing and thereby to assess whether it is consistent with their own goals and ideals.

Every democracy faces these issues, and as many of the contributions to this volume underscore, most democracies are confronting them more frequently and in a wider range of settings in the twenty-first century than ever before. What was unthinkable before Al Qaeda's terrorist attack on United States (US) civilians on September 11, 2001, is now thinkable. The transnational nature of the threat posed by Al Qaeda, a loosely organized movement that spans many countries, means that inter-state coordination and intelligence sharing is essential to identifying and neutralizing the threat. The condition of cooperation is often a promise of confidentiality, thus multiplying the potential grounds for secrecy claims. Thus, the United Kingdom (UK) may refuse to disclose information not because it considers it a secret, but because the US considers it a secret and shared it with the UK only on condition that the UK also treat it as secret.

The challenges posed by secrecy are not unique or *sui generis*. They are largely the same across democracies world-wide. Thus, we all have a lot to learn from each other, and from how different democracies have sought to strike a balance between transparency and confidentiality, between due process and secret evidence, between executive discretion and accountable, checked government. The contributions to this volume explore these questions from a multiplicity of perspectives, drawing on experiences from many jurisdictions, including Australia, Canada, the European Union (EU), Finland, Germany, India, Israel, Italy, the UK and the US. Comparative constitutionalism across so many jurisdictions is often made difficult by the substantial differences in legal culture, governmental structure, and the like. But on the issues of secrecy, what emerges is a common set of problems, and common attempts to address those problems. There are many differences, to be sure. But this is an area where cross-national learning and borrowing may be especially fruitful, precisely because the problems are so common.

This book, which developed from a conference held at the Bocconi University in Milan in December 2011, sponsored by the International Association of Constitutional Law Research Group on 'Constitutional Responses to Terrorism', is divided into five parts. Parts 1 and 2 address the issue of secrecy from an institutional point of view, examining the capacity of courts and legislatures to control the use and prevent the abuse of secrecy claims by the executive branch in national security contexts. After this broad perspective, focused on questions of structural relations, Parts 3, 4 and 5 focus on three substantive areas of anti-terrorism law – detention, criminal trials and administrative measures – and explore how in each of these cases assertions of secrecy and national security distort the functioning of the legal system and can undermine fundamental principles of procedural justice and fairness.

Part 1 begins with a chapter by Lord Justice Stephen Sedley, on the role of the judiciary in the oversight of secrecy in the UK. Lord Sedley, a retired judge of the Court of Appeal of England and Wales, examines a number of key decisions by British courts, including several cases in which he was directly involved as a judge, and explains how, over the last decade, the British judiciary has attempted to improve its standards of procedural justice, constraining the recourse by the government to secret evidence in a variety of settings. His contribution emphasizes the fundamental roles that the jurisprudence of the European Court of Human Rights (ECtHR) and of the European Court of Justice (ECJ) have had on the position of British courts, often forcing the UK Supreme Court to overrule the deferential decisions of lower courts. Nevertheless, Lord Sedley concludes his essay with a sober note on the UK government's 2011 proposal, initially contained in a 'Green Paper' entitled *Justice and Security*, to expand the use of classified evidence and cleared counsel – a development he regards as fundamentally incompatible with the principles of the British Constitution.

The role of the judiciary in checking abuse of secrecy is also at the core of the chapters by Stephen Schulhofer and Mindia Vashakmadze, focusing respectively on the US and Germany. Stephen Schulhofer's contribution examines the three main legal regimes for judicial oversight of secrecy in the US: the Classified Information Procedure Act (CIPA), applicable in criminal cases; the 'state secrets' privilege, which operates primarily in civil damages suits; and the Freedom of Information Act (FOIA), a statute that grants citizens the right to obtain official documents from their government, but contains many exemptions that preserve secrecy. While Schulhofer regards the CIPA and FOIA regimes as granting more adequate instruments of review to US courts, he concludes that executive branch demands for deference generally inhibit the willingness of the judiciary to use their existing capacities effectively to oversee executive recourse to secrecy. He advances a plea for a reconsideration of the role of courts in the field of national security, based on a more informed understanding of the characteristics of judicial expertise and of the comparative advantage of courts vis-à-vis the other branches of government in balancing security needs with public interest values.

A more optimistic assessment of the willingness of courts to rein in executive abuse of secrecy emerges from Mindia Vashakmadze's analysis of the jurisprudence of the German Constitutional Court (GCC). As Vashakmadze accounts, the GCC has, albeit with some limits, reinforced the right of the German Parliament to obtain classified information from the executive and at the same time annulled legislation which unduly restricted privacy rights in the interests of surveillance and public safety. Part 1 concludes with a chapter by Sudha Setty, which offers a worrying comparative summary of the institutional weakness of the judiciary as a counter-weight to governmental claims of secrecy in the field of counter-terrorism. Surveying the practice of courts in the US, the UK, Israel and India, Setty reveals substantial limitations in the capacity of courts to provide relief, even to individuals subject to the most disgraceful human rights abuses, when governments invoke the state secrets privilege. While formalistic reasoning discarding review of secrecy claims appears to be at its height in the US and India, Setty suggests that structural reforms would be needed in most legal systems to invert the trend of judicial deference vis-à-vis the executive when reasons of secrecy are asserted to thwart litigation.

In light of the difficulties encountered by the judiciary in overseeing recourse by the executive branch to secrecy, Part 2 explores the potential role played by legislatures. Kathleen Clark and Nino Lomjaria compare legislative access to intelligence information in the US and Canada. The US and Canada have different institutional regimes: while the latter is a parliamentary system, the former is characterized by separated institutions sharing power. As Clark and Lomjaria's chapter emphasizes, legislatures tend to be more effective in controlling the executive branch in separation-of-powers systems than in parliamentary systems. Nevertheless, the US Congress faces significant practical difficulties in accessing and managing intelligence information that may significantly limit its capacity to operate as an effective check on executive agencies.

Analyzing the state secrets privilege in Italy, Arianna Vedaschi identifies a potential expansion of it use through Prime Ministerial decrees, which are exempt from parliamentary review. Vedaschi maintains that this expansive trend is neither lawful nor consistent with the fact that secrecy is a constitutional exception and should therefore not permit expansive interpretations and applications. In addition, Vedaschi criticizes both the weakness of parliamentary scrutiny and the excessively cautious approach adopted by the Italian Constitutional Court in overseeing the state secrets privilege. The political dynamics at play in Italy's parliamentary system have substantially reduced the incentive for the Parliamentary Committee to scrutinize the use of the state secrets privilege, while at the same time the Constitutional Court has so far failed to exercise judicial review. Vedaschi concludes her contribution with a plea for more robust oversight – a recommendation, however, that in its most recent rulings the Italian Constitutional Court has failed to follow.

Part 3 turns to an analysis of secrecy in a number of distinct substantive national security settings, and particularly to an evaluation of the consequences of procedures relying on secret evidence for the protection of due process. As Kent Roach explains, the need to protect secret information existed already during the Cold War. Nevertheless, the use of secrecy has widely expanded since 9/11, triggering a number of unprecedented problems. Secret information is used to justify military and immigration detention, to blacklist individuals suspected of financing terrorism and freeze their assets and, more recently, even to decide targeted killings with drones. At the same time, as Roach accounts, secrecy is not static: national governments and international institutions gather and share information in dynamic and polycentric ways. This raises entirely new challenges. As Roach says, information that originates in a dark torture cell in one part of the world can be transmitted and cause secrecy-based legal and political decisions in Washington and London. In this context, a particularly worrying development is the use of secret evidence to justify detention or other restrictive measures on the personal liberty of individuals – a theme at the heart of the chapters by Shiri Krebs and Andrew Lynch, Tamara Tulich and Rebecca Welsh.

Shiri Krebs's contribution focuses on the use of secret evidence in preventive detention in Israel. Her chapter defies conventional wisdom on the jurisprudence of the Israeli Supreme Court and reveals a worrying picture of widespread acceptance of secret evidence as a justification for administrative detention. On the basis of the analysis of hundreds of court cases between 2000 and 2010, Krebs lifts the veil of secrecy that surrounds judicial proceedings reviewing the lawfulness of security detentions and provides a useful glimpse into the dynamics that drive judicial oversight, casting some doubts about the capacity of courts to uphold core due process values when directly assessing secret evidence in an inquisitorial way. Andrew Lynch, Tamara Tulich and Rebecca Welsh's chapter compares the use of control orders based on secret evidence in the UK and Australia. As the authors explain, control orders cause a profound restriction on personal freedom, amounting to a form of quasi-detention. Yet, judicial review of control orders based on secret evidence has been at best uneven in both countries. As Lynch, Tulich and Welsh argue, UK courts have been more demanding in pushing for disclosure of secret evidence through special advocates, mostly because of the pressures of the ECtHR, while Australian courts lacked analogous capacity, thus raising serious concerns about the vulnerability of constitutional values.

Wrapping up the themes addressed throughout Part 3 is the contribution by David Cole and Steve Vladeck, which offers a comprehensive analytical framework on the use of secret evidence and cleared counsel in detention proceedings. By comparing the US, the UK and Canada, Cole and Vladeck explain how all three countries have faced the challenge raised by the use of secret evidence to deprive individuals of their liberty and have addressed it through the use of cleared counsel (i.e. attorneys with special permission to access security files). Yet each country has adopted distinct practices with respect to the limits on, and powers of, these cleared counsel. The authors compare the cleared counsel models in place in the US for the Guantanamo proceeding, in the UK for the adoption of control orders and in Canada for immigration proceedings and underline the advantages and the disadvantages that each model has vis-à-vis the others. Moreover, after demonstrating that all three countries are governed by common constitutional principles of due process and fair justice, Cole and Vladeck argue that each country could – and indeed, as a constitutional matter, should – borrow from the experiences of the others to improve the fairness of the proceedings without undermining legitimate security concerns.

Part 4 focuses on the role of secrecy in criminal trials. Jason Mazzone and Tobias Fischer explore the use of anonymous testimony in criminal trials and the implications that a normalization of this practice may have. The authors compare the increasing use of anonymous testimony in recent years in three common law countries, the UK, Australia and New Zealand, and discuss the advantages and disadvantages that the institutionalization of a practice that remains exceptional elsewhere, such as in the US, may have. In their account, Mazzone and Fischer refrain from providing definitive answers to the question whether normalization of anonymous testimony should be encouraged or resisted but clearly illustrate the competing interests at stake in the debate, thus opening an important avenue of research on how to balance transparency and secrecy in criminal law. Clive Walker's contribution analyzes the role that secrecy has played in the criminal prosecution of suspected terrorists in the UK legal system, as well as the range of constitutional and international law questions that the UK's increasing reliance on secret evidence has raised.

Ori Aronson, instead, compares the use of military tribunals in the US and Israel and discusses what may be the hidden significance of a resort to adjudicatory bodies that operate outside the ordinary judicial system (founded on principles of transparency and open justice) and instead follow a logic of secrecy and exceptionality. Drawing on Michel Foucault's notion of *heterotopia* (literally: a diverse place), Aronson argues that the establishment of military tribunals to try national security cases may paradoxically have the effect of making these (apparently invisible) institutions more visible to the public. To substantiate his claim, Aronson contrasts two recent examples – the US decision to try Khalid Sheikh Mohammed in military tribunals and Israel's decision to prosecute Marwan Barghouti in civilian courts – and suggest that the former may have had the effect of securing much more visibility to the trial than the latter. Aronson's philosophical and multidisciplinary perspective aims to enrich our understanding of the complex interplay of secrecy and constitutional values.

Part 5 addresses the use of secrecy in administrative counter-terrorism measures. As Tuomas Ojanen explains in his contribution, an increasing resort to administrative measures has taken place in the last few years to tackle the threat of national and international terrorism. Administrative measures have a number of advantages: they are preventive in character; they can generally be adopted by the executive with lighter standards of proof; and they do not require prior judicial involvement or adversarial proceedings. For these reasons, they can be a flexible, proactive instrument to fight terrorism. Yet administrative measures have profound repercussions on the constitutional rights of targeted individuals and entities. Human rights concerns are heightened when administrative measures are based on secret information. In these situations, according to Ojanen, courts should abandon the traditional deference that is adopted in administrative law cases and demand greater disclosure of evidence. Ojanen takes Finland as a case study. Despite its solid tradition of respect for human rights, since 9/11 the Finnish government has increasingly resorted to secrecy in immigration proceedings to justify expulsion of foreign nationals based on national security reasons. Nevertheless, in its most recent case law the Supreme Administrative Court has resisted executive claims of secrecy developing a positive judicial practice against government abuses.

While Ojanen's chapter focuses on the use of secrecy in administrative measures at the *national* level, Cian Murphy considers the issue from a *supranational* perspective. In his chapter, Murphy analyzes the most recent case law of the ECJ on the use of secrecy in counter-terrorism cases and discusses the option of introducing special advocates in EU law – a proposal he regards as unconvincing, given the unsatisfactory experience of special advocates in the UK. Federico Fabbrini takes the topic one step further, by analyzing the interplay between secrecy and administrative measures on a *global* scale. In his chapter, Fabbrini describes the emergence at the level of the United Nations (UN) of an administrative regime to freeze the assets of individuals and entities suspected of financing terrorism and the challenges that judicial review of these measures raises. As Fabbrini explains, courts in the EU have increasingly demanded disclosure of the evidence that is said to justify terrorist listings. Yet, judicially mandated access to classified information has thus far been impossible because the UN itself does not possess the evidence, which is held as secret by individual states, most often the US. Given the central role played by the US in the global fight against terrorism and the similarities between the US and UN sanctions regimes, Fabbrini's chapter explores the possibilities for listed persons to seek due process in US courts, as well as the obstacles that emerge along this road.

The use of secrecy in the administrative arena is also at the core of the last contribution of Part 5: Deirdre Curtin's chapter on secrecy regulation in the EU. Rather than focusing on EU administrative sanctions based on secret evidence and judicial review by the ECJ, Curtin's work adopts an original stand and examines from an institutional point of view the emergence of a web of secret administrative practices within the action of the EU bodies. Building on her previous work on the institutionalization of an executive power in the EU, Curtin examines the expansion of regulatory instruments that provide for the classification of documents and the sharing of confidential information among EU agencies and between the EU institutions and the member states. EU integration in the economic, political and security realm has inevitably increased the need for EU institutions to adopt internal administrative measures to manage and classify information. But Curtin maintains that a risk of overclassification arises from the practice of the EU political branches in the last decades. To counter this development, Curtin argues in favor of stronger oversight by the EU Parliament, whose role ought to be precisely to check the executive branch in the EU separation-of-powers system.

The book concludes with a chapter by Justice Lech Garlicki, whose essay can rightly be considered as a sort of *rapport de synthèse*. Garlicki, until November 2012 a judge and President of Chamber at the ECtHR, offers a historical account of the use of secrecy in political societies and at the same time illuminates the gradual but substantive improvements that constitutional law has made over time to address the challenges that executive assertions of secrecy raise. In particular, according to Garlicki, the emergence of layers of constitutional norms beyond the state has significantly enhanced the protection of core values of constitutionalism, such as transparency, fairness and procedural justice. This is supported by the jurisprudence of the ECtHR, and by its positive influence in many domestic jurisdictions. Garlicki's conclusion thus nicely echoes the opening chapter by Lord Sedley, who expressly acknowledged the lead of the ECtHR in changing the practice of the UK judiciary. As the dialogue between the two judges reminds us, secrecy, national security, and the challenge of assuring fundamentally fair procedures will remain a certain feature of our uncertain era. The chapters in this volume suggest that the vindication of constitutional law will turn on both the comparative study of, and the joint interaction between, national and supranational legal regimes.

PART 1

Secrecy and courts

2. Terrorism and security: back to the future?

Lord Justice (retired) Stephen Sedley

This book will be very different from the book which might have been written ten years ago under the auspices of the International Association of Constitutional Law on the same topic. Then, the world was still reeling from the enormity of Al Qaeda's attack on its arch-enemy, the United States (US). President Bush, like King Lear, was promising to 'do such things…'. What they would be we knew not, though they turned out to include a war on a state which had had nothing to do with the attack, stimulating a still unsatisfied appetite for enforced regime change. They have also more recently come to include the use of transnational assassination, with major implications for international law as well as for domestic principles of due process which may, however, lie at or beyond the perimeter of this volume.

But this time ten years ago the first constitutional steps, following the Security Council resolutions calling upon member states to inaugurate tougher regimes of surveillance and repression were already being taken. The distinguished South African jurist Richard Goldstone called them a tyrant's dream – a licence to every undemocratic regime to repress its dissidents. Ten years later, we are beginning to survey and appraise the consequences for constitutional democracy.

Nobody doubts the continuing need for a new level of vigilance. At one pole this has produced a pseudo-jurisprudence which holds that persons suspected of terrorism have no rights: they can be held indefinitely without trial and tortured freely to extract information. A recent book by an American scholar made the mistake of arguing that piracy furnished a precedent for this.[1] Unfortunately for him, piracy has for centuries been governed by an elaborate code, a significant part of the law of nations, which has required captured suspects to be rendered to

---

[1] Heller-Roazen, Daniel, *The Enemy of All: Piracy and the Law of Nations* (Zone, 2009).

the judicial authority at the nearest port and to be tried by due process of law. The US is in fact currently doing this with suspected Somali pirates, who are being delivered by US warships to Kenya for trial in Mombasa.

At the other pole is the stance, both principled and pragmatic, that you do not defend your fundamental values by sacrificing them. This, I would guess, is where the majority of contributors to this volume start from. But it is also here that the real difficulties start. To sacrifice your values is one thing; to modify or qualify them is another; and if there is a pivotal question for us, it is the extent to which the processes of open government and fair trials may legitimately be recast in order to meet the threat of terrorism.

The debate tends sometimes to overlook the fact that in these ten years we have had considerable success in using traditional police methods – observation, information, investigation, interrogation, charge, trial and proof in open court before a judge and jury. In the United Kingdom (UK), in a succession of cases, this has worked well. So far as we know, we have no black holes into which suspects disappear, though there is evidence that we have helped some to disappear into those of the US. Nevertheless, one undoubted counterweight to the insistence on enhanced interrogation as a necessary evil is the evidence that conventional methods are not only ethically acceptable but work better.

But the devastating attack by suicide bombers on London's public transport in July 2005 demonstrated that this was not enough. As we have more recently learned from the public inquest into the 52 deaths it caused, it also demonstrated something to which I shall return – the inability of the security services to fill the gaps in conventional policing, sometimes because of their own incompetence.

Even so, prevention – the critical issue – lies largely upstream of the criminal justice process. The law of attempt may catch some planned offences, and the law of conspiracy others. But terrorist crime characteristically originates in social, religious and cultural strata in which policing and law have no role, and whose autonomy good constitutions and human rights instruments protect. Can prevention work without invading this protected terrain? And if not, can it be done without what would otherwise be unacceptable discrimination?

The answer to both questions is probably no. But it is worth recalling that the possible need to secure tabulated rights against abuse by means of other such rights is specifically contemplated by Article 30 of the Universal Declaration:

> Nothing in this Declaration may be interpreted as implying for any State, group or person any right to engage in any activity or to perform any act aimed at the destruction of any of the rights and freedoms set forth herein.[2]

The provision sets a useful matrix for this book, because it applies to states as well as to individuals and groups. None of these may use human rights to destroy human rights; but there the restriction ends. It plainly means, for example, that the freedoms of association and expression may not be used by some to deny the right of others to life – classically the core aim of terrorism. But it does not mean that states may not, within limits, constrict those rights for some in order to assure them for all. The question which Article 30 does not and cannot answer, but which is our present concern, is where and how the balance is to be struck.

The UK has in recent years been a test-bed for working out this conflict of principle. I propose to limit the rest of what I have to say to what has become – depending on how you look at it – either a dialogue or a conflict between the UK's courts and its executive government. It is a process in which, as always, Parliament has the last word; but national security is a field in which the executive, through ministers, maintains pretty firm control of what Parliament eventually does. The dialogue has been possible only because the UK – and, as I shall have occasion to mention, the European Union and the Council of Europe – have strong and independent judiciaries. That of the UK is empowered by the common law to gauge the legality of executive action, and by a constitutional instrument – the Human Rights Act 1998 – to gauge the compatibility of Parliamentary legislation with fundamental rights; and I will take the liberty, since this chapter is in the nature of a personal swansong, of mentioning in one or two places my own role in the process. But while the common law might well have supplied as much substance for the right to a fair trial as does article 6 of the European Convention on Human Rights, it is the latter which has furnished the courts in Strasbourg and Luxembourg with the materials which have given international support to the long-established principles of the common law.

In a landmark decision in 2004,[3] the Appellate Committee of the House of Lords struck down as arbitrary and discriminatory the use of the power of detention contained in the immigration legislation to indefinitely imprison foreign nationals who were suspected of involvement in terrorism but could neither be tried nor deported. The response of

---

2 Declaration of Human Rights, Art. 30.

3 *A v Home Secretary* [2004] UKHL 56.

government was to introduce by primary legislation[4] a system of control orders, to all intents and purposes a system of house arrest, save that, by a judicial rule of thumb, it was confined to a maximum of 16 hours a day. This had the desired effect of distinguishing it from formal arrest, but in doing so it forfeited part of its purpose, namely control.

The system, however, had a more fundamental vice. The formal judicial oversight which was built into it was said to be subject to such wide limits on disclosure of evidence to the controlee that his right to challenge the control order might become completely nugatory. Since the legal test was the existence of no more than reasonable grounds for suspecting involvement in terrorism, the withheld evidence might not only be wide in scope but uncertain in its significance and capable of an innocent explanation. But in a decision on three linked cases, from which I dissented, the Court of Appeal[5] held that it was lawful, where the sensitivity of the evidence made it necessary, to withhold disclosure to the suspect of the entirety of the evidence placed before the judge.

The statutory system also includes provision for the use of 'special advocates', an innovation purportedly borrowed from Canada and approved in principle by the European Court of Human Rights (ECtHR). The special advocate is a security-cleared lawyer whose role is to make up so far as possible for the individual's own exclusion from the evidentiary process. He or she will have access to the closed material and can challenge its exclusion, its relevance or its reliability. The one thing the special advocate cannot do is tell the individual, even in outline, what the case is against him, or therefore present any coherent answer on his behalf.

My two colleagues in the Court of Appeal considered that this, though no substitute for a proper defence, was sufficient to assure due process, at least where 'the cogency of the closed material is such as to satisfy the judge that no effective challenge could be made to it'. In common with two of the three judges who had decided the cases at first instance, I disagreed. I said:

> Far from being difficult, as Lord Brown tentatively suggested it was, it is in my respectful view seductively easy to conclude that there can be no answer to a case of which you have only heard one side. There can be few practising lawyers who have not had the experience of resuming their seat in a state of hubristic satisfaction, having called a respectable witness to give apparently cast-iron evidence, only to see it reduced to wreckage by ten minutes of

---

4 The Prevention of Terrorism Act 2005.

5 *Home Secretary v AF (No. 3)* [2008] EWCA Civ 1148.

well-informed cross-examination or convincingly explained away by the other side's testimony. Some have appeared in cases in which everybody was sure of the defendant's guilt, only for fresh evidence to emerge which makes it clear that they were wrong. As Mark Twain said, the difference between reality and fiction is that fiction has to be credible. In a system which recruits its judges from practitioners, judges need to carry this kind of sobering experience to the bench. It reminds them that you cannot be sure of anything until all the evidence has been heard, and that even then you may be wrong. It may be, for these reasons, that the answer to Baroness Hale's question – what difference might disclosure have made? – is that you can never know.

This is why Megarry J's celebrated dictum in *John v Rees* about the fallibility of judgment based on partial evidence matters so much. Judges are not proof against the human delusion that one has heard enough to be sure that there is no answer. They have to guard themselves against it, and the way in which the law ensures they do so – not only the common law but all the systems governed by the European Convention on Human Rights and many others beside – is to insist, not that everything must be known before judgment is given, but that everyone affected must have had a proper chance (which they may of course forfeit) to advance as much material as may help the tribunal in reaching a judicious conclusion. No member of the House in *MB* suggested otherwise. If neither disclosure nor gist can enable the controlee to exercise this right, he is not getting a fair hearing because, however sure the court may feel on the material his accuser has placed before it, it simply cannot know whether there is a tenable answer, and the special advocate in the nature of things cannot tell them. The recent judgment of the ECJ in *Kadi v Council of the European Union* (3 September 2008) reiterates this principle, and it is rightly not suggested that a special advocate can always be depended on to fill the fairness gap.[6]

A week before the three cases came on further appeal before the Supreme Court (as the House of Lords Appellate Committee had now become), the ECtHR decisively changed the landscape. In *A v United Kingdom*,[7] a challenge to the forensic use of closed material in the UK, the ECtHR spelt out what Lord Hoffmann, grumpily but accurately, described as 'a rigid rule that the requirements of a fair hearing are never satisfied if the decision is "based solely or to a decisive degree on closed material"'.[8] In consequence, as Lord Hope wrote in relation to my dissent:

I think there is much force in his protest that the answer to the question what difference disclosure might have made is that you can never know, and that

6 Paras 113–14.

7 [2009] ECHR 301.

8 [2009] UKHL 28, para 71 (Hoffman); 84 (Hope).

> for a judge to hold that a hearing in which the party affected has had no opportunity to answer is a fair hearing negates the judicial function which is crucial to the control order system … The consequences of a successful terrorist attack are likely to be so appalling that there is an understandable wish to support the system that keeps those who are considered to be most dangerous out of circulation for as long as possible. But the slow creep of complacency must be resisted. If the rule of law is to mean anything, it is in cases such as these that the court must stand by principle. It must insist that the person affected be told what is alleged against him.

A second principal area where due process has faced compromise to the point of extinction is in the making of freezing orders – orders which put the state in total control of an individual's assets and make him, as I suggested in the Court of Appeal and as the Supreme Court agreed, effectively a prisoner of the state. The power to do this was intended by the Security Council to stop funds reaching Al Qaeda, but the control exercised by virtue of a freezing order extended to preventing the suspect from buying a packet of fish fingers without official permission. There were two regimes which ran in tandem: the Security Council regime by which individuals were designated on the nomination of member states, and a domestic regime which allowed the executive to list individuals suspected on reasonable grounds of involvement in terrorism. Ignoring two extant domestic regimes contained in primary legislation, the Treasury had taken advantage of the power to implement United Nations (UN) measures contained in the 1946 United Nations Act, and had introduced by Order in Council an asset-freezing regime startling in its disregard for due process and the rule of law.

Here again I was in the minority in the Court of Appeal,[9] but was upheld by the Supreme Court.[10] Here, too, a European decision, this time in the Court of Justice in Luxembourg, had intervened.[11] Mr Kadi had been listed by the Security Council without the shadow of an opportunity to learn why, much less to contest it. (It is relevant to record here a strong possibility that the UK, during its brief flirtation with the Gaddafi regime, did the Colonel a favour by getting the Security Council sanctions committee to list some of his exiled critics.) The EU had its own regulation implementing the UN system, but the Court of Justice held that, while it could not adjudicate on the legality of the UN measure, the Council of the EU, by simply implementing the sanctions committee's listing, had itself failed to accord Mr Kadi a fair hearing. In response, the

9 *Ahmed v HM Treasury* [2008] EWCA 1187.
10 [2010] UKSC 2.
11 *Kadi v UK* (2008) C-402/05 P.

Council supplied Mr Kadi with a summary of the reasons for listing him, but on a fresh appeal, the General Court of the EU[12] held that this was insufficient to meet the requirements of fairness: what was required was access to the evidence relied on to justify listing.

One important aspect of this decision is that the Luxembourg court adopted the jurisprudence of the Strasbourg court in *A v United Kingdom*. Its immediate consequence was that when the *Ahmed* case reached the UK Supreme Court, the executive was once again faced with a supranational decision that made its position untenable – or would have done had the Supreme Court not, in broad agreement with my dissent in the Court of Appeal, struck down the Orders in Council as an abuse of the executive's powers in domestic law, both because they blocked effective access to the courts and because they violated the principle of legal certainty. Once again it was the Scottish judge Lord Hope who spoke out most firmly:

> If the rule of law is to mean anything, decisions as to what is necessary or expedient in this context cannot be left to the uncontrolled judgment of the executive … Conferring an unlimited discretion on the executive as to how those [UN] resolutions, which it has had a hand in making, are to be implemented seems to me to be wholly unacceptable. It conflicts with the basic rules that lie at the heart of our democracy.[13]

This then is the situation in which ministers and their executive departments have had to stand back and consider where to go next. It is by now evident that the use of prerogative or delegated powers to thwart basic norms of due process is going to encounter principled judicial resistance both domestically and in Europe. The only solution is primary legislation which, apart from the possibility of a declaration of incompatibility with the human rights convention, is constitutionally judge-proof. Hence the consultation document, the Green Paper[14] entitled *Justice and Security*, published in 2011 by the British Government. Its tone is respectful of judicial decision-making, but its undisguised objective is to institutionalise the forensic use of damaging material without letting the party most closely affected by it know what it is – an aim incompatible with what most civilised systems understand by due process. The question is whether this is justified by a greater end – the frustration and eradication of terrorism.

---

[12] *Kadi v Commission* [2010] ECR-II.

[13] [2010] UKSC 2, para 45.

[14] Cm 8194, October 2011.

Before I say more about the Green Paper, it is necessary to pay some attention to the role of the security services in the formulation of its proposals. It is a frequent objection that even revealing the gist of a case may disclose, at least to a guilty suspect, the means of surveillance or information-gathering which have been used. Precisely because they have to operate clandestinely, the security services have this field to themselves. They have resisted repeated pressure from within and outside government to relax the present statutory bar on revealing in open court the fact, let alone the content, of electronic intercepts, even where the evidence might be decisive and no appreciable harm be done to the surveillance system. Government is again looking at the need for this, but – in an unfortunate division of labour – is doing it separately from the closed material proposal in the Green Paper. Meanwhile, one result is the use of opaque 'gisting' (one of the ugliest contributions of the modern legal system to the English language) to convey the purport but not the substance of evidence secured by electronic interception; but this can only be done in proceedings which can lawfully accord less than full disclosure. Another result, therefore, is the constant search for methods of trying proceedings behind closed doors in order to allow the court but not the suspect to see the products of interception.

The entitlement of the security services to call the shots is contested. Like every state institution, they have an interest in justifying their own existence; unlike other state institutions, on the other hand, they have to be accorded a very large measure of autonomy and trust. But when, on rare occasions, they emerge into daylight, their credentials sometimes look poor. Although we are still waiting to see what the Chilcot Committee makes of their advice to ministers about the threat posed by Saddam Husain's regime on the eve of the Iraq war, we now know from the Hallett inquest into the 7/7 deaths which I mentioned earlier that the leader of the suicide bombers had been followed and photographed by the security services, but that the picture taken of him was then so incompetently transmitted for showing to a supergrass in the US who might well have identified him as a dangerous individual, that it became useless. Such amateurism does not inspire confidence.

It is against this backdrop, as well as the judicial backdrop which I have been describing, that the Government has now issued its Green Paper. Its core proposal is to generalise the use of a form of trial known as closed material proceedings – CMPs. The extension of such procedures to civil damages claims is at present blocked by the Supreme Court's ruling in *Al Rawi v Security Service*[15] that there is no power at common law to introduce CMPs into regular civil actions. The Green Paper's key proposal is that new legislation should permit the introduction of CMPs into regular court proceedings, accompanied by the use of special advocates, wherever the judge is satisfied that sensitive material needs to be used which cannot be disclosed to the party affected by it. If adopted, this is likely to make redundant the longstanding public interest immunity process.

It is almost a century since Lord Shaw of Dunfermline, in a famous judgment on the primacy of open justice,[16] said

> To remit the maintenance of constitutional right to the region of judicial discretion is to shift the foundations of freedom from the rock to the sand.

Closed material proceedings were first introduced in the UK in 1997,[17] well before 9/11, and were restricted to immigration cases raising national security issues: they were truly exceptional. The proposal to generalise them carries a sinister baggage train, including a proposal to extend what is insouciantly called 'light touch vetting' from criminal juries, where it is supposed to be confined to weeding out jurors with criminal records, to coroners' juries which may be required to see sensitive material.

What we are now approaching may thus be the tipping point at which the exception becomes the rule. That in itself is troubling; but what is more troubling is that the coming rule is one which will place the legal system on a continuing emergency footing and will transfer an important tranche of command from Parliament and the courts to the executive. The Green Paper is breezily confident that this will not happen, and it may be right; but to the extent that it does happen, concomitantly sapping both the democratic process and the rule of law, terrorism will be able to congratulate itself on a significant victory.

In 1628, when the English Parliament was discussing the legality of billeting of troops on civilians, Sir Edward Coke said in the debate:

> God send me never to live under the law of conveniency or discretion … Shall the soldier and the justice sit on one bench, the trumpet will not let the crier [i.e. the usher] speak … Where the common law can determine a thing, the martial law cannot.[18]

---

15 [2011] UKSC 34.

16 *Scott v Scott* [1913] AC 417.

17 The Special Immigration Appeals Commission Act 1997.

18 Commons Debates 1628, ed. R.C. Johnson et al., Yale 1977.

3. Oversight of national security secrecy in the United States

Stephen Schulhofer

INTRODUCTION

In a constitutional system, the legislature is expected to play an active role in formulating policy, and the courts are expected to play an active role in protecting individual rights. But nonetheless, where issues affecting national security are concerned, executive officials in virtually all constitutional democracies typically exercise unchecked power to conceal information that is essential to the effective exercise of those legislative and judicial functions. In its actual practices, the United States (US) largely conforms to this pattern of *de facto* executive dominance, even though its formal laws grant substantial power to regulate secrecy to Congress and the courts.

Although some secrecy in national security matters is appropriate and inevitable, unilateral executive control over decisions *whether* to impose secrecy is not. American law provides five separate processes for overriding executive secrecy judgments. Along with semi-independent review within the executive branch and oversight by Congress, three distinct bodies of law grant a checking function to the courts: the Classified Information Procedures Act (CIPA, applicable in criminal cases), the state secrets privilege (SSP, applicable in civil suits), and the Freedom of Information Act (FOIA, a statute that creates a free-standing cause of action to demand disclosure of information held by the government). These five systems differ considerably in the degree to which they involve deference to the executive, or – in contrast – active, independent judgments about the need for secrecy. American law thus provides broad scope to compare competing approaches. In addition, where American adversary procedures for the review of executive-branch secrecy are at their height (in CIPA), they permit full-fledged representation by security-cleared counsel, a more vigorous checking capability than appears possible through the 'special advocate' approach favored in the UK. This chapter describes these American oversight systems and assesses them by focusing on the expertise and incentives of the participants in each.[1]

Executive control over sensitive information presumes a unique and highly specialized executive expertise, a notion not only touted by the intelligence community but widely accepted by members of Congress, judges and the general public. Yet this common conception involves a mixture of truth, hyperbole, misunderstanding and myth.

The executive branch is not the exclusive repository of the knowledge and experience necessary to make sound judgments about when to maintain secrecy in national security affairs. Congress has considerable expertise in military, foreign policy and intelligence matters. While judges typically do not, courts have solid *institutional* capacities to elicit expertise. Nor is national security expertise the only proficiency required. Information-access judgments demand an appreciation for the value of both secrecy and transparency. Members of Congress and judges may not have deep familiarity with the former, but they thoroughly understand the latter. National security officials, in contrast, are predisposed by training and experience to abhor transparency; in this crucial expertise they are markedly deficient. Courts therefore have an indispensable place in a sound system for making information-access decisions. They offer not only the obvious advantage of independence from self-interested incentives, but also the rarely noticed point that they are in fact superior in some essential forms of expertise.

In one domain of American practice, criminal cases governed by CIPA, US courts routinely provide active oversight of classification decisions, an experience that demonstrates the capacity of the CIPA model to afford a fully adversarial and yet workable judicial check.

This chapter builds on this adversarial judicial model and integrates it with a more robust legislative role, in order to propose a framework for effective oversight of executive branch judgments about access to national security information.

Section 1 describes the existing executive secrecy apparatus. Section 2 examines the present structure of legislative and judicial oversight, and Section 3 assesses the extent to which Congress and the courts currently are able to prevent unjustified secrecy. As Sections 2 and 3 show, these outside institutions have considerable legal powers, but they now operate

---

[1] For more detailed discussion of these issues, with more detailed citations, see Stephen J. Schulhofer, Secrecy and Democracy: Who Controls Information in the National Security State?, available at http://ssrn.com/abstract=1661964.

under self-imposed, informal constraints; their willingness to thwart improper secrecy is episodic and feeble. Section 4 develops an oversight framework more consonant with constitutionalism – a framework that combines robust national security safeguards with maximum feasible transparency and accountability.

1. THE EXECUTIVE SECRECY APPARATUS

Despite the WikiLeaks phenomenon and the more selective revelations accomplished by journalists and whistleblowers, the executive secrecy system remains powerful and largely effective.

For many, this is exactly as it should be. The fact that individuals outside the executive branch cannot nullify classification decisions simply reflects the supposed fact that outsiders lack the capacity to make such decisions wisely. Yet the hypothesis of executive expertise and the converse hypothesis of outsider incompetence are often made with little understanding of how the classification system works. In fact, the executive secrecy apparatus is purposely designed for over-classification. Officials are required to disregard many relevant interests in transparency, and they have largely unchecked freedom to impose secrecy, when doing so serves their political and personal self-interest, even if such secrecy is not called for by national security concerns. This section describes the framework for initial classification decisions and the available systems for review of those decisions by officials within the executive branch.

1.1 Initial Classification

In the American Government, millions of individuals are allowed to impose secrecy on documents in which they insert classified material.[2] An executive order promulgated by the President provides that information controlled by the US Government can be classified whenever its disclosure 'reasonably could be expected to cause damage to the national security'.[3] The order prohibits classification to 'conceal violations of law, inefficiency or administrative error'.[4] Of course, that restriction can easily be ignored in practice. But even on paper, the regime doesn't work against over-classification and in fact serves to enable it.

---

[2] See Comm'n on Protecting and Reducing Gov't Secrecy, Report, S. Doc. No. 105-32, at 4, 31 (1997) [hereinafter President's Comm'n.].

[3] Exec. Order No. 13526, 75 Fed. Reg. 707 (Jan. 2, 2010) at §1.2(a)(3).

[4] Id. at §1.7(a)(1).

One reason for this is that classifiers are charged with reducing possible national security damage to the lowest achievable minimum, suggesting zero tolerance for risk. The costs of secrecy (not only for society at large but for the classifying agency itself) are expressly excluded from the calculus. The executive order provides only one avenue for taking into account 'the public interest in disclosure'. For the 'exceptional' cases in which transparency might be called for, public-interest balancing is permitted, but only when a classification is appealed to the head of the agency, who alone is permitted to weigh the relative benefits of secrecy and disclosure.[5] Thus, public-interest balancing cannot occur at the time of initial classification, and in cases that are not 'exceptional', the value of disclosure cannot be considered at any point at all.

This decision to constrain public-interest balancing is intentional, reflecting the intelligence community's view that '[i]f this weighing of interests were required for every decision to keep classified information secret, it would bring the … process to a virtual halt'.[6] Thus, the American classification system opts for over-classification as a matter of principle. It does not, even in theory, aim to generate the degree of secrecy that would optimally serve the wider public interest.

1.2 Oversight Within the Executive Branch

In an effort to counterbalance the over-classification dynamic, the executive branch has instituted several mechanisms to push back.[7] All of them, however, are structurally weak, and they have had little impact. For example, the procedure for automatic declassification, normally after 10 or 25 years, is subject to numerous exceptions.[8] Government archives contain billions of pages of classified material that is more than 25 years old.[9]

---

[5] Id. at § 3.1(b).

[6] PUBLIC INTEREST DECLASSIFICATION BOARD, IMPROVING DECLASSIFICATION: A REPORT TO THE PRESIDENT FROM THE PUBLIC INTEREST DECLASSIFICATION BOARD 29 (Dec. 2007) [hereinafter PIDB REPORT], www.archives.gov/declassification/pidb/improving-declassification.pdf (last visited July 9, 2009).

[7] Id. at 13–14.

[8] Exec. Order 13526, *supra* note 3, at §3.3(a), (b).

[9] INFORMATION SECURITY OVERSIGHT OFFICE, 2008 ANNUAL REPORT TO THE PRESIDENT (Jan. 12, 2009) [hereinafter ISOO 2008 REPORT], at 9–11.

Any individual can request mandatory declassification review (MDR) within the classifying agency.[10] MDR amounts to a non-judicial version of the Freedom of Information Act and has become an attractive alternative to FOIA, because it is generally faster. Yet MDR declassification remains trivial in relation to the volume of classified material. The pages declassified in 2008 represent less than 1 per cent of the pages classified that year.[11]

A challenger dissatisfied with intra-agency review can appeal to an Interagency Security Classification Appeals Panel (ISCAP) consisting of senior officials from the principal national security agencies. By majority vote, ISCAP can order declassification over the objection of the classifying agency. But ISCAP appeals are rare (less than 100 per year), in part because public-interest balancing is permitted only by the head of the classifying agency. Thus, ISCAP cannot declassify when disclosure benefits outweigh risks; it must assume that such benefits are always trumped by national-security dangers, no matter how slender.

By almost every measure, oversight within the executive branch affords only a slight counterweight to the built-in preference for over-classification.[12] The operational reality is simply that 'agencies face very little internal pressure to minimize secrecy'.[13] Reinforcing that difficulty, the prerequisite to well-founded government action – an effort to balance benefits against costs – is largely precluded. Thus, a classification decision that survives all phases of executive branch reassessment does not, even in theory, reflect an expert judgment that secrecy is in the public interest, all things considered. Absent pressure from outside the executive branch, too much information inevitably will be concealed; accountability as well as national security itself are bound to suffer.

The next section examines the outside sources of countervailing pressure.

2. CHECKS ON THE EXECUTIVE BRANCH

The executive branch does not have unchallenged control over national security secrets. American law sometimes requires disclosure of classified information to a judge or to certain members of Congress. Social and

---

[10] Exec. Order 13526, *supra* note 3, at §3.5.

[11] PIDB Report at 14.

[12] Id. at 8–12.

[13] Meredith Fuchs, Judging Secrets: The Role Courts Should Play in Preventing Unnecessary Secrecy, 58 Ad. L. Rev. 131, 149 (2006).

political realities generate leaks and sometimes force the executive branch to disclose information that outsiders have no legal right to see. Informal factors also can push in the opposite direction, neutralizing checks that the law supposedly affords. That tempering effect may prevent excessive oversight, but it also may disable essential oversight.

The press plays a large but typically overstated role in this process. Reporters have a first amendment right to publish what they know but no constitutional right to obtain information or to shield sources who leak information confidentially. In national security matters, moreover, potential sources are largely confined to security-cleared officials, an exceptionally reticent group, and officials responsible for unwelcome leaks, if identified or suspected, face exclusion from both government and most private employment in the areas of their expertise; they may face criminal prosecution as well. The press deserves credit for many legendary national security revelations, but its contributions inevitably will be episodic and (relative to the stock of classified material) rare. On national security matters, its principal contribution is to transmit information made available in other ways. Far more often than not, therefore, legal powers to force disclosure become the essential tools that allow the press to do its job. Two institutions have formal authority to pierce the executive information monopoly – Congress and the courts.

2.1 Congress

Congress has formidable tools for obtaining access to classified information. But it often lacks the will to deploy its tools effectively. Though critics of 'rights-based' litigation typically consider the political process a preferable source of accountability,[14] they often idealize its potential,[15] overlooking limitations that can make congressional oversight pallid in national security matters.

Congress controls the intelligence community budget and has substantial influence over amounts spent for particular activities. Under present

---

[14] E.g., Samuel Issacharoff and Richard H. Pildes, Between Civil Libertarianism and Executive Unilateralism: An Institutional Process Approach to Rights During Wartime, 5 THEORETICAL INQUIRIES IN LAW 5, 14, 42–44 (2004) (rights-based adjudication is often 'abstract', in contrast to legislative endorsement, which is often made in 'informed, deliberative manner').

[15] Compare Cass Sunstein, Minimalism at War, 2004 SUP. CT. REV. 47, with Daryl J. Levinson and Richard H. Pildes, Separation of Parties, Not Powers, 119 HARV. L. REV. 2312 (2006) (questioning premises of separation-of-powers model).

conditions, however, Congress lacks the practical tools necessary to effectively oversee the substance of those activities. Its committees know too little, and they lack the capacity and the motivation to critically examine whatever they learn. Under unitary government (when a single party controls both the legislative and executive branches), and even under divided government (when control of the two branches is split between the parties), oversight of substantive policy has been weak, misdirected or both. Among those who have studied national security oversight, there is no significant dissent from this view.[16]

Expenditure levels and the substance of agency activity are understandably the salient areas of national security policy. A third domain – the judgment *whether* to impose secrecy – is at least equally important, because decisions about what the public can know govern its ability to hold the executive branch accountable on budgetary and substantive matters. Yet in this third area of national security policy, congressional oversight is virtually non-existent. Although Congress may press an agency to declassify documents, the decision whether to disclose – the *sine qua non* of public accountability – traditionally has not been subjected to formal oversight at all.

The dangers of this executive monopoly are tempered to a degree by the fact that Senators and Representatives with a 'need to know' have considerable (though not unlimited) access to classified secrets. Thus congressional oversight of expenditures and activities does not always occur in an information vacuum. But the information sometimes provided to congressional leaders at best gives only the opportunity for oversight; it does not supply the motivation. And in politics, the only reliable source of motivation (apart from self-interested lobbyists) is an engaged public. Bentham put the point clearly: '[I]n comparison to publicity, all other checks are of small account.'[17]

Executive management of public disclosure therefore places most incentives for legislative oversight under presidential control. Technically, the executive does not oversee itself, but it can regulate what its ostensibly independent overseer (Congress) cares about. As a result, Congress currently does not and cannot supply sufficient countervailing pressure.

---

[16] See, e.g., U.S. NAT'L COMM. ON TERRORIST ATTACKS UPON THE UNITED STATES, THE 9/11 COMMISSION REPORT 419 (2004) (unanimous finding that congressional oversight of intelligence is dysfunctional).

[17] Quoted in ROBERT M. PALLITTO AND WILLIAM G. WEAVER, PRESIDENTIAL SECRECY AND THE LAW 88 (2007).

2.2 The Courts

Like Congress, the courts have many tools to challenge executive control. But the courts also resemble Congress in another respect, for they are typically unwilling to deploy their checking powers effectively. This section examines the judicial checking function in the three contexts where it arises most often: criminal litigation, civil damage suits, and the Freedom of Information Act.[18]

2.2.1 Criminal cases

The Classified Information Procedures Act[19] provides detailed procedures to reduce the conflict between secrecy needs and due process requirements. It also deals with security clearances for court personnel (other than judges and jurors) and the security of courthouse quarters where proceedings involving classified material occur.[20]

Under CIPA, when a defendant seeks classified information for pre-trial preparation or for use at trial, the judge reviews the information in a closed pre-trial hearing, to determine if it is relevant. If it is, CIPA permits the government to avoid compulsory disclosure by replacing sensitive information with an unclassified 'substitution' – for example, a redacted version. But substitution is permissible only when it 'provide[s] the defendant with substantially the same ability to make his defense';[21] the judge must compare the original documents with the proposed substitution, to insure that an effective defense is not compromised.

If no substitution can meet legitimate defense needs without risk to national security, CIPA provides other devices for avoiding a secrecy/due process conflict. The judge may order that classified material be made available to the defense under a protective order, to prevent public disclosure. If the government is unwilling to accept disclosure under a

---

[18] Habeas corpus review of Guantánamo detentions has proceeded as a rough version of criminal litigation; judges and counsel for the detainees by and large appear to have had substantial access to the relevant facts. Where the process has fallen short is primarily in two domains. First, the rules of law imposed by the US Court of Appeals have been unjustifiably favorable to the government. Second, even if defense counsel's access to information has been adequate, public access has been woefully inadequate.

[19] Classified Information Procedures Act, Pub. L. 96-456, 4 Stat. 2025, reprinted at 18 U.S.C. app. 3 [hereinafter cited as CIPA].

[20] See Security Procedures Established Pursuant to Pub. L. 96-456, reprinted following 18 U.S.C. app. 3.

[21] CIPA, *supra* note 19, at §6(c).

protective order, and if no other remedy will adequately protect defense interests, *the judge must dismiss the prosecution.*

In a terrorism prosecution, these procedures confront the CIPA judge with a daunting task. A discovery request may require judicial review of thousands of pages of classified material, with difficult judgments to be made on every page about relevancy, substitution and other options for meeting the defense needs. Courts working with CIPA quickly realized that they needed help. The solution most readily available was to insist that members of the defense team obtain security clearance (under the CIPA procedures already in place for clearance of courthouse personnel) and then to provide the classified material to cleared defense counsel under protective order. This approach was successfully used pre-9/11 for vast amounts of material in the 'embassy bombings' trial, in order to narrow the issues in dispute and enable the judge to make a well-informed ruling after an adversarial presentation; it is now the common practice.[22]

Cleared counsel is not a 'special advocate' in the UK conception – that is, a lawyer appointed by and responsible to the court. Cleared counsel is the defendant's lawyer and is ethically obliged to provide zealous representation. He is fully engaged in trial strategy, pretrial preparation and the trial itself, all on the defendant's behalf.

The principal limitation of cleared counsel – by comparison to the American defense attorney's role in conventional pretrial discovery – is that cleared counsel normally cannot share classified information with his client and therefore may not be able adequately to assess its import. There is a presumption that counsel-only review is sufficient, but the presumption can be overcome and client consultation permitted if defense counsel shows that the defendant's personal input is necessary to evaluate the information.[23]

Since its enactment, CIPA has affected hundreds of espionage and terrorism prosecutions. There were 62 espionage prosecutions during the 1980s alone,[24] and there have been over 100 international terrorism prosecutions since September 11, 2001, most of them with the potential to expose considerable amounts of classified information.[25]

---

22 See SERRIN TURNER AND STEPHEN J. SCHULHOFER, THE SECRECY PROBLEM IN TERRORISM TRIALS 25–27 (2005).

23 Id. at 28.

24 Id. at 22.

25 RICHARD B. ZABEL AND JAMES J. BENJAMIN, JR., IN PURSUIT OF JUSTICE 84–85 (2009).

These developments call into question many conventional assumptions about judges' supposed lack of national security expertise. CIPA practice has drawn judges deeply into the details of classified files. Judges have evaluated reams of material, assessing relevancy and crafting fine-grained substitutions. In this iterative process, government claims about the need for secrecy often shrink or collapse, while the judge's less specialized but more independent perspective prevails. In criminal litigation, federal judges seem especially cognizant of their responsibility to serve as the independent buffer between government and the individual, and they have become increasingly self-confident in performing this familiar role, even when national security concerns are implicated.[26] Yet there are no known instances in which a significant security breach attributable to CIPA has ever occurred.[27]

In theory, CIPA leaves disclosure decisions entirely within executive hands. But unless the government is willing to forgo prosecution entirely, CIPA procedures force the disclosure of classified files to the judge and sometimes to defense counsel. That process provides a degree of accountability and a deterrent to self-serving classification decisions. Moreover, the threat of CIPA dismissal obliges the executive to internalize part of the social cost of secrecy. Inevitably that dynamic leads the government to realize that some information need not have been classified and to accept that some properly classified material nonetheless can be released.

In these ways CIPA has generated voluminous disclosures that the government would normally resist. When a matter is sufficiently sensitive, however, the executive branch can opt to preserve secrecy, and pay the price by declining to prosecute. CIPA thus affords only modest accountability to the general public when disclosures are subject to a protective order. Moreover, because dismissal is always an available option for the government, CIPA cannot invariably force disclosure, and it therefore does not offer any accountability at all when the executive is determined to avoid it. Those, of course, are the times when accountability may be most needed.

2.2.2 Civil litigation

Civil suits against the government provide the natural mechanism to fill that gap. Yet state secrets privilege gives the government a wide-ranging license to veto unwanted disclosures in any civil case having national

---

26 See id. at 84–85.

27 Id. at 88.

security implications.[28] The privilege, as currently interpreted, prevents civil litigation from providing any meaningful check on overbroad or unjustified secrecy decisions.[29]

2.2.3 The Freedom of Information Act (FOIA)

FOIA establishes the principle that all government records must be publicly available, unless specifically exempted.[30] Exemption 1 protects all information that 'in the interest of national defense or foreign policy [is] properly classified'.[31] But unlike the state secrets privilege, exemption 1 procedures permit active judicial oversight. FOIA requires agencies to identify classified material page-by-page and section-by-section.[32] And FOIA imposes a CIPA-like filtering process, requiring that '[a]ny reasonably segregable portion of a record shall be provided ... after deletion of the portions which are exempt'.[33] Moreover, FOIA discourages automatic judicial deference to executive preferences, because it requires the court to 'determine the matter de novo, ... and the burden is on the agency to sustain its action'.[34]

In practice, however, a widely perceived imperative to defer to the executive often migrates into FOIA cases, despite Congress's expressly stated preference to the contrary.[35] Thus, a former Chief Judge of the US Court of Appeals for the D.C. Circuit acknowledged that, despite Congress's mandate for *de novo* review, oversight in Exemption 1 cases 'often seems to be done in a perfunctory way'.[36] Indeed the 'reasonable basis' standard expressly rejected by Congress (in favor of the *de novo*

---

[28] See United States v. Reynolds, 345 U.S. 1 (1953).

[29] For detailed discussion, see Schulhofer, *supra* note 1.

[30] 5 U.S.C. §552(a),(b) (2009).

[31] 5 U.S.C. §552(b)(1) (2009). Other exemptions are available as well, but because these largely duplicate Exemption 1 in national security cases, they will not be discussed separately.

[32] See, e.g., Allen v. CIA, 636 F.2d 1287, 1293 (D.C. Cir. 1980).

[33] 5 U.S.C. §552(b) (2009).

[34] 5 U.S.C. §552(a)(4)(B) (2009).

[35] When the Supreme Court held that FOIA did not authorize judicial review of Exemption 1 claims, EPA v. Mink, 410 U.S. 73 (1973), Congress amended the statute to require courts to decide whether records 'are in fact *properly* classified'. 5 U.S.C. §552(b)(1)(B) (2009) (emphasis added). Nonetheless, deference has remained the dominant pattern. See Adam M. Samaha, Government Secrets, Constitutional Law, and Platforms for Judicial Intervention, 53 UCLA L. Rev. 911, 940 (2006).

[36] Patricia M. Wald, Two Unsolved Constitutional Problems, 49 U. Pitt. L. Rev. 753, 760 (1988).

alternative) has become 'ironically, a good summation of post-1974 practice'.[37] Federal judges have posited that agency decisions are motivated solely by concern for national security harm, even when circumstances strongly suggest the contrary.[38] And when agencies invoke the 'mosaic' argument,[39] courts have even allowed 'seemingly innocuous'[40] information – in other words, *any* information – to be shielded, with essentially no judicial review at all. Mosaic theory shuts down any possibility of review, deferential or otherwise, because it attributes reality to risks that only an intelligence expert – or not even an intelligence expert – can detect. And it implies extreme but one-sided risk aversion: zero-tolerance for any risk of imprudent disclosure but unlimited tolerance for unnecessary secrecy. Because the mosaic theory cannot be falsified, deference becomes abdication, an abdication many courts make no effort to disguise.[41]

Although the FOIA review typically afforded is therefore far from robust, a minority of judges insist on taking a hard look, a valuable check regardless of its outcome.[42] And because FOIA requests trigger intra-agency review and settlement pressure, FOIA indirectly generates voluminous national security disclosures that almost certainly would not occur otherwise.[43] In the past six years, tens of thousands of pages of previously classified material have been released in response to FOIA litigation.[44]

That said, FOIA's value, though not trivial, is fragile. Judicial oversight, even in its currently episodic form, depends on the forbearance of

---

37 Samaha, *supra* note 35, at 940.

38 E.g., ACLU v. Dept. of Defense, 389 F. Supp.2d 547, 564–66 (S.D.N.Y. 2005) (upholding exemption despite 'concern that CIA's purpose … is less to protect intelligence activities … than to conceal possible violations of law').

39 The 'mosaic' argument posits that enemy intelligence experts can piece together small details, insignificant in themselves, in order to construct a revealing picture of sensitive US secrets.

40 CIA v. Sims, 471 U.S. 159, 179 (1985).

41 E.g., *Halperin*, 629 F.2d 144, 148 (D.C. Cir. 1980) (judges may not 'second-guess'). Compare Cntr. for Nat. Security Studies, 331 F.3d, at 951 (Tatel, J., dissenting) (mosaic reasoning 'drastically diminish[es], if not eliminat[es] the judiciary's role').

42 See STEPHEN DYCUS, et al., NATIONAL SECURITY LAW 1013 (4th ed. 2007).

43 Id. at 1014.

44 Over 100,000 pages of classified material have been released in just one subset of these cases, those seeking records relating to abuse at detention centers overseas. See www.aclu.org/national-security/aclu-v-department-defense-torture-foia.

the executive, which retains wide discretion to neutralize FOIA through obfuscating mosaic arguments and unrelenting appeals. Equally worrisome, effective oversight depends on the wavering commitment of the judges themselves and on the extent to which they are willing to resist the mystique of agency expertise.

3. ASSESSING THE OVERSIGHT SYSTEM

Ideally, oversight bodies might be designed to complement one another, each operating where it is best suited and filling oversight gaps left by the others. If this is the aspiration, however, the American system falls far short of meeting it. The oversight mechanisms leave wide spaces where executive control of information is unrestrained in practice.

Although the press, for example, plays an indispensable role, its successes in ferreting out secrets represent a minute percentage of the classified material that the public deserves to see. Unlike the press, which is highly motivated but lacks dependable means for obtaining information, Congress has potent tools but usually lacks the motivation to use them constructively. And even when Congress obtains sensitive information for itself, it has virtually no authority to require that classified documents and testimony be made public. Thus, Congress cannot convey noteworthy material to the press, which must (but normally cannot) obtain it elsewhere. And that gap weakens the significance of the access Congress itself enjoys, because Congress's motivation to seek information and to act on it is a function of political incentives, which in turn are a function of the public awareness that neither the press nor Congress can normally supply.

That leaves the courts. In criminal cases, courts have been assertive, and CIPA gives them authority to subject secrecy claims to fine-grained inspection. But prosecutors' charging discretion gives the executive branch substantial control over the scope of the material that faces CIPA scrutiny. FOIA is more promising, as it permits any person to initiate a request for disclosure of any document. Nonetheless, FOIA has one major limitation. FOIA judges can override improper classification decisions, but the substantive standard for classification is exceedingly permissive – national security interests are defined broadly and the most slender national security concern can qualify, without regard to the public value of disclosure. As a result, a national security exemption from FOIA is typically easy to justify, regardless of its real motivation. And beyond that formal obstacle, FOIA's potential is easily neutralized by the willingness of judges to be seduced by calls for deference to supposed agency expertise. Overall, FOIA, as currently applied, offers only a modest, unreliable means to challenge executive information control.

In sum, each of the checking institutions – the press, Congress and the courts – has either feeble tools for forcing disclosure or little willingness to insist upon it. And because these weaknesses reinforce one another, the overall apparatus of information oversight is weaker than the sum of its parts. It does not provide dependable mechanisms for assuring accountability and democratic governance in matters that touch the national security.

4. REFORM

Debates over access to national security secrets – whether they concern the broad principle or just a particular document – ultimately center on conflicting judgments about competency. This section examines the expertise and other strengths of the executive, legislative and judicial branches and then proposes mechanisms to move toward a more meaningful system of checks and balances.

4.1 Institutional Assets and Liabilities

4.1.1 Congress

Despite the potential benefits of legislative oversight, Congress supposedly has significant shortcomings in the national security arena. It is said that secrets are not safe in congressional hands and that Congress lacks the necessary expertise. Finally, for many observers, political accountability – Congress's strength – entails (or degenerates into) a low politics of partisanship and pettiness, distorting policy rather than improving it.

The danger of leaks, however, has little substance. Each chamber has detailed procedures to securely store and handle classified material. Congressional staff who need access to classified information must obtain clearances; there is no reason to consider them less trustworthy than security-cleared employees of the executive branch. Members of Congress are not required to hold security clearances, but there is no indication that security breaches emanating from Congress have ever been a significant problem.[45] And because any given secret is known to far more executive officials than to individuals in the congressional

---

[45] HAROLD HONGJU KOH, THE NATIONAL SECURITY CONSTITUTION 173 (1990). In ERIC A. POSNER AND ADRIAN VERMEULE, TERROR IN THE BALANCE (2007) 170, the authors assert the opposite but offer no basis for that position.

offices on Capitol Hill, leaks from Congress are more easily identified and deterred.

The charge of incapacity in national security matters is more justified but highly exaggerated. Intelligence committee staff develop specialized knowledge and experience, often more than enough to put them on a par with their counterparts in the executive branch. It is not even accurate to picture Congress and the executive as distinct teams. Intelligence committee staff often are recruited from the executive agencies and vice versa. George Tenet had spent almost his entire career in congressional staff positions before President Clinton named him to lead the CIA. Porter Goss, his immediate successor, had high-level national security experience only during his seven-year stint as chair of the House Intelligence Committee. Yet both were widely seen to have impressive intelligence expertise. They were not transformed from novices into national security authorities the moment they left Capitol Hill to join the executive branch.

In any case, whatever Congress's lack of expertise, it remains a mystery why its deficiencies are so widely considered incurable. Members tend to lack expertise because their tenure on the intelligence committees is limited. Congress could easily extend or abolish those term limits, and larger staffs can help offset lack of expertise among members. Instead, Congress has opted for the worst of both worlds, saddling the intelligence committees with the combined burden of small staffs (to limit the danger of leaks) and rotating committee assignments (to prevent members from amassing too much power). The resulting oversight structure is dysfunctional but not beyond repair.

Justified mistrust of Congress must therefore rest less on concerns about its skills, which are easily improved, and more on its incentives, which are highly flawed and hard to fix. The difficulties center on two problems – incentives to act badly and incentives not to act at all. The President's party has strong reasons to protect the executive branch and help it shield embarrassing information. The opposition party should (in theory) be motivated to restrain the administration. But the opposition party is also – and more strongly – motivated to win elections, a goal that imposes different priorities. The opposition may use information access to expose embarrassing but inconsequential executive actions – as happened under divided government during the late 1990s. Conversely, the goal of electoral success may push the opposition to ignore its national security prerogatives. It may prefer to avoid confronting the President on issues of national security, almost always his safest terrain – as happened in the years immediately following the 9/11 attacks. Either way, Congress often will have no appetite for the kind of scrutiny that national security oversight requires.

The challenge for Congress is to serve its (and the nation's) interest in sustaining checks and balances, in the face of distorting incentives and deficits in expertise. But this predicament is not unique to the national security domain: it pervades the modern legislative agenda. Lack of time or knowledge and unwelcome political pressures exist throughout. And Congress has ways to overcome these obstacles – delegating authority to independent agencies and transferring oversight responsibilities from its committees to its specialized cadre of auditors, the Government Accountability Office. The appropriate response to oversight obstacles therefore cannot be for Congress simply to withdraw from the field. As I develop below, Congress can craft mechanisms that address its deficiencies and permit accountability to be restored.

4.1.2 The courts

In the case of judges, oversight raises not only pragmatic doubts but also objections of principle. Congress's political accountability may be a mixed blessing, but critics charge that courts have no political mandate at all. The same feature that many see as a virtue – judicial independence – represents for others the sin of undemocratic power. The concern is heightened, of course, when the safety of the nation may be at stake.

Several factors narrow this concern. First, courts have their own mandates, not necessarily political but constitutional – for example, their mandate to uphold the rule of law, by affording some remedy when officials exceed statutory or constitutional bounds. In addition, courts often do have a political mandate, in the form of duties conferred by Congress. FOIA and CIPA are obvious examples. And Congress can at any time instruct the courts to do more. The decisive questions for reform, then, are ones of workability and practical effects.

A familiar advantage of courts, relative to Congress, is their independence. A second strength, seldom appreciated, is their attention span. Congress can exercise oversight if it wishes, and its actions carry a political imprimatur that courts lack. But Congress's incentives do not generate – and usually undercut – motivations to act with regularity and persistence. In that regard, courts have a decisive advantage.

Its dimensions are worth making explicit. If courts were self-contained, self-propelled mechanisms, swinging into action when and as they please, they could hardly provide sustained or legitimate checks. Discussions that disparage judicial review sometimes portray judicial oversight as little more than a right of intervention conferred on certain individuals who happen to wear robes.[46] But 'courts' are not just collections of judges. They represent an institutional practice, involving parties who present specific complaints, which are probed, narrowed and resolved through multi-stage adversarial processes. Citizens concerned about official misconduct may or may not get Congress to take notice, but when a judicial forum is available, they are assured that the oversight agency will not have the prerogative to lose interest or move on to the next day's hot topic. The judiciary offers staying power that Congress can seldom match, even on matters that arouse majoritarian concern.

Closely related is the judicial capacity for detail. Courts often cannot see, or do anything about, 'the big picture'. But they are skilled at examining narrow issues in depth. Congress itself is well aware of courts' superior attention span and aptitude for specifics; it often delegates oversight functions to the judiciary, to take advantage of this ability to consider discrete questions in a sustained way.[47]

Two of the principal difficulties for courts are counterparts to their advantages – political insulation and inability to address the big picture. The other major concerns are that they lack expertise and are vulnerable to leaks – assumptions that figure prominently in *United States v. Reynolds*,[48] the 1953 decision establishing a broad state secrets privilege, and *E.P.A. v. Mink*,[49] the 1973 decision barring judicial review of classified material under FOIA. Many lower courts continue to make the same assumptions; they seldom note that subsequent statutes overruled *Mink* and transformed the environment that prompted the Court's fears in *Reynolds*.

Since CIPA's enactment in 1980, judges in criminal cases have often found themselves deeply immersed in classified material. Aided by security-cleared counsel, they have evaluated enormous quantities of classified material. Likewise, FOIA judges have made available mountains of improperly classified material, with no known national security damage or unintended leaks attributable to these processes. Those achievements are tempered, however, by the fact that judges typically use FOIA powers cautiously. Current FOIA practice cannot definitively

---

46 E.g., Posner and Vermeule, *supra* note 45, at 240–44 (analyzing 'institutional features of the judiciary' solely in terms of selection process and motivations for individuals who hold judicial office).

47 Examples include the Tort Claims Act and the Administrative Procedures Act. See Pallitto and Weaver, *supra* note 17, at 106–107.

48 345 U.S. 1 (1953).

49 410 U.S. 73 (1973).

determine whether robust judicial oversight would produce similar benefits on a wider scale or instead generate significant national security costs (or both).

FOIA nonetheless moves the debate about expertise out of the domain of abstraction into the setting of concrete disputes over specific documents. The lessons of that experience are mixed. In most situations, judges do not believe they have enough knowledge to determine *de novo* whether material is properly classified. The 1974 Congress thought otherwise, but we cannot dismiss the views of the judges themselves; they are, of course, experts in what they themselves know. On the other hand, judges have their own self-interested reasons to avoid confronting the national security establishment. They may therefore overestimate the relevance of their conceded lack of national security expertise.

Indeed, the debate about expertise has been dominated by a misconception. To be sure, judges (with rare exceptions) have no specialized training in intelligence analysis. That fact is routinely cited as the decisive objection to any active judicial role. Yet the observation is largely beside the point.

Judges have no particular training in many, perhaps most, of the subjects they are called upon to adjudicate. Typically, they know nothing about how to perform open-heart surgery, build bridges, or diagnose mental illness. But their outstanding proficiency is their *ability to listen.* They are skilled in learning from professionals and critically assessing divergent claims. Whether the topic is familiar or arcane, judges specialize in separating well-grounded from flimsy contentions. Secrecy decisions are no different; they require much more than just an understanding of national security effects. Ultimately they require an ability to appraise rival claims, an appreciation for the value of robust public debate, and an instinct for fine-grained solutions that leave maximum feasible scope for all competing interests.

Intelligence analysts have no claim to excel in these qualities – far from it. If anything, their background and training steer them away from developing such skills. The pervasive assumption that judges lack expertise is therefore either exaggerated or irrelevant. In several of the crucial abilities – the *generalist's perspective*, the *ability to listen*, and the *capacity to arbitrate between interests in conflict* – judges are the quintessential experts, while the national security professionals have no expertise at all.

Military and foreign policy matters are distinctive because they can involve very high stakes. Even so, concern about imprudent disclosure cannot justify the complete suspension of accountability. Judges know that unwarranted disclosures may have grave consequences; they can be instructed (superfluously) to take that danger into account. It is the other side of this coin that needs emphasis – that national security experts have powerful incentives to seek *unjustified* secrecy, that unjustified secrecy poses a grave threat to the national welfare, and that only the judiciary has the independence and skill necessary to reach appropriate, narrowly tailored conclusions about when and where concealment is needed. Error costs should influence judgment – of course. But they cannot be permitted to displace it, because oversight is essential to insure that official claims are truly based on expertise, not on self-interest.

4.1.3 Inter-branch comparative advantage

The executive holds the lion's share of the nation's national security expertise, and it is uniquely well positioned to appreciate 'the big picture' in military matters and foreign affairs. On the debit side, the executive branch has an exceptionally myopic perspective. National security concerns are uppermost (appropriately so), but other important objectives, such as nurturing a well-informed public, normally do not further executive interests and thus command little attention. Transparency is not an interest that national security officials can be expected to value, even when they make secrecy decisions in good faith.

And often secrecy decisions are not made wisely or in perfectly good faith. Executive officials lack objectivity. Intimate involvement with the issues, the primary source of their expertise, almost inevitably undermines impartiality. Compounding that problem, national security officials have a multitude of improper reasons to keep information secret. Secrecy shields error and inefficiency, preserves freedom of action, protects agency turf, enhances status vis-à-vis other bureaucrats or outsiders, and prevents public interference with unpopular or controversial policies. Inappropriate incentives are so many and so strong that credible observers often consider unnecessary classification to be the dominant pattern, not the isolated exception.

Congressional strengths could offset some of these executive-branch weaknesses. With its staff and supporting agencies, Congress as an institution is a far different body from the mercurial, unsophisticated amateur portrayed in the common caricature. Congress can bring to bear significant expertise, and through its oversight committees, it sees much of the big picture. Its detachment from operational involvement gives it a degree of objectivity that executive officials lack, while its preoccupation with constituent interests and with the full menu of legislative business gives it accountability, political legitimacy and a broad, generalist's perspective. Detracting from these advantages, however, are Congress's distorted incentives, which impair oversight during divided and unitary government alike.

Courts offer different assets and liabilities. Judges can claim no national security expertise and typically cannot see the big picture. They arguably lack political legitimacy and are entirely unaccountable. But these endlessly-repeated points convey only part of the story. First, as CIPA experience demonstrates, the adversary process goes far toward mitigating judges' familiar deficiencies in national security expertise. Second, in many of the capabilities required for sound decisions about secrecy, courts are superior to the executive, to Congress or to both.

Courts, together with Congress, have two essential qualities that the executive lacks – a generalist's perspective and the capacity to arbitrate between security needs and public-governance values. The manner in which courts mediate this conflict differs from that of Congress, as judges lack political accountability. But in terms of independence and objectivity, courts outrank both the executive and legislative branches. Judicial mechanisms also are less likely to slight the interests of politically weak minorities and are more fine-grained, reflecting courts' greater attention span and capacity for detail. Most importantly, the last two qualities, along with judges' comparatively few distorting incentives, increase the likelihood that oversight functions assigned to the courts will actually be performed.

4.2 Implementing Reform

Proposals to attack over-classification through reform within the executive branch are a perennial favorite, because they escape any need to question conventional wisdom about executive expertise and outsider incompetence. Despite repeated attempts, however, that path has produced few improvements.[50] Further efforts in that direction are worth considering, but the core of the problem is the absence of strong, fully independent checks.

4.2.1 Strengthening Congress

Two issues need to be considered – the flow of information to Congress itself and the flow of information to the public.

Facilitating congressional access is relatively simple, because it can be achieved without jeopardizing the classified status of sensitive information. Congress can, for example, strengthen its oversight structures by

---

50 See PRESIDENT'S COMM'N, *supra* note 2; PIDB REPORT, *supra* note 6.

expanding intelligence committee staffs and permitting longer terms of service for committee members. Another straightforward step would be to reinforce safeguards for whistleblowers who turn to Congress when classification is used to cover up inefficiency and abuse. The failure to provide effective protection for intelligence community employees who alert Congress to matters warranting oversight is inexcusable and profoundly undemocratic.

The other area of concern is over-classification. Congress's own access to classified information seldom translates into an effective check, in part because – so long as information remains classified – members cannot mobilize public opinion by sharing their knowledge. One way to address this problem would be to tighten the classification *criteria* – for example by narrowing such manipulable categories as 'critical infrastructure' and by stipulating that public-interest balancing must be a factor in the classification decision, so that classification cannot be considered proper when slender national security risks are outweighed by substantial public benefits of disclosure.

Congress also needs to strengthen declassification procedures. One approach might be to allow declassification by the opposition party, at least when it can muster significant support across the aisle. But declassification by congressional coalition would almost always be stymied by the President's party. And in any event it could not meet the need for an ongoing check on the thousands of classification actions taken every working day. A more promising option, therefore, would be to create a permanent agency, with its own staff and joint executive-legislative membership, in order to consider declassification appeals on an ongoing basis. Such an agency, of course, could not defy the President when executive branch preferences are strongly held, and it therefore should not supplant recourse to the judiciary through FOIA. But in thousands of noteworthy but less politically fraught cases, such a panel could furnish independent yet expert judgment, providing considerable pressure for transparency.

4.2.2 Strengthening the courts

Existing barriers to judicial oversight are primarily psychological rather than doctrinal. In criminal cases, judges seem instinctively comfortable with their checking function, but in FOIA cases, most judges simply refuse to exercise the *de novo* review authority they already possess. Ultimately, therefore, any effort to make judicial review more effective will depend on educating the judiciary. Tunnel vision now leads most judges to see only the value of national security expertise (which they lack). FOIA judges must be reminded that along with that expertise, equally necessary attributes are impartiality, an appreciation for transparency, and an ability to provide a fine-grained accommodation of conflicting claims. The message must be communicated to judges – and to the public at large – that courts represent our preeminent repository of the indispensable capacity to provide objective, narrowly tailored reconciliation of the competing values – security and transparency – on which the survival of a healthy democracy depends.

CONCLUSION

In the domain of national security, American executive officials ordinarily are left free to control and conceal whatever information they choose to consider sensitive. The press represents a significant but easily exaggerated source of countervailing power, because American reporters have no legal leverage and (despite WikiLeaks) only episodic practical success in obtaining classified information. Formal information-access powers are therefore indispensable, in their own right and as enabling mechanisms that permit the press to function.[51]

In practice, therefore, formal legislative and judicial checks remain essential, even where public opinion and informal political pressure ultimately will be decisive. In fact, however, most of the legal powers required have already been conferred on Congress and the courts. The deployment of these powers is almost invariably hobbled not by formal obstacles but by a lack of will, fueled in turn by the mystique of executive expertise and the myth of outsider incompetence. What nearly all discussion of the over-classification problem overlooks, however, is that much of the expertise necessary for sound secrecy decisions is notably absent in the executive branch; it can be found only in legislative bodies or the courts. Mechanisms identified in this chapter are readily available to harness that expertise, promote wider public recognition of it, and thus insure accountability. Such steps are imperative if we are to close the information loophole that permits so much national security activity to escape the rule of law.

---

[51] *See* Bill Keller, *The Times & the Internet*, N.Y. REV. BOOKS, September 24, 2009, at 93 (noting importance of FOIA to reporters).

4. Secrecy vs. openness: counterterrorism and the role of the German Federal Constitutional Court

Mindia Vashakmadze

INTRODUCTION

Germany is no newcomer to counterterrorism. In fact, it has struggled with terrorists since the early 1970s. But 9/11 tested Germany's approach to counterterrorism in a special way. The fact that a number of Islamist terrorists had spent considerable time within Germany planning their attacks was a harrowing discovery for the authorities. It was therefore not surprising that the German state reacted swiftly to 9/11.[1] In 2002, the legislature adopted two counter-terrorism packages that extended the competences of the security and intelligence agencies.[2]

Notions of openness and transparency underlie much of German constitutional-legal practice (though not explicitly mentioned in the Basic Law).[3] These themes are especially relevant with respect to counter-terrorism – an area in which the tensions between openness and secrecy are extensive. Transparency, among others, implies clarity of legal regulation and democratic accountability of decision-making. The German Parliament (Bundestag) has the power to legislate in areas relating to the exercise of fundamental rights. This power is exclusive to the legislature, which means that the executive may not regulate such matters by way of delegation.[4] Moreover, Parliament exercises oversight

[1] See on this Oliver Lepsius, Liberty, Security, and Terrorism: The Legal Position in Germany, 5 GERMAN L. J. 435, 459–60 (2004).

[2] Gesetz zur Bekämpfung des internationalen Terrorismus (Terrorism Law) of Jan 9, 2002 (BGBl I p. 361).

[3] See JÜRGEN BRÖHMER, TRANSPARENZ ALS VERFASSUNGSPRINZIP (2004).

[4] See, for example, BVerfGE 33, 125; BVerfGE 49, 89.

over the actions of the executive. However, the power of parliamentary oversight is not limitless, especially in the area of counterterrorism.

The German Federal Constitutional Court (FCC) resolves disputes that arise between branches of the Federal Government.[5] It also deals with constitutional complaints and examines the constitutionality of laws. Although the FCC has not declared the extension of the powers of the intelligence and security agencies unconstitutional, it has handed down a considerable number of judgments concerning security legislation. This chapter will address the case law that has evolved after 9/11. More specifically, this chapter focuses on the role of the FCC in terms of its impact on the counter-terrorism measures that have been introduced since 9/11. While doing so, it will highlight the tension that exists between parliamentary powers and government competences, as well as the tension that exists between the right to a free development of personality[6] and government secrecy. The FCC cases are reviewed briefly because of the limited scope of the present contribution.

1. TRANSPARENCY THROUGH DEMOCRATIC ACCOUNTABILITY – THE TENSION BETWEEN PARLIAMENTARY SCRUTINY AND CORE EXECUTIVE COMPETENCES

Although the executive has far-reaching powers in the area of foreign and security policy, it is the Parliament that has the ability to bring to light wrongdoing on the part of the Government and to ensure the accountability of the executive. For example, the legislature can question the Ministers, use its budgetary powers to control the government's security agenda and elect a new government with a vote of no confidence. Additionally, standing committees have the ability to inquire into government activities.

One important tool the legislature may use to ensure government accountability is the power to appoint an investigative committee according to Article 44(1) of the Basic Law.[7] This power, which has been the

---

[5] Bundesverfassungsgerichtsgesetz, Aug. 11, 1993 (BGBl. I p. 1473).

[6] Article 2(1) of the Basic Law reads: 'Every person shall have the right to free development of his personality insofar as he does not violate the rights of others or offend against the constitutional order or moral law.'

[7] 'The Bundestag shall have the right, and on the motion of one quarter of its members the duty, to establish a committee of inquiry, which shall take requisite evidence at public hearings. The public may be excluded.'

subject of several rulings of the Constitutional Court,[8] is a minority right that enables the representatives of the opposition to effectively oversee executive action. In essence, it allows the opposition to conduct investigations into the government's activities independently from the parliamentary majority.

1.1 Reinforcing the Rights of Parliamentary Investigation

One case that highlights the tension between the rights of Parliament to obtain pertinent information from the executive and the need for government secrecy concerned the alleged German participation in extraordinary renditions that were subject to parliamentary investigation.[9] Here, the FCC found that the right of Parliament to obtain the information in accordance with Article 44 of the Basic Law had been violated.

Shortly after 9/11 the Federal Intelligence Service (Bundesnachrichtendienst) began cooperating with the Central Intelligence Agency (CIA) in its counterterrorism efforts. In 2004, however, accusations began to swirl about the possible involvement of the German secret agencies in extraordinary renditions. Thus, in 2005 the Parliament requested a report from the Federal Government related to its involvement in the Iraq war and the fight against international terrorism. On 15 February 2006, the Federal Government issued this report at the behest of the parliamentary control organ, which is in charge of ensuring the Government's accountability for the security services.[10] The report detailed the Bundesnachrichtendienst's cooperation with the CIA and other services. However, certain questions remained unanswered and thus the parliamentary factions of Liberal, Green and the Left Party representatives, together with a group of three members of Parliament, created an investigative committee. The committee was tasked with clarifying the political directives that had been issued to the Bundesnachrichtendienst, the Federal Domestic Intelligence Service (Bundesamt für Verfassungsschutz), the Military Intelligence Service

---

[8] See, for example, Volker Röben, Federal Constitutional Court Defines the Power of Parliamentary Minorities in the Constitutionally Established, Parliamentary Investigative Committees, 3 GERMAN L. J. (2002), available at http://germanlawjournal.com/index.php?pageID=11&artID=194.

[9] BVerfG, 2 BvE 3/07, 17 June 2009, BVerfGE 124, 78.

[10] Bericht der Bundesregierung (offene Fassung) gemäß Anforderung des Parlamentarischen Kontrollgremiums vom 25. Januar 2006 zu Vorgängen im Zusammenhang mit dem Irakkrieg und der Bekämpfung des Internationalen Terrorismus, 15 February 2006.

(Militärischer Abschirmdienst), the General Prosecutor (Generalbundesanwalt) and the Federal Investigative Police Agency (Bundeskriminalamt). The committee was also set up to investigate how political control was structured and ensured.[11]

To implement its mandate, the committee questioned the representatives of the Federal Government and a range of state bodies subordinate to the executive. However, on many occasions the Government refused to submit the requested documents and granted only limited permission to witnesses to testify before the investigative committee. As a result, a constitutional claim was lodged with the FCC.[12] In the course of proceedings, the executive invoked the notion of core executive competences and public weal (Staatswohl) to justify its withholding of pertinent information.

The Court took a balanced approach to analysing the claim, setting legal limits to parliamentary investigation while also carving out the scope of the Government's prerogative to keep certain information concealed. The Court held that Parliament's right to investigate suspicious governmental action is limited to the mandate for investigation.[13] According to the Court, reasons for withholding information from the investigative committee can be derived from the principle of the separation of powers between the branches of government.[14] According to this principle, there is a core area of government competences guaranteeing the executive's functionality and effectiveness. To defend the core executive competence, the Court held that parliamentary oversight does not extend to internal decision-making processes of the executive, especially when they are still ongoing.[15] Furthermore, the Court held that public weal might also justify limitations on investigative powers of Parliament.[16] Finally, basic rights[17] and the prohibition of abuse of rights[18] also serve to limit parliamentary investigations.

---

11 See also *supra* note 9, at 85–8.

12 Article 93(1) Basic Law. Constitutional organs of Germany have the capacity to bring a claim. In constitutional practice, part of Parliament (parliamentary faction) is entitled to claim the right of Parliament in relation to other constitutional organs before the Constitutional Court.

13 *Supra* note 9, at 118–20.

14 Id. at 120–23.

15 Id.

16 Id. at 123–5.

17 Id. at 125–8.

18 Id. at 128.

Although core executive competences may not serve as a justification to shield the legislature from access to pertinent information, the Parliament may not impede the Government's flexibility. Stated differently, the Parliament's interest in having access to information must be balanced against the Government's interest in keeping things running. Thus, in order to trump an executive demand for secrecy, parliamentary requests for information must be of special importance, particularly where the Government's internal decision-making processes are involved. However, the reverse is true when parliamentary requests for information concern possible violations of the law by the executive.[19] In these instances, the Government must give substantial justification for any refusal to submit the requested information.

In the end, the Court concluded that the executive failed to adequately justify its withholding of information and evidence. According to the Court, the information on intelligence cooperation with foreign services could not be withheld only by reference to a possible threat to public weal.[20] The executive must demonstrate that the release of the information would threaten US secrecy interests and strain future intelligence cooperation between the US and Germany.[21] The fact that the release of such information would be inconvenient to the German Government was an insufficient reason for withholding the information. The Court held that it should be regarded as a consequence of the exercise of a right to parliamentary investigation, which must be accepted by the Government.[22]

The Court addressed the scope of the committee's mandate in the context of inter-governmental intelligence sharing. Here, the German Government justified its nondisclosure by emphasizing the importance of inter-state intelligence sharing in the fight against global terrorist threats. The Court was not impressed by this rather abstract argument. It held that the activities of the security agencies would be exempt from parliamentary scrutiny only in certain circumstances. For example, it noted that special protection would be required when the release of foreign intelligence information would have a detrimental impact in the international sphere.

However, it seems difficult to draw a line between the domestic and international impact of the release of intelligence information provided by the foreign services, or to determine precisely when such action would

19 Id. at 123, 132.
20 Id. at 134
21 Id.
22 Id.

strain inter-state intelligence co-operation. It seems equally problematic to assess precisely when such a release may negatively affect the legitimate secrecy interests of the respective foreign services. This, therefore, remains an area in which the Government has leeway to explain its concerns and to present its arguments to the legislature.

In sum, the Court balanced the interests of parliamentary oversight with core executive responsibility. The Court, while reinforcing the right of parliamentary investigation, based its analysis on the principle of separation of powers.[23] It held that a general appeal to the executive functions and core responsibilities does not suffice to justify non-disclosure of relevant information. It has also paid sufficient attention to the protection of core executive responsibilities from unjustified parliamentary intrusions. Thus, the effectiveness of the security agencies has not been called into question. At the same time, the Court sent a message to the wider public that its legitimate interest in reining in clandestine government activities remains adequately protected through respective constitutional means.

2. MORE TRANSPARENCY THROUGH THE PROTECTION OF PERSONAL LIBERTY? THE TENSION BETWEEN PERSONALITY RIGHTS AND GOVERNMENT CONTROL AND SURVEILLANCE

The complexity of the government's security measures can lead to a non-transparency, which increases the chance that violations of personality rights will go unchallenged. An individual who is unaware of continuous state surveillance, for example, is unlikely to seek an effective legal remedy guaranteed by Article 19(4) of the Basic Law. However, restrictions can lawfully be imposed to address serious security threats or to protect an important public good, such as the free democratic state order, or the existence of a Federation or of a Federal State (Bundesland).

It can be argued, however, that after 9/11 the Court's rulings managed to enhance the right to 'informational self-determination', which is derived from the right to the free development of personality enshrined in Article 2(1) of the Basic Law. The FCC demonstrated its awareness that the increasing complexity of government measures targeted at the early

[23] On the separation of powers see CHRISTOPH MÖLLERS, GEWALTENGLIEDERUNG – LEGITIMATION UND DOGMATIK IM NATIONALEN UND INTERNATIONALEN RECHTSVERGLEICH (2005).

prevention of security threats might widen the range of infringements upon fundamental rights. The concept of informational self-determination, developed by the FCC in its long-standing jurisprudence,[24] is not compatible with unrestricted government surveillance and control of the individual. In the following section, those cases will be briefly discussed, in which the Court had the opportunity to address the tensions between the need to increase subjection of the individual to state surveillance and control due to new security threats and the right to the free development of personality of Article 2(1) of the Basic Law.

2.1 Right to a Free Development of Personality and 'Informational Self-Determination' – Dragnet Investigation

The grid search was first introduced in the 1970s and was used against the members of RAF. Although it did not prove very effective, its legislative framework was maintained and it was thus able to be subsequently re-activated after 9/11. The grid search permits the Government to gather personal information about its citizens in order to effectively identify and track so-called sleepers. The North Rhine-Westphalia (NRW) Police Act allows a dragnet investigation to be instituted to avert a present threat to the Federation, the Bundesland or the life or safety of an individual. Such measures need to be ordered by a judge. Indeed, in October 2001 the Düsseldorf First Instance Court authorized a data-mining operation (which did not lead to any criminal proceedings). The First Instance Court found that there was a 'present threat' to overriding public and individual values. The court order, based on section 31(1) of the NRW Police Act, was challenged by a Moroccan student who claimed that the court violated his basic right to informational self-determination.

The Constitutional Court concluded that the First Instance Court had violated the student's right to 'personal self-determination' under Article 2(1) in connection with Article 1(1) of the Basic Law (which guarantees the inviolability of human dignity).[25] According to the Court, the person's right to control as to when and which parts of personal information are disclosed was infringed.[26] Nevertheless, the Court concluded that Section 31(1) of the NRW Police Act was proportional and in conformity with the Constitution. The Court held, however, that the 'present threat' language of the Act has to be interpreted narrowly to apply only to

[24] See, for example, BVerfGE 65, 1 at 43 et seq.

[25] 1 BvR 518/02, April 4, 2006 (BVerfGE 115, 320).

[26] Id. see esp. at 367 et seq.

'concrete threat(s)'. The general threat persistent after 9/11 did not meet the standard of a concrete threat.[27] The FCC regarded its narrow construction of 'present threat' as necessary to fulfil the constitutional requirement of certainty and clarity, which is the standard for imposing restrictions on the exercise of basic rights.[28]

The FCC emphasized the intensity of the state's intrusion upon the basic right to a free development of personality.[29] The Court pointed out that certain persons would be stigmatized because of the selection process.[30] Moreover, the intrusion was also problematic because only persons against whom further action was taken had to be informed of the data collection and only after the data analysis was finished.[31] In this context, the Court also referred to an indiscriminate invasion of personal rights without suspicion. The transfer and use of the data so collected constituted an intrusion in the right to a free development of personality, which was largely used to identify suspects, and not to strengthen existing suspicion.[32] Accordingly, the FCC concluded that there must be a concrete threat to justify any intrusion in the right to informational self-determination. Such threat shall be based on facts and not on mere presumptions.[33]

The decision has been subject to criticism. Commentators have argued that the decision left the State largely defenceless, depriving it of the capacity to take effective preventive measures in the face of global terrorist threats.[34]

---

27 Id.

28 Id. at 365 et seq.

29 Id. at 347 et seq.

30 Id. 351–3.

31 Id. at 353–4.

32 Id. at 354–6.

33 Id. at 367 et seq.

34 See the dissenting opinion by Judge Evelyn Haas of 4 April 2006, who argued that the Court's decision left the state defenceless because the legislature was deprived of the opportunity to issue preventive measures below the threshold of the concrete threat. She emphasized that the Court shall exercise judicial self-restraint in its relations to the legislature. Id. at 371–81; see also Winfried Bausback, Fesseln für die wehrhafte Demokratie, NEUE JURISTISCHE WOCHENSCHRIFT 1922 (2006).

2.2 From Informational Self-Determination to Individual IT Rights – Protecting the Integrity and the Confidentiality of Personal Computer Systems

The Constitutional Court had one further opportunity to demonstrate its approach to protecting personal liberty from government intrusion. The case dealt with the constitutionality of provisions of the North Rhine-Westphalia Constitution Protection Act, which allowed secret internet surveillance and access.[35] Under the Act, the police were permitted to use special software technology to infiltrate personal computers and collect personal information for criminal law and threat prevention purposes. The Court found that the Act violated the general right of personality enshrined in Article 2(1)[36] and Article 10(1) of the Grundgesetz, which guarantees the privacy of correspondence, post and telecommunications.[37] The Court also found that the Act violated Article 19(1) of the Basic Law, which requires that the legislature specify the basic right affected.[38]

The FCC argued that the respective provision of the Constitution Protection Act did not satisfy the standards set by the constitutional requirement of clarity of norms; the principle of proportionality was violated; moreover, the provision did not envisage the appropriate procedural measures to protect the core of private life. The Court recognized a citizen's right to a guarantee of confidentiality and integrity in information-technology systems. In other words, the Constitutional Court by enhancing the protection range for personal information established a new information technology right of the individual. However, this right may be restricted for threat prevention and crime prosecution purposes. The FCC considered the infiltration of personal computers permissible if there is a concrete threat to an important legal interest, which must be carried out pursuant to a law. While differentiating between the security agencies and the police, the FCC emphasized that the proportionality requirement shall be fully applicable to both institutions.

The Court found that there was no adequate statutory protection against the encroachments upon the core of private life, which is

---

35 BVerfG, 1 BvR 370/07, 27 February 2008, BVerfGE 120, 274.

36 Id. at 302–40.

37 Id. at 340–46.

38 Id. at 340. Article 19(1) states: 'Insofar as … a basic right may be restricted by or pursuant to a law, such law must apply generally and not merely to a single case. In addition, the law must specify the basic right affected.'

protected by Article 19(2) of the Grundgesetz.[39] The secrecy of the access diminished the opportunity for the respective person to ensure, before or during the investigation, that the core area of private life was protected through appropriate legal remedies. Accordingly, the FCC concluded that the approval by the judiciary would be necessary, which would establish a mechanism of preventive control of the state's secret access to the information-technology systems. Thus, the FCC established two preconditions for lawful online snooping: First, there must be clear evidence of a concrete threat to public good. Second, the judiciary must approve the search. If both elements are met, then the authorities are allowed to access a suspect's personal computer.

2.3 Right to Privacy of Communication (Article 10(1) of the Basic Law). Overturning the Data Retention Legislation

The legislation on data retention was issued in implementation of the EU Data Retention Directive.[40] It amended the German Telecommunications Act and the Code of Criminal Procedure.[41] The amendments permitted the retention and transmission of personal data to the authorities to prosecute criminal offences, to prevent dangers to public security and to perform the intelligence tasks. The amendments triggered a public debate in Germany and soon reached the FCC in Karlsruhe after about 34,000 people lodged a complaint with the Constitutional Court.[42] The FCC found that data retention rules incorporated in paragraphs 113 a and b of

[39] This provision reads: 'In no case may the essence of a basic right be affected.'

[40] Directive 2006/24 on the retention of data generated or processed in connection with the provision of publicly available electronic communications services or of public communications networks and amending Directive 2002/58/EC, OJ [2006] L 105/54, April 13, 2006. See also Report from the Commission of the Council and the European Parliament (Evaluation Report on the Data Retention Directive (Directive 2006/24/EC)), April 8, 2011COM(2011) 225 final.

[41] Gesetz zur Neuregelung der Telekommunikationsüberwachung und anderer verdeckter Ermittlungsmaßnahmen sowie zur Umsetzung der Richtlinie 2006/24/EG (BGBl. I p. 3198).

[42] Anna-Bettina Kaiser, German Data Retention Provisions Unconstitutional in Their Present Form; Decision of 2 March 2010, NEUE JURISTISCHE WOCHENSCHRIFT 2010, p. 833, 6 EUROPEAN CONSTITUTIONAL L. REV. 503–17 (2010).

the Telecommunications Act[43] and paragraph 100 of the Code of Criminal Procedure were not compatible with Article 10(1) of the Grundgesetz, which protects the privacy of communication.

The Court examined the constitutionality of the issue in light of the principle of proportionality. Although the Court concluded that prosecution of crimes, prevention of threats and intelligence activities constituted legitimate goals,[44] it emphasized that the procedure of preventive data retention must constitute an exception to remain in line with the Constitution.[45] Interestingly, the Court went further and concluded that 'it is part of the *constitutional identity of the Federal Republic of Germany* that the citizens' enjoyment of freedom may not be totally recorded and registered, and the Federal Republic must endeavour to preserve this in European and international connections'.[46] Thus, the policy of total and comprehensive oversight over the citizens' enjoyment of their freedoms cannot be reconciled with the constitutional foundations of the Federal Republic.

In this case, too, the Court proceeded to define the requirements for a legislative framework. While doing so, the Court placed its emphasis on data security, scope and purposes of the use of data, transparent data transfer and legal remedy. According to the FCC, the legislature must not apply any unspecified notion of 'serious crimes'. The Court concluded that a list of the criminal offences must be formulated; thus, the clarity of the legislative basis must be ensured. In this context, the court emphasized that a general threat to public security cannot justify data transmission. This would require the existence of a concrete threat to the protected public and individual values (the life, limb or freedom of a person, the existence or the security of the Federal Government or of a Bundesland).

The Court concluded that the Parliament has to take legislative measures regarding the use of the data.[47] In addition, the Court regarded the open and transparent use of data as a pre-requisite for an effective legal remedy.[48] However, the Court admitted that the intelligence activity might require some secrecy in the use of data. In this case, the person

---

[43] Telekommunikationsgesetz (TKG) of 22 June 2004 (BGBl. I p. 1190); recently amended by the Law of March 24, 2011 (BGBl. I p. 506).

[44] BVerfG, 1 BvR 256/08, 2 March 2010, BVerfGE 125, 260, at 316.

[45] Id. at 317.

[46] Id. at 324, emphasis added.

[47] Id. at 325 et seq.

[48] Id.

concerned has to be informed subsequently. Exceptions to this obligation have to be authorized by the judiciary.[49]

Any use of personal data, which is kept secret continuously (and without necessary institutional safeguards) would be in contravention of the Constitution. Thus, the Court reinforced the procedural transparency with respect to the use of personal data in this case. Another major contribution of the Court was to enhance data security, and to define a central role for the legislature in shaping the required legal framework.[50]

CONCLUSION

In its case law under review, the Federal Constitutional Court gave teeth to a rather vague notion of transparency through the means of a functional separation of powers and the protection of basic rights. The Court set standards for clarity of legal regulation and for transparency in their implementation. It also elaborated on the reasons for issuing regulations and decisions by state authorities, and reinforced the transparency in proceedings.

The FCC set significant limits to legislative and executive preventive action in the area of counterterrorism by determining that a concrete threat is required to justify any intrusion into basic rights. Moreover, the Court stressed the importance of a substantiated justification of any limitations/modifications of basic rights. The Court's position that the executive shall give reasons for its decisions related to threat prevention would also contribute to more transparency.

The principle of democratic accountability as well as the status of the individual in the constitutional system is not compatible with expansive secrecy, and the jurisprudence of the Federal Constitutional Court demonstrates as much. The adherence to the principle of a functional separation of powers would ensure that the democracy is able to defend itself within the bounds of the Constitution and would not convert itself into an extra-constitutional preventive state.

Parliament has to ensure the rule of law in counterterrorism through legislative action; however, the legislation may not cover all possible scenarios and responses to new security threats. In cases that are not

---

[49] Id. at 336–7.

[50] It is worth noting that the EU Data Retention Directive remains unimplemented so far. This generated some criticism from Brussels. EU rügt Deutschland, SÜDDEUTSCHE ZEITUNG, Oct. 28, 2011, at 5.

clearly defined in legislation, the mechanisms of democratic accountability shall re-establish the balance of power among the branches of government.[51] Parliament will have to exercise its oversight over the Government's counterterrorist policies most effectively. This would serve the legitimate interest of the broader public in controlling the Government's anti-terrorist activities, especially when they have a direct bearing on basic rights.

[51] See also Andreas L. Paulus and Mindia Vashakmadze, Parliamentary Control over the Use of Armed Forces Against Terrorism – In Defence of the Separation of Powers, 38 NETHERLANDS YEARBOOK OF INTL'L L. 113, 159 (2007).

5. Formalism and state secrets

Sudha Setty

INTRODUCTION*

The state secrets privilege has received a tremendous amount of scholarly attention in the US in the last decade, initially prompted by the administration of President George W. Bush seeking early dismissals of lawsuits that dealt with allegations of serious constitutional and human rights violations.[1] The administration's litigation posture was troubling – but the judicial acceptance of these claims, largely based on the judiciary's own formalistic view of its own role in engaging the executive branch on national security secrecy[2] – allowed the executive branch to make virtually unilateral secrecy determinations that shielded it from civil suits.

In September 2009 the Obama administration created a new policy that mandated a more rigorous internal administrative review prior to invoking the state secrets privilege.[3] In the years since the new policy took effect, it appears as though this internal review process has resulted in little difference with regard to the invocation of the privilege at the

* This chapter is drawn from a previous work: Sudha Setty, Judicial Formalism and the State Secrets Privilege, 38 WM. MITCHELL L. REV. 1629 (2012).

1 Press Release, Office of Sen. Edward M. Kennedy, Kennedy Introduces State Secrets Protection Act (Jan. 22, 2008) (internal quotation marks omitted), available at 2008 WLNR 1256008; e.g., William G. Weaver and Robert M. Pallitto, State Secrets and Executive Power, 120 POL. SCI. Q. 85, 100 (2005) (claiming that the Bush administration is using the state secrets privilege with 'offhanded abandon').

2 E.g., El-Masri v. Tenet, 437 F. Supp. 2d 530 (E.D. Va. 2006), aff'd, 479 F.3d 296 (4th Cir. 2007) (dismissing suit seeking damages for extraordinary rendition and torture upon upholding the government's invocation of the state secrets privilege).

3 See Memorandum from Eric Holder, Attorney Gen., on Policies and Procedures Governing Invocating of the State Secrets Privilege to Heads of Exec.

pleadings stage in cases that allege torture and other human rights abuses.[4]

One high-profile case, that of Binyam Mohamed and other plaintiffs claiming that they had been subject to extraordinary rendition, torture, and prolonged detention, offers evidence of a disturbing trend of US courts retreating to formalistic reasoning[5] to extend unwarranted deference to the executive branch in security-related[6] contexts.[7] In this chapter, I consider the state secrets privilege and place the formalist decision-making of the *Mohamed* court in juxtaposition with other nations' jurisprudence – including the English courts that dealt with a separate

---

Dep'ts & Agencies (Sept. 23, 2009) [hereinafter Holder Memorandum], (establishing layers of internal review regarding invocations of the state secrets privilege).

4 See Sudha Setty, Litigating Secrets: Comparative Perspectives on the State Secrets Privilege, 75 BROOK. L. REV. 201, 257–8 (2009) (identifying the continuity between the Bush and Obama administrations in their approach to the state secrets privilege).

5 I use judicial formalism to refer to a methodology that gives primacy to narrow rule-following rather than consideration of the role of the courts to act in a way that is infused with morality when necessary to preserve individual rights. See Richard H. Pildes, Forms of Formalism, 66 U. CHI. L. REV. 607, 612–16 (1999) (describing one form of formalism as 'apurposive rule-following'). Justice Antonin Scalia has supported use of a formal approach to maximize stability and credibility in the Supreme Court's decision making, opining that a 'discretion-conferring approach is ill suited … to a legal system in which the supreme court can review only an insignificant proportion of the decided cases'. See Antonin Scalia, The Rule of Law as a Law of Rules, 56 U. CHI. L. REV. 1175, 1178 (1989).

6 Cass Sunstein has offered three categories of judicial decision-making in wartime: national security maximalism, in which courts defer broadly to executive branch claims of Article II authority; liberty maximalism, in which courts maintain a peacetime approach to constitutional liberty questions; and minimalism, in which courts use a narrow approach to creating precedent to weigh security and liberty interests. See Cass R. Sunstein, Minimalism at War, 2004 SUP. CT. REV. 47, 50–52 (2004). I suggest that *Mohamed* and similar decisions should be conceived of differently, reflecting a formal and narrow adherence to procedures and rules as a means of enabling deference to executive claims and avoiding meaningful engagement in underlying civil liberties concerns.

7 E.g., Arar v. Ashcroft, 585 F.3d 559 (2d Cir. 2009) (dismissing suit seeking damages for extraordinary rendition and torture upon a finding that constitutional and international law obligations did not apply); Al-Aulaqi v. Obama, 727 F. Supp. 2d 1 (D.D.C. 2010) (dismissing suit seeking injunctive relief for the listing of plaintiff's son on the US targeted killings list based on standing and political question grounds).

lawsuit brought by Mohamed there. This case exemplifies the US shift away from the flexible, rule of law-oriented approach that courts in the United Kingdom and Israel take, and toward the formalistic rigidity that the Indian Supreme Court often employs in government secrecy cases.[8]

Given the Obama administration's aggressive invocation of the state secrets privilege and the judiciary's unwillingness to defend the ability of individuals to litigate their basic human and civil rights, I conclude that for meaningful change to occur, the United States Congress must re-introduce state secrets reform legislation that infuses the litigation process with procedural and substantive fairness,[9] and that courts must step away from judicial formalism and instead take on the complex and difficult task of providing a venue for government accountability.

1. THE OBAMA ADMINISTRATION AND THE STATE SECRETS PRIVILEGE

In his prefatory language to the Obama administration's 2009 state secrets policy, Attorney General Eric Holder emphasizes that the policy's goals include 'provid[ing] greater accountability and reliability in the invocation of the state secrets privilege in litigation … [and] strengthen-[ing] public confidence that the U.S. government will invoke the privilege in court only when genuine and significant harm to national defense or foreign relations is at stake and only to the extent necessary to safeguard those interests'.[10] The policy also includes important limitations such as a prohibition against using the privilege to conceal violations of the law or prevent embarrassment to the government.[11] Unfortunately, the promise

---

8 These four nations – the United States, England, Israel and India – are useful comparators because of their shared common law traditions and the shared roots of evidentiary privileges such as the state secrets privilege in English law and policy.

9 Congress's reform attempts, albeit unsuccessful, have attempted to improve procedural and substantive justice for plaintiffs. See, e.g., 154 CONG. REC. S198–201 (daily ed. Jan. 23, 2008) (statement of Sen. Kennedy on the State Secrets Protection Act).

10 Holder Memorandum, *supra* note 3, at 1.

11 Holder Memorandum, *supra* note 3, at 2. The rest of the policy establishes the layers of review with the Department of Justice with regard to satisfying the procedural requirements for invoking and defending the privilege. These procedural requirements are first laid out in the seminal US state secrets case of United States v. Reynolds, 345 U.S. 1, 6–8, 10–11 (1953). For an in-depth account of

of these reforms has not yet been fulfilled, as the case of Binyam Mohamed exemplifies.

In *Mohamed*, the Northern District of California dismissed a suit brought by five detainees against a Boeing subsidiary allegedly involved in the transportation of the detainees for government-directed rendition and torture.[12] Binyam Mohamed, a British resident, claimed that he traveled to Afghanistan in 2001 to escape a lifestyle that led to drug addiction in England.[13] US authorities alleged that Mohamed trained with the Taliban in Afghanistan to prepare for an attack within the US. Mohamed was arrested in Pakistan in 2002 and claims he was detained and tortured in various locations under US control until February 2009, when he was released without charge.[14] Mohamed and similarly situated plaintiffs filed suit in 2007 against Jeppesen Dataplan, the Boeing subsidiary that operated detainee transport airplanes to and from detention centers.[15]

In granting the government's motion to dismiss, the district court used the same reasoning that other US courts dealing with the privilege have relied upon,[16] primarily the need to dismiss the suit because the subject matter at issue – the government's extraordinary rendition program – was itself a state secret that could jeopardize national security interests if revealed.[17] A Ninth Circuit panel reversed, rejecting the government's claims that the suit needed to be dismissed outright based on its subject matter.[18] The administration appealed to the Ninth Circuit to hear the case *en banc*, where it prevailed in having Mohamed's suit dismissed.

---

the *Reynolds* case, see LOUIS FISHER, IN THE NAME OF NATIONAL SECURITY: UNCHECKED PRESIDENTIAL POWER AND THE *REYNOLDS* CASE (2006).

12 Mohamed v. Jeppesen Dataplan, Inc., 539 F. Supp. 2d 1128, 1130 (N.D. Cal. 2008).

13 Profile: Binyam Mohamed, BBC NEWS (Feb. 23, 2009), http://news.bbc.co.uk/2/hi/7870387.stm.

14 Id. Mohamed alleges that he was beaten, scalded, and suffered cuts on his genitals with a scalpel by his captors.

15 Amended Complaint at 1–6, Mohamed v. Jeppesen Dataplan, Inc., 563 F.3d 992 (9th Cir. 2009) (No. 07-2798).

16 E.g., El-Masri v. Tenet, 437 F. Supp. 2d 530, 535 (E.D. Va. 2006), aff'd, 479 F.3d 296 (4th Cir. 2007) (dismissing based on the state secrets privilege a suit in which plaintiff alleged extraordinary rendition and torture).

17 Mohamed v. Jeppesen Dataplan, Inc., 539 F. Supp. 2d 1128, 1134–36 (N.D. Cal. 2008).

18 Mohamed v. Jeppesen Dataplan, Inc., 563 F.3d 992, 997, 1009 (9th Cir. 2009).

2. FORMALISM IN JEPPESEN

The Ninth Circuit *en banc* dismissed the plaintiffs' suit in a formalistic opinion that failed to acknowledge the reality of the gross human rights abuses that plaintiffs suffered. The majority began its evaluation of the government's invocation of the privilege by finding that the procedural requirements were met and that the information is privileged.[19] The court then reasoned that it is obligated to dismiss a suit if it appeared that privileged information would be necessary to litigate the case.[20] The majority found that even if plaintiffs were able to prove their case relying solely on publicly available evidence, dismissal of the suit was still warranted because Jeppesen Dataplan would have found it difficult to mount a defense without implicating privileged material.[21] It is particularly ironic that the majority, while claiming to have struggled with the tension between human rights and security concerns, ultimately retreated to rigid and formalist reasoning that turned on its concern that a company allegedly complicit in the torture of innocent civilians is able to adequately defend itself in a civil matter.[22]

The majority opinion abdicated its structural responsibility to uphold the rule of law and check government abuse, instead offering only hollow platitudes and unlikely avenues for redress: at one point the court conjectures that the executive branch may decide someday to compensate the victims of the extraordinary rendition program, akin to the compensation for the rendition and internment of individuals of Japanese descent during World War II.[23] At other points, the court bizarrely shifted responsibility to Congress to provide redress to plaintiffs, noting that

---

[19] Id. at 1080, 1085–6 (relying on the test articulated in United States v. Reynolds, 345 U.S. 1, 7–8 (1953)).

[20] Id. at 1083.

[21] Id. at 1089–90.

[22] The veracity of the plaintiffs' claims about Jeppesen Dataplan's complicity in the torture is not factored into the majority opinion, a point raised by the dissent. See id. at 1095 n 5 (Hawkins, J., dissenting) (noting that former Jeppesen employees understood that their extraordinary rendition flights resulted in the torture of detainees).

[23] Id. at 1091. It is remarkable that the majority considered the reparations awarded to Japanese internees during World War II as a potentially appropriate model of compensation. Those reparations came decades after the harm to the internees, and only after a national soul-searching as to how such poor national security policy was validated by all branches of government and the public. Further, hearkening back to the internment evokes comparisons to the deferential formalism of Korematsu v. United States, 323 U.S. 214 (1944), which most

Congress has the power to investigate government abuses, could enact private bills to compensate the plaintiffs or take up state secrets reform.[24]

The dissent by Judge Hawkins included a critique of the narrowness of the majority opinion, noting the veracity of Mohamed's claims of Jeppesen Dataplan's role in rendition and torture, and that the majority's failure to give weight to these claims undermines an appropriate analysis.[25] Judge Hawkins observed that the majority 'disregard[ed] the concept of checks and balances' and abdicated its responsibility by suggesting that the executive or Congress should act to provide compensation, characterizing the majority's suggestion regarding reparations as 'elevat[ing] the impractical to the point of absurdity' and noting the need to preserve an avenue for the tortured plaintiffs to seek redress in the courts if possible.[26]

3. FORMALISM IN THE COMPARATIVE CONTEXT

The Supreme Court established the standard for evaluating a claim of the state secrets privilege in the 1950s, drawing from English precedent during World War II. English public interest immunity, used akin to the state secrets privilege, evolved in a different direction than that of the U.S. since that time; this dynamic is illustrated clearly in the contemporaneous treatment of Binyam Mohamed's lawsuit in the English courts. To further contextualize the analysis of judicial formalism in the application of the privilege, I briefly consider how Israel and India deal with questions of state secrecy during litigation.[27]

3.1 England

English courts generally afford high levels of deference to government officials claiming public interest immunity,[28] although the 2009 and 2010

---

modern commentators view as a profound failure of the judiciary to uphold the rule of law and curb abuses by the national security state.

[24] Id. at 1091–92.

[25] Id. at 1095–96.

[26] Id. at 1101.

[27] India and Israel are useful comparators as functioning democracies with constitutionally mandated separation of powers and serious ongoing national security threats, and, like the US in the context of the state secrets privilege, derive some legal processes from the United Kingdom.

[28] See Air Canada v. Sec'y of State for Trade [1983] 2 AC 394 at 395 (Eng.) (stating that when a government official has proffered a good faith affidavit as to

decisions in the case of Binyam Mohamed illustrate a potential shift. The backdrop of the English litigation in *Mohamed* relates to proceedings in the US. In May 2008, the US charged Mohamed under the Military Commissions Act[29] with conspiracy to commit terrorism,[30] relying on confessions which Mohamed alleged were elicited under the threat of torture.[31] Mohamed began proceedings in English courts seeking release of evidence in the possession of the British government that the US had compiled against Mohamed. In August 2008, a court ruled in Mohamed's favor,[32] but redacted a summary of intelligence gleaned from US intelligence sources after the Foreign Secretary issued a public interest immunity certificate claiming that state secrets were at issue.[33]

The Divisional Court of the Queen's Bench Division reconsidered in early 2009 whether the public interest immunity certificate issued by the Foreign Secretary was compelling.[34] The public interest immunity certificate asserted that the summary report must remain undisclosed because the US government had threatened to 're-evaluate its intelligence sharing relationship with the United Kingdom' and possibly withhold vital national security information from the United Kingdom should the summary be disclosed to Mohamed's attorneys.[35]

The English court laid out the test for balancing the public interest in national security and the public interest in 'open justice, the rule of law

---

the need for the public interest immunity to apply, the court should give absolute deference).

[29] 10 U.S.C. §§ 948–50 (2006).

[30] This proceeding was later dropped, as the convening judge determined the prosecution could not proceed without the use of evidence obtained through torture. See William Glaberson, U.S. Drops Charges for 5 Guantánamo Detainees, N.Y. TIMES, Oct. 21, 2008, www.nytimes.com/2008/10/22/washington/22gitmo.html?adxnnl=1&adxnnlx=1328130327-WTFkFvw3ue0Rn9QlvAuLHQ.

[31] Mohamed v. Sec'y of State for Foreign & Commonwealth Affairs, [2008] EWHC (Admin) 2048, [38]–[47] (Eng.).

[32] Id. at [105].

[33] Id. at [150]–[160].

[34] The court noted that the information in question was '7 very short paragraphs amounting to about 25 lines' of text which summarized reports by the US government to British intelligence services on the treatment of Mohamed during his detention in Pakistan. See Mohamed v. Sec'y of State for Foreign & Commonwealth Affairs, [2009] EWHC (Admin) 152, [14] (Eng.).

[35] Id. at [62]. See Glenn Greenwald, Obama Administration Threatens Britain to Keep Torture Evidence Concealed, SALON.COM (May 12, 2009), www.salon.com/2009/05/12/obama_101.

and democratic accountability'.[36] The test involved balancing the public interest in disclosure of the information and the possibility of serious harm to a public interest such as national security if disclosure is made, and determining whether national security interests can be protected by means other than nondisclosure.[37]

Considering factors in support of disclosing the information, the court noted the need to uphold the rule of law,[38] comport with international and supranational standards,[39] ensure that allegations of serious criminality are not inappropriately dismissed,[40] maintain accountability over the government,[41] and protect the public and media interest in disclosure of government activities.[42] The court also appeared surprised that the U.S. government was apparently interfering in a matter of the rule of law and government accountability in another country.[43] Nonetheless, the court relied on its long-standing precedent of deference to the executive branch in matters of national security[44] and upheld the Foreign Secretary's issuance of the public interest immunity certificate.[45]

However, in October 2009 the court reversed its previous decision to withhold the information regarding Mohamed's treatment.[46] The court

---

[36] *Mohamed*, [2009] EWHC (Admin) 152, [18] (Eng.) (noting that this case revolved around a question of the rule of law, not around the rights of an individual litigant).

[37] Id. at [34] (citing Regina v. H, [2004] 2 AC 134 (HL) [36(3)] (Eng.)).

[38] *Mohamed*, [2009] EWHC (Admin) 152, [18]–[19] (Eng.).

[39] See *Mohamed*, [2009] EWHC (Admin) 152, [20]–[21], [26], [30], [101]–[105].

[40] Id. at [26(iv)], [26(ix)].

[41] Id. at [32].

[42] Id. at [37] ('Where there is no publicity there is no justice ... There is no greater danger of usurpation than that which proceeds little by little, under cover of rules of procedure, and at the instance of judges themselves' (quoting Scott v. Scott, [1913] AC 417 (HL) 477 (Lord Shaw of Dunfermline) (appeal taken from EWCA (Civ) (UK)).

[43] Id. at [69].

[44] See id. at [63]–[67]. However, the court noted that such deference needed to be limited to instances of genuine national security, and not cases in which 'it appears that while disclosure of the material may cause embarrassment or arouse criticism, it will not damage any security or intelligence interest'. Id. at [66] (quoting R. v. Shayler, [2003] AC 247 (HL) 272 (Lord Bingham of Cornhill) (appeal taken from EWCA (Crim) (UK)).

[45] Id. at [79].

[46] Mohamed v. Sec'y of State for Foreign & Commonwealth Affairs, [2009] EWHC (Admin) 2653, [7] (Eng.) (noting that reopening of a case should be done in 'exceptional circumstances' if necessary in the 'interests of justice').

reasoned that there was an extremely low likelihood that the Obama administration would actually withhold intelligence from the United Kingdom,[47] and noted that 'a vital public interest requires, for reasons of democratic accountability and the rule of law in the United Kingdom, that a summary of the most important evidence relating to the involvement of the British security services in wrongdoing be placed in the public domain in the United Kingdom'.[48]

The October 2009 decision ultimately rejected formalistic reasoning in favor of maintaining the rule of law, open justice and the possibility of public accountability. In February 2010, the Court of Appeal upheld the divisional court's decision, noting the veracity of Mohamed's claims of torture.[49] Specifically, the appellate decision looked to dicta in the US habeas corpus matter of *Mohammed v. Obama*.[50] In that case, Judge Kessler weighed the habeas corpus petition of detainee Farhi Saeed bin Mohammed and considered evidence proffered by the government that Binyam Mohamed, while in detention at Guantánamo Bay, told the government that bin Mohammed had trained with him at an al-Qaeda base.[51] Judge Kessler described the harrowing detention and torture of Binyam Mohamed while in US custody that rendered his testimony regarding bin Mohammed unreliable and inadmissible.[52] She further noted that '[t]he Government does not challenge or deny the accuracy of Binyam Mohamed's story of brutal treatment'.[53]

The English Court of Appeal used this revelation as one basis for upholding the order for the UK government to disclose information

---

47 Id. at [39], [49], [69vi], [104]. The court noted that the objections made by the Obama administration to disclosing the information in question were not as strong as the threats made by the Bush administration.

48 Id. at [105].

49 Mohamed v. Sec'y of State for Foreign & Commonwealth Affairs, [2010] EWCA (Civ) 158, [2011] QB 218 (Eng.). See Adam Tomkins, National Security and the Due Process of Law, 64 Current Legal Problems 215, 229 (2011) (noting that allegations of horrific torture weighed significantly in the court's decision-making).

50 Mohammed v. Obama, 704 F. Supp. 2d 1 (D.D.C. 2009). This citation refers to the de-classified opinion that was made publicly available on December 16, 2009. The original version of the opinion, dated November 19, 2009, is cited at Mohammed v. Obama, 689 F. Supp. 2d 38 (D.D.C. 2009).

51 *Mohamed*, 704 F. Supp 2d. at 2, 18–19.

52 Id. at 20–23, 29.

53 Id. at 24.

regarding Mohamed's mistreatment.[54] This willingness of the English Court of Appeal to engage in a realist analysis serves as a sharp contrast to the Ninth Circuit *en banc* decision in *Mohamed*, where the majority does not appear to concern itself with evidence of the veracity of Mohamed's claims and instead limits itself to an overly formalistic interpretation of the state secrets privilege.[55]

3.2 Israel

Israeli courts, like their English counterparts, offer an example of how the courts balance imperatives of security with the rule of law when they refuse to accept a narrow interpretation of their own role. Courts, akin to the English reasoning in the *Mohamed* case, use a flexible, realist approach to analyzing these questions, giving significant weight to plaintiffs' allegations of human rights violations. In Israel almost any complaint against the executive branch is considered justiciable.[56] Although justiciability is no guarantee of ultimate success in litigation against the government, the institutionalization of hearing such cases reflects, at its best, a judicial willingness of the courts to engage in critical thinking about government claims regarding national security.

In *Public Committee Against Torture in Israel v. Israel*,[57] plaintiffs challenged the preventative strikes undertaken by the Israeli military in response to alleged terrorist attacks based on the ensuing loss of civilian life and Israel's international law obligations. As an initial matter, the court considered a challenge by the government that the suit was not justiciable based on national security concerns.[58] The Israeli Supreme

---

[54] Mohamed v. Sec'y of State for Foreign and Commonwealth Affairs, [2010] EWCA (Civ) 65 [138], [2011] QB 218 (Eng.).

[55] In fact, the only reference to Judge Kessler's decision comes in a footnote referencing the *Mohammed* case, in which the court notes that Binyam Mohamed's allegations have been discussed elsewhere. See Mohamed v. Jeppesen Dataplan, Inc., 614 F.3d 1070, 1074 n.1 (9th Cir. 2010).

[56] Aharon Barak, Foreword: A Judge on Judging: The Role of a Supreme Court in a Democracy, 116 HARV. L. REV. 16, 153 (2002) ('Our Supreme Court – which in Israel serves as the court of first instance for complaints against the executive branch – opens its doors to anyone with a complaint about the activities of a public authority.').

[57] HCJ 769/02 Public Comm. Against Torture in Isr. v. Israel [2005] (Isr.), available at http://elyon1.court.gov.il/files_eng/02/690/007/A34/02007690.a34.pdf.

[58] Id. at 5 ¶ 9 (arguing against justiciability, the government cites Israeli High Court of Justice precedent, HCJ 5872/01 Barakeh v. Prime Minister 56(3)

Court applied a four-pronged test to determine justiciability, reasoning that a case involving the impingement of human rights is always justiciable;[59] that a case in which the central issue is one of political or military policy and not a legal dispute is not justiciable;[60] that an issue that has already been decided by international courts and tribunals to which Israel is a signatory must be justiciable in Israel's domestic courts; and that judicial review is most appropriate in an *ex post* situation.[61]

In this case, the Israeli Supreme Court found that the claims were clearly justiciable.[62] Ultimately, the Israeli Supreme Court concluded that the targeted killings at issue were not per se illegal, but that they must be evaluated on an individual basis.[63] Although the holding in *Public Committee Against Torture* raises important and concerning questions as to the substantive justice of these decisions, a baseline structural benefit exists in having access to courts for grievances involving allegations of human rights violations.

3.3 India

Whereas England and Israel illustrate the ability of courts to utilize a rule of law analysis, India represents a hard line of formalism that the US is at risk of veering toward. Indian courts have historically granted the utmost deference to the executive branch as to when national security policy should be disclosed.[64] When cases raise issues of individual rights being

---

[2002], for the proposition that 'the choice of means of war employed by [the government] in order to prevent murderous terrorist attacks before they happen, is not among the subjects in which this Court will see fit to intervene').

[59] HCJ 769/02 Public Comm. Against Torture in Isr. v. Israel 34–35 ¶ 50 [2005] (Isr.), available at http://elyon1.court.gov.il/files_eng/02/690/007/A34/02007690.a34.pdf (citing HCJ 606/78 Oyeb v. Minister of Def. 33(2) Isr SC 113, 124 (Isr.)).

[60] Id. at 35 §51 (citing HCJ 4481/91 Bargil v. Israel 37(4) Isr SC 210, 218 [1993] (Isr.)).

[61] Id. at 36 §§ 53–4.

[62] Id. at 1–2 §§1–3.

[63] Id at 41–2 § 63. This decision is particularly notable given the recent decision dismissing a suit challenging the U.S. targeted killing program. See Al-Aulaqi v. Obama, 727 F. Supp. 2d 1 (D.D.C. 2010) (dismissing, based on standing grounds, the suit of Nasser al-Aulaqi to enjoin the US government from keeping his son, US citizen Anwar al-Aulaqi, on its targeted killing list).

[64] E.g., State of Uttar Pradesh v. Raj Narain, A.I.R. 1975 SC 865 (India) (carving out national security as the area in which the Prime Minister can unilaterally decide what information to disclose); see Mrinal Satish and Aparna Chandra, Of Maternal State and Minimalist Judiciary: The Indian Supreme

compromised by government secrecy, courts purport to undertake a balancing test to determine whether the public interest or individual rights at stake should override executive secrecy; however, government claims regarding the necessity of secrecy consistently prevail.[65] Deference to executive branch decision-making is deep-rooted in national security-related cases,[66] and is consistent with India's history of granting the executive branch sole power to determine whether to disclose information in any number of contexts, including enforcement of its Official Secrets Act, a legacy of British colonial rule in India.[67]

In *Dinesh Trivedi v. Union of India*,[68] the Indian Supreme Court considered whether to order the publication of background documents underlying a commissioned report on government corruption over which the government had claimed secrecy. Members of Parliament, including petitioner Dinesh Trivedi, alleged that the Home Minister refused disclosure to avoid government embarrassment.[69] The Indian Supreme Court began with the need for transparency, noting that 'Sunlight is the best

---

Court's Approach to Terror-Related Adjudication, 21 NAT'L L. SCH. INDIA REV. 51, 65 (2009) (describing the history of Indian courts deferring to executive decisions regarding security matters).

65 E.g., People's Union for Civil Liberties & Anr. v. Union of India & Ors., (2004) 2 S.C.C. 476 (India) (upholding denial of request for disclosure of information).

66 This deference has been consistent, despite the adoption of right to information legislation in recent years and judicial statements about the importance of government transparency. Freedom of Information Act, No. 5 of 2003; INDIA CODE (2009), available at http://indiacode.nic.in; e.g., S.P. Gupta v. President of India, A.I.R. 1982 S.C. 234, § 66 (India) ('The concept of an open government is the direct emanation from the right to know which seems to be implicit in the right of free speech and expression guaranteed under Article 19(1)(a) [of the Indian Constitution]. Therefore, disclosure of information in regard to the functioning of Government must be the rule and secrecy an exception justified only where the strictest requirement of public interest so demands.').

67 India operates under the edicts of the Official Secrets Act of 1923 (OSA), enforced in India by the British colonial government. Under the OSA, any disclosure of information – intentional or inadvertent – likely to affect the sovereignty, integrity or security of India is punishable by imprisonment for up to fourteen years.

68 Dinesh Trivedi v. Union of India, (1997) 4 S.C.C. 306 (India). The Court in *Trivedi* relies heavily on the balancing test articulated in S.P. Gupta, *supra* note 65, to find that government secrecy claims ought to be upheld despite rule of law concerns.

69 *Trivedi*, 4 S.C.C. 306, §§6, 8.

disinfectant. But it is equally important to be alive to the dangers that lie ahead.'[70] The Indian Supreme Court accepted with little question the government's claim and hypothesized that the public furor toward individuals named in the report – should it be published in full – could lead to harassment and violence. Based on its own speculative concerns that appear grounded in historical deference to executive decision-making,[71] the court upheld government secrecy claims.[72] Similar reasoning has been used in other secrecy matters,[73] bolstered by claims of consistency with English public interest immunity jurisprudence.[74] The level of deference offered by the Indian Supreme Court is higher than that of any of the other nations considered here, but is seemingly more consistent with the recent state secrets cases in the US than that of the English courts in the *Mohamed* litigation.[75] The Indian Supreme Court, consistent with its security-related jurisprudence, has consistently reverted to a formalistic analysis that offers a rhetorical nod to the rule of

---

[70] Id. § 19.

[71] See SHYLASHRI SHANKAR, SCALING JUSTICE: INDIA'S SUPREME COURT, ANTI-TERROR LAWS, AND SOCIAL RIGHTS 61–71, 90–91 (2009) (arguing that whereas social rights is considered an area in which the judiciary is expected to take an active role, security and secrecy are areas in which the constitutional framers and Parliament have purposefully curtailed the judiciary's ability to curb executive power).

[72] Id. §§ 16–20.

[73] E.g., People's Union for Civil Liberties & Anr. v. Union of India & Ors., (2004) 2 S.C.C. 476 (India). The Court in this case upheld the government's secrecy claim over a report on nuclear reactors, reasoning that secrecy was sometimes necessary because '[i]f every action taken by the political or executive functionary is transformed into a public controversy and made subject to an enquiry to soothe popular sentiments, it will undoubtedly have a chilling effect on the independence of the decision-maker'. See the Right of Information section of the *People's Union* opinion, id.

[74] See the Criteria for Determining the Question of Privilege section of the *People's Union* opinion, id. (citing Uttar Pradesh v. Raj Narain, A.I.R. 1975 S.C. 865, which held that 'the foundation of the law behind Sections 123 and 162 of the Evidence Act is the same as in English law').

[75] There is no indication that the adoption of a Right to Information statute in 2005 has substantially affected the reasoning of the courts with regard to security-related secrecy, particularly since the statute contains a carve-out for national security matters. See The Right to Information Act, No. 22 of 2005, INDIA CODE (2009), available at http://indiacode.nic.in.

law and individual rights, but no avenue of relief for those who seek to chip away at government secrecy.[76]

CONCLUSION

In the US, the state secrets cases illustrate what may be becoming the new normal in security-related jurisprudence: formalistic reasoning that allows the court to bow out of its counter-majoritarian role of protecting individual rights and justice. Certainly the approach taken by India and the US is not the only viable one – England and Israel are evidence of that. The *Mohamed* case illustrates that England's current application of the state secrets privilege – however historically deferential – reflects at least in some cases the prioritization of various rule of law principles by the English courts, including the need for open justice, government accountability, and the opportunity for redress by individual litigants. The flexible approach used by the English court to determine that secrecy ought not prevail in the *Mohamed* case is reassuring to those concerned with rights protection. Yet the larger specter of the US exerting pressure regarding the state secrets privilege serves as a warning that even though the US was not successful with regard to applying pressure on England,[77] US soft power may successfully pressure courts in nations where courts would otherwise apply a narrower privilege.

Such a dynamic makes it all the more important that structural reform occur. Passage of strong state secrets reform legislation should become a

---

76 See Satish and Chandra, *supra* note 64, at 63 (critiquing the Indian Supreme Court's terrorism jurisprudence for focusing on procedural and technical questions and abdicating its role as a protector of fundamental rights).

77 The US government's displeasure at the English treatment of Binyam Mohamed's case motivated the British government to propose the stripping of judicial review over similar cases in which sensitive information may be disclosed. See SECRETARY OF STATE FOR JUSTICE, JUSTICE AND SECURITY GREEN PAPER, 2011, Cm. 8194, § 2.91 (UK), available at www.statewatch.org/news/2011/oct/uk-justice-and-security-green-paper.pdf. The Green Paper notes that such measures are necessary because '[s]ince *Binyam Mohamed*, the Government and its foreign government partners have less confidence than before that the courts will accept the view of Ministers on the harm to national security that would result from disclosure'. Id. § 1.43; cf. United Kingdom House of Lords, Joint Committee on Human Rights, Twenty-Fourth Report, Justice and Security Green Paper, at §§ 99–103 (Mar. 27, 2012) (emphasizing the importance of courts in weighing government claims of the need for secrecy).

priority,[78] and courts should resist being cowed by assertions that judicial involvement in security matters is unwarranted or undermines the safety of the nation.[79] Although genuine access to the courts is no guarantee of substantive justice, substantive justice is unlikely to be achieved if the judiciary continues to retreat behind a wall of formalism.

---

[78] Arguments that high levels of deference are unwarranted continue to grow. E.g., See Aziz Rana, Who Decides on Security? 44 Conn. L. Rev. 1417, 1424, 1445–46 (2012); Stephen J. Schulhofer, Secrecy and Democracy: Who Controls Information in the National Security State? (NYU Sch. of Law, Pub. Law Research Paper No. 10-53), available at http://ssrn.com/abstract=1661964.

[79] Such assertions are sometimes offered by the judiciary itself. E.g., *Boumediene v. Bush*, 553 U.S. 723, 802 (2008) (Roberts, C.J., dissenting) (critiquing the level of judicial involvement in detention decisions endorsed by the Court and noting that, '[a]ll that today's opinion has done is shift responsibility for those sensitive foreign policy and national security decisions from the elected branches to the Federal Judiciary').

PART 2

Secrecy and legislatures

6. Direct and indirect access to intelligence information: lessons in legislative oversight from the United States and Canada

Kathleen Clark and Nino Lomjaria

INTRODUCTION

In theory, legislatures can perform critical oversight functions regarding nearly all government agencies, including those that conduct intelligence activities, if they have access to information about those activities. Legislators gain access to information in several different ways: directly when information is provided to the legislators themselves; or indirectly when the information is provided to their staff members, to legislative offices that conduct studies for the legislature, or to non-legislative offices that report to the legislature.

This chapter examines legislative access to intelligence information in the United States and Canada – two countries that have taken radically different approaches to intelligence accountability.[1] Section 1 describes how, after intelligence abuse scandals erupted in the mid-1970s, the US Congress increased its access to intelligence information from limited direct access of legislators themselves to expanded access through all four of these methods. While this chapter highlights some of the limitations on Congressional oversight, Congress has the ability to

[1] Some passages in this chapter are based on other publications: Kathleen Clark and Nino Lomjaria, Limited Oversight: Legislative Access to Intelligence Information in the United States and Canada, 6 J. PARLIAMENTARY & POLITICAL L. 523 (2012); Kathleen Clark, Congress's Right to Counsel in Intelligence Oversight, 2011 U. ILL. L. REV. 915 (hereinafter Clark, Congress's Right to Counsel); Kathleen Clark, The Architecture of Accountability: A Case Study of the Warrantless Surveillance Program, 2010 B.Y.U. L. REV. 357.

engage in relatively robust review of intelligence activities.[2] Section 2 explains that the Canadian Parliament generally obtains information about intelligence activities only when non-legislative offices provide it with reports, and those reports generally omit classified information. As a result, Canadian parliamentarians have generally had no more access to intelligence information than the Canadian public at large, limiting their ability to assess and control the government's intelligence activities.

1. UNITED STATES CONGRESS'S ACCESS TO INTELLIGENCE INFORMATION

1.1 Members of Congress

Congress performs most of its work through its committees. Until the mid-1970s, congressional oversight of intelligence was handled by intelligence subcommittees of the House and Senate Armed Services and Appropriations Committees.[3] Their oversight was quite lax[4] and intelligence agencies provided oral (rather than written) briefings.[5] The members of Congress who chaired the intelligence subcommittees apparently saw themselves as allies (rather than adversaries) of the intelligence agencies, and saw no need for additional staff resources or more formal oversight mechanisms.[6]

---

[2] EUROPEAN PARLIAMENT DIRECTORATE-GENERAL FOR INTERNAL POLICIES, PARLIAMENTARY OVERSIGHT OF SECURITY AND INTELLIGENCE AGENCIES IN THE EUROPEAN UNION 87 (2011) (describing the US Congress as 'the best example' of a bicameral legislature with specialized intelligence oversight committees in each house); Stephen J. Schulhofer, Democratic Governance and Constitutional Rights: Oversight of Secrecy Decisions in the National Security State ('The existing system at best gives Congress only the *opportunity* for oversight; it does not supply the *motivation*.').

[3] L. BRITT SNIDER, CENT. INTELLIGENCE AGENCY, SHARING SECRETS WITH LAWMAKERS: CONGRESS AS A USER OF INTELLIGENCE 1 (1997) (hereinafter SNIDER, SHARING SECRETS WITH LAWMAKERS).

[4] CECIL V. CRABB, JR. AND PAT M. HOLT, INVITATION TO STRUGGLE: CONGRESS, THE PRESIDENT AND FOREIGN POLICY 137 (1980), at 137.

[5] L. BRITT SNIDER, THE AGENCY AND THE HILL: CIA'S RELATIONSHIP WITH CONGRESS, 1946–2004, at 306 (2008) (hereinafter SNIDER, THE AGENCY AND THE HILL) ('[T]he lack of a professional staff capable of independently probing and assessing what the Agency was being directed to do … hampered the CIA subcommittees.').

[6] See Clark, Congress's Right to Counsel, *supra* note 1, at 924.

This arrangement changed in the mid-1970s, amid public revelations of intelligence agency abuses. In December 1974, Congress formalized the regulation of one particular type of intelligence activity: covert actions, which are intended 'to influence political, economic, or military conditions abroad, where it is intended that the role of the United States Government will not be apparent or acknowledged publicly'.[7] Congress mandated that the President report 'in a timely fashion, a description and scope of … [covert actions] to the appropriate committees of the Congress'.[8]

That same month, Seymour Hersh started publishing a series of newspaper articles detailing extensive illegal activity by intelligence agencies.[9] Hersh's articles led to the creation of ad hoc investigative committees in the Senate (colloquially known as the 'Church Committee' for its chair, Senator Frank Church) and the House (known as the 'Pike Committee' for its chair, Representative Otis Pike).[10] These committees hired large staffs, held hearings and wrote lengthy reports revealing widespread illegal activities by the intelligence agencies.[11] Both committees recommended enhanced congressional oversight of the intelligence community.

In May 1976, less than a month after the Church Committee issued its final report, the Senate created the Senate Select Committee on Intelligence and passed a nonbinding resolution that department heads should keep that committee 'fully and currently informed' of the agency's intelligence activities.[12] The following year, the House created its own

---

7 50 U.S.C. § 413b(e).

8 Foreign Assistance Act § 32, 88 Stat. at 1804. The 'appropriate committees' were the House and Senate Foreign Relations, Armed Services and Appropriations Committees. STEPHEN F. KNOTT, SECRET AND SANCTIONED: COVERT OPERATIONS AND THE AMERICAN PRESIDENCY 163 (1996) at 166.

9 Seymour M. Hersh, Huge C.I.A. Operation Reported in US Against Antiwar Forces, Other Dissidents in Nixon Years, N.Y. TIMES, Dec. 22, 1974, at 1.

10 FRANK J. SMIST, JR., CONGRESS OVERSEES THE UNITED STATES INTELLIGENCE COMMUNITY 1947–1994, at 9–10 (2d ed. 1994).

11 The Church Committee issued seventeen volumes of reports and hearings. CRABB AND HOLT, *supra* note 4, at 149; see S. SELECT COMM. TO STUDY GOVERNMENTAL OPERATIONS WITH RESPECT TO INTELLIGENCE ACTIVITIES AND THE RIGHTS OF AMERICANS, S. REP. NO. 94-755 (1976). The Pike Committee issued recommendations. HOUSE SELECT COMM. ON INTELLIGENCE, 94TH CONG., RECOMMENDATIONS OF THE FINAL REPORT OF THE HOUSE SELECT COMMITTEE ON INTELLIGENCE, H.R. Rep. No. 94-833 (1976).

12 S. Res. 400, 94th Cong. § 11(a) (1976) (as amended).

intelligence committee.[13] President Carter partially endorsed the Senate resolution by issuing an executive order requiring intelligence agencies to keep the intelligence committees 'fully and currently informed' of their activities.[14] But the executive order was fundamentally ambiguous because it included language about the protection of intelligence 'sources and methods'. The order stated that disclosures to Congress must be undertaken 'consistent with applicable authorities and duties, including those conferred by the Constitution upon the Executive and Legislative Branches and by law to protect sources and methods'.[15] In 1980, Congress codified the requirement that the executive branch keep the intelligence committees 'fully and currently informed' of intelligence activities (including covert actions),[16] but it also included limiting language similar to that in Carter's executive order.[17]

Ambiguity about the extent of Congress's right to intelligence information can be found not just in these early enactments, but also in later statutes in this field. When Congress re-codified the duties of the Director of Central Intelligence (DCI) in 1992, it set out in statute a requirement that the DCI 'provid[e] national intelligence' to Congress.[18] But it also stated that this requirement applied only 'where appropriate', a term that Congress did not define.[19] When Congress created the office of Director of National Intelligence (DNI) in 2003, it mandated that DNI 'ensur[e] that national intelligence is provided' to Congress, and omitted the 'where appropriate' language.[20] Yet the effect of this statute is unclear, for it does not purport to mandate that the DNI share all national intelligence with Congress. Like the earlier version, this statutory mandate for disclosure leaves substantial discretion in the hands of the executive branch to determine which information to disclose. On the

---

13 H.R. Res. 658, 95th Cong. (1977) (enacted).

14 Exec. Order No. 12,036, § 3-401, 3 C.F.R. 112, 132 (1979).

15 Id. § 3-4, 3 C.F.R. at 132.

16 Intelligence Authorization Act for Fiscal Year 1981, Pub. L. No. 96-450, sec. 407(b)(1), § 501(a), 94 Stat. 1975, 1981 (1980) (known as the Intelligence Oversight Act of 1980) (codified as amended at 50 U.S.C. § 413(a)). For a visual representation of these congressional intelligence oversight statutes have evolved over time, see As the Code Changes, http://asthecodechanges.wustl.edu.

17 50 U.S.C. § 413(a) (1988) (amended 1991).

18 Intelligence Authorization Act for Fiscal Year 1993, Pub. L. No. 102-496, sec. 705, § 103(a), 106 Stat. 3180, 3190–91 (1992).

19 Id.; see also SNIDER, SHARING SECRETS WITH LAWMAKERS, *supra* note 3, at 14 (1997).

20 National Security Intelligence Reform Act of 2004, Pub. L. No. 108-458, sec. 1011, § 102A(a), 118 Stat. 3643, 3644 (codified at 50 U.S.C. § 403-1).

other hand, Congress passed legislation in 2010 requiring the executive branch to provide the intelligence committees with 'the legal basis under which … intelligence activit[ies are] being … conducted',[21] and specifically requires disclosure of the legal basis for intelligence interrogations,[22] and cybersecurity programs.[23]

With respect to covert actions, the 1980 statute implicitly required intelligence agency heads to provide prior notification of such actions to the full intelligence committees,[24] but explicitly allowed prior notice to be limited to eight congressional intelligence leaders (the chairs and ranking members of the intelligence committees, the Speaker and minority leader of the House of Representatives, and the majority and minority leaders of the Senate) 'if the President determines it is essential to limit prior notice to meet extraordinary circumstances affecting vital interests of the United States'.[25] Where the President does not provide *prior* notice, the statute requires him to 'fully inform the intelligence committees *in a timely fashion*' about these actions and to 'provide a statement of the reasons for not giving prior notice'.[26]

The limits of this approach and the issue of timing are illustrated by one aspect of the Iran-Contra controversy. In January 1986, President Reagan issued presidential findings in connection with the sale of arms to Iran, but did not notify any members of Congress until ten months later,

---

[21] Intelligence Authorization Act for Fiscal Year 2010, Pub. L. No. 111-259, § 331(b), 124 Stat. 2654, 2685 (amending 50 U.S.C. § 413a(a)(2)).

[22] Id. § 333(a)(3), 124 Stat. at 2687.

[23] Id. § 336(a)(2)(A), 124 Stat. at 2689. This legislation also requires the executive branch to report the legal basis for covert actions.

[24] The statute does not explicitly require the executive branch to provide the intelligence committees with prior notification of covert actions, but refers to covert actions as 'significant *anticipated* intelligence activit[ies]'. Id. § 407(a)(2), 94 Stat. at 1981 (emphasis added). The statute's two mentions of 'prior notice' seem to assume that prior notice is generally required. See 50 U.S.C. § 413(a)(1), (b) (1988) (amended 1991); see also S. REP. NO. 96-730, at 4 (1980) (repealing the earlier requirement that the executive branch report covert actions to Congress 'in a timely fashion', and replacing it with a requirement that the intelligence committees be given prior notice of covert actions); SNIDER, THE AGENCY AND THE HILL, *supra* note 5, at 59–60.

[25] 50 U.S.C. § 413(a)(1). The Senate Report on this legislation asserted that withholding of prior notice to the full committees would occur 'in rare extraordinary circumstances'. S. REP. NO. 96-730, at 12.

[26] Intelligence Authorization Act for Fiscal Year 1981, § 407(b)(1), § 501(b), 94 Stat. at 1982 (codified at 50 U.S.C. § 413(b)) (emphasis added).

after a Lebanese newspaper revealed those operations to the world.[27] Eventually, the Justice Department's Office of Legal Counsel (OLC) issued an opinion reviewing these events and asserting that this delay in notification was legal despite the statutory requirement that notice be given 'in a timely fashion'.[28] The opinion reasoned that the '"timely fashion" language should be read to leave the President with virtually unfettered discretion to choose the right moment for making the required notification'.[29] In response to Congressional requests that he repudiate this OLC opinion, the first President Bush indicated that 'in almost all instances', he would provide prior notice; in 'those rare instances' when he did not provide prior notice, he 'anticipate[d] that notice will be provided within a few days'; and if he withheld notice for longer than that, he would be doing so 'based upon [his] assertion of authorities granted [his] office by the Constitution'.[30] In effect, Bush asserted that the Constitution granted him authority to act contrary to the statutory requirement of 'timely' notice.[31]

In 1991, following recommendations of the joint committee responsible for investigating the Iran-Contra scandal,[32] Congress enacted legislation stating that presidential findings in support of covert actions may not authorize covert actions that have already occurred, must be in writing, and must be provided to the chairs of the intelligence committees.[33] In that legislation, Congress left the nonspecific 'timely fashion'

---

[27] See Marshall Silverberg, The Separation of Powers and Control of the CIA's Covert Operations, 68 TEX. L. REV. 575, 603 (1990); see also EXECUTIVE SUMMARY, in REPORT OF THE CONGRESSIONAL COMMITTEES INVESTIGATING THE IRAN-CONTRA AFFAIR, H.R. REP. NO. 100-433, S. REP. NO. 100-216 (1987).

[28] Memorandum from Charles J. Cooper, Assistant Attorney Gen., Office of Legal Counsel, Dep't of Justice, to the Attorney Gen., The President's Compliance with the 'Timely Notification' Requirement of Section 501(b) of the National Security Act (Dec. 17, 1986) at 2, 24.

[29] Id. at 24.

[30] Letter from President George Bush, President of the United States, to the Chairman of the House Intelligence Comm., reprinted in H.R. REP. No. 102-166, at 27 (1991) (Conf. Rep.).

[31] Under the analysis in Justice Jackson's concurrence in Youngstown Sheet & Tube Co. v. Sawyer, 343 U.S. 579, this would fall into Jackson's third category: executive power that exists after Congress has legislated a prohibition. 343 U.S. at 637–8 (1952) (Jackson, J., concurring).

[32] William E. Conner, Congressional Reform of Covert Action Oversight Following the Iran-Contra Affair, 2 DEF. INTELLIGENCE J. 35 (1993)

[33] Intelligence Authorization Act, Fiscal Year 1991, Pub. L. No. 102-88, sec. 602, § 503(a), 105 Stat. 429, 442 (codified at 50 U.S.C. § 413b).

requirement, rather than replacing it with a more specific requirement.[34] The conference report accompanying this legislation asserted that re-enactment of 'the phrase "in a timely fashion" ... should not in any way be taken to imply agreement or acquiescence in the' OLC memorandum's position, and that the phrase should properly be understood to mean 'within a few days'.[35] The conference report, however, disclaimed any congressional ability to authoritatively interpret this law. It asserted that '[n]either the legislative [n]or executive branch authoritatively interpret the Constitution, which is the exclusive province of the judicial branch'.[36] Yet this assertion ignored the fact that the judicial branch never has the opportunity to interpret the Constitution with respect to many issues related to intelligence.[37] Oftentimes in the national security sphere, the responsibility for interpreting the Constitution falls on the political branches, rather than the judicial branch. Faced with a President who asserted constitutional authority to ignore a statutory requirement, Congress blinked when given the opportunity to devise a statutory mandate for 'timely notification'.

While Congress has imposed statutory requirements that the executive branch provide it with information, these requirements are fundamentally ambiguous. In effect, they leave the executive branch with the discretion to disclose or not. The consequences of nondisclosure are merely political rather than legal. Although the executive branch shares a wide range of intelligence information with Congress,[38] it also asserts its

---

[34] Id.

[35] H.R. REP. No. 102-166, at 28 ('[T]he President's stated intention ... to make a notification "within a few days" ... is consistent with what the conferees believe is its meaning and intent').

[36] Id.

[37] Recent examples of courts refusing to address the constitutionality of executive branch intelligence-related activities include Al Haramain Islamic Foundation v. Obama, 2012 U.S. App. LEXIS 16379 (9th Cir. 2012) (dismissing on the basis of sovereign immunity case alleging illegal warrantless surveillance); Padilla v. Yoo, 678 F.3d 748 (9th Cir. 2012) (dismissing on the basis of qualified immunity case alleging torture); and Fazaga v. Federal Bureau of Investigation, 2012 WL 3327092 (C.D. Cal.) (dismissing on state secrets grounds counts alleging that FBI's investigation of Muslim Americans violated their constitutional rights).

[38] In 2004, the CIA provided Congress with 1,000 briefings and 4,000 documents. ALFRED CUMMING, CONG. RESEARCH SERV., CONGRESS AS A CONSUMER OF INTELLIGENCE INFORMATION 7–8 n.40 (2009).

authority not to disclose to Congress some intelligence information.[39] The intelligence committees have 'been willing to limit access to particularly sensitive information to members and/or a few senior staff, [and] to limit the number of committee members with access to especially sensitive information'.[40] Some of these limits – such as notifying only congressional intelligence leaders of covert actions – are statutorily authorized, but other limits – such as restrictions on consulting staff – have no statutory basis.[41]

1.2 Members' Staff

Members of Congress delegate to their staff members the initial fact-finding and analysis that result in hearings, reports, and ultimately, legislation. While members may provide the vision and goals for this work, their staff carry out essential functions in investigating the executive branch's activities and enabling members to understand the legal framework in which those activities occur.

Just as members' access to intelligence information increased in the mid-1970s, so too did access for their staffs. The subcommittees that conducted intelligence oversight until the mid-1970s had only minimal staff.[42] In the Senate, only one staff member was allowed to attend briefings conducted by intelligence agencies.[43] The subcommittees did not have secure facilities to store classified documents, so they did not keep written records of the executive branch's briefings or of subcommittee meetings. Staff members who wanted to examine documents had to travel to Central Intelligence Agency (CIA) headquarters in Langley, Virginia, and were prohibited from removing any documents or even their own notes about the documents.[44]

The Church and Pike Committees, on the other hand, had large staffs who underwent security background checks so that they could gain

---

[39] The executive branch does not generally share intelligence sources or methods, raw intelligence, or the President's Daily Brief with Congress. Id. at 4.

[40] S. Rep. No. 103-88, at 10.

[41] Intelligence committee leaders have also acquiesced in the executive branch's desire to limit some information to the committee chairs and ranking members. There is no statute, committee rule, or chamber rule support for these limited notifications Alfred Cumming, Cong. Research Serv., 'Gang of Four' Congressional Intelligence Notifications 6–7 (2010) at 6–7.

[42] Snider, The Agency and the Hill, *supra* note 5, at 306 (2008)

[43] Crabb and Holt, *supra* note 4, at 141.

[44] Smist, *supra* note 10, at 4–5, 7–8.

access to intelligence information.[45] These security-cleared staff members' enabled the Church and Pike Committees to conduct extensive hearings and produce lengthy reports about intelligence abuses. The National Security Agency (NSA) initially took the position that its information was so sensitive that it would be provided only to the chair and ranking member, rather than to staffers, but it eventually abandoned this position and provided information to committee staffers.[46] Staffers were instrumental in uncovering the NSA's program of warrantless surveillance of telegram traffic in and out of the country.[47]

Since enactment of the congressional intelligence leader notification procedures in 1980, the executive branch has asserted that those leaders may not consult their staff members – even those with high-level security clearances – regarding the covert action information that the executive branch provides them.[48] Congressional intelligence leaders have also acquiesced to the executive branch position on this issue. The intelligence oversight statutes are silent on this question, as are the intelligence committee rules.

While intelligence committee members are able to consult their staff regarding many intelligence activities, they have not been able to do so with respect to some of the most sensitive intelligence programs. This hobbles Congress's ability to understand and analyze key executive branch programs. Executive branch officials have asserted that these programs – such as warrantless surveillance – are legal, but they have not permitted Congress to review the executive branch's own legal analysis.[49] In addition, the executive branch asserts that these members may not consult their own security-cleared lawyers and other expert staff, which would enable these members to draw their own independent conclusions about the legality of these programs.[50]

---

[45] The Church Committee had 135 staff members, LOCH K. JOHNSON, A SEASON OF INQUIRY: THE SENATE INTELLIGENCE INVESTIGATION 25 (1985), and the Pike Committee had 32 staff members. SMIST, *supra* note 10, at 136.

[46] L. Britt Snider, Recollections from the Church Committee's Investigation of NSA: Unlucky Shamrock, STUD. INTELLIGENCE, Winter 1999–2000.

[47] Id.

[48] Heidi Kitrosser, Congressional Oversight of National Security Activities: Improving Information Funnels, 29 CARDOZO L. REV. 1049, 1059 (2008).

[49] See, e.g., Letter from William E. Moschella, Assistant Attorney Gen., to Senator Patrick J. Leahy, Ranking Member, Comm. on the Judiciary (Apr. 4, 2005) (on file with author) ('[T]he Executive Branch has substantial confidentiality interests in OLC opinions, and our longstanding practice is not to disclose non-public OLC opinions outside the Executive Branch').

[50] See Kitrosser, *supra* note 48, at 1059.

Executive branch insistence that Congress not consult its staff has occurred not just in connection with congressional oversight of intelligence activities, but also with respect to congressional authorization for war. In the fall of 2002, the Bush administration was seeking congressional authorization for its planned invasion of Iraq. The executive branch made available to all members of Congress – but not their staffs – a ninety-two page document assessing Iraq's weapons of mass destruction.[51] All members of Congress were free to go to a secure room and read the document, but they could not take notes and could not consult staff about its contents.[52] Prior to voting to authorize the US invasion of Iraq, only a few members of Congress took the time to read past the five page executive summary.[53]

1.3 Congress's Indirect Servants: Government Accountability Office and Inspectors General

In monitoring the activities of the executive branch, Congress relies not just on its own staffers, but also on other offices that it has created in the legislative and executive branches. These include the Government Accountability Office (GAO) and offices of Inspector General (IG) in dozens of executive branch agencies.

The GAO has over 3000 employees who audit and analyze the operation of the executive branch, responding to specific requests for such analysis from members of Congress.[54] GAO employees engage in long-term – if often low-profile – investigations and analyses of executive branch programs, producing hundreds of detailed and often technical reports every year.[55] The GAO helps Congress carry out its oversight functions by conducting long-term studies and developing expertise regarding executive branch programs. Despite – or perhaps because of – this record of robust, staff-enabled oversight, the executive branch has

---

[51] Dana Priest, Congressional Oversight of Intelligence Criticized: Committee Members, Others Cite Lack of Attention to Reports on Iraqi Arms, Al Qaeda Threat, WASH. POST, Apr. 27, 2004, at A1.

[52] Id.

[53] Id.; see also Leslie Gielow Jacobs, Bush, Obama and Beyond: Observations on the Prospect of Fact Checking Executive Department Threat Claims Before the Use of Force, 26 CONST. COMMENT. 433, 450–51 (2010).

[54] US GOV'T ACCOUNTABILITY OFFICE, GAO-09-2SP, CITIZENS' REPORT: FISCAL YEAR 2008 SUMMARY OF GAO'S PERFORMANCE AND FINANCIAL RESULTS 1 (2009), www.gao.gov/new.items/d092sp.pdf.

[55] In Fiscal Year 2008, the GAO provided Congress with over 1200 reports (including written testimony) analyzing executive branch programs. Id. at 3.

traditionally insisted that Congress not consult the GAO in connection with certain intelligence information. The executive branch asserts that the GAO does not have the authority to analyze intelligence activities.[56] During the Reagan administration, the DOJ's OLC asserted that while the GAO's mandate is to evaluate executive branch programs that have been authorized by statute, intelligence activities are undertaken pursuant to the President's constitutional foreign policy responsibilities rather than statute.[57] In light of the statutory authorization for, and regulation of, intelligence operations, this OLC opinion is not particularly persuasive. Until recently, Congress has acquiesced in the executive branch's insistence that intelligence oversight be conducted only by the intelligence committees and not by the GAO. But legislative developments in 2010 suggest that this may be changing, at least to a limited degree. The Intelligence Authorization Act for Fiscal Year 2010 required the DNI to 'issue a written directive governing the access of the Comptroller General', who is the leader of the GAO, to intelligence information,[58] and required the Comptroller General to ensure the confidentiality of that information.[59]

Another less direct agent of Congress exists in the offices of Inspector General (IG) that Congress has created in dozens of agencies.[60] Congress gave IGs the ability to directly access an agency's records in order to investigate allegations of waste, fraud, and abuse. IGs' direct access to agency documents gives them the ability to provide intensive oversight in response to specific allegations.[61] While IGs are embedded within the

---

[56] Investigative Authority of the General Accounting Office, 12 Op. O.L.C. 171 (1988).

[57] Id. at 172 ('[GAO's statutory mandate covers] only ... activities carried out pursuant to statute, and not activities carried out pursuant to the Executive's discharge of its own constitutional responsibilities').

[58] Pub. L. No. 111-259, § 348(a)(1), 124 Stat. 2654, 2700 (codified at 50 U.S.C. § 403-9).

[59] Id. § 348(b)(1), 124 Stat. at 2700. The legislation also indicates that GAO employees will be subject to 'the same statutory penalties for unauthorized disclosure or use of such information as' executive branch employees. § 348(b)(2), 124 Stat. at 2700.

[60] Inspector General Act of 1978, Pub. L. No. 95-452, § 6, 92 Stat. 1101, 1104–05 (codified at 5 U.S.C. app. 3 § 6); but see id. §§ 8D, 8E (permitting Treasury Secretary and Attorney General to restrict IGs' access to information relating to ongoing investigations, confidential sources, and other matters).

[61] See, e.g., UNCLASSIFIED REPORT ON THE PRESIDENT'S SURVEILLANCE PROGRAM PREPARED BY THE OFFICES OF INSPECTORS GENERAL OF THE DEPARTMENT OF

executive branch and are appointed by the President or agency head, they may be thought of as servants of Congress, gathering information about alleged wrongdoing within the executive branch and providing that information to Congress on a regular basis.

Every six months, IGs issue detailed reports to the agency head and Congress.[62] IG reports have become a particularly important source of information for congressional committees investigating the executive branch.[63] The publicity that accompanies issuance of an IG report sometimes spurs political pressure for changes in such processes. For example, after concerns were raised about the FBI's extensive use of National Security Letters (NSLs) to collect information, Congress required the Justice Department IG to audit the FBI's use of NSLs.[64] Those audits revealed widespread problems in the FBI's administration of NSLs,[65] and helped spur legislation narrowing the FBI's authority to issue them.[66]

2. CANADIAN PARLIAMENT'S ACCESS TO INTELLIGENCE INFORMATION

Canada has three main agencies that engage in intelligence activities: the Canadian Security Intelligence Service (CSIS), the Communications Security Establishment (CSE) and the Royal Canadian Mounted Police (RCMP). CSIS provides security assessments to all federal departments

---

DEFENSE, DEPARTMENT OF JUSTICE, CENTRAL INTELLIGENCE AGENCY, NATIONAL SECURITY AGENCY AND DIRECTOR OF NATIONAL INTELLIGENCE (2009).

62 Id. at § 5.

63 PAUL C. LIGHT, MONITORING GOVERNMENT: INSPECTORS GENERAL AND THE SEARCH FOR ACCOUNTABILITY 39, 56 (1993).

64 USA PATRIOT Improvement and Reauthorization Act of 2005, Pub. L. No. 109-177, § 119, 120 Stat. 192, 219 (2006).

65 US DEPT. OF JUSTICE, OFFICE OF INSPECTOR GENERAL, A REVIEW OF THE FEDERAL BUREAU OF INVESTIGATION'S USE OF NATIONAL SECURITY LETTERS (2007); US DEPT. OF JUSTICE, OFFICE OF INSPECTOR GENERAL, A REVIEW OF THE FEDERAL BUREAU OF INVESTIGATION'S USE OF NATIONAL SECURITY LETTERS: ASSESSMENT OF CORRECTIVE ACTIONS AND EXAMINATION OF NSL USAGE IN 2006 (2008).

66 After the first Inspector General report, Representative Jerrold Nadler introduced a bill to place limits on the use of National Security Letters, H.R. 3189, 110th Cong. (2007), and Senator Russ Feingold introduced a companion bill in the Senate. S. 2088, 110th Cong. (2007).

and agencies except the RCMP.[67] CSE provides 'foreign signals intelligence in support of defence and foreign policy' and protects electronic information and communication.[68] The RCMP, which is Canada's federal police force, dramatically increased its role in intelligence after the Canadian Parliament passed the post-9/11 Anti-Terrorism Act, which criminalized terrorist support, terrorist financing and participation in terrorist groups.[69]

This section describes parliamentarians' direct and indirect access to intelligence information. Traditionally, members of Parliament have not had access to classified information. Instead, they have had access only to unclassified information that is made public by the offices that conduct reviews of intelligence agencies and by ad hoc inquiries that the Canadian Government establishes in response to specific scandals.

2.1 Parliamentary Members and Offices

Members of the Canadian Parliament – other than those who are government ministers – have generally not had direct access to classified security information. Both the House of Commons and the Senate have committees that review national security affairs, but the members of those committees do not have access to classified information about intelligence activities.[70] The House of Commons has a Standing Committee on Public Safety and National Security, whose mandate is to review the effectiveness of the CSIS and RCMP.[71] The committee can compel the appearance of officials, including ministers, and its members are regularly briefed on national security issues.[72] While the Committee could potentially be a potent review body, its members do not have

---

67 SECURITY INTELLIGENCE REVIEW COMMITTEE, ANNUAL REPORT TO THE HOUSE OF COMMONS, 2009–2010 (available at www.sirc-csars.gc.ca/pdfs/ar_2009-2010-eng.pdf).

68 National Defence Act, R.S.C. 1985, s. 273.62.

69 S.C. 2001, c. 41; TIM RIORDAN RAAFLAUB, CIVILIAN OVERSIGHT OF THE RCMP'S NATIONAL SECURITY FUNCTION (2006) (available at www.parl.gc.ca/content/LOP/ResearchPublications/prb0409-e.htm).

70 Craig Forcese, National Security Law: Canadian Practice in International Perspective 109 (2008); Special Senate Committee on Anti-terrorism, Security, Freedom and the Complex Terrorist Threat: Positive Steps Ahead 42 (2011) (hereinafter Special Senate Committee, Positive Steps Ahead).

71 Standing Order, s.108(2). Available at www.parl.gc.ca/About/House/StandingOrders/chap13-e.htm

72 Forcese, *supra* note 70, at 109.

access to intelligence information.[73] Similarly, the Senate has a Special Committee on Anti-Terrorism, but like its House counterpart, its members do not have access to classified information.[74] As a result, committee review of intelligence programs has been described as 'perfunctory'.[75]

The parliamentary officer responsible for auditing federal government programs, the Auditor General, has asked the key question: 'How can Parliament scrutinize the spending and performance of security and intelligence activities if key information must be kept secret' from Parliament?[76] She has noted the contrast between Parliament's legislative authority to control and review intelligence agencies and the inability of parliamentarians to carry out these functions.[77] While 'parliament needs objective information to determine whether public funds have been spent properly and managed well', the need for secrecy 'create[s] special problems for … providing information to Parliament'.[78] An ad hoc committee of parliamentarians has recommended the creation of a parliamentary committee to conduct reviews of the security and intelligence communities, but Parliament has failed to pass legislation that would create a permanent National Security Committee of Parliamentarians to provide oversight for the intelligence agencies.[79]

Against this background of no permanent parliamentary access to intelligence information, in 2009, the House of Commons responded to an intelligence-related scandal regarding the alleged mistreatment of detainees by Canadian forces in Afghanistan by creating a Special Committee to conduct an investigation, and that Committee demanded

---

[73] Special Senate Committee, Positive Steps Ahead, *supra* note 70, 45–6.

[74] *Id.*

[75] Forcese, *supra* note 70, at 109 (describing Standing Committee on Public Safety and National Security).

[76] *Id.*

[77] Auditor General of Canada, A Message from the Auditor General of Canada 1 (April 2005) (hereinafter 2005 Auditor General Message), available at www.oag-bvg.gc.ca/internet/English/parl_oag_200504_00_e_14931.html (last visited August 9, 2012).

[78] 2005 Auditor General Message, *supra* note 77, at 1.

[79] Bill C-81 is available at www.parl.gc.ca/HousePublications/Publication.aspx?DocId=2333974&Language=E&Mode=1&File=14.

The Auditor General also recommended creating 'a committee of Parliament, bound to secrecy and acting on behalf of the whole, that could receive reports containing classified information from security and intelligence agencies'. 2005 Auditor General Message at 2.

that the Government produce documents.[80] After the Government resisted and asserted national security secrecy, the Speaker of the House of Commons ruled that the Government must turn over the information, asserting that the House of Commons has a fundamental right to hold the Government to account for its actions.[81] The Speaker found that 'accepting an unconditional authority of the executive to censor the information provided to Parliament would jeopardize the separation of powers'.[82] Eventually, the Government agreed to a procedure involving the appointment of an Ad Hoc Committee of Parliamentarians who would obtain security clearances and take a confidentiality oath.[83] In 2011, this Committee received the first set of requested documents, which was the first time that members of Parliament had been provided with classified information.[84]

While members of Parliament have not generally had direct access to classified information, a parliamentary officer, the Auditor General, has had such access. The Auditor General audits federal government departments, Crown corporations, and other federal organizations, reporting publicly to the House of Commons on matters that the Auditor General believes should be brought to its attention. The Auditor General can require the federal government to provide all information that she considers necessary to fulfill her responsibilities.[85] But when the Auditor

---

[80] Craig Forcese, Parliamentary and Specialised Oversight of Security and Intelligence Agencies in Canada, in European Parliament Directorate-General for Internal Policies, Parliamentary Oversight of Security and Intelligence Agencies in the European Union (Annex A.XI) (2011).

[81] Ruling on the Questions of Privilege Raised on March 18, 2010 Concerning the Order of the House of December 10, 2009, Respecting the Production of Afghan Detainee Documents (available at www.canada.com/pdf/lee-ruling-2010-04-27-english.pdf).

[82] *Id.*

[83] Memorandum of Understanding between the Right Honourable Stephen Harper, Prime Minister, The Honourable Michael Ignatieff, Leader of the Official Opposition and Gilles Duceppe, Leader of the Bloc Quebecois, June 2010 (available at www.scribd.com/doc/33138988/Final-agreement-to-release-detainee-related-documents).

[84] Mark Kennedy and Althia Raj, Government Releases Afghan Detainee Documents, NATL. POST (June 22, 2011); THE HONOURABLE CLAIRE L'HEUREUX-DUBÉ AND THE HONOURABLE FRANK IACOBUCCI, AFGHAN DETAINEE DOCUMENT REVIEW: REPORT BY THE PANEL OF ARBITERS ON ITS WORK AND METHODOLOGY FOR DETERMINING WHAT REDACTED INFORMATION CAN BE DISCLOSED (April 15, 2011).

[85] *Id.*

General reports to Parliament, her reports do not include classified information.

As the next section shows, members of Parliament and of the public have had access to some information about Canadian intelligence activities through the publicly available reports of several government offices that review the intelligence-related agencies.

2.2 Non-Parliamentary Offices that Review Intelligence Activities

Each of the three main agencies that engage in intelligence activities has an office responsible for reviewing those activities. The activities of the CSIS are reviewed by the Security Intelligence Review Committee (SIRC) and an Inspector General (IG). The CSE is reviewed by the Office of the Communications Security Establishment Commissioner. The RCMP is reviewed by the Commission for Public Complaints Against the RCMP (CPC). In general, these executive review offices have access to classified information, but all references to classified information are removed before their reports are provided to Parliament.

2.2.1 SIRC and IG Review of the CSIS

CSIS is subject to an independent review body, the Security Intelligence Review Committee (SIRC) that investigates complaints, conducts reviews of CSIS's activities and reports to the Canadian Parliament.[86] SIRC's members are appointed from the Queen's Privy Council,[87] and have access to all CSIS information except confidences of the Queen's Privy Council.[88] SIRC is small in size relative to CSIS and operates on the basis of risk management. It develops a plan to review particular programs, and a typical review requires hundreds of staff hours over the course of several months. The results of these staff reviews are then presented to the SIRC members. Most of SIRC's reports and recommendations are submitted to the director of CSIS rather than to Parliament, but once a year, SIRC produces an annual report on its activities and that report is submitted to both CSIS and Parliament.[89] That annual report

---

[86] Security Intelligence Review Committee annual report to the House of Commons, 2009–2010, available at www.sirc-csars.gc.ca/pdfs/ar_2009-2010-eng.pdf.

[87] The Queen's Privy Council for Canada is the group of cabinet ministers, former cabinet ministers and other prominent Canadians appointed to advise the Queen on issues of importance to the country.

[88] CSIS Act, s. 39 (3).

[89] CSIS Act, ss. 52, 54.

summarizes its reports and recommendations, but all references to classified information are removed before it is provided to Parliament.[90]

CSIS is also subject to oversight by an Inspector General (IG) who is appointed by the Governor General and answers to a deputy minister.[91] The IG reviews the operational activities of CSIS, monitoring its compliance with its operational policies[92] and certifying whether activities involve an unreasonable or unnecessary exercise of any of its powers.[93] It serves as 'the Minister's eyes and ears in the [CSIS] ... to maintain an appropriate degree of ministerial responsibility'.[94] The IG has access to all information relating to CSIS's performance of its functions[95] except confidences of the Queen's Privy Council and Cabinet documents.[96] The IG reports to the Minister of Public Safety, and those reports may contain classified information. Those reports are made public only after the classified information is removed.

To summarize, SIRC has authority to review the activities of the CSIS, but all classified information is removed from its reports before they are provided to Parliament or the public. The IG has access to extensive information about the CSIS, but reports to the Minister rather than to Parliament.

2.2.2 Commissioner Review of the CSE

The review body for the CSE is the Office of the Communications Security Establishment Commissioner, who is appointed by the Governor General.[97] The Commissioner has access to all of CSE's information and reviews CSE's activities for compliance with the law.[98] He reports annually to the Minister regarding these reviews and the Minister

---

90 The annual reports to the Parliament are available at www.sirc-csars.gc.ca/anrran/index-eng.html.

91 Canadian Security Intelligence Service Act, R.S.C., 1985, c. C-23, s. 30 (available at laws-lois.justice.gc.ca/eng/acts/C-23/index.html). The current Canadian government plans to disband the IG. Craig Forcese, Fewer Eyes on the Spies: Going Backwards on Accountability (May 8, 2012) (available at cips.uottawa.ca/fewer-eyes-on-the-spies-going-backwards-on-accountability/).

92 CSIS Act, s. 30.

93 Id. s. 33.

94 RAAFLAUB, *supra* note 69.

95 CSIS Act, s. 31 (1).

96 CSIS Act, s. 31 (2).

97 National Defence Act, s. 273.63 (1).

98 COMMISSION OF INQUIRY INTO THE ACTIONS OF CANADIAN OFFICIALS IN RELATION TO MAHER ARAR, REPORT OF THE EVENTS RELATING TO MEHER ARAR, ANALYSIS AND RECOMMENDATIONS (ARAR INQUIRY) 283 (2006).

forwards the annual report to both houses of Parliament, but the annual report is not made public.[99] He also has the power to undertake investigations in response to complaints, and must report any illegal activity to the Minister and (if appropriate) the Attorney General.[100]

2.2.3 CPC Review of RCMP

The review body for the RCMP is the Commission for Public Complaints Against the RCMP (CPC). CPC members are appointed by the Governor General,[101] and the CPC reports to the Minister of Public Safety and Emergency Preparedness, who then forwards those reports to each House of Parliament.[102] The CPC has the authority to review RCMP behavior in individual cases,[103] but its review powers are quite limited in scope.[104] Its role is to respond to specific complaints from the public, and it rarely initiates investigations itself.[105] It has access only to information that is relevant to a specific complaint (unlike SIRC's broader access to CSIS's information).[106] Shirley Heafey, former CPC Chair, has publicly complained about the CPC's inability to properly review RCMP's work and called for new powers so that it can review the RCMP's anti-terrorism activities more effectively.[107]

While the RCMP's intelligence activities increased dramatically after adoption of the Anti-Terrorism Act, the role of the RCMP's review body, the CPC, has not changed. The CPC's ability to provide accountability is

---

99 *Id.* at 282.

100 National Defence Act, s. 273. 63 (2).

101 RCMP Act, s. 45.29(1).

102 *Id.* s. 45.34.

103 Exhibit 1.1, AUDITOR GENERAL OF CANADA, MARCH 2009 STATUS REPORT, Chapter 1, National Security: Intelligence and Information Sharing, available at www.oag-bvg.gc.ca/internet/English/parl_oag_200903_01_e_32288.html#hd3a.

104 RAAFLAUB, *supra* note 69.

105 CRMP Act, s. 45.37 (1). The RCMP is not obligated to follow recommendations made by the Chair or by a public interest hearing panel.

106 RAAFLAUB, *supra* note 69.

107 The thin line of oversight, THE GLOBE AND MAIL (Dec. 14, 2009) http://circ.jmellon.com/docs/view.asp?id=1256 (last visited August 11, 2011); Jim Bronskill, Arar inquiry urges more scrutiny of Canada's intelligence activities, THE CANADIAN PRESS, December 12, 2007, http://circ.jmellon.com/docs/view.asp?id=1068 (last visited August 11, 2011).

quite limited. This has created a disparity between the review mechanisms for CSIS and those for the RCMP, with the RCMP being subject to less rigorous scrutiny.[108]

2.3 Ad Hoc Inquiries Regarding Intelligence Abuses

While neither the Canadian Parliament nor the specific review offices engage in robust oversight of intelligence activities, the Canadian Government does have an additional oversight mechanism that has produced significant information: ad hoc inquiries led by judges with the power to compel both testimony and the production of evidence.[109] Since 2001, two of these inquiries have investigated alleged misconduct by intelligence agencies and produced important reports that have been available to Parliament as well as the public. A 2006 inquiry report concluded that the RCMP provided misleading information about Canadian citizen Maher Arar to the United States Government, which sent Arar to Syria, where he was tortured.[110] Similarly, a 2008 inquiry examined the role of Canadian Government officials in the detention and torture of three Canadian citizens, Abdullah Almalki, Ahmad Abou-Elmaati and Muayyed Nureddin, by Syria and Egypt, and concluded that the actions of Canadian officials contributed to their detention or mistreatment.[111] Both inquiries discussed the lack of oversight of national security activities.[112] While the inquiries uncovered problems with the intelligence agencies, they did not result in any changes in parliamentary oversight for these agencies.

---

[108] RAAFLAUB, *supra* note 69.

[109] See Kent Roach, Review and Oversight of National Security Activities and Some Reflections on Canada's Arar Inquiry, 29 CARDOZO L. REV. 53 (2007); Kent Roach, Uneasy Neighbors: Comparative American and Canadian Counter-Terrorism, 38 WM. MITCHELL L. REV. 1701 (2012).

[110] ARAR INQUIRY, *supra* note 98, at 13–16 (2006).

[111] INTERNAL INQUIRY INTO THE ACTIONS OF CANADIAN OFFICIALS IN RELATION TO ABDULLAH ALMALKI, AHMAD ABOU-ELMAATI AND MUAYYED NUREDDIN (2008).

[112] STANDING COMMITTEE ON PUBLIC SAFETY AND NATIONAL SECURITY, REVIEW OF THE FINDINGS AND RECOMMENDATIONS ARISING FROM THE IACOBUCCI AND O'CONNOR INQUIRIES, 40th Parliament, 2nd session, 1 (2009) (available at http://dsp-psd.pwgsc.gc.ca/collection_2009/parl/XC76-402-1-1-03E.pdf).

CONCLUSION

The United States Congress has adopted a multi-channel approach to intelligence oversight. Members of Congress have access to classified information about intelligence activities both directly and indirectly. The executive branch shares some of its most sensitive information directly with only a few members of Congress. While this kind of direct access to information might seem ideal, competing demands on members' time and restrictions on consulting staff regarding some of this information may actually hobble their ability to process and respond to this information. Members of Congress also gain access to a wider range of intelligence information indirectly through their staff members and review offices found in the legislative branch (the Government Accountability Office) and the executive branch (Inspectors General) that report to Congress. This indirect access to information has proven to be critically important to Congress's ability to conduct oversight because staff members and oversight agencies become force multipliers, enabling Congress to more effectively monitor and control executive branch intelligence activities.

Members of the Canadian Parliament have traditionally not had access to any classified information about the nation's intelligence activities. While one parliamentary office, the Auditor General, has access to classified information, her reports to Parliament are stripped of such information. Similarly, several non-parliamentary review offices have access to classified information, but their reports to Parliament do not include any classified information. Thus, members of Parliament are in no better position than a member of the public to evaluate the conduct of Canadian intelligence agencies. In a recent break with this approach, the House of Commons demanded and a few members were eventually given access to classified information about alleged wrongdoing regarding the Canadian forces' treatment of detainees in Afghanistan. The Memorandum of Understanding between the Prime Minister and leaders of three parliamentary parties that formed the basis for this information-sharing was unprecedented. But it was also an *ad hoc* response to a specific demand for information, and it is not clear whether it will become a precedent for future information sharing with Parliament.

7. *Arcana Imperii* and *Salus Rei Publicae*: state secrets privilege and the Italian legal framework

Arianna Vedaschi

INTRODUCTION

This chapter focuses on the state secrets privilege within the Italian legal framework. The Italian experience is particularly interesting because the state secrets privilege is specifically regulated by a law that has encompassed the principles decided by the Italian Constitutional Court. The first section examines the compatibility of the state secrets privilege with a democratic framework, while investigating the constitutional basis of the state secrets privilege according to the Italian Constitution. It also gives an account of the various scholarly stances on this issue. The second section analyzes the legislation on state secrets privilege, which has been partially amended by Law 133/2012 and more widely revised through Law 124/2007. The aim of the second section is to highlight Law 124/2007's main innovations in relation to previous Law 801/1977 – approved thirty years earlier. The third section focuses on rulings of the Constitutional Court on state secrets,[1] and criticizes the Court's failure to fully carry out its oversight of the state secrets privilege. In my concluding remarks, I consider this failure of the Constitutional Court in a broader context and call for a change in the trend in the constitutional

[1] See judgment 106/2009 and the very recent judgment 40/2012, both are available at www.cortecostituzionale.it. On judgment 106/2009 see: Adele Anzon, Il segreto di Stato ancora una volta tra Presidente del Consiglio, autorità giudiziaria e Corte costituzionale, 2 GIURISPRUDENZA COSTITUZIONALE, 1020 (2009). Vittorio Fanchiotti, Il gusto (amaro) del segreto, 2 GIURISPRUDENZA COSTITUZIONALE, 1039 (2009). Fabrizio Ramacci, Segreto di Stato, *salus rei publicae e* «sbarramento» ai p.m., 2 GIURISPRUDENZA COSTITUZIONALE, 1015 (2009).

jurisprudence, in the direction of greater and more effective oversight by both the Constitutional Court and an autonomous body.[2]

1. STATE SECRETS PRIVILEGE AND ITS CONSTITUTIONAL BASIS: A SCHOLARLY DEBATE

A preliminary discussion of the compatibility of the state secrets privilege with a democratic framework is important to understand this chapter's argument. One of the cardinal principles of a democracy lies in the transparency of its government's political action, which presupposes openness and access to information (i.e., facts, documents, etc.). The right of citizens to be informed of the activities of their governments derives from this general principle. When citizens are informed, they can better exert control and, if need be, hold government bodies accountable for any decision or action taken while carrying out their duties.[3]

Secrecy is in tension with this general principle of transparency, which is instrumental to democratic accountability. In fact, because secrecy is in direct contrast with openness, and therefore democratic systems generally, it appears to be more representative of dictatorships or illiberal regimes.

However, state secrecy is not wholly incompatible with a democratic framework, and every democracy resorts to secrecy when national security or other compelling interests so require. Thus, the need arises to find a balance between state secrecy and other legitimate fundamental needs of the community.

Before considering the problem of a necessary balance, it is important to identify the constitutional basis of the state secrets privilege. Constitutional scholars are divided on this issue.[4] Some believe the state secrets privilege lies in the sacred duty to defend the homeland found in article

---

[2] Although I am aware that a desirable reversal of case law is unlikely at least in the short term, future decisions by the European Court of Human Rights (ECHR) may bring it about. On the ECHR's jurisprudence see Giuseppe Arconzo & Irene Pellizzone, Il segreto di Stato nella giurisprudenza della Corte costituzionale e della Corte europea dei diritti dell'uomo, available at www.associazionedeicostituzionalisti.it.

[3] Norberto Bobbio, La democrazia e il potere invisibile, II RIVISTA ITALIANA DI SCIENZA POLITICA, 181 (1980).

[4] See Paolo Caretti, Limiti costituzionali alla tutela del segreto di Stato, DEMOCRAZIA E DIRITTO, 815 (1980) and Margherita Raveraira, Segreto nel diritto costituzionale, XIV DIGESTO ITALIANO DELLE DISCIPLINE PUBBLICISTICHE, 27 (1999).

52 of the Constitution,[5] while others claim that this provision addresses only military secrets, and prefer to locate the constitutional basis for secrecy in the broader obligation of allegiance to one's home country demanded by article 54.[6] Still others see these provisions operating jointly to support secrecy claims.[7] And other scholars claim that the above-mentioned provisions are unsatisfactory and maintain instead that the basis for state secrecy is found in article 117.2(d) of the Constitution, which identifies national security as within the exclusive remit of the national Parliament.[8]

Identifying the constitutional basis for state secrecy provides the starting point for striking a balance between secrecy and other constitutional values. Questions remain about how to offset national security interests (and its related institution, i.e., secrecy) against the exercise of the judicial function for the purpose of criminal prosecution.[9] As far as criminal matters are concerned, specific national security requirements, for which secrecy is essential, can very well collide with an individual's fundamental rights, such as the right to counsel (article 24 Const.).

Both perspectives[10] evoke potential conflict between the executive and the judiciary due to their different interests. The judiciary,[11] which in Italy is separate from and fully independent of any political power, must seek to further justice by prosecuting those charged with crimes in full compliance with their right to a defense. The executive, by contrast, aims to protect national security and, as a result, is more likely to resort to the

---

5 Article 52 of the Italian Constitution. Adele Anzon, Segreto di Stato e Costituzione, I GIURISPRUDENZA COSTITUZIONALE, 1755–1800, 1784 (1976). For an English translation of the Italian Constitution see The Italian Constitution. Text and notes (Lucio Pegoraro and Justin O. Frosini eds., Clueb 2008).

6 Article 54 of the Italian Constitution. Silvano Labriola, Segreto di Stato, XLI ENCICLOPEDIA DEL DIRITTO, 1031 (1989).

7 Paolo Barile, Democrazia e segreto, 1 QUADERNI COSTITUZIONALI 29, 37 (1987); Giovanni Pitruzzella, Segreto. Profili costituzionali, XVIII ENCICLOPEDIA GIURIDICA, 5 (1992).

8 Alessandro Pace, L'apposizione del segreto di Stato nei principi costituzionali e nella legge n. 124 del 2007, 5 GIURISPRUDENZA COSTITUZIONALE, 4041 (2008).

9 In Italy the exercise of prosecution is not referred to a judge's discretionary decision making, but is instead mandatory as provided for by articles 25 and 112 of the Constitution.

10 Articles 24 and 25 of the Italian Constitution.

11 Please note that according to the Italian legal system the role of public prosecutor is not exercised by government officials but is assigned to members of the judicial power.

state secrets privilege. Hence there is a need to find the correct balance between the needs underlying those values and rights protected by the Constitution through the duty of loyal cooperation between those very same powers.

2. THE STATE SECRETS PRIVILEGE AND ITALIAN LEGISLATION

The state secrets privilege is currently regulated by Law 124/2007,[12] as amended by Law 133/2012.[13] Law 124/2007[14] replaced Law 801/1977,[15] which was adopted thirty years earlier to modify a number of articles of the Italian code of criminal procedure (ccp). The 2007 statute, as amended, was designed to codify all previous constitutional jurisprudence relating to this subject matter.[16]

Article 39.1 of Law 124/2007 defines the substantive scope of the state secrets privilege. It must cover documents, information, activities and any other matter whose disclosure may jeopardize the integrity and the independence of the Italian Republic, even with regard to international agreements and relations with other nations, or harm the defense of the homeland and of those institutions lying at the heart of the Constitution.

In 2008, according to article 39.5 of Law 124/2007, the Prime Minister (PM) promulgated a regulation to identify more specifically the criteria on whose basis documents and information are liable to be covered by

---

[12] Law 3 August 2007, no. 124 on Intelligence System for the Security of the Republic and new provisions governing state secrets privilege, in Official Journal, 13 August 2007, no. 187. The text in force was amended by Decree Law 85/2008, confirmed – with amendments – by Law 121/2008, Decree Law 78/2009, confirmed – with amendments – by Law 102/2009, by Legislative Decree 104/2010 and lastly by Law 133/2012.

[13] Law 7 August 2012, no. 133, in Official Journal, 10 August 2012, no. 186.

[14] For a commentary on this Law see Federico Fabbrini and Tommaso Giupponi, Intelligence agencies and the state secret privilege: the Italian experience, 4 ICL-JOURNAL 443, 463 (2010). See also Tommaso Giupponi, La riforma del sistema di informazione per la sicurezza della Repubblica e la nuova disciplina del segreto di Stato, in Nuovi profili del segreto di Stato e dell'attività di intelligence 53–128 (Giulio Illuminati ed., Giappichelli 2010).

[15] Law 24 October 1977, no. 801. For a commentary on this Law see Vittorfranco Pisano, The Italian Intelligence Establishment: A Time for Reform?, 21 PEN STATE INT'L L. REV., 263 (2002).

[16] See judgments 82/1976 and 86/1977.

secrecy. Specifically, article 5 of the Prime Ministerial decree of 8 April 2008 refers to the inclusion of those areas liable to be covered by the state secrets privilege. These areas are specifically listed in a dedicated annex. This decree actually broadens the scope of the state secrets privilege, because it extends the areas liable to be covered by secrecy to include 'the protection of interests of an economic, financial, industrial, technological, health and environmental nature' – interests not encompassed in the original statutory language. In fact, this had been deliberately subtracted from the area of secrecy during parliamentary debate in 2007. Against this background some reservations can be expressed on the legitimacy of the implementation of Law 124/2007 given its tendency to amplify the scope of the state secrets privilege.[17]

Lastly, as far as its substance is concerned, the Law expressly forbids placing the seal of state secrecy on documents, information or matters relating to terrorist or subversive acts that may endanger the constitutional order or on facts constituting devastation and ransacking,[18] Mafia-style criminal organization,[19] political–Mafia exchange[20] and mass murder.[21]

As for the rules of procedure, a central role is played by the PM, who has exclusive competence and who is entitled to place the seal of state secrecy on specific facts and proceedings in addition to providing evidence for and confirming the applicability of the state secrets privilege when invoked by other institutions.[22]

In general, placing the seal of state secrecy is ineffective unless a written provision complete with signature and verifiable date is submitted.[23] When a public official invokes the state secrets privilege as part of a criminal procedure, the PM must confirm the assertion of secrecy.[24] Moreover, the Constitutional Court has ruled that 'the executive [must] indicate the basic reasons underlying the state secret'.[25]

---

[17] Armando Spataro, Abuse of state secrecy and national security, contribution to meeting in Tbilisi 1 (Sep. 16, 2010), available at www.assembley.coe.int.

[18] Article 285 cc.

[19] Article 416 bis cc.

[20] Article 416 ter cc.

[21] Article 422 cc.

[22] Article 1 Law 124/2007.

[23] Article 39.4 Law 124/2007.

[24] Article 202.5 ccp, amended by Article 40 Law 124/2007. Carlo Bonzano, Il segreto di Stato nel processo penale (Cedam 2010).

[25] Judgment 86/1977. See Adele Anzon, Interrogativi sui riflessi sostanziali della nozione di segreto di Stato individuate dalla Corte costituzionale, GIURISPRUDENZA COSTITUZIONALE, 866–9 (1977).

The secrecy privilege, once properly invoked, presumptively lasts for fifteen years, but may be extended to thirty years on a sufficient showing that secrecy remains necessary.[26]

2.1 State Secrets Privilege and Criminal Investigations

Italy's case law makes it useful to briefly outline the set of rules and regulations on the state secrets privilege, specifically those involving criminal investigation.[27] In particular, according to article 202.1 ccp, public officials and civil servants must refrain from testifying or giving evidence on matters covered by the state secrets privilege. This provision concerns witnesses, though the Constitutional Court[28] extends it also to defendants thanks to a very broad interpretation.[29]

When a witness invokes the state secrets privilege before a prosecutor, the prosecutor must ask the PM to confirm whether or not the requested information is secret.[30] The PM must reply within 30 days of being notified.[31]

If the PM denies the existence of any secret (or lets the 30-day deadline lapse without giving a statement), the prosecutor may acquire

---

26 Articles 39.7, 39.8 and 39.9 Law 124/2007, unlike the previous Law 801/1977 which did not set a time limit. On the other hand, whenever the need for secrecy has lapsed, the PM will order the cessation of the bonds of secrecy. In the case of a 'supranational secret', i.e., a secret that arises from an international agreement, the provision aimed at dispensing with secrecy must derive from a previous agreement with the relevant foreign or international authorities (article 39.10 Law 124/2007).

27 Article 202 ccp.

28 See judgment 106/2009. Notwithstanding, according to the Supreme Court of Cassation, because article 51 of the Italian criminal code (cc) excludes any liability for exercising a right and because the right to counsel is a fundamental right recognized by article 24 of the Constitution, the defendants violating the prohibition would not be punishable because it would be for the purpose of their defense during the trial. See sez. VI, 10 March 1987, CASSAZIONE PENALE, 1897 (1988).

29 For a critical analysis see Alessandro Pace, Sull'asserita applicabilità dell'imputato dell'obbligo di astenersi dal deporre sui fatti coperti dal segreto di Stato e sull'inesistenza dei fatti eversivi come autonoma fattispecie di reato, 1 GIURISPRUDENZA COSTITUZIONALE, 526 (2012) and also available at www.giurcost.org.

30 Article 202.2–6 ccp.

31 Article 202.4 ccp. It is worth noting that the deadline has been brought forward to halve the time compared to the previous legislation in an effort to expedite the decision-making process.

the information and proceed with the criminal investigation. By contrast, if the PM confirms that the requested information is secret, the prosecutor may not acquire or use, directly or indirectly, the information covered by the privilege. Where the privileged material is central to the investigation, the case must be dismissed 'due to the existence of the state secrets privilege'.[32]

However, the proceedings may continue if the prosecutor finds that the classified elements are not essential and there is other evidence upon which the criminal investigation may be based and thus resolved.[33] To this end, it must be noted that the Constitutional Court has repeated time and again that 'the reassertion of the state secrets privilege' by the PM may not 'prevent prosecutors from investigating crimes relating to the reported crime (*notitia criminis)* in their possession',[34] but may only 'forbid the prosecutors acquiring and consequently using any elements or evidence covered by secrecy'.[35]

2.2 State Secrets Privilege and its Control Mechanism

In Italian law, there are two types of checks against the abuse of the state secrets privilege. One is essentially political in nature and is the province of the Italian Parliament. The legislative branch must continually keep the executive under check according to the Italian form of government. Therefore the outcome (of this verification on the state secrets privilege) may even entail the resignation of the executive due to a vote of no confidence. It is common knowledge that in Italian parliamentary government the executive must have the confidence of Parliament.[36]

However, Parliament may neither replace the executive nor modify any decision taken by the PM, even when Parliament disagrees with the reasons for asserting a state secrets privilege. Thus, even when scrutinized by the Parliament, the PM remains the sole 'keeper' of the secret.

The parliamentary check is quite weak because it can only verify (1) the reason – however formulaic – for justifying invocation of the privilege and (2) the prohibition to invoke secrecy with respect to

---

32 Article 202.5 ccp.

33 Article 202.6 ccp.

34 This is often impossible for the judge.

35 See judgment 110/1998.

36 On the general characteristics of the Italian legal system and, in particular, the form of government, the sources of law and the Italian Constitutional Court see the chapters by Justin O. Frosini and Arianna Vedaschi in Introduction to Italian Public Law, 31, 211 and 183 (ed. Giuseppe F. Ferrari, Giuffré, 2008).

subversive plots that may endanger the constitutional order or on documents relating to terrorist acts or on facts constituting those crimes mentioned in section 2.[37]

Nevertheless, a report is submitted to the plenary assembly of Parliament only if the Parliamentary Committee for the Intelligence and Security Services (COPASIR) – a political body typically presided over by a member of the opposition[38] – deems the assertion of state secrecy invalid. The recent Law 133/2012 states that, during a specific secret hearing, the PM must provide, at the request of the Chairman of the COPASIR, all useful information to allow the COPASIR to verify whether the state secrets privilege confirmation is lawful and legitimate. Only if the COPASIR deems it unlawful, will the matter be reported to Parliament.[39]

The other type of check is the province of the Constitutional Court, which – in the case of conflict of powers – may be asked to verify the legitimacy of the state secrets privilege and, if necessary, revoke it.

Unlike the previous check, this verification is only carried out whenever the executive and the judiciary cannot agree on the state secrets privilege. For example, if a prosecutor or a judge presiding over a criminal trial believes that the state secrets privilege was not invoked in compliance with the law or if the invocation is deemed invalid, the prosecutor or the judge will raise a jurisdictional dispute before the Constitutional Court.[40]

The Constitutional Court then determines the legitimacy of the asserted secrecy privilege. If deemed invalid, the PM may not assert it with reference to the same act or document and the criminal procedure resumes. By contrast, the Court may resolve the conflict by assessing the legitimacy of the state secrets privilege, in which case the prosecutor or

---

37 Article 39.11 Law 124/2207; as already Article 12 Law 801/1977 previously in force.

38 This political body is made up of ten MPs (five from the Chamber of Deputies and five from the Senate). See Articles 30 and 31 Law 124/2007.

39 In no case can secrecy be invoked by the government when a majority of two thirds of COPASIR's members decide to investigate the operations of the intelligence services, in order to verify if these operations are in compliance with the law (see Article 31.9 Law 124/2007, as modified by Article 6 Law 133/2012). Therefore, COPASIR must have the right to access to all information and documentation in order to be able to proceed with its investigations. It is worth noting that before this recent new Law 133/2012 was enforced, COPASIR had to vote unanimously in order to have access to the aforementioned information and documentation.

40 Article 31.7 Law 124/2007.

judge may neither acquire nor utilize (directly or indirectly) any documents or proceedings that are classified through the state secrets privilege.

3. STATE SECRETS PRIVILEGE AND THE ITALIAN CONSTITUTIONAL COURT

The Constitutional Court has addressed the state secrets privilege in about ten rulings. The vast majority of these rulings concern the Italian intelligence services. Indeed, if I were to narrow down my focus to the most significant ones, I could concentrate my attention on fewer than five rulings. This shortlist would certainly include the last two rulings, one of which concerns Abu Omar, which has had international resonance.[41] Thus, few rulings have been made on the state secrets privilege and these are predominantly concerned with intelligence activities.

Before dealing with the merits of the Constitutional Court's jurisprudence, another aspect must be taken into account: the type of ruling. Most of the case law is the result of the conflict of powers between branches of the government and not the result of the traditional constitutional review.[42]

More specifically, a number of issues addressed by the Court are particularly useful in sketching out the jurisprudential picture regarding this subject. Additionally, such an exercise is helpful to understand

---

[41] On the Abu Omar case see Michele Nino, The Abu Omar Case in Italy and the Effects of CIA Extraordinary Renditions in Europe on Law Enforcement and Intelligence Activity, REVUE INTERNATIONAL DE DROIT PÉNAL, 113 (2007). Federico Fabbrini, Extraordinary Renditions and the State Secret Privilege: Italy and the United States Compared, 3 ITALIAN JOURNAL OF PUBLIC LAW, 2, 255 (2011).

[42] Following article 37 of Law 87/1953 'conflicts between branches of government shall be resolved by the Constitutional Court provided that the conflict arises between bodies that have the competence to express the final will of the branches of government they belong to' and 'whose competences are regulated by the Constitution'. A consequence of this conflict resolution is that the Constitutional Court will declare the annulment of the concrete act that provoked the dispute. This annulment will have an *erga omnes* effect. In other words, jurisdictional disputes consist of conflicts between branches of government and the Constitutional Court acts as arbiter by entering into the merits of the case and resolution of the dispute. See Justin O. Frosini, Constitutional Justice, in Introduction to Italian Public Law, 183 (ed. Giuseppe F. Ferrari, Giuffré, 2008).

whether the Court really does control the state secrets privilege. Lastly, this approach will allow me to understand, upon reaching my conclusions, whether the state secrets privilege as defined by the Italian lawmaker and by the constitutional jurisprudence is compatible with democracy.

One of the crucial issues addressed by the Court is the constitutional basis for the state secrets privilege. The Court addressed the question of the constitutional basis for secrecy in ruling 86/1977 – which may be considered, under many aspects, the leading case – and previously in ruling 82/1976, before revisiting the same issue in its last two rulings on the subject.[43] According to the Court, the state secrets privilege is legitimate only if it serves the 'paramount interests' of the community (citizenry) and it is the 'necessary instrument' to guarantee national security. The Court establishes in even more specific terms that the seal of secrecy may only be given if its goal is to guarantee the territorial integrity, the independence, or the democratic framework. In other words, the seal may be given only if it is to protect the existence of the State, which is always understood as a social community (Nation-State) and not as a government structure (Organizational-State). In sum, the Court identifies the constitutional basis for secrecy in articles 1, 5 and 52 of the Constitution, which protect the democratic framework, the national unity and independence of the Nation as well as the sacred duty to defend the homeland, respectively.[44]

The Court's reasoning clearly acknowledges the importance of secrecy, that is, to protect national security. Hence the centrality of the definition put forward by the Constitutional Court in relation to the idea of national security, which, in the last analysis, coincides with the survival of the Nation, independently of the interests of the Government and of its political majority.[45] As a matter of fact, according to the Court, the state secrets privilege is an 'instrument aiming to protect the *salus rei*

---

[43] Judgments 106/2009 and 40/2012: the Constitutional Court reiterates the principles legitimizing the state secrets privilege, by expressly bringing the previous jurisprudence to the fore (see also judgments 110 and 410/1998). These principles, which have not only been consistently confirmed by the Court, have also – as mentioned earlier – been implemented by the legislation enforced over time (see Law 801/1977 and Law 124/2007).

[44] See judgment 40/2012, point 5, but also see judgment 106/2009. Constitutional jurisprudence of the 1970s insists on article 52 of the Italian Constitution (marginally articles 87 and 126), then touches on articles 1 and 5 of the Italian Constitution, before explicitly referring to a set of articles and not only on one article.

[45] Judgment 86/1977.

publicae', because it is linked with national security intended as 'a community's essential and insuppressible interest'. In light of this assumption, the Court recognizes the 'pellucid quality of absolute predominance' inherent in this interest 'over any other, in that it affects ... the very existence of the State'.[46] Consequently, the other constitutional values are doomed to perish or recede when confronted with national security.[47] The national security interest has therefore been articulated and made explicit by the lawmaker,[48] according to the Court's latest ruling, which establishes the undisputed preeminence of 'self-preservation' of the State over other basic rights, such as the right to defense in a trial.[49]

Against this background, the ruling on whether and how to guarantee national security through the seal of secrecy appears to be of great importance. As mentioned earlier, the decision to grant the seal of secrecy is the exclusive competence of the PM.[50] The Constitutional Court stresses 'the wide discretionary quality and the essentially political nature' of such a decision, which allows the PM to single out the information that must be classified in the interest of *salus rei publicae*.[51] However, the PM's wide discretionary powers[52] are solely limited to the need to express the 'basic' (or rather formulaic) reasons underlying his decision and to the prohibition against classifying subversive plots that may endanger the constitutional order.[53] These limits, established by the Court's earlier judgments, are now legislatively enforced (see section 2).

With the political nature of the decision leading to secrecy having been established, the Court emphasizes that only Parliament can review its merits and legitimacy. This check can be traced back to the natural relationship between the legislative power and the executive power. In fact, in an even broader sense, the Government must, according to the

---

46 Judgments 40/2010, 106/2009, 110/1998 and 86/1977.

47 Judgment 40/2012.

48 Judgments 82/1976 and 86/1977; these two judgments were handed down in the context of a legislative vacuum. The principles established by these judgments have been incorporated by the lawmaker in 1977 and 2007.

49 By protecting the defendant through acquittal whenever the defendant's right to counsel is hampered.

50 Judgments 82/1976 and 86/1977 for the first time mentioned by the Court and then received by the lawmaker.

51 Judgments 40/2012 and 106/2009.

52 Identifying the facts that may jeopardize national security requires an assessment which goes beyond administrative discretion and which encroaches on political discretion (judgment 86/1977).

53 Judgment 86/1977 and so forth.

Court, be held accountable for its decisions or actions before the Italian people. The latter exerts full sovereignty through its representatives in Parliament. Parliament, in turn, holds the executive accountable.[54]

According to the Constitutional Court, the assertion of secrecy is not subject to judicial review. In fact, the Court has decidedly excluded any judicial review of whether and how secrecy applies.[55] More overtly, in its last ruling the Court specifies that the reason for secrecy must be received by both Parliament and the judiciary. Parliament must be allowed to review the merits of the PM's decision while the judiciary must be presented with the reasons for 'barring' the trial – whenever secrecy is invoked and asserted during a criminal procedure. Then, the Court may, in its capacity, circumscribe its review to whether the formulaic reason exists or not.

The constitutional basis and reason for the state secrets privilege accounts for the other constraint mentioned earlier: the prohibition against placing the seal of secrecy on subversive acts that may endanger the constitutional order. Indeed, concealing subversive acts or plots would clash with the aim of ensuring the existence of the nation.

In this regard, it is worth pointing out the Court's restrictive interpretation in its two most recent rulings. Indeed, the Court deems subversive only those acts meant to 'overthrow the democratic order or the institutions of the Italian Republic', that is, those meant 'to damage the primary good of the State's international legal personality'. The Court considers subversive those acts that are liable to demolish 'the overall democratic structure of the institutions'.[56] In other words, any action aimed at overthrowing the Government or at attacking the constitutional bodies would be considered subversive. Interestingly, the Court rules that a single event, however serious,[57] may not constitute a subversive act.[58]

Thus, the Court has limited its supervisory role with regard to the state secrets privilege. For example, in its verification as to 'the existence or non-existence of the premises underlying the state secrets privilege … invoked and asserted', the Court reviews only the legitimacy of the institution that asserts the state secrets privilege, whether there is formulaic reason for it and, finally, whether it complies with the prohibitions codified by article 39.11 of the Law 124/2007.

---

[54] Judgment 86/1977. The Constitutional Court refers to Article 95 of the Italian Constitution.

[55] Judgments 106/2009 and 40/2012, point 3.

[56] Judgment 40/2012, point 8.5.

[57] The Constitutional Court refers to the Abu Omar case.

[58] Judgment 106/2009.

As discussed in the conclusion that follows, there are a number of points in the jurisprudence of the Constitutional Court that raise questions. But it is the overarching result, which translates into the Court's effective resignation to act as the reviewer of the state secrets privilege, that is most disappointing.

CONCLUSION

The above analysis leads to several conclusions. First of all, as regards the legislative aspects, it must be noted that a potential expansion of the use of the state secrets privilege is made possible thanks to the executive's sources of law, that is PM decrees, which are exempt from parliamentary review.[59] According to Italian law, the PM's decrees cannot complement statutes (approved by Parliament). The PM's decree can only specify what the statute already says. I think that on this point the PM's decree of April 8, 2008 is not lawful. My opinion takes also into account the fact that the expansive trend of the PM's decree 2008 is not consistent with the fact that secrecy is a constitutional exception and should therefore not admit extensive interpretations and applications.

Furthermore, the danger posed by the expansion of secrecy is amplified on account of the role granted to the PM in matters relating to the state secrets privilege.[60] In essence, the problem is that the Head of Government is given full decision-making powers, with little or no political oversight exercised by the COPASIR. Hence, for example, this Committee has yet to pronounce on the seal of secrecy placed on the Abu Omar case. Unfortunately, the latest amendments of 2012 did not introduce any specific deadline[61] that would oblige the COPASIR to expand its control on the state secrets privilege. Indeed, the very political

---

[59] Decree of 8 April 2008 on criteria to identify information, data, documents, records, activities, things and places liable to be subject to state secrets privilege, in Official Journal, April 16, 2008, no. 90.

[60] Judgment 86/1977. This exclusive role of the PM was decided by the constitutional jurisprudence dating back to the 1970s. The statement of this judgment was then formalized by Law 801/1977 and further reinforced by Law 124/2007.

[61] I think that it would be desirable to require the COPASIR to meet tighter time schedules. See Armando Spataro, Segreti. 'Segreto di Stato fabbrica di impunità'. Abu Omar, Telecom, Magdi Allam: come si ostacolano le indagini, IL FATTO QUOTIDIANO, October 14, 2010 and Armando Spataro, Se si dilata il segreto di Stato, LA REPUBBLICA, August 9, 2010.

makeup of the Committee does not offer reassurance about the effectiveness of its oversight. The various MPs who have alternately chaired the COPASIR, for example, were former vice PMs during the Prodi administration. Mr. Prodi himself confirmed the state secrets privilege on the Abu Omar case. In other words, the law does not recognize the potential issue that the decision maker and the supervisory overseer may be one and the same. And the new Law 133/2012 has not amended this critical point. I call for an amendment of the Law which must introduce a new kind of oversight by an autonomous body or at least partially autonomous from Parliament.

In addition, until now, COPASIR's control is exercised purely on basic reasons given by the PM. However, thanks to an amendment added by Law 133/2012, during a specific secret hearing, the PM must disclose any and all useful information to allow COPASIR to be better placed to verify whether the state secrets privilege confirmation is lawful and legitimate. But it is worth noting that this opportunity is only granted at the request of the Chairman of the Committee. So I suggest amending the Law so as to diclose always any useful information for the autonomous oversight body.

Moreover, as regards controversial classified cases, no power of inquiry has ever been exerted, irrespective of the COPASIR supervisory oversight. This shows the weakness inherent in the political oversight, which in practice turns out to be unsatisfactory because it seems to defer to the PM's discretionary power rather than curbing it.

The legislative prohibitions on invoking secrecy with respect to subversive plots that may endanger the constitutional order or on documents relating to terrorist acts also fail to achieve their goal due to the restrictive interpretation given by the Italian Constitutional Court. In fact, the Constitutional Court's restrictive interpretation of the definition of subversion must be criticized. The latter should not be forcibly traced back to specific criminal offences with the result of excluding the crime in question,[62] nor should it be only connected with the subversion of the institutions, but should instead apply also to violations of those founding principles underlying the Italian democratic order, first and foremost those human rights that can be encapsulated in the notion of human dignity.

---

[62] Judgment 106/2009 and Article 270 cpp. Alessandro Pace, I 'fatti eversivi dell'ordine costituzionale' nella legge n. 801 del 1977 e nella legge n. 124 del 2007, in Studi in onore di Lorenza Carlassarre, 1099 (Giuditta Brunelli, Andrea Puggiotto, Paolo Veronesi eds., Cedam 2009).

From a logical point of view, these prohibitions should be interpreted extensively rather than restrictively, since the state secrets privilege is by definition an exception to the principle of transparency in the areas of public action.

I disagree with the excessively cautious approach adopted by the Constitutional Court to its role in the oversight of state secrets privilege – a role that was expressly given to the Constitutional Court by the lawmaker.

It is worth noting that under no circumstances may the Court be challenged with the state secrets privilege.[63] In fact, the Court must always comply with the necessary secrecy guarantees and the law when reviewing proceedings covered by secrecy. Consequently, the Court may acquire any classified information while doing so.

Nevertheless, the Court's constitutional jurisprudence indicates that it has resigned from the role of reviewer. Indeed, the most recent rulings, namely rulings 40/2012 and 106/2009, highlight the self-restraint firmly embraced by the Court. As pointed out earlier, the Court confines its review to the mere presence of the formulaic reason and the existence of any prerequisites for secrecy, while refusing to ascertain the connection between the object of secrecy (classified information) and the aims set by the lawmaker, which are meant to reflect the constitutional rights warranting secrecy.

The result is therefore the Court's resignation from effectively reviewing the use of the state secrets privilege. However, from my perspective, the Court should not have given up its reviewing role, but it could and should have verified the constitutional legitimacy of the state secrets privilege, at least to ensure compliance with the principle of legality and proportionality in relation to the reasonableness of the PM's decision. Thus, the Court would have ensured its compliance with the constitutional principles and values underlying the use of secrecy. Instead, the Court's prudent behavior has led to the dangerous amplification of the executive's discretionary power, despite the fact that, as noted earlier, the executive already has ample leeway, which is hardly ever curbed by the parliamentary oversight,[64] even in light of the most recent changes to Law 124/2007.

---

63 See Article 40.8 Law 124/2004: 'In no circumstances may state secrets privilege be invoked against the Constitutional Court. The Court shall adopt the necessary measures to ensure the secrecy of its proceedings.'

64 Adele Anzon, La Corte abbandona definitivamente all'esclusivo dominio dell'autorità politica la gestione del segreto di Stato nel processo penale, 1

The risk clearly consists of the executive abusing the state secrets privilege leading to a distorted use of the state secrets privilege in the interest of the Government rather than that of the Nation-State.[65]

Furthermore, the current system of checks fails to prevent such gross violations. The Parliament may not be interested in sanctioning the PM and the judiciary is unable to identify such violations. In the mean time, the Constitutional Court has relinquished its role as reviewer of the state secrets privilege.

This leads to the further dangerous consequences of having national security – discretionarily placed by the executive power at the heart of secrecy – as the strong value at the apex of the formal hierarchy of constitutional values.

In fact, according to the Court's reasoning, national security always appears to be automatically preeminent over other constitutional values.[66] The constitutional jurisprudence underpins the idea that there is effectively a preference for a rigid hierarchy of constitutional values culminating in national security.[67] Indeed, the latter always prevails when it is at stake but only the PM can decide whether it is at stake.

This theoretical edifice is far removed from a system of checks and balances. In the case of a system of checks and balances, the importance of constitutional values is ascertained on a case-by-case basis and the reasonableness of the PM's decision is placed under review, once the actual compliance of the object of secrecy with the laws has been verified.

Within this theoretical edifice, international terrorism becomes incorporated into the more general and potentially broader definition of national security. This, at least in theory, makes the Italian system more vulnerable to the potential misuse of the state secrets privilege.

GIURISPRUDENZA COSTITUZIONALE, 534 (2012) and also available at www.giurcost.org.

[65] This effect has been condemned by the Constitutional Court since 1977.

[66] Judgment 40/2012, point 5.

[67] For a critical analysis see Arianna Vedaschi, Has the balancing of rights given way to a hierarchy of values?, 1 COMPARATIVE L. REV., 1–40 (2010). In fact, over the last few years the interest of national security has been increasingly put forward by democracies to the point that it has become a legitimate right, see Ginevra Cerina Feroni & Giuseppe Morbidelli, La sicurezza: un valore superprimario, 1 PERCORSI COSTITUZIONALI, 31 (2008). On balancing see Andrea Morrone, Il nomos del segreto di Stato, in Nuovi profili del segreto di Stato e dell'attività di intelligence 1–52, 23 (Giulio Illuminati ed., Giappichelli 2010).

Finally and from a more general perspective, it is worth pointing out that all these findings can be read to trace the boundary between the areas of the Italian constitutional bodies, that is in the broader context of the Italian form of government. As it is well known, challenges posed in the most delicate moments of a democracy's life are particularly meaningful in examining the form of government and its democratic level. The latest cases of the assertion of the state secrets privilege have always provoked a conflict of powers decided by the Constitutional Court. This conflict has shown the executive and the judiciary do not agree on the use of secrecy so the assertion of the state secrets privilege highlights a breaking point between the executive and the judiciary, and the consequent break in the loyal cooperation between branches of the government. Indeed, this breaking point fails to achieve a fair solution within the Italian legal system because an effective oversight of the PM's assertion or confirmation of state secrets privilege does not exist. The lack of a litmus test for secrecy brings out the weakness of the system of checks and balances that ultimately affects the same form of government.

PART 3

Secrecy and detention

8. Managing secrecy and its migration in a post-9/11 world

Kent Roach

INTRODUCTION

Secrecy has emerged as a different type of legal and political problem since 9/11. Secrecy has always presented a threat to fairness and to transparent governance. Governments have always had an incentive to overclaim secrecy. Nevertheless, the post-9/11 focus on terrorism has changed the nature of the competing interests. In the Cold War era, secret information could generally remain secret forever so long as it was not leaked to the other side. Secret information was used to inform the strategic decisions of both sides and as a basis for removing suspected spies from a country or removing their security clearances. Such spies, however, were rarely prosecuted and they were not detained on the basis of secret evidence. Courts generally deferred to the government's claims of secrecy and did not attempt to reconcile the competing values of secrecy and disclosure.

Today, secrecy is more complex and challenging. In the immediate aftermath of 9/11, many democracies used secret evidence that was not disclosed to the detainee or the public to justify military and immigration detention. Such secret evidence is now used to justify targeting decisions under the US's program for killing suspected terrorists with drones. The Security Council of the United Nations, as well as most domestic executives, use secret evidence to blacklist individuals and groups suspected of involvement in al Qaeda and the Taliban. Courts no longer blindly defer to governmental claims of secrecy. The creation of many new terrorist crimes designed to prevent terrorism means that what was once intelligence that could always remain secret may now be evidence of a crime or material that must be disclosed to the accused to ensure a fair trial.

The desire to use information to impose severe legal consequences on individuals while also keeping it secret has gained increased prominence since 9/11. The use of secret evidence has been legally and politically controversial. There have been many court cases challenging governmental claims to secrecy and much litigation over the adequacy of correctives to secrecy such as the use of security-cleared special advocates to challenge secret evidence and the use of public interest immunity proceedings to prevent the disclosure of secret material that might be relevant in legal proceedings. The ongoing military commissions at Guantanamo are controversial in part because of the continued role of secrecy and the related issue of the mistreatment of the detainees. Secrecy can be used to cover up misconduct. A *Justice and Security Bill*[1] introduced in the UK Parliament on May 28, 2012 would allow the use of secret evidence only seen by special advocates in civil proceedings. It also would allow the government to prohibit the disclosure of material that reveals wrongdoing about third parties such as the US and other allies.

Secrecy is also more challenging today because of its dynamic, polycentric and contingent nature. The issue is no longer the binary one of whether one agency, nation or tight Bloc of nations will classify and keep information secret or not. Rather, secrecy is often a product and a precondition of information sharing relationships between agencies within countries and between countries. These relationships and the conditions of secrecy are not static. They evolve over time. What is secret at one point in time may well become public at another time. Intelligence investigations of suspected terrorists can quickly change into criminal investigations given the nature of broad new terrorism offences. Secrecy also has a new public relations dimension as secrecy may erode the legitimacy of various counter-terrorism measures. This in turn may promote perhaps false but nevertheless damaging perceptions that those targeted are not really involved in terrorism and/or that the secret information is derived from torture or is otherwise unreliable. Secrecy should be seen less as a noun that describes a thing and more as a verb that describes processes and ongoing relationships. Secrets migrate between countries in the same way that infectious diseases and computer viruses migrate. Information that originates in a dark torture cell in one part of the world can instantly be transmitted and cause secrecy-based legal and political problems in Washington and London. Secrets also migrate into public evidence and public intelligence. Secrecy is a problem that must be managed along with the relationships between domestic and international agencies with security responsibilities.

---

1 HL Bill 27 (introduced May 28, 2012).

1. SECRECY HAS BECOME MORE LEGALLY AND POLITICALLY CONTROVERSIAL SINCE 9/11

Much commentary has focused on the increasing role of secrecy and intelligence as governments attempt to prevent another 9/11.[2] These are important developments as surveillance capabilities expand with technology and as the distribution of secret intelligence increases to agencies, corporations and other nations often escaping effective review. At the same time, however, the increased legal and political contestation of secrecy should not be ignored. In the Cold War era, courts and even the media were much more deferential to state secrecy claims than they are today. To be sure, there were exceptions, such as the Supreme Court's refusal to enjoin the publication of the leaked Pentagon Papers,[3] but they pale in comparison to post-9/11 developments such as WikiLeaks[4] or court decisions in both England and Canada that have rejected governmental claims of secrecy.

1.1 Guantanamo, Targeted Killings and Secrecy

Since 9/11, American courts have been very receptive to state claims of secrecy and have used them to reject several legal challenges to extraordinary renditions and to targeted killings.[5] Even in the US, however, there has been some judicial push back to secrecy. In *Hamdan v. Bush*,[6] the Supreme Court held that military commissions at Guantanamo violated both Common Article 3 of the Geneva Convention and the

---

[2] See for example Gabriel Schoenfeld *Necessary Secrets, National Security, the Media and the Rule of Law* (New York: Norton, 2010); Dana Priest and William Arkin *Top Secret America* (New York: Little Brown, 2011). For interesting comments on these two books see Lawrence Friedman and Victor Hansen 'Secrecy, Transparency and National Security' (2012) 38 William Mitchell L.Rev.1610.

[3] *New York Times v. Sullivan* 403 U.S. 713 (1971).

[4] For arguments that internet technology has changed the nature of leaks since the Pentagon Papers case by making prosecution less realistic see Patricia Bellia 'WikiLeaks and the Institutional Framework for National Security Disclosures' (2012) 128 Yale Law Journal 1448.

[5] For descriptions of how American courts have used broad state secrets doctrine as a form of 'extra-legalism' in which law has been used in an exceptional way to shield extra legal conduct from review see Kent Roach *The 9/11 Effect: Comparative Counter-Terrorism* (Cambridge: Cambridge University Press, 2011) at 223–7.

[6] 548 U.S. 557 (2006).

Uniform Code of Military Justice in part because evidence could be presented without the defendant being present. This issue is related to secrecy because the absence of the accused from the proceedings could ensure that the information was only seen by security-cleared counsel and military judges. Indeed, the impossibility of using secret evidence in American criminal trials given the accused's constitutional confrontation rights was one of the reasons why the Bush administration was attracted to military commissions. The *Military Commissions Act of 2006*, enacted in response to *Hamdan*, provided that the accused should be present in the proceedings unless he was disruptive or dangerous.[7] The *Military Commissions Act of 2009* prohibits military judges from ordering the release of classified information,[8] but also ensures that the accused has access to any information that is introduced into evidence in military commissions.[9] There are also provisions drawn largely from the Classified Information Proceedings Act (CIPA) that govern the use and disclosure of classified or secret information on a public interest immunity model. They allow the use of non-classified substitutes for classified information and they provide for the withdrawal or termination of certain charges as a remedy for non-disclosure of classified information.[10] There seems to be a growing albeit grudging recognition of the unfairness of the use of secret evidence.

At the same time, the taint of prior uses of secret evidence as well as public suspicion that secrecy will be used to cover up torture and other misconduct lingers. Although Congress decided at the end of 2011 to create a rebuttable presumption in favor of military detention and trial of alien terrorists suspected of involvement in al Qaeda, President Obama has indicated that he will waive this option when it might prevent other countries from extraditing or transferring terrorist suspects to the United States. Secret evidence as it was previously used at Guantanamo stands a potent and easily understood symbol of unfair counter-terrorism. The unfairness of secret evidence towards those targeted may have strategic as well as normative costs. Many believe that al Qaeda has morphed into an ideology that builds on grievances and a sense that Muslims are under attack throughout the world. In such a context, the public relations costs of using secret evidence should be taken seriously because it may promote a sense that innocent people have been unfairly detained, convicted or targeted as terrorists.

---

7 *Military Commissions Act of 2006* 120 Stat 2611 s.949d(e).
8 *Military Commissions Act of 2009* H.R. 2647-385 s.949p-1(a).
9 Ibid s.949p-1(b).
10 Ibid subchapter V.

Secret evidence is used by the US military and the CIA in decisions about targeted killing. Attorney General Holder has stressed that the evidence supporting such decisions is carefully reviewed within the government and has argued that the process satisfies due process because due process need not be judicial process.[11] The problem with this approach is that it requires people to trust the government that the secret evidence has been thoroughly tested and vetted even though the executive has an incentive to err on the side of security. In contrast to the Israeli courts, American courts have taken a hands-off approach to review of targeted killing.[12] The Israeli courts have in one prominent case reviewed targeted killings and have stressed the importance of both ex ante and ex post review within the military and involving the courts.[13] To be sure, Israel has not gone as far as the United Kingdom in giving security cleared special advocates access to secret information, but it has provided a process that goes beyond the executive simply reviewing itself. The Obama administration does not seem to think that anyone could seriously challenge the legitimacy of their attempts to keep strategic military information behind targeted killings secret. In a sense, this is a return to a Cold War strategy where the need to preserve secrets from the other side was widely accepted. What has changed since 9/11, however, is that terrorism as opposed to invasion or nuclear war is widely accepted as the prime threat to national security. Terrorism is seen by many as a crime and the use of war-like secrecy is much more problematic in responding to a crime than to a threat of invasion or nuclear war. Hence, the legitimacy of the US's use of secrets to kill people in its controversial war against al Qaeda has been challenged. It may become a liability in the US's dealings with the Muslim world.

1.2 The United Kingdom and Secrecy

Secret evidence was also used in the United Kingdom under Part IV of the *Anti-Terrorism Crime and Security Act, 2001.* It provided for the indeterminate detention of non citizen terrorist suspects who could not be deported. Cases were heard by the Special Immigration Appeals Commission which allowed security cleared lawyers called 'special advocates' to examine and challenge secret evidence that was not disclosed to

---

[11] Eric Holder 'Speech at Northwestern Law School' March 5, 2012 available at www.justice.gov/iso/opa/ag/speeches/2012/ag-speech-1203051.html.

[12] *Al-Aulaqi v. Obama* 727 F.2d 1 (Dist Ct, 2010).

[13] *Public Committee against Torture v. Israel* (HCJ 769/92) in Judgments of the Israel Supreme Court on Terrorism Vol 3 at 88.

detainees or their lawyers. Special advocates are, however, restricted from communicating with detainees once they have seen the secret material because of concerns that they may inadvertently disclose secrets to the detainee. This raises concerns that detainees may not have a fair trial because they are unable fully to assist special advocates in their defence. The fear of inadvertent disclosure by special advocates is related to the Cold War concept of the mosaic[14] effect in which the detainee could potentially fit together the pieces of the puzzle about sources and methods from even innocuous pieces of information.

The provisions for indeterminate detention without trial in Part IV of the *Anti-Terrorism, Crime and Security Act of 2001* were repealed after the House of Lords in 2004 declared them incompatible with the Human Rights Act, 1998 incorporating parts of the European Convention on Human Rights.[15] They were replaced by control orders which also allowed secret evidence to be used. The use of secret evidence has continued to be controversial and the House of Lords, following authority from the European Court of Human Rights, has ruled that the use of secret evidence to support control orders is invalid if the controlee is not afforded sufficient detail about the case against him to permit him to instruct his defense counsel and participate in his defense. Although secret evidence can still be used, subject to this 'gisting' requirement and challenge by special advocates, much of it must be disclosed to allow persons to defend themselves.[16] The UK government has now replaced control orders with a new regime that also allows the use of secret evidence. The spread of special advocates has been controversial in the UK.[17]

---

[14] The mosaic theory assumes that professional experts on the other side such as the KGB for the former Soviet Union will collect information so that the disclosure of seemingly innocuous information will provide a clue or fill in the missing piece of the mosaic. See *Henrie v. Canada* (1988) 53 D.L.R. (4th) 568 at 580 stressing the danger that 'the informed reader' will put together the pieces of the mosaic. For discussion see Kent Roach *The Unique Challenges of Terrorism Prosecutions* (Ottawa: Public Works, 2010) at 195–204, For pre-9/11 uses of the mosaic theory in American law see David Pozen 'The Mosaic Theory, National Security and the Freedom of Information Act' (2005) 115 Yale L.J. 628.

[15] *A. v. Secretary of State* [2004] UKHL 56.

[16] *Secretary of State v. AF (no. 3)* [2009] UKHL 28 at para 59 following *A v. United Kingdom* App no 3455/05 19 February 2009 para 220.

[17] Justice, *Secret Evidence* (London: Justice, 2009); see also UK Green Paper *Justice and Security* Cmnd 8194 (London: Stationery Office, 2011); Justice and Security Bill HL Bill 27.

1.3 Canada and Secrecy

Secret evidence is used in Canada to support the administrative detention and deportation of non-citizens thought to be a security threat. In 2002, a judge of the Federal Court which reviews such procedures commented in an extra-judicial speech that the judges of his Court 'do not like this process of having to sit alone hearing only one party and looking at the materials produced by only one party and having to try to figure out for ourselves what is wrong with the case that is being presented before us and having to try for ourselves to see how that witnesses that appear before us ought to be cross-examined'. The judge ended his speech with an extraordinary confession – 'I sometimes feel a little bit like a fig leaf'.[18] Security certificates have been controversial in Canada, often being branded as 'secret trials'. This controversy illustrates some of the legal and political costs of secrecy.

In 2007, the Supreme Court of Canada held that the absence of any adversarial challenge to the secret evidence submitted to the judge in security certificate proceedings violated the right to a fair trial under section 7 of the Canadian Charter of Rights and Freedoms.[19] The Court rejected the idea that searching review of secret evidence by specially designated Federal Court judges, many of whom had long experience in intelligence matters,[20] could make up for the use of secret evidence. The Court held that the right to a fair hearing could be met only by an adequate substitute for disclosure and that there was none under the regime then in place. Parliament responded with a regime of security cleared special advocates who, like British special advocates, could not communicate with anyone including the detainee after having seen the secret evidence, absent court approval. The new regime has been challenged under the Canadian Charter of Rights and Freedoms, but has been

---

[18] James Hugessen 'Watching the Watchers: Democratic Oversight' in D. Daubney et al eds., *Terrorism, Law and Democracy* (2002) at 384, 386.

[19] Section 7 provides that a person's life, liberty and security of the person can only be taken away in accordance with the principles of fundamental justice. *Charkaoui v. Canada* [2007] 1 S.C.R. 350. On this case and legislative responses to it see generally the collection of essays in (2008) 42 S.C.L.R,(2d) 251–440.

[20] For further discussion of the judicial management model used in Israel and elsewhere see Daphne Barak-Erez and Mathew Waxman 'Secret Evidence and the Due Process of Terrorist Detentions' (2009) 48 Colum. J. of Transnational Law 1 at 20–27.

upheld with the courts stressing that judges have allowed special advocates in appropriate cases to consult with the detainees and others even after they have seen the secret evidence.[21]

1.4 New Developments in Secrecy in Malaysia

The use of secret evidence in the UK and Canada has echoes of reliance on British colonial emergency legislation used in Israel and Malaysia to justify preventive administrative detention. As discussed above, 'secret trials' have become controversial in the US, UK and Canada. As will be seen, they have even become controversial in Malaysia which in 2012 repealed its infamous Internal Security Act that allowed indeterminate detention without trial on the basis of secret evidence; Malaysia replaced this legacy of British colonial emergency laws with the Security Offences (Special Measures) 2012 Act.[22] As will be seen, it borrows quite liberally from democratic legislation like the US Classified Information Procedures Act and its Commonwealth counterparts by placing duties on criminal defendants to notify the state if they intend to adduce 'sensitive information' broadly defined to include any material relating to national security, national defence, international relations but also 'public order' and 'sovereignty' regardless of whether it has been classified as secret or even confidential.[23] Section 8 of the act allows the court to authorize the prosecutor to use a summary or a statement setting out the relevant facts that the sensitive information would establish. The accused may never know the details of the information, including the identity of witnesses or informers, and thus be unable to challenge the credibility of the material on which a summary or statement of facts is based. Section 8(4) borrows from CIPA practice and contemplates that the accused's lawyer but not the accused may be able to examine the underlying sensitive information and argue that it should be disclosed to the accused or that a summary should not be used against the accused. At the same time, the new law does not cede as much control to the judiciary over secret evidence as the legislation of many democracies because section 11(4) allows the Minister for Home Affairs to prevent the disclosure of any sensitive information or summary on the basis that it would be 'prejudicial to national security or national interest'. Section 28 of the new law also prohibits the disclosure of the identity of informers even in circumstances where a

---

[21] *Harkat v. Canada* 2012 FCA 122.

[22] Laws of Malaysia 2002 Act 747 available at http://malaysianlaw.my/attachments/Act-747-Security-Offences_85130.pdf.

[23] Ibid s.3

court may determine that the accused's innocence may be at stake. The new Malaysian law is more rights sensitive than the infamous Internal Security Act that allowed for indeterminate detention on the basis of secret evidence without trial.[24] At the same time, increased acceptance of secrecy in Western terrorism trials has made it possible for more authoritarian countries such as Malaysia to use more modern laws to pursue aggressive security agendas that include the use of secret evidence.[25]

1.5 The UN Security Council and Secrecy

Secrecy is not only controversial domestically. The UN Security Council relies on secret evidence in its listing of terrorists under the regime established by Resolution 1267. The European Court of Justice held in the *Kadi* case that this procedure, which afforded the listed party no opportunity whatsoever to respond, lacked basic fairness and could not be implemented at the European level.[26] The European Court of General Instance subsequently held that a narrative summary designed to provide Kadi with some information about why he was listed while also protecting intelligence sources and methods did not provide enough information to afford a judicial remedy.[27] Canadian and British courts

---

24 Section 4(3) of the new law helpfully provides that 'no one shall be arrested and detained under this section solely for his political belief or political activity' while at the same time following the British example of allowing preventive arrest for a maximum 28 day period. One important difference is that British law requires some judicial review and authorization whereas the new Malaysian law does not. Similarly s.14 of the new law allows anonymous witnesses, as is also allowed in the United Kingdom. One difference, however, is that the European Court of Human Rights has placed restrictions on relying on anonymous witnesses for the whole of the prosecution's case which would of course not apply in Malaysia.

25 The general theme of the old style security agendas of more authoritarian countries being transformed into more modern laws based on Western models is explored in Roach *The 9/11 Effect: Comparative Counter-Terrorism* (Cambridge: Cambridge University Press, 2011) at 440–42.

26 *Yassin Abdullah Kadi and Al Barakaat International Foundation v Council of the European Union and Commission of the European Communities,* Cases C-402/05 P and C-415/05 P, *Yassin Abdullah Kadi and Al Barakaat International Foundation v. Council and Commission,* 3 September 2008.

27 *Kadi v. European Commission* judgment of the General Court (7th Division) 30 September 2010 available at http://eur-lex.europa.eu/LexUriServ/LexUriServ.do?uri=CELEX:62009A0085:EN:HTML.

have also made adverse comments about the use of secret evidence in the 1267 regime and have even compared it with the position faced by Josef K. in Kafka's *The Trial*.[28] The Security Council has responded to these criticisms with a number of reforms including the creation of an Ombudsperson to consult with those seeking de-listing and the nations that may have supplied the secret information, and by giving the Ombudsperson's delisting recommendations presumptive force.[29] The Security Council's attempts to respond to its secret evidence problems are particularly telling because it has responded more to concerns about the political legitimacy of the use of secret evidence than to threats that domestic or supra-national courts would actually interfere with its listing processes given that these courts have all admitted that they do not have jurisdiction to review the actions of the Security Council. The collection and exchange of secret intelligence and the use of such information to impose serious legal consequences has significantly increased since 9/11, but so too have the legal and political controversies surrounding secrecy.

2. MANAGING SECRECY DOMESTICALLY

Domestically, secrecy involves the dynamic and contingent relationship between intelligence and evidence. The 9/11 Commission in the United States,[30] the Air India Commission in Canada[31] and the Haneef Commission in Australia[32] all stressed the importance of ensuring that intelligence is better distributed in efforts to make better informed counter-terrorism decisions. These commissions did not understand secrecy as static or immutable. The 9/11 Commission and the Air India Commission especially were drawn towards recommending new management structures. The former recommended a Director of National Intelligence and the latter recommended an enhanced role for the Prime Minister's National Security Advisor respectively to govern the relations between intelligence agencies and between such agencies and other parts of government. These recommendations have been criticized by some as

[28] *Abousfian Abdelrazik v The Minister of Foreign Affairs and the Attorney General of Canada* [2009] FC 580; *Treasury v. Ahmad* [2010] UKSC 2.

[29] Security Council Resolutions 1904 and 1989.

[30] *The 9/11 Report* (New York: Norton, 2004).

[31] Commission of Inquiry into the Investigation of Bombing of Air India Flight 182, *A Canadian Tragedy* Vol 3 (Ottawa: Public Works, 2010).

[32] *Report of the Inquiry into the Investigation of Dr. Mohammed Haneef* (Canberra: Government Services, 2008).

attempting to centralize and impose too much institutional structure,[33] but they recognize that secrecy can only be controlled if the relationships between agencies that share information are overseen and managed. The Air India Commission recognized that intelligence agencies had legitimate concerns to fear the disclosure of intelligence sources and methods if they shared intelligence with policing and other security officials, but concluded that it was not acceptable in light of the failure to share intelligence that might have prevented the 1985 bombing of Air India Flight 182 for intelligence agencies to have unilateral discretion not to disclose intelligence. Instead, they recommended that intelligence agencies be required to disclose intelligence that might reveal evidence of a terrorist crime to the Prime Minister's National Security Advisor (NSA). The information would be protected by a new national security privilege, but the NSA would be able to decide whether the public interest required keeping the intelligence secret or risking its disclosure by sharing it with policing, transportation or border officials. The Canadian government rejected this proposal, but the point is that the Commission recognized that secrecy was not static and required the management of information sharing relations between domestic agencies with security responsibilities.

Although the United States does not have a separate domestic civilian intelligence agency, administrative barriers known as 'the wall' were constructed to regulate the sharing of intelligence with prosecutors working on criminal prosecutions. Concern about the barriers reportedly played some, albeit limited, role in at least one investigation of the 9/11 hijackers. One FBI agent working on the intelligence side rebuffed an inquiry from another FBI agent working on the law enforcement side, in part because the file contained signals intelligence. The rebuffed FBI agent replied that 'someday someone will die – and wall or not – the public will not understand why we were not more effective'.[34] The 9/11 Commission found that the law enforcement agent had been wrongly denied the intelligence because the suspect was already subject to a law enforcement investigation. It also concluded that more information sharing could have identified at least two of the hijackers and possibly disrupted the 9/11 plot.[35] The 9/11 Commission recommended a radical restructuring of government to encourage information sharing, including the creation of a National Counterterrorism Centre with a National

---

[33] Richard Posner *Preventing Surprise Attacks: Intelligence Reform in the Wake of 9/11* (Boston: Little Brown, 2005).

[34] 9/11 Commission Report at 8.2.

[35] 9/11 Commission Report at 3.2.

Intelligence Director with powers to oversee and resolve disputes between intelligence agencies. Leaving aside the workability of such proposals, the main point is that they recognize that secrecy needs to be managed and controlled.

Domestic agencies are under increasing pressure to share secret information in an attempt to prevent another 9/11. Both the 9/11 Commission in the US and the Air India Commission in Canada were critical of the lack of sharing of information. The sharing of information, especially with law enforcement agencies, however, presents real risks that secret intelligence might eventually be disclosed and with that confidential sources and methods of intelligence gathering. Both commissions were drawn, not to defining new bright lines between what was secret and what was not, but to recommending new structures to manage the relationship between domestic agencies that may share information. They also recognized the need in some circumstances for intelligence to be shared and used even if that meant that the secret material might eventually be disclosed. The very nature of secrecy has changed as we have moved out of a Cold War era with its focus on keeping information secret from the other side to a new era where terrorism is seen as the greatest national security threat. Today, what was once secret may have to be disclosed in order to prosecute terrorists or inform front line officials to take security precautions.

3. MANAGING SECRECY INTERNATIONALLY

If the challenges of managing secrecy domestically are great, they are even greater internationally. In Canada, the Arar Commission was appointed because a failure by Canadian officials to place caveats or restrictions on information shared with American agencies contributed to the detention and torture of Maher Arar and other Canadians in Syria. The Arar Commission did not recommend that security information no longer be shared with foreign partners, but stressed the importance of using caveats in an attempt to manage the use of shared information. It also stressed the need for effective and wide ranging review of information sharing practices.[36] Both the Arar and Air India commissions

---

[36] Commission of Inquiry into the Activities of Canadian Officials in Relation to Maher Arar *Report of the Events Relating to Maher Arar* (Ottawa: Public Works, 2006); *Report on a New Review Mechanism for the RCMP's National Security Activities* (Ottawa: Public Works, 2006).

were drawn towards recommendations that attempt to oversee the relationships between agencies that shared information both domestically and internationally. Neither commission saw secrecy as static. They recognized that what was secret at one point in time might not be secret at another point in time and secrecy depended on evolving relationships and circumstances.

Canadian courts have started not to take secrecy claims based on the third party rule of control over shared intelligence at face value. They have required Canadian agencies to request foreign agencies to amend the restrictions or caveats that they originally placed on the disclosure of shared intelligence.[37] They also have required intelligence agencies to retain material collected in targeted investigations because of its potential evidential value.[38] These changes have not been a comfortable experience for Canadian agencies which rely on foreign intelligence and worry that such requests might make foreign countries hesitate to share intelligence.[39]

The Canadian approach to secrecy is more proportionate than that contemplated in the Justice and Security Bill introduced in May 2012 in the UK Parliament.[40] This bill contemplates that the executive can simply designate that material must not be publicly disclosed because its disclosure 'would be damaging to the interests of national security'[41] and would prohibit judges from considering public interest immunity proceedings as a more proportionate alternative.[42] It also would allow the executive to dictate that material that reveals misconduct by third parties such as foreign intelligence agencies should not be disclosed simply because that material was or had been held by any UK intelligence service.[43] Both types of executive designations are subject to judicial review, albeit fairly deferential review. Although draconian in many respects, the Justice and Security Bill at least recognizes the need to manage secrecy through review of the activities of the security services by pairing the provisions for secret evidence and non-disclosure with

---

37 *R. v. Khawaja* 2007 FC 490.

38 *Charkaoui v. Canada* [2008] 2 S.C.R. 326.

39 Kent Roach 'When Secret Intelligence Becomes Evidence' (2009) 47 Sup.Ct.L.Rev. 2d 147.

40 HL Bill 27.

41 Ibid s.6(2)(b).

42 Ibid s.6(3).

43 Ibid s.13(3).

reforms to strengthen review by parliamentary committees and the Intelligence Services Commissioner.[44]

The UN Security Council has encountered many problems with respect to its use of secret evidence to list individuals and groups associated with al Qaeda and the Taliban under Resolution 1267. The reform process remains a work in progress. As with domestic processes, the UN reforms attempt to manage secrecy in the context of evolving relationships, in this case the relationships between the 1267 Committee, the Ombudsperson and the countries that supply the intelligence that support the listings.

The post-9/11 management of secrecy has been further complicated by the frequent sharing of information and counter-terrorism between democracies and countries with poor human rights records. Canada appointed two inquiries into whether Canadian information sharing practices made Canada complicit with the torture of Canadians held in Syria. The United Kingdom appointed but then abandoned a similar inquiry, in part because of ongoing police investigations, but also because the legitimacy of the inquiry had been threatened by giving the Cabinet a veto over what sensitive information the inquiry could disclose.

Canada's Arar Commission severely criticized Canadian officials for sharing complete investigative files with American agencies without vetting the accuracy of the shared information or attaching restrictions or caveats on what use the US could make of the information, including whether it could be shared with other countries such as Syria. The Commission stressed the importance of caveats not as a means to hinder information sharing, but as a means of establishing a relationship between Canadian agencies and the foreign agencies with which they shared information. It stressed that caveats could in appropriate cases be amended but that the process of seeking an amendment should have alerted Canadian officials to the dangers that the Americans would render Maher Arar to Syria or share information with Syria.[45] The emphasis is on managing the use of secret information and thereby reducing the risk of information contributing to torture and other forms of mistreatment. The Arar Commission and a follow-up commission are also noteworthy

---

44 Ibid ss.1–5. These reforms include allowing Parliament to appoint members to the Intelligence and Security Committee and allowing it to review operational matters. The reforms are, however, heavily constrained by requirements that the Prime Minister continue to nominate members and can prohibit review of operational matters.

45 Commission of Inquiry into the Activities of Canadian Officials in Relation to Maher Arar *Report of the Events Relating to Maher Arar* (Ottawa: Public Works, 2006).

because they demonstrate how information sharing can become both legally and politically controversial. Mr Arar sued both Canada and the United States, and lawsuits against the Canadian government by other Canadians tortured in Syria are still pending. Unlike during the Cold War, governments now have to be aware that their information sharing practices may make them legally responsible for misdeeds committed by other governments.

Managing secrecy at the transnational level will remain challenging. There is a danger that information that is potentially very valuable in preventing acts of terrorism will be tainted by torture or other forms of mistreatment. This creates a danger that caveats and secrecy may simply shield mistreatment or alternatively that governments may ignore tainted information that could help prevent acts of terrorism. Governments that exchange information with regimes that do not respect human rights may be subject to lawsuits alleging complicity with torture. Such litigation may generate further cycles of controversy and secrecy as democratic governments may raise state secrets claims in such litigation or settle claims to avoid revealing secrets that may embarrass themselves and their partners. There are no easy solutions. Democracies must be careful when they share information because of concerns about complicity in misconduct. As in the domestic arena, secrecy should not be seen as a static fact, but rather as a contingent classification with both costs and benefits. Moreover, secrecy is subject to re-evaluation as the relationships between producers and consumers of information evolve. The fact that both sharers of secret information are sovereign nations, often not subject to much if any judicial review, greatly complicates the international management of secrecy. That said, developments such as the mediating role of the delisting Ombudsperson for the 1267 committee suggests that some progress can be made. A failure to manage secrecy will result in the continued legal and political controversy that has affected the 1267 committee.

CONCLUSION

The first decade after 9/11 has had significant effects on secrecy. Courts have in general become less deferential to state claims of secrecy, if only because of their recognition that the use of secret evidence to justify prolonged military and immigration detention has drastic effects on the detainees. Much of the post-9/11 debate on secrecy has focused on correctives within the legal system to accommodate demands for secrecy. Thus the role of special advocates in the United Kingdom and Canada has loomed large as has the respective merits of public interest immunity and closed proceedings. The recent *Security Offences* law in Malaysia and the *Justice and Security* Bill introduced in the UK suggest that it would be unwise to conclude that sustainable progress towards greater openness has been made. The Malaysian law allows the use of secret evidence in criminal trials albeit subject to a thin veneer of public interest immunity or CIPA-type language frequently used in the UK and the US. The UK government has responded to fears that intelligence received from American and other foreign agencies might be disclosed in civil proceedings by proposing to allow the use of secret evidence confronted only by special advocates in civil proceedings and executive prohibitions on the disclosure of material held by British intelligence agencies that reveals misconduct by third parties. This bill will rightly be controversial. If the war against terror is in part a war against ideologies that may become more widely accepted because of perceptions of unfair treatment, then the public relations harms of 'secret trials' need to be more seriously considered.

Legal systems will continue to evolve in their quest to balance the competing interests in disclosure and secrecy, but more attention needs to be paid to the demands for secrecy by domestic and foreign intelligence agencies. Such agencies should not be allowed to remain comfortable in Cold War habits of secrecy where disclosures of sources and methods were absolutely prohibited and sources and foreign agencies could routinely be promised absolute secrecy. Intelligence agencies and others should not be able to claim secrecy simply to prevent the disclosure of misconduct and complicity in misconduct. They must resist the temptation to engage in over-classification and unnecessary claims of secrecy. At the same time, the state will continue to have a legitimate interest that some intelligence be kept secret. Secrecy may be necessary to protect vulnerable sources, ongoing investigations and promises made to other countries. There can be no once and for all decisions about secrecy; much will depend on circumstances and the evolving relations between those who share secret information.

The costs of secrecy will vary depending on the uses of secret information. The cost of secrecy will be much less when secret intelligence is used for the traditional purposes of warning governments but much more when it used as evidence to impose legal consequences on individuals and/or when it leads to complicity and cover-ups with respect to human rights abuses. In addition, the post-9/11 decade has also demonstrated that it is wrong to equate secrecy with achieving greater security, as so often was thought to be the case in the Cold War era. For example, secrecy may impose security costs if it prevents intelligence from being passed on to those who are in the best position to take immediate on the ground steps to prevent acts of terrorism. In addition, the use of secret evidence poses real risks to the legitimacy of domestic and international legal systems, especially when combined with the danger that secrecy will also cover up human rights abuses that may cast doubt on the reliability of the intelligence. Targeted killings based on secret evidence can be defended on the basis that no country reveals such secret information used for military targeting, but many view such killings not as legitimate acts of war, but as executions of suspected criminals who have been tried only by the executive on the basis of secret evidence that has never been subject to adversarial challenge. The legitimacy of legal systems has both normative and instrumental values. Secret trials are inherently unfair to those subject to them, but they also sap verdicts, even if well supported by the secret evidence, of public support and legitimacy. Secret trials fail to expose and denounce those who are prepared to use violence for political or religious ends.

A demand side approach to secrecy suggests that more attention should be paid to the relationships between producers and consumers of potentially secret information. Ultimately, the demands for secrecy and the legitimacy of those demands will depend on how such relationships are managed. Domestically, as both the 9/11 Commission and the Air India Commission stressed, intelligence agencies should not be able to demand secrecy as a good in itself or because they are uncomfortable with perhaps remote risks of disclosure. The demand to break down walls within governments can serve as a positive force in making agencies re-think instinctive reliance on secrecy that may have made sense during the Cold War but no longer makes sense in an age where terrorism is seen as the greatest threat to national security.

The increased information sharing promoted since 9/11 may have security benefits, but it comes with dangers. In Canada, the Arar Commission revealed that information sharing can result in complicity in torture and similar findings might well have emerged had the UK's Detainee Inquiry been allowed to complete its work. The answer to these dangers must, however, lie between the extremes of simply not sharing information or requiring full WikiLeaks-style transparency with respect to all information sharing. As the Arar Commission recommended, governments need to be better aware of the dangers of sending and receiving information that may make them complicit in misconduct. They should also attempt, as best as possible, to use caveats, memorandums of understandings and other instruments to manage relationships with their information sharing partners. Secrecy is not static. It has to be continually justified and must be re-evaluated in light of its political costs and legal risks.

9. National security, secret evidence and preventive detentions: the Israeli Supreme Court as a case study

Shiri Krebs*

1. INTRODUCTION

The 'war on terror' gave rise to various harmful state-sponsored means, including preventive detentions, designed to stop suspected terrorists from committing future atrocities. Judicial review provides the main protection against arbitrary and unjustified preventive detention, which is often based on secret evidence.

In the first decade of the twenty-first century, the Israeli Supreme Court reviewed hundreds of preventive detention cases. Scholars have argued – based on the Court's rhetoric in a few renowned cases – that Israel's judicial review of preventive detentions is robust and effective.[1] However, there has been little scrutiny of the Court's actual review practice beyond a handful of high-profile, oft-quoted cases. This chapter presents, for the first time, a systematic empirical analysis of the Israeli Supreme Court's case law regarding preventive detention from 2000 to 2010. The analysis encompasses all of the relevant judgments, including hundreds of short, laconic and unpublished decisions. The findings reveal a meaningful gap between the rhetoric of a few renowned cases and actual practice. On the one hand, this study reveals that out of the 322 cases decided by the Israeli Supreme Court in this period, not a single case resulted in a release order, and in no case did the Court openly reject

* The author wishes to thank Prof. Jenny Martinez for her guidance, advice and inspiration. A thorough description of this research and its findings was published as: Shiri Krebs, *Lifting the Veil of Secrecy: Judicial Review of Administrative Detentions in the Israeli Supreme Court*, 45(3) VANDERBILT JOURNAL OF TRANSNATIONAL LAW 639 (2012).

[1] Stephen J. Schulhofer, *Checks and Balances in Wartime: American, British and Israeli Experiences*, 102 MICH. L. REV. 1

the secret evidence. On the other hand, more subtle Court dynamics were detected, such as 'bargaining in the shadow of Court' and 'mediation' efforts on behalf of the Court.

In order to lift the veil of secrecy that typically characterizes judicial proceedings regarding preventive detentions, the study involved seventeen in-depth interviews, with all of the relevant stakeholders, including Supreme Court Justices, defense lawyers, state attorneys, Israeli Security Agency (ISA) representatives, and former detainees. These interviews provide a unique glimpse into the judicial review process and reveal some of the behind-the-scenes dynamics of that process.

Put together, the comprehensive case law analysis and in-depth interviews offer extensive information on the actual practice and the inherent difficulties of judicial review of preventive detention cases, and reveal the unique methods the Court has developed to confront them. Fundamentally, they cast doubt on arguments that Israel's detention model is one that should be emulated by other countries.

2. JUDICIAL REVIEW OF PREVENTIVE DETENTIONS: THE NORMATIVE FRAMEWORK

This chapter focuses on a specific preventive detention regime, also referred to as 'executive detention',[2] 'administrative detention',[3] or 'security detention'.[4] This type of detention is a proactive mechanism operated by the Executive or military authorities in order to prevent future harm to national security.[5] In accordance with this mechanism, individuals can be preventively detained although they have never committed any crime; they are being detained in order to prevent them from committing future crimes or offenses.

In the first decade after the emergence of a global 'war on terror', preventive detention without criminal charge has become an increasingly

---

[2] Marc D. Falkoff, *Back to Basics: Habeas Corpus Procedures and Long-Term Executive Detention*, 86 DENV. U. L. REV. 961, 961 (2009).

[3] Derek P. Jinks, *The Anatomy of an Institutionalized Emergency: Preventive Detention and Personal Liberty in India*, 22 MICH. J. INT'L L. 311, 313 (2000).

[4] John McLoughlin, Gregory P. Noone & Diana C. Noone, *Security Detention, Terrorism and the Prevention Imperative*, 40 CASE W. RES. J. INT'L L. 463, 463 (2007).

[5] Rinat Kitai-Sangero, *The Limits of Preventive Detention*, 40 MCGEORGE L. REV. 903, 905 (2009).

popular counter-terrorism mechanism.[6] The Guantánamo detainees are perhaps the most infamous example,[7] but they are not alone. All around the globe, from India,[8] to Israel,[9] to the Russian Federation,[10] to Australia,[11] states facing terrorist threats are employing some sort of preventive detention regime. Interestingly, even states such as Israel, which has used preventive detention for decades, introduced new preventive detention regimes and began using them more widely after the terrorist attacks in the US on September 11, 2001.[12]

Judicial review of preventive detention is particularly important for several reasons: (a) the inherent imbalance between the state and the detainee; (b) the state's reliance on secret evidence[13] and ex parte proceedings;[14] (c) the Court's deference to the state's discretion in issues

---

6 Kenneth Anderson, *U.S. Counterterrorism Policy and Superpower Compliance with International Human Rights Norms*, 30 FORDHAM INT'L L.J. 455, 474–81 (2007); Jenny Hocking, *Counter-Terrorism and the Criminalisation of Politics: Australia's New Security Powers of Detention, Proscription and Control*, 49 AUSTL. J. POL. & HIST. 355, 355–71 (2003); Dominic McGoldrick, *Security Detention – United Kingdom Practice*, 40 CASE W. RES. J. INT'L L. 507, 509 (2009). For an analysis of preventive detentions in international law and in armed conflict situations, see Ashley S. Deeks, *Preventive Detention in Armed Conflict*, 40 CASE W. RES. J. INT'L L. 403 (2009).

7 *See* Johan Steyn, *Guantanamo Bay: The Legal Black Hole*, 53 INT'L & COMP. L.Q. 1 (2004) (providing background and analysis on Guantánamo Bay detention center).

8 Jinks, *supra* note 3.

9 Itzhak Zamir, *Preventive Detention*, 18 ISR. L. REV. 150 (1983).

10 Todd Foglesong, *Habeas Corpus or Who Has the Body? Judicial Review of Arrest and Pre-Trial Detention in Russia*, 14 WIS. INT'L L.J. 541 (1996).

11 Jenny Hocking, *Counter-Terrorism and the Criminalisation of Politics: Australia's New Security Powers of Detention, Proscription and Control*, 49 AUSTL. J. POL. & HIST. 355, 355–71 (2003); Katherine Nesbitt, *Preventative Detention of Terrorist Suspects in Australia and the United States: A Comparative Constitutional Analysis*, 17 B.U. PUB. INT. L.J. 39 (2007).

12 *See infra*.

13 Daphne Barak-Erez & Matthew Waxman, *Secret Evidence and the Due Process of Terrorist Detentions*, 48 COLUM. J. TRANSNAT'L L. 3, 5 (2009); Sarah H. Cleveland, Hamdi *Meets* Youngstown*: Justice Jackson's Wartime Security Jurisprudence and the Detention of 'Enemy Combatants'*, 68 ALB. L. REV. 1127, 1132–34 (2005).

14 Barak-Erez & Waxman, *supra* note 12, at 21; Hamish Stewart, *Is Indefinite Detention of Terrorist Suspects Really Constitutional?*, 54 U.N.B. L.J. 235, 245 (2005).

of national security;[15] and (c) the bias of all decisionmakers in favor of detention, given the differential risks of false positives and false negatives. An incorrect decision is revealed only when the Executive or the judge releases from custody a dangerous individual who is later involved in a terrorist activity. An incorrect decision that approves detention of an innocent individual who would never have committed a terrorist act is invisible, and indeed, unknowable.[16] This is substantially different than criminal proceedings, which deal with past offenses. If an offense has already occurred, a defendant *can* materially prove his or her innocence as to that offense. But an innocent person wrongly detained can never prove that he would not have engaged in illegal acts even if he had been free.

Since one of the basic characteristics of preventive detentions is the reliance on privileged intelligence information provided by undisclosed sources, and collected, secretly, by state security agencies, the Court's judicial review in these cases becomes even more challenging.[17]

In order to confront the difficulties posed by the use of secret evidence, two distinct models of judicial review have emerged in preventive detention cases: the 'judicial management' model and the 'special advocate' model. The former rests on ex parte proceedings, in which the judge plays a cardinal role in executing an independent, inquisitorial scrutiny of the secret evidence.[18] The latter model introduces 'special advocates' or government attorneys approved by state authorities, whose role is to represent the detainee's interests with respect to the secret evidence, and are permitted to confront that evidence in closed proceedings.[19] The special advocate communicates with the detainee before seeing the evidence, but generally cannot once he has been exposed to

---

[15] DAVID KRETZMER, THE OCCUPATION OF JUSTICE: THE SUPREME COURT OF ISRAEL AND THE OCCUPIED TERRITORIES 118 (2002); Kitai-Sangero, *supra* note 5, at 912.

[16] Kitai-Sangero, *supra* note 5, at 909.

[17] Van Harten elaborates on three different weaknesses in this regard: (1) the judge is precluded from hearing additional information that the individual could have supplied had he known the Executive's claims; (2) courts are uniquely reliant on the Executive to be fair and forthcoming about confidential information; and (3) the dynamic or atmosphere of closed proceedings may condition a judge to favor unduly the security interest over priorities of accuracy and fairness. Gus Van Harten, *Weaknesses of Adjudication in the Face of Secret Evidence*, 13 INT'L J. EVID. & PROOF 1, 1 (2009).

[18] *See* Barak-Erez & Waxman, *supra* note 13, at 21–2.

[19] *See id.* at 27–31.

the secret evidence.[20] While the judicial management model is employed in the Israeli preventive detention regime, the special advocate system was adopted in the United Kingdom and Canada.[21]

Comparing and analyzing these two models, Professor (and now Supreme Court Justice) Daphna Barak-Erez and Professor Matthew Waxman recently opined that, roughly speaking, the special advocate model enhances participation, while the judicial management model is designed to enhance accuracy – and can better regulate the detention system across many cases.[22] This chapter will assess the validity of this proposition by empirically analyzing the Israeli Supreme Court judicial review of preventive detentions.

3. PREVENTIVE DETENTIONS IN ISRAEL

Israel currently holds more than 300 detainees under three different preventive detention regimes.[23] *In the Israeli Territory* applies the Emergency Powers (Detentions) Law of 1979 (IDL).[24] Under the IDL regime, the Minister of Defense is vested with the authority to order a person's detention without trial for the protection of state security and public safety for a period of up to six months. The detention may be extended indefinitely by repeatedly issuing new orders.[25] The IDL mandates judicial review by the civilian court system;[26] initially, within forty-eight hours from the time of arrest,[27] and then repeatedly every three months.[28] Since detention orders are often based on secret evidence, the IDL specifies that while assessing the secret evidence, the reviewing judge is

---

20 *Id.*

21 *See id.* at 18–24; Maureen T. Duffy & Rene Provosi, *Constitutional Canaries and the Elusive Quest to Legitimize Security Detentions in Canada*, 40 CASE W. RES. J. INT'L L. 531, 541–43 (2007); Derek McGhee, *Deportation, Detention & Torture by Proxy: Foreign National Terror Suspects in the UK*, 29 LIVERPOOL L. REV. 99, 105 (2008).

22 Barak-Erez & Waxman, *supra* note 13, at 36–46.

23 As of May 2012.

24 Emergency Powers (Detention) Law, 5739-1979, 33 LSI 89 (1979) (Isr.).

25 *Id.* § 2(a).

26 Mara Rudman & Mazen Qupty, *The Emergency Powers (Detention) Law: Israel's Courts Have a Mission – Should They Choose to Accept It?*, 21 COLUM. HUM. RTS. L. REV. 469, 470–71 (1989); *see also* Zamir, *supra* note 9, at 153.

27 Emergency Powers (Detention) Law § 4(a).

28 *Id.* § 5.

not bound by the regular rules of evidence.[29] In particular, the judge may 'admit evidence not in the presence of the detainee or his representative, or without revealing it to them', if he is convinced that disclosure of the evidence is liable to 'harm the security of the region or public security'.[30]

In the West Bank (and until recently also in Gaza) – an area regarded by Israeli courts as subject to belligerent occupation – military law applies and independently authorizes preventive detention.[31] The most recent military order governing preventive detentions in the West Bank is Preventive Detentions Order No. 1591 (MDO).[32] The MDO authorizes IDF's military commanders to detain a person for a maximum period of six months when there is 'a reasonable basis to believe that the security of the region or public security' requires it.[33] Here too, the detention may be extended indefinitely, six months at a time.[34] The detainee must be brought before a military judge within eight days to determine whether the detention is justified.[35] Similar to the IDL regime, the MDO includes a provision permitting the use of secret evidence that is not revealed to the detainee or his (or her) representative, and permits deviations from the regular rules of evidence.[36] The military court's decision may be appealed to the Military Court of Appeals by either the detainee or the military commander.[37] Although, according to the MDO, the decision of the Military Court of Appeals should be the last instance of review for the military commander's decision, a practice developed over the years of submitting habeas corpus petitions to the Israeli Supreme Court, sitting

---

[29] *Id.* § 6. For discussion on secret evidence in Israeli preventive detention proceedings, see Barak-Erez & Waxman, *supra* note 13, at 19.

[30] Emergency Powers (Detention) Law § 6(c).

[31] *See, e.g.*, HCJ 7957/04 Mara'abe v. Prime Minister of Isr., 45 I.L.M. 202, 207 (2006) (Isr.); HCJ 2056/04 Beit Sourik Vill. Council v. Gov't of Isr. 58(5) PD 807, para. 23 [2005] (Isr.); HCJ 3799/02 Adalah Legal Ctr. for Arab Minority Rights in Isr. v. GOC Cent. Command, 45 I.L.M. 491, 498 (2006) (Isr.); *see also* Aharon Barak, *A Judge on Judging: The Role of a Supreme Court in a Democracy*, 116 HARV. L. REV. 16, 148–60 (2002); Daphne Barak-Erez, *Israel: The Security Barrier – Between International Law, Constitutional Law, and Domestic Judicial Review*, 4 INT'L J. CONST. L. 540, 542–48 (2006).

[32] Military Order Regarding Preventive Detention (Judea and Samaria) (No. 1591), 5767-2007, § 1 (Isr.), available at www.btselem.org/sites/default/files/preventive_detention_military_order_1591_eng.pdf.

[33] *Id.* § 1(a).

[34] *Id.* § 1(b).

[35] *Id.* § 4(a).

[36] *Id.* §§ 7–8.

[37] *Id.* § 5.

as High Court of Justice, to review the decisions of the Military Court of Appeals.[38]

In 2002, the Israeli parliament introduced a new preventive detentions law: the *Incarceration of Unlawful Combatants* Law of 2002 (UCL).[39] The UCL gives state authorities the power to detain 'unlawful combatants', who are as defined in § 2 of the law as persons who have taken part in hostilities against the State of Israel, directly or indirectly, or who are members of a force carrying out hostilities against Israel, and who do not satisfy the conditions of prisoner of war status under international humanitarian law.[40] According to the UCL, persons identified as unlawful combatants may be subject to preventive detention for an unlimited period of time if the Chief of Staff believes that their release will harm state security.[41] Article 5(a) determines that within fourteen days from the date of arrest, the detainee must be brought before a district court judge to determine if the detention is justified.[42] A district court judge must then review the detention every six months.[43] Article 5(e) permits the court to depart from the rules of evidence, including the admittance of evidence without the presence of the detainee or the detainee's lawyer.[44] In June 2008, the Israeli Supreme Court ruled on several appeals that attacked the constitutionality of the UCL based on Israeli constitutional law and international humanitarian law.[45] While upholding the law and dismissing the appeals,[46] the Court interpreted the law narrowly, thus minimizing its scope of application.[47]

---

38 Esther Rosalind Cohen, *Justice for Occupied Territory? The Israeli High Court of Justice Paradigm*, 24 COLUM. J. TRANSNAT'L L. 471, 471 (1986).

39 Incarceration of Unlawful Combatants Law, 5762-2002, SH No. 1834 p. 192, *reprinted in* 32 ISRAELI Y.B. ON HUM. RTS. 389 (Yoram Dinstein & Fania Domb eds., 2003).

40 *Id.* art. 2.

41 *Id.* art. 3(a).

42 *Id.* art. 5(a).

43 *Id.* art. 5(c).

44 *Id.* art. 5(e).

45 CrimA 6659/06 A v. State of Israel, 47 I.L.M. 768, para. 3 (2008) (Isr.).

46 *Id.* para. 53.

47 *Id.* para. 21.

4. THE JUDICIAL REVIEW PROCESS

4.1 The Reasoned and Renowned Judgments

Israeli and international scholars alike generally accept that the Israeli Supreme Court's judicial review of preventive detention cases is robust and effective.[48] The Israeli judicial review model is characterized as 'interventionist',[49] and the Israeli Supreme Court was commended for asserting judicial review over government actions that affect Palestinians, both within Israel and the West Bank and Gaza, even in the midst of the Palestinian uprising.[50] In spite of the common criticism that the use of secret evidence contradicts basic requirements of fairness and due process,[51] the Israeli Supreme Court has been praised for developing 'an activist approach in its review role of the non-disclosed evidence'.[52]

Indeed, some of the Court's landmark cases in this regard created meaningful legal constraints on the Executive. The extraordinary decision in the *Bargaining Chips* case,[53] for example, which prohibited detention

---

48 Barak, *supra* note 31, at 500–501; Barak-Erez & Waxman, *supra* note 13, at 20–21; Stephanie Cooper Blum, *Preventive Detention in the War on Terror: A Comparison of How the United States, Britain, and Israel Detain and Incapacitate Terrorist Suspects*, HOMELAND SECURITY AFF., Oct. 2008, at 8; Yigal Mersel, *Judicial Review of Counter-Terrorism Measures: The Israeli Model for the Role of the Judiciary During the Terror Era*, 38 N.Y.U. J. INT'L L. & POL. 67, 110–113 (2006); Zamir, *supra* note 9, at 391.

49 Stephen J. Schulhofer, *Checks and Balances in Wartime: American, British and Israeli Experiences*, 102 MICH. L. REV. 1906, 1918 (2004).

50 PHILIP B. HEYMANN, TERRORISM, FREEDOM, AND SECURITY: WINNING WITHOUT WAR 95–96 (2004).

51 Am.–Arab Anti-Discrimination Comm. v. Reno, 70 F.3d 1045, 1069 (9th Cir. 1995) (quoting Anti-Fascist Comm. v. McGrath, 341 U.S. 123, 170 (1951) (Frankfurter, J., concurring)); David Cole, *Judging the Next Emergency: Judicial Review and Individual Rights in Times of Crisis*, 101 MICH. L. REV. 2565, 2592–93 (2003); Tracy L. Conn, *The Use of Secret Evidence by Government Lawyers: Balancing Defendants' Rights with National Security Concerns*, 52 CLEV. ST. L. REV. 571, 571 (2004).

52 Barak-Erez & Waxman, *supra* note 13, at 23–4.

53 In this case, the petitioners were Lebanese citizens held by Israeli authorities as bargaining chips in an attempt to release an Israeli navigator from captivity. In its decision – reversing its previous judgment on the matter – the Supreme Court held that the desire to release Israelis from captivity does not justify preventive detention. The Court determined that administratively detaining the petitioners may only be justified by their individual dangerousness. CrimFH 7048/97 Anonymous v. Minister of Def. 54(1) PD 721, 743 [2000] (Isr.).

for the purpose of using detainees as bargaining chips to trade for release of Israeli captives, was undoubtedly a courageous decision that was not easily received by state authorities or the Israeli public. In other well-known cases, the Court stressed the significance of judges thoroughly examining the materials, ensuring that every piece of evidence connected to the matter at hand is submitted to them, and never allowing the high volume of cases to affect either the quality or the extent of the judicial examination.[54] In a more recent case, the Court dealt specifically with the problem of secret evidence, stating that the state's use of secret evidence imposes on the Court a special duty to take extra care in reviewing the confidential material and to act as the detainee's 'mouth'.[55] These and similar high profile decisions have been cited by legal scholars in Israel and in other countries as demonstrating a rigorous and activist judicial approach to preventive detention cases.[56] As appealing as this image may be, the legal scholarship thus far has been deficient in asking whether the practice matches the rhetoric. While the Court's review of the normative legal framework is indeed powerful, its ability to review concrete detention orders is much less meaningful. When the actual practices are examined, it becomes clear that the reasoning of these few cases offers a misleading description of the actual judicial review practice and its outcomes.

4.2 The Actual Practice of the Court – All of the Relevant Decisions

In the first decade of the twenty-first century, the Israeli Supreme Court performed judicial review of 322 preventive detention cases. Out of these, not even a single case resulted in a judicial decision to release the detainee,[57] and only 14 percent received an elaborated and reasoned judgment, while the rest received only a summary order of affirmance.

---

[54] HCJ 3239/02 Marab v. IDF Commander in the W. Bank 57(2) PD 349 [2002] (Isr.), at para. 33 (quoting *Sajadiya* 42(3) PD at 821).

[55] HCJ 11006/04 Khadri v. IDF Commander in Judea & Samaria para. 6 [2004] (unpublished decision) (Isr.).

[56] *See, e.g.*, Barak-Erez & Waxman, *supra* note 13; Blum, *supra* note 48; Mersel, *supra* note 48.

[57] With the exception of the Lebanese *Bargaining Chips* case, which originated in 1994 in an appeal that was denied. In 1997, the Court agreed to rehear the case, and in April 2000 accepted the petitioner's legal claim that the IDL does not authorize the state to detain non-dangerous aliens as 'bargaining chips' for purposes of future negotiations. *Anonymous*, *supra* note 53.

Ninety-five percent of the Court judgments were based on secret evidence that was presented by the state during ex parte hearings.[58] Below are some of the main findings.

4.2.1 The outcomes of the cases

One of the most interesting and surprising findings relates to the results of the cases; in particular, to the striking gap between the robust language of the published cases and the complete absence of actual intervention regarding individual detention orders. In the 282 MDO cases, the Court granted only two petitions (less than 1 percent); the first being the state's petition to reverse the Military Court of Appeals' decision to release a detainee.[59] The only successful petition submitted by a detainee against specific military detention orders is the *Marab* case, in which the Court invalidated military detention orders that authorized IDF officers in the West Bank to order the detention of a detainee for a period of twelve days (under one order) and eighteen days (under another order), without any judicial involvement.[60] However, this declaration of nullification was suspended for a six month period and the Court did not actually order the release of any of the detainees.[61]

Regarding the thirteen IDL appeals, four (31 percent) were partly successful: in two cases, the Supreme Court shortened the length of the detention orders;[62] in another two cases the Court reversed part of the district court's legal analysis, thus setting out a binding legal framework for the lower court in accordance with the detainees' legal arguments.[63]

---

[58] This detail relates to the 220 cases that were heard in Court (as will be explained hereinafter, 102 of the cases were withdrawn before the Court's hearing). In the remaining 5 percent the Court did not conduct ex parte proceedings since the case concerned only legal questions, was dismissed *in limine* or due to the objection of the detainee.

[59] HCJ 1389/07 Commander of IDF Forces in the Judea & Samaria Area v. Military Court of Appeals [2007] (Isr.).

[60] Military Commander in the W. Bank v. Military Court of Appeals [2007] (unpublished decision) (Isr.); HCJ 3239/02 Marab v. IDF Commander in the W. Bank 57(2) PD 349 [2002] (Isr.).

[61] *Id.* para. 36.

[62] ADA 10198/09 Anonymous v. State of Israel [2010] (unpublished decision) (Isr.); ADA 2627/09 Osama Rashek v. State of Israel [2009] (unpublished decision) (Isr.).

[63] ADA 4794/05 Ufan v. Minister of Def. para. 41 [2005] (unpublished decision) (Isr.); ADA 4414/02 Anonymous v. State of Israel 57(3) PD 673, 677 [2002] (Isr.).

Of the twenty-seven UCL appeals, only one was partly successful. In *A v. State of Israel*,[64] the Court accepted the detainee's argument that he did not fall under the UCL's definition of 'unlawful combatant'. But instead of ordering his immediate release, the Court suspended its judgment for twenty-one days to enable the state to consider other alternatives.[65] Additionally, in five of the cases, the Court shortened the time periods between judicial reviews.[66]

4.2.2 Rate of withdrawals

The research identified a significant rate of withdrawals: 36 percent of the MDO cases were withdrawn by the petitioners (the detainees) a short period of time before the court hearing. Moreover, in 19 percent of the MDO cases, the petitions were withdrawn after the Court had examined the secret evidence ex parte.[67] An explanation for this unique and surprising phenomenon will be offered hereinafter, in section 5.2.

4.2.3 The length of the decisions

Out of the remaining MDO cases (which were not withdrawn by the detainees), only 12 percent ended in detailed and reasoned judgments (of more than three pages), while 70 percent resulted in very short (one to six lines), summary decisions offering little or no analysis of the evidence or law. In contrast, IDL and UCL appeals never resulted in such short judgments; most resulted in a detailed, reasoned and fully-elaborated decision of more than three pages (85 percent in the UCL appeals and 69 percent in the IDL appeals), while the remaining cases resulted in short (one to three page) decisions.

---

[64] Ron Avital, Ido Rosenzweig & Yuval Shany, The Israeli Democracy Inst., *A.D.A. [Administrative Detention Appeal] 7750/08* Anon. v. State of Israel (Jan. 2009).

[65] *Id.*

[66] ADA 2595/09 Sofi v. State of Israel para. 27 [2009] (unpublished decision) (Isr.) (ordering to hold the next judicial review process within three months); ADA 6409/10 Al-Amudi v. State of Israel para. 5 [2010] (unpublished decision) (Isr.); ADA 6406/10 Sarski v. State of Israel para. 5 [2010] (unpublished decision) (Isr.); ADA 2156/10 Anonymous v. State of Israel para. 13 [2010] (unpublished decision) (Isr.); ADA 9257/09 Anonymous v. State of Israel para. 6 [2009] (unpublished decision) (Isr.). In the last four cases the Court did not intervene in the timing of the judicial review process per se, but ordered the state security authorities to review the necessity of the detention every month.

[67] The reasons for this finding will be discussed in section 6, *infra*.

4.2.4 The length of the detention

Although the length of a detention is one of the most crucial and relevant factors for judicial review, in 66 percent of its MDO decisions the Court never mentions it. In contrast, all decisions in UCL cases include the length of the detention, and only one IDL decision omitted this important detail. More importantly, in the decisions that did not review the detention's length, 32 of the cases involved preventative detentions longer than two years. All of these cases concerned non-Israeli detainees, either Palestinians or Lebanese citizens.

4.2.5 The nationality of the detainees

Ninety-five percent of the cases concerned Palestinian detainees from the West Bank and Gaza, with the remaining 5 percent divided almost equally between Israeli Palestinians, Israeli Jews, and Lebanese nationals.

4.2.6 The court's 'recommendations' to the parties

In 15 percent of the cases heard by the Court, the Court included in its decision specific instructions, recommendations or suggestions regarding the case. These included requests for the state to reconsider its position, recommendations not to prolong the detention in the future, or statements that new and updated materials would be required in order to issue future detention orders. Additionally, in 9 percent of the MDO cases the Court successfully mediated between the parties and memorialized their agreement or the state's concessions. A typical such agreement is that the state will not issue a new detention order at the end of the current detention order, as long as no new intelligence information will be gathered against the detainee during the current detention period. In other cases, although upholding the detention order, the Court's judgment included general future legal instructions on preventive detention, such as instructions to the state to interrogate detainees immediately after their arrest (invalidating the state's practice of holding Palestinians in preventive detention for long periods of time without conducting any interrogation).[68]

---

[68] *See, e.g.*, HCJ 1546/06 Gazawi v. Military Commander in the W. Bank para. 6(3) [2006] (unpublished decision) (Isr.); HCJ 6068/06 El-Afifi v. Military Commander in the W. Bank para. 6(5) [2006] (unpublished decision) (Isr.); HCJ 9015/06 Taweel v. Military Commander in the W. Bank para. 4(2) [2006] (unpublished decision) (Isr.).

5. 'BEHIND THE SCENES' OF THE JUDICIAL REVIEW PROCESS

The case law analysis revealed a surprising increase in the number of petitions and appeals to a court that has not released a detainee from preventive detention in the last ten years; as well as a high and unexplained rate of withdrawals. In order to suggest some possible explanations for these findings, the author conducted seventeen in-depth interviews with the various stakeholders that participate in the judicial review process, namely: Supreme Court Justices, state attorneys, defense lawyers, ISA representatives and Palestinian (former) detainees. Due to the sensitivity of the discussed issues and the limited amount of information contained in the relevant judgments, these interviews provide a rare opportunity to witness the actual dynamics of the judicial review process.

5.1 Secret Evidence, Ex Parte Proceedings, and the Judicial Management Model

The analysis of the Court's decisions revealed an almost absolute reliance on ex parte proceedings and on secret evidence during the preventive detention hearings. In the interviews, almost all of the former Supreme Court Justices expressed at least some level of discomfort with the use of secret evidence, as well as with the Court's ability to question the state's position. One of the Justices expressed a feeling of profound unease in handling such cases,[69] and explained that these hearings are extremely difficult due to their unique ex parte and preventive character.[70] Justice B added a similar description:

> You have a feeling of discomfort. I never enjoyed sitting in preventive detention cases. No one enjoys it. Judges don't like these cases, because we are trained to criminal proceedings, with witnesses, cross-examination … It is not pleasant. You want to run away from it as fast as you can, but you know that it is necessary for the sake of your people and country.[71]

More specifically, one justice noted the difficulty judges have differing with the ISA assessment of the secret evidence:

---

[69] Interview with Justice A, Supreme Court of Isr. (Dec. 20, 2010).
[70] *Id.*
[71] Interview with Justice B, Supreme Court of Isr. (Dec. 21, 2010).

> The judges cannot differ with the ISA story. How can I? I don't have the defense lawyer jumping to say 'it never happened,' 'this is not true.' My ethos, as a judge, is that I have two parties. Of course, I can think by myself, but I need tools, which are missing ... at most I have very limited tools.[72]

Defense lawyers considered the hearings wholly inadequate. Defense Lawyer C demonstrated the dynamics of such proceedings, stating that:

> The state attorneys should also come to the hearing nervous and tense – but they are always very relaxed. They know that no matter what they say or do, they will always win.[73]

All of the defense lawyers that participated in the research expressed frustration with the way that the reliance on secret evidence and ex parte proceedings undermined their ability to 'fight back' and to challenge the ISA narrative. 'I feel like a blind defense lawyer', and 'I represent my client with two hands tied behind my back' were common metaphors during the interviews.[74] The detainees themselves expressed similar views. 'The ISA determines everything',[75] Detainee B explained. Detainee A felt the same:

> I never knew what the case against me was, or what the evidence against me was. I had no information, and therefore had nothing to say in my defense.[76]

Even the state attorneys felt that the judicial review of preventive detentions is 'handicapped'[77] by the reliance on secret evidence presented during the ex parte hearing. 'In some cases even I felt that it was too easy',[78] said State Attorney A. Another state's attorney further clarified:

> With all the good will on the part of everybody, there is no way to conduct a fair ex parte hearing. The human nature and the dynamic of the process prevent fair hearing of the case.[79]

---

[72] Interview with Justice D, Supreme Court of Isr. (Dec. 22, 2010).
[73] Interview with Defense Lawyer C (Dec. 22, 2010).
[74] Interview with Defense Lawyer A (Dec. 19, 2010); Interview with Defense Lawyer B (Dec. 20, 2010).
[75] Interview with 'Mohamed', Admin. Detainee. (Jan. 12, 2011).
[76] Interview with 'Yusuf', Admin. Detainee (Jan. 12, 2011).
[77] Interview with State Att'y B (Dec. 23, 2010).
[78] Interview with State Att'y A (Dec. 21, 2010).
[79] Interview with State Att'y B, *supra* note 77.

As revealed by the interviews, the absence of the defense lawyer and the detainee from the hearing is problematic not only because it makes challenging the ISA evidence difficult, but also because the presence of an adversary is critical to the development of a unique courtroom dynamic. Both state attorneys and ISA representatives felt that the unique atmosphere and dynamics of the ex parte proceedings created a trust-based relationship between the Justices and themselves. As explained by State Attorney C:

> The ex parte proceedings create intimacy between the state representatives and the Justices.[80]

State Attorney A stated the interactions created a 'secret dialogue' between the state attorneys and the Court.[81] ISA Representative A added his impression that the closed-door hearings and the repeated interaction created a 'shared language' used by the ISA representatives, the state attorneys, and the Supreme Court Justices.[82]

Surprisingly, and in stark contrast to the scholarly view of these proceedings as rigorous and thorough, almost all of the interviewees – including the Justices themselves – agreed that the judicial management model suffers from inherent weaknesses that prevent, at least to some extent, meaningful and independent judicial assessment of the secret evidence. Interestingly, almost all of the Justices and state attorneys strongly supported the special advocate model and favored its implementation in the Israeli system. The interviews suggest, along with the finding that in ten years the Court has never rejected the use of secret evidence or released a detainee based on the insufficiency of the secret evidence, that the judicial management model may be less robust and effective than is currently believed.

5.2 Bargaining in the Shadow of the Court

Two of the most interesting and surprising findings previously discussed are the increasing number of petitions to the Court, despite the fact that the Court has not released an individual in the past ten years, and the high withdrawal rate of petitions. The interviews shed some light on these findings and suggest possible explanations that link these issues together.

---

[80] Interview with State Att'y C (Jan. 26, 2011).
[81] Interview with State Att'y A, *supra* note 78.
[82] Interview with ISA Legal Advisor A, Isr. Sec. Agency (Feb. 14, 2011).

Regarding the prehearing dynamics, many of the MDO petitions appeared to be submitted not to initiate a judicial review process, but rather to instigate some sort of negotiations with the state's representatives and prompt a settlement. Apparently, as is evident from the interviews with state attorneys and ISA members, the submission of a petition to the HCJ instigates an internal state process, in which the ISA reassesses the necessity of the detention.[83] If, at the end of this process, the ISA insists on the necessity of the detention, a specific state attorney is assigned to examine the strength of the case, and in some cases pressures the ISA to reach a settlement.[84] The relevant attorneys – both state attorneys and defense lawyers – described at length this process of 'bargaining in the shadow of the Court',[85] and explained the 'behind the scenes' impact of the Court on the state's position.[86] As was revealed by the interviews, this 'bargaining' process is pursued by detainees' lawyers not only to reach a beneficial settlement, but also to acquire some information regarding the strength and nature of the secret evidence.[87] The high withdrawal rate – 36 percent of the MDO cases – is therefore explained by either a settlement ending the detention (usually not immediately, but within a couple of months), or an 'understanding' on the detainee's part that the secret evidence is strong, and it is therefore useless, and maybe even harmful, to continue with the judicial review process and present the secret evidence to the Court.[88]

Without ignoring the advantages of this practice, mainly the state's internal inspection that sometimes leads to ending the detention, there are some inherent deficiencies. First, there is a meaningful imbalance between the state and the detainee. The detainee and his or her lawyer come to the negotiation table knowing nothing at all regarding the quality, reliability, and quantity of the state's information, and therefore may be pressured to agree to poor settlements. Second, the Court is not aware of the majority of these cases, does not scrutinize them, and

---

[83] Interview with ISA Legal Advisor A, Isr. Sec. Agency (Feb. 14, 2011); Interview with State Att'y A, *supra* note 78.

[84] Interview with State Att'y A, *supra* note 78.

[85] A phrase coined by Robert H. Mnookin & Lewis Kornhauser, *Bargaining in the Shadow of the Law: The Case of Divorce*, 88 YALE L.J. 950 (1979).

[86] Interview with Defense Lawyer A, *supra* note 74; Interview with Defense Lawyer B, *supra* note 74; Interview with Defense Lawyer C, *supra* note 73; Interview with State Att'y A, *supra* note 78; Interview with State Att'y B, *supra* note 77; Interview with State Att'y C, *supra* note 80.

[87] Interview with Defense Lawyer B, *supra* note 74.

[88] *Id.*

therefore cannot exercise its relative advantage in regulating the detention system. Moreover, it is precisely in these cases – in which the ISA prefers not to go to Court – that judicial review would be the most necessary and useful.

This bargaining dynamic is not restricted to the prehearing stage of the process. In many MDO cases the Court itself was involved in the bargaining process, suggesting to both the detainee and the state various alternatives to the continuation of the detention (including deportation).[89] In 13 percent of the MDO cases the Court stated specific recommendations for the state, including recommending that the state not issue a prolonged detention order or that a senior ISA officer be involved in such a decision. While the state does not automatically implement such recommendations, the Supreme Court's statements can potentially influence the military courts' judicial review. Accordingly, ISA Representative A emphasized the restraining effect of the Court, and the desire of the ISA to avoid 'bad decisions'.[90]

Many of the interviewees emphasized the effective shift of judicial review from the main stage, the courtroom, to the behind-the-scenes actions: internal state proceedings and negotiations with the defense lawyers, either before or after the court hearing. In this context, State Attorney B emphasized the shift of the review from the Court to the state authorities, and expressed discomfort with having to play this dual role:

> A part of the judicial review is transferred from the Court to the state attorneys, and since they represent the ISA – they are under conflict of interests.[91]

State Attorney C added his own impression, explaining that this duality does not produce a robust state scrutiny of the necessity of the detention:

> The state attorney's power should not be overstated or idealized. We represent the ISA even in borderline cases, especially when we are dealing with masses of cases, and the idea that we are conducting a meaningful review is not more than a myth.[92]

---

[89] *See, e.g.*, HCJ 8142/10 Ayad Dudin v. Military Commander in the W. Bank [2010] (unpublished decision) (Isr.); HCJ 9456/05 Tsubach v. Military Judge [2005] (unpublished decision) (Isr.).

[90] Interview with ISA Legal Advisor A, *supra* note 83.

[91] Interview with State Att'y B, *supra* note 77.

[92] Interview with State Att'y C, *supra* note 80.

ISA representatives affirmed this assertion, stating that the ISA conducts an independent assessment when a petition is submitted to the Supreme Court, and offers a settlement only if it coincides with its own agenda.[93]

In short, although the bargaining process may sometimes lead to releases of detainees, it is not necessarily desirable due to its several weaknesses, including: the inherent imbalance of the process; the blindness of the detainee regarding the secret evidence and its strength; and the finding that, indeed, in many of the cases, the settlement represents ISA interests alone.

5.3 'Law in the Books' vs. 'Law in Action'

The case law analysis revealed a significant gap between the rhetoric of a few renowned cases and actual practice; between legal reasoning and meaningful interpretation of, and sometimes even intervention in, the normative framework of the detention regimes and the overall acceptance of secret evidence and detention orders. Moreover, as the case law analysis revealed, most of the decisions concerning detention orders are short and laconic, ignoring most of the unique circumstances and specific details of the case. In the interviews, both defense lawyers and former detainees expressed their frustration with this practice, which ignores the individual characteristics of the detainees and tends to neglect crucial details, such as the detention's length. As one defense lawyer stated

> There is no human being in the case: not where he is from, not how old he is, not even how long his detention is; nothing.[94]

The state attorneys shared this feeling of discomfort and opined that the entire process of preventive detentions, from the detention order, to the appeal, to the military court, to the petition to the HCJ, is merely 'a copy–paste from the beginning to the end'.[95] This description was affirmed by ISA Representative A, who characterized the process as an 'assembly line', and expressed discomfort with the effects of this process on the ISA methods:

---

[93] Interview with ISA Legal Advisor A, *supra* note 83.
[94] Interview with Defense Lawyer A, *supra* note 74.
[95] Interview with State Att'y A, *supra* note 78.

> I am not a fan of preventive detentions not because it infringes the right to liberty, but rather because of its effect on the ISA work ... This is, of course, a very convenient tool, but when you use it too much it becomes dull.[96]

These assessments may shed light on why, in many of the cases, the detainees did not request to be present at their own hearings, and preferred to remain locked up in their prison cells rather than participate in the judicial review process.[97] Defense Lawyer B, who represented the detainee in one of the few cases that received a fully elaborated legal decision, did not feel any joy of success. On the contrary, she felt even more frustrated because she was unable to share this partial success with her client:

> My client was very much disappointed, since the decision wasn't at all about him.[98]

Moreover, the gap between the rhetoric of the few full opinions and the everyday practice in hundreds of summary, boilerplate decisions, casts a shadow over the reasoning and legal instructions articulated in some of the more detailed decisions:

> The more reasoned judicial decisions are no more than a bunch of clichés, since they are not implemented ... the Justices talk highly about being the 'detainee's mouth,' but they can't. How can they be his mouth, when they know nothing at all about his side of the story?[99]

The above analysis emphasizes the gap between the legal reasoning of the Court and its ability to implement its normative framework in concrete cases. While the Court's expertise in setting the relevant rules and limitations, and in striking the general balance between liberty and security is evident, the implementation of these rules as to specific cases is much more difficult.

---

[96] Interview with ISA Legal Advisor A, *supra* note 83.

[97] The database I created recorded fifty-nine such requests, all MDO cases, which are about 30 percent of the MDO cases that reached the stage of a courtroom hearing.

[98] Interview with Defense Lawyer B, *supra* note 74.

[99] *Id.*

6. CONCLUSION

The combination of security crisis, secret evidence and preventive detentions poses unique challenges to effective judicial review. In Israel, a quasi-inquisitorial judicial management model has emerged to confront these challenges and to provide strong guarantees against arbitrary and unjustified detentions. The Israeli model of judicial management, widely discussed as a model to be emulated, has been praised for achieving the desired balance between individual liberty and national security. It was commended for its robust scrutiny of secret evidence and for safeguarding individual liberty in times of national emergency.

Nonetheless, as this research reveals, the actual practice is much more complex and may lead us to be less optimistic. The Court systematically avoids issuing release orders and gives secret evidence only minimal scrutiny. As both the case law analysis and the interviews demonstrate, the Court refrains from openly questioning the ISA assessment of the secret evidence, and prefers to either focus on general legal arguments or to be satisfied with nonbinding 'recommendations'. At the same time, a 'bargaining in the shadow of the Court' phenomenon has emerged: negotiations occur between the defense lawyers, ISA representatives, and state attorneys, which lead to agreements between the state and the detainee and to the withdrawal of many of the petitions before they reach the courtroom hearing stage. While in some of these cases the agreements improve the detainee's situation and lead, eventually, to his or her release, it should be remembered that these mediation or negotiation efforts suffer from significant weaknesses – such as the inherent imbalance of the process and the blindness of the detainee regarding the secret evidence and its strength. As a result, some detainees are pressured to agree to 'bad settlements', weighted unfairly in the state's favor, which are not reviewed by the Court.

The findings summarized here should prompt doubt about the widely accepted scholarly view regarding the advantages of the judicial management model, which include revealing the 'actual truth' and regulating detention systems. First, the empirical analysis suggests that the Court's ability to regulate the detention system is much more meaningful as to the legal interpretation of the statutory regime, than as to the assessment of the secret evidence and the individual circumstances of the case. The findings demonstrate that, indeed, the Court's main impact in these cases is through crafting legal limitations by narrowly interpreting statutory language, and not by analyzing the credibility and strength of secret evidence. Moreover, as revealed by this research, most of the borderline cases are withdrawn before they reach a courtroom. The outcomes of these cases are the result of settlements between the detainee and the state, not meaningful judicial review. Therefore, the Court's regulatory capacity is limited because the cases that could have potentially instigated such a regulatory intervention are left undecided.

Second, regarding inquisitorial fact-finding, this research identified a 'bargaining phenomenon', where parties resolve individual detention cases through alternative dispute resolution mechanisms, such as mediation and negotiation. These mechanisms do not focus on rigorous fact-finding or verification of the justifications for detention, and, instead promote practical solutions in the immediate interest of the parties.

Finally, the research findings demonstrate the vulnerability of democracies, in times of national security crisis, to illiberal mechanisms, and the dear price they pay to uphold schemes of secrecy and confidentiality. Specifically, the research highlights the unique challenges posed by secret evidence to fair judicial proceedings. Unfortunately, detention proceedings become an 'assembly line' in which 'enemies', 'terrorists' or just 'others' are constantly losing their most basic and valued human right: their freedom.

10. Secrecy and control orders: the role and vulnerability of constitutional values in the United Kingdom and Australia

Andrew Lynch, Tamara Tulich and Rebecca Welsh

1. INTRODUCTION

This chapter compares the role that constitutional values according individuals the right to a fair process when the state seeks to restrict their liberty have played in the development of terrorism control order schemes in the United Kingdom (UK) and Australia. The respective schemes are similar and both illustrate constitutional values under considerable tension. However, there are salient differences in the ways those values have managed to provide some resistance to incursions on liberty. These different reactions stem from broader jurisdictional distinctions, including the manner in which those values are articulated in law, that affect the capacity of constitutional values to ameliorate, if not eliminate, measures that are hostile to them. The systemic features in question expose the vulnerability of constitutional values, normalizing government incursions into areas beyond national security.

The difference in the way that constitutional values have been used to limit state excess in the two jurisdictions is stark. In the UK, procedural rights are expressly protected by both the European Convention on Human Rights ('ECHR')[1] and the *Human Rights Act 1998* (UK) ('HRA'). Consequently, 'control orders' – which impose a range of diverse restrictions, including substantial periods of home detention, upon

[1] Convention for the Protection of Human Rights and Fundamental Freedoms, *opened for signature* 4 November 1950, E.T.S 5, 213 U.N.T.S. 221 (entered into force 3 September 1953) ('ECHR').

suspected terrorists, often on the basis of secret evidence not disclosed to the 'controlee' – have been subject to significant challenge in the UK's domestic court system and the European Court of Human Rights ('ECtHR'). Significantly bolstered by the decisions of the latter, UK courts have diminished the executive's ability to rely on secret evidence when issuing control orders by insisting on a minimum standard of disclosure to allow the controlee to meaningfully challenge the case against him or her. Articulation of the relevant values has also facilitated political review, notably by the UK Parliament's Joint Committee on Human Rights ('JCHR'), and provided a framework for debates about the continuation of the scheme.

By contrast, discourse around even the most basic concerns about control orders in Australia has been abstract, due in large part to the lack of any formal legal instrument for human rights protection at the national level.[2] Given that absence, the implied constitutional separation of judicial power has been increasingly appreciated by the courts as a significant source of rights protection,[3] though it only operates indirectly as such. Control orders in Australia have been challenged as infringing upon the independence of federal courts protected by Chapter III of the Commonwealth Constitution. Consequently, the challenge focused on the powers of federal courts to issue control orders and the historical authority to make similar preventive orders such as bail and 'binding over' orders. Crucially, the possible use of secret evidence in the application and issuing of a control order in Australia has received scant attention.

Controlees in the two countries may be denied full access to information used to support the order over them in different ways. The slow, but steady, development of procedural protections for controlees under human rights legislation in the UK stands in contrast to Australia, where controlees must rely on vague and comparatively fragile constitutional implications and common law principles. Both the rise in preventive models of justice and the associated reliance on intelligence as evidence colour our comparison of the two systems. The use of secret evidence in control order proceedings is an important and illuminating aspect of the preventive paradigm that challenges fundamental constitutional values – and how we think about the best means of protecting these.

---

[2] The Parliamentary Scrutiny (Human Rights) Act, 2011 (Austl.) is a recent development but depends on entirely political, rather than judicial, review of rights infringement.

[3] JAMES STELLIOS, THE FEDERAL JUDICATURE – CHAPTER III OF THE CONSTITUTION 98–102 (LexisNexis Butterworths, 2010).

2. SECRET EVIDENCE AND CONTROL ORDER PROCEEDINGS

Intelligence-led approaches to anti-terrorism law, whether manifested as preparatory criminal offences or civil preventive orders, creates a blurring of the traditional distinction between intelligence and evidence,[4] leading courts to rely increasingly on 'secret evidence'. Secret evidence is material introduced in judicial proceedings but not disclosed to an affected party or his or her legal representative. It may be heard in closed hearings from which the affected party and his or her representative are excluded (unless, in Australia, the latter enjoys a security clearance), or it may be in the form of documentary evidence that is not made available to them in whole or part. Secret evidence need not, in all instances, challenge constitutional values, including the independence of the judiciary. For example, applications for public interest immunity typically occur in open court, albeit the content of the information is not disclosed to the other party.[5] Significantly, while the court receives this secret evidence, a successful claim of public interest immunity results in that material being excluded from the body of evidence that may be adduced at trial and, therefore, cannot supply a ground for the judge's decision.[6]

Australian courts regularly receive material gathered primarily for intelligence purposes as evidence in criminal proceedings. This evidence is, however, subjected to the usual tests of the adversarial system. Still, non-disclosed evidence, in whole or in part, will generally be comprised of confidential intelligence. The most troubling characteristic of intelligence is not simply the manner in which it may have been gathered, nor even the need to keep it secret, but its strong focus on identifying future risks. It is this that challenges courts as they are called upon to engage with the preventive law model constructed around national security.

---

[4] Kent Roach, *The Eroding Distinction Between Intelligence and Evidence in Terrorism Investigations*, in COUNTER-TERRORISM AND BEYOND: THE CULTURE OF LAW AND JUSTICE AFTER 9/11 (Nicola McGarrity, Andrew Lynch and George Williams eds., Routledge, 2010).

[5] Langer and Roach acknowledge that in some cases 'these proceedings are even conducted at least in part on an ex parte basis without full participation from the accused for fear of revealing the secrets': Máximo Langer and Kent Roach, *Rights in connection with criminal process*, in, HANDBOOK ON CONSTITUTIONAL LAW 9 (Mark Tushnet et al eds., Routledge, 2012 (forthcoming)) available at: http://ssrn.com/abstract=1942423.

[6] Australian Law Reform Commission, *Keeping Secrets: The Protection of Classified and Security Sensitive Information*, Report No 98 10.8 (2004).

Although some have argued that better regulation of the use of intelligence generally is possible,[7] attention has largely focused on designing measures that aim to curb the unfairness of processes that rely on secret information. Examples include provision for redacted summaries of secret evidence, security-cleared counsel to represent the interests of the affected person at closed hearings relating to secret evidence, and disclosure only to counsel.[8] Measures of this sort have been applied under the control order regimes of the UK and Australia.

3. THE UNITED KINGDOM – EXECUTIVE ORDERS, SECRET EVIDENCE AND SPECIAL ADVOCATES

Terrorism control orders were introduced in the UK by the *Prevention of Terrorism Act 2005* (PTA), enacted in response to the decision of the House of Lords in *A v Secretary for the Home Department*. In that case, the Lords ruled that a statute authorizing indefinite detention, without charge or trial, of foreign nationals reasonably believed by the Home Secretary to be terrorists and a risk to national security was incompatible with the right to liberty and prohibition on discrimination under the ECHR.[9] The PTA authorized the imposition of control orders on British citizens and foreign nationals alike, for 'purposes connected with protecting members of the public from a risk of terrorism'.[10] Most commonly, control orders required their subjects to remain in their homes during specified hours of the day, denied them access to telephone and internet, and severely limited their permissible visitors and associations. After several years of highly controversial operation, the control order scheme was supplanted by a new system of Terrorism Prevention and Investigation Measures, referred to as 'TPIM notices'.[11] These are less intrusive of individual liberty but share sufficient procedural similarities with the earlier scheme, especially with respect to disclosure, that judicial decisions on the control order process enjoy a continued relevance in respect of TPIM notices. Obviously, UK control orders still provide a logical

[7] Clive Walker, *Intelligence and Anti-Terrorism Legislation in the United Kingdom*, 44 CRIME, LAW AND SOCIAL CHANGE 387, 409–10 (2005).

[8] See, John Ip, *The Rise and Spread of the Special Advocate*, P.L. 717, 717 (2008).

[9] A v. Secretary for the Home Department, [2005] 2 A.C. 68 (H.L.).

[10] Prevention of Terrorism Act, 2005, § 1 (UK) ('PTA').

[11] Terrorism Prevention and Investigation Measures Act, 2011 (UK) ('TPIM Act'),

comparison with the Australian control order regime, considered in the next section.

The PTA established two types of control orders: derogating and non-derogating. Of the former, which enabled the imposition of obligations inconsistent with the right to liberty under Article 5 of the ECHR,[12] none were ever issued. Non-derogating control orders could be made by the Home Secretary, with prior permission of the High Court, when he or she had 'reasonable grounds for suspecting the individual is or has been involved in terrorist related activity'.[13] The High Court also retained a supervisory role that involved the application of standard principles of judicial review. When the control order scheme was replaced by the new regime of TPIM notices, there were nine non-derogating control orders in place in the UK, all of which lapsed with the legislation.[14] As at 31 May 2012, nine British nationals were subject to TPIM notices, all of whom were subject to control orders when the TPIM Act commenced.[15]

The TPIM Act provides for the imposition of specified measures upon individuals where the Home Secretary 'reasonably believes that the individual is, or has been, involved in terrorism-related activity', some of which is 'new terrorism-related activity', and the Home Secretary reasonably considers the measures necessary to protect the public from a 'risk of terrorism'.[16] The measures available under a TPIM notice are generally less extreme than those previously available under the control order regime. For example, forced relocation is no longer permitted and the more flexible curfew condition has been replaced with an overnight residency measure.[17] The process for issuing a TPIM notice is similar to that which governed the making of non-derogating control orders: the notice is made by the Home Secretary with prior permission of the court in non-urgent cases and the court's role is limited to judicial review.

Control orders and now their successors, TPIM notices, are civil preventive orders[18] that impose restrictions, prohibitions and obligations upon individuals who have not necessarily been charged with any criminal offence for the conduct that gives rise to the order. Although the lower civil standard of proof applies to the facts upon which the

---

[12] PTA, § 4 .

[13] PTA, § 2(1)(a).

[14] 19 DEC. 2011, PARL. DEB., HC (2011) 143WS (UK) (Theresa May).

[15] 19 JUNE 2012, PARL. DEB., HC (2012) 57WS (UK) (Theresa May).

[16] TPIM Act, §§ 2–3.

[17] *Id.*, sch 1.

[18] Secretary of State for the Home Department v. MB and others, [2007] UKHL 46.

determination to make the order rests, criminal sanctions are imposed for a breach of its conditions. This hybrid nature led the House of Lords to conclude in the case of *Secretary of State for the Home Department v. MB* that even though the orders are civil, the seriousness of their potential consequences should increase the measure of procedural protection afforded to the controlee in order to comply with Article 6 of the ECHR's guarantee of a right to a fair trial.[19]

Precisely what that ruling in the *MB* case meant in practice took further litigation to illuminate. The particular procedural focus in *MB* and the subsequent cases was upon the use by the UK of special advocates to represent the controlee at closed hearings in which secret evidence is raised. As special advocates are also now a key feature of the TPIM scheme, these decisions remain influential. Special advocates are used in a range of settings with the aim of mitigating the unfairness to the person affected by non-disclosure of evidence against them. Their use first arose in the UK in the review of deportation orders made on the basis of national security.[20] Under TPIMs, as was the case under the control order regime, if the Home Secretary wishes to rely upon secret evidence in proceedings before the UK courts, a special advocate must be appointed to represent the interests of the TPIM subject in closed material hearings.[21] Special advocates serve both a 'disclosure' and 'representative' function.[22] In the former, they 'test to the full the cogency of the case put forward by the Home Secretary for non-disclosure of material'.[23] In the latter, special advocates represent the interests of affected persons in closed hearings. However, once closed material is disclosed to the special advocate he or she may not take instructions from or speak to the affected person.

The inability to consult with the affected party is the chief subject of complaints regarding the use of special advocates. In addition, special advocates object to the lack of access to independent experts or evidence,

---

19 *Id.* [44] (Lord Bingham), [72] (Baroness Hale), [84] (Lord Carswell), [92] (Lord Brown).

20 CONSTITUTIONAL AFFAIRS COMMITTEE, THE OPERATION OF THE SPECIAL IMMIGRATION APPEALS COMMISSION (SIAC) AND THE USE OF SPECIAL ADVOCATES, 2004–05, H.C. (UK).

21 Civil Procedure Rules, 1998, Pt 76 (UK), as made under the PTA sch 1, § 4.

22 Constitutional Affairs Committee, *supra* note 20, 23–4.

23 Constitutional Affairs Committee, *id.*, 23; Aileen Kavanagh, *Special Advocates, Control Orders and the Right to a Fair Trial*, 73(5) THE MODERN LAW REVIEW 836 (2010).

and the practical inability to call witnesses.[24] The JCHR has been a frequent critic of the scheme for these and other reasons.[25] As the reaction to the UK government's Security and Justice Green Paper of October 2011 ('Green Paper') has demonstrated, the use of special advocates remains deeply controversial within the legal profession.[26]

The use of secret evidence in control order proceedings was challenged as an infringement upon the right to a fair trial under Article 6 of the ECHR, as incorporated in domestic law by the HRA. Although in the *MB* case of 2007 the House of Lords determined that the provisions of the PTA could be read consistently with the Article 6 guarantee, differences in reasoning across the bench meant that lower courts were not given clear guidance as to what procedural protections were required as a result of that decision.[27] Subsequently, the Law Lords had the benefit of clear guidance from the ECtHR in *A v United Kingdom*, which ruled that those subject to restraints based on secret evidence must be given sufficient details about that information to allow them to meaningfully instruct their counsel and participate in their defence.[28] As the Court stated:

> While in certain circumstances it might be permissible for a court to sanction non-disclosure of relevant evidence to an individual on grounds of national security, it could never be permissible for a court assessing the lawfulness of detention to rely on such material where it bore decisively on the case the detained person had to meet and where it had not been disclosed, even in gist or summary form, sufficiently to enable the individual to know the case against him and to respond.[29]

---

[24] Kavanagh, *id*, 838; Al Rawi and others (Respondents) v. The Security Service and others (Appellants), [2011] UKSC 34, [37].

[25] Joint Committee on Human Rights Ninth Report of Session 2009-10, *Counter-Terrorism Policy and Human Rights* (Sixteenth Report): Annual Renewal of Control Orders Legislation 2010, H.C. 395 (London: TSO), 18–25.

[26] Angus McCullough QC et al, Justice and Security Green Paper Response to Consultation From Special Advocates (16 December 2011) http://adam1cor.files.wordpress.com/2012/01/js-green-paper-sas-response-16-12-11-copy.pdf at 29 January 2012.

[27] [2007] UKHL 46. See the majority opinions of [44] (Lord Bingham), [72] (Baroness Hale), [84] (Lord Carswell), [92] (Lord Brown). See, also, Adam Tomkins, *National Security and the Role of the Court: a Changed Landscape?*, L.Q.R. 543, 550 [2010]; and, Helen Fenwick and Gavin Phillipson, *Covert Derogations and Judicial Deference: Redefining Liberty and Due Process Rights in Counter-Terrorism Law and Beyond*, 56(4) McG. L.J. 863 (2011), 899–900.

[28] A v. United Kingdom (European Court of Human Rights, Grand Chamber, Application No 3455/05, 19 February 2009).

[29] *Id.* [195].

The ECtHR further ruled that special advocates 'could not perform this function [of providing a fair hearing to the detainee] in any useful way unless the detainee was provided with sufficient information about the allegations against him to enable him to give effective instructions to the special advocate'.[30] As a result, the use of special advocates would not achieve procedural fairness where the 'open material consisted purely of general assertions and … [the] decision to uphold … and maintain the detention was based solely or to a decisive degree on closed material'.[31]

In *Secretary of State for the Home Department v AF (No. 3)* handed down shortly afterwards, the House of Lords followed this lead and held that for control order proceedings to be fair 'the judge must insist in every case that the controlled person is given sufficient information to enable his special advocate effectively to challenge the case that is brought against him'.[32] This decision entitled controlees to know at least the 'gist' of the case against them. Rather than deliver on this requirement, the government's response to the *AF (No. 3)* decision included the adoption of defensive strategies to avoid disclosure of sensitive information, while continuing use of the existing control order scheme.[33] Even so, the excesses of the scheme were significantly tempered by the decision. Fenwick and Phillipson suggest that while traces of the UK's long tradition of extreme judicial deference to the executive on national security matters has been discernible in the control order litigation, 'overall the courts have displayed a relative boldness that contrasts strongly with the approach taken in much earlier decisions'.[34] Although they note that the change in approach has occurred 'with considerable assistance' from the ECtHR, this does not detract from the fact that although the values in play were originally articulated in European Community law, they are firmly part of the UK's contemporary constitutional settlement, as evidenced by their application in the *AF (No. 3)* decision.[35]

30 *Id.* [220].
31 *Id.*
32 Secretary of State for the Home Department v. AF (No. 3), [2009] UKHL 28, [85] (Lord Hoffmann).
33 Kavanagh, *supra* note 23, 852–3.
34 Fenwick and Phillipson, *supra* note 27, 916.
35 Fenwick and Phillipson, *id.*

The use of secret evidence in judicial proceedings generally has attracted attention in the government's 2011 Green Paper.[36] Controversially, its central suggestion was to extend use of closed material procedures ('CMPs') to make them 'available wherever necessary in civil proceedings'.[37] The Green Paper also invited comment and consideration on the option of providing legislative clarification of the minimum disclosure requirement (or 'gisting') set out in *AF (No. 3)* and the contexts in which the decision does not apply.[38] In a joint response, the special advocates voiced opposition to the 'unsound premise' on which the Green Paper proposals rest, namely, that CMPs are fair and effective as currently used and are 'capable of delivering procedural fairness'.[39] The special advocates also caution against employing the terminology of 'gisting' as shorthand for the minimum disclosure requirement articulated in *AF (No. 3),* as that 'may go well beyond' what the term 'gisting' involves.[40] Following the Green Paper, the *Justice and Security Bill* was introduced into the House of Lords on 28 May 2012.[41] The Bill provides for CMPs in civil proceedings where disclosure of information would damage national security.[42] Despite the government's attempt to institute a comprehensive solution to the tension between secrecy and fairness through its Green Paper and subsequent Bill, currently before the UK Parliament, this debate clearly still has a long way to go.

4. THE AUSTRALIAN SCHEME – JUDICIAL ORDERS, SECRET EVIDENCE AND THE NSIA

Following the London bombings of 7 July 2005, the Commonwealth of Australia legislated for a national control order regime to deal with suspected terrorists.[43] Although the Australian control order provisions were modelled on the UK scheme, little regard was paid to the legal,

---

36 19 OCT. 2011, PARL. DEB., H.C. (2011) 899 (UK) (Kenneth Clarke).

37 Ministry of Justice, *Justice and Security Green Paper*, 2011, Cm. 8194 (London: TSO), 22.

38 *Id.*, 27–8.

39 McCullough et al, *supra* note 26, 2 [2], 7 [17].

40 McCullough et al, *id.*, 17 [35].

41 Justice and Security Bill, 2012–13, H.L. Bill [27] (Eng.).

42 *Id.* § 6.

43 This was amongst a suit of anti-terror measures that amended the Criminal Code Act 1995 (Austl.) ('Criminal Code') by the Anti-Terrorism Act (No. 2) 2005 (Austl.).

security and cultural context in which control orders arose in the UK.[44] In particular, the creation of control orders in a constitutional setting that lacks an express articulation of human rights values has resulted in a rather different reaction to the use of secret material in issuing those orders.

Superficially, Australia's control orders bear strong similarities to the original scheme in the UK, especially insofar as the list of possible restrictions on the liberty of the controlee is concerned. Both countries allow control orders to require that the controlee must remain at specified premises between specified times each day or on specified days, providing for de facto 'detention'. Only two Australian control orders have been issued and the terms of those orders include relatively modest restrictions, especially when compared to those of the UK.[45] Just as in the UK's regime, a person who contravenes any of the terms of a control order commits an offence punishable by up to five years' jail.

The Australian control order regime provides the Australian Federal Police ('AFP') with a three-tiered process to obtain a control order: first, the AFP receives consent from the Attorney-General; then an ex parte application for an interim control order from an issuing court is submitted; and finally proceedings to confirm the control order at which the controlee is able to appear. At each stage, information may be withheld 'if disclosure of that information is likely to prejudice national security (within the meaning of the *National Security Information (Criminal and Civil Proceedings) Act 2004*)'.[46] The *National Security Information (Criminal and Civil Proceedings) Act* ('NSIA') defines 'likely to prejudice national security' as 'a real, and not merely a remote, possibility that the disclosure will prejudice national security'. In turn, 'national security' is defined as including 'Australia's defence, security, international relations or law enforcement interests'.[47]

Interim control orders are issued ex parte and without notice to the affected person. They may be issued when a court is satisfied, on the balance of probabilities, that the order would 'substantially assist in preventing a terrorist act' or 'that the person has provided training to,

[44] Andrew Lynch, *Control Orders in Australia: A Further Case Study in the Migration of British Counter-Terrorism Law*, 8 OXFORD U. COMMW. L.J. 159 (2008).

[45] Jabbour v. Thomas, [2006] FMCA 1286; Jabbour v. Hicks, [2007] FMCA 2139; Jabbour v. Hicks, [2008] FMCA 178.

[46] Criminal Code, s 104.2(3A).

[47] National Security Information (Criminal and Civil Proceedings) Act, 2004 (Austl.) §§ 8, 17 ('NSIA').

or received training from, a listed terrorist organisation', and that each of the terms of the control order is 'reasonably necessary, and reasonably appropriate and adapted, for the purpose of protecting the public from a terrorist act'.[48] These terms are broader than those in the UK, as Australian law authorizes control orders without any showing that the controlee had any personal involvement in terrorism or terrorism-related activity.[49] Additionally, although any interim order that is made by an issuing court must include, among other things, a summary of the grounds on which the order was made,[50] any information likely to prejudice national security is not required to be included in the summary.[51]

If the AFP seeks confirmation of the interim order, it must serve the controlee, in person, with copies of the documents contained in the initial request and 'any other details required to enable the person to understand and respond to the substance of the facts, matters and circumstances which will form the basis of the confirmation of the order'.[52] Again, material likely to prejudice national security within the meaning of the NSIA need not be provided.

The NSIA is clearly of crucial importance to the Australian control order scheme, but the full extent of its impact upon *all* federal criminal and civil proceedings must be appreciated. As detailed below, the direct operation of the NSIA in any proceeding, including those relating to the making of a control order, has the benefit of exposing claims that information is likely to prejudice national security to the prospect of adversarial challenge. But additionally, its incorporation by reference in the tests applied in respect of control order proceedings enables the standards of the NSIA to be used by the executive to determine that information should be withheld from the controlee and his or her legal representative. Those decisions, in distinction to the direct operation of the NSIA's provisions upon judicial proceedings, may be made without affording the affected individual any review of that non-disclosure.

Even through its direct application, the protections afforded by the NSIA show a low regard for the important constitutional value of fair process. The Act allows the Commonwealth Attorney-General to issue a

---

48 Criminal Code, § 104.4(1)(c)–(d).

49 Thomas v. Mowbray, (2007) 233 CLR 307, 352 (Gummow and Crennan JJ). See Denise Meyerson, *Using Judges to Manage Risk: The Case of Thomas v Mowbray*, 36 F. L. Rev. 209, 223 (2008).

50 Criminal Code, § 104.5(1)(h).

51 *Id.*§ 104.5(2A).

52 *Id.*§ 104.12A(2).

certificate opposing the release of information in a court proceeding that he or she believes will be detrimental to national security. This certificate may be challenged by the affected individual's legal representative, provided he or she has security clearance, at a closed hearing. Given the absence of a formal legal instrument for the protection of rights in Australia, it is only at this hearing that the value of procedural fairness, that enjoys a clear constitutional status in many other jurisdictions, finally enters the picture as a possible counter-weight to the executive's preference for secrecy. But while the law requires a balancing of interests, it ultimately subjugates the individual's right to a fair and open judicial hearing to the interest of national security. Assuming control order proceedings are purely civil, in closed hearings under the NSIA the court will be called upon to determine disclosure based on:[53]

- whether, having regard to the Attorney-General's certificate, there would be a risk of prejudice to national security if the information were disclosed or the witness called;
- whether such an order would have a substantial adverse effect on the substantive hearing; and,
- any other relevant matter.

The criminal jurisdiction equivalent of this provision, § 31(8), places in the balance the risks of prejudice to national security on one hand and 'a substantial adverse effect on the defendant's right to receive a fair hearing, including in particular on the conduct of his or her defence' on the other. Crucially, the Act provides that, in both civil and criminal matters, the court 'must give the greatest weight' to national security considerations in making its decision.[54]

In *R v Lodhi,* a criminal defendant facing terrorist charges challenged this prioritizing of state interests over the right of the individual to a fair process. Justice Whealy dismissed the claim, stating 'that the legislation does no more than to give the Court guidance as to the comparative weight it is to give one factor when considering it alongside a number of others ... the discretion remains intact'.[55] On appeal, the higher Court confirmed that this 'tilted' balancing exercise did not amount to 'legislative usurpation of judicial process', nor did it 'impinge upon the integrity of the process by which the judgment is formed. It may affect the

---

53 NSIA, § 38L(7).

54 NSIA, § 38L(8).

55 *R v Lodhi* [2006] NSWSC 571, [108] (N.S.W).

outcome of the process, but not in such a way as to affect its integrity.'[56] The Court applied a high threshold to determine whether judicial integrity has been 'usurped' or unduly compromised, in keeping with the general approach of Australian courts to the principle of judicial integrity under Chapter III of the Constitution.[57]

Quite apart from its direct operation upon control order proceedings, the real significance of the NSIA is its indirect and pre-emptive effect on the information that is provided to the controlee at the key stages in making an order, as outlined earlier. The control order scheme adopts NSIA standards to empower authorities to regulate, in the first instance, the material they provide to a controlee. As a result, challenging the resultant exclusions would be much more difficult than through the review that normally occurs in the special hearing process after the Attorney-General has issued a certificate in accordance with the provisions of the NSIA. This is because the extent to which reliance on non-disclosed material occurs in the making of the order may be highly opaque. In this regard, it is notable that § 104.13(2)(b) permits a controlee's lawyer only a copy of the order itself and expressly denies any entitlement to other related materials. While the NSIA may be brought to bear in the adversarial process for confirming an interim order, this will not necessarily expose to challenge the earlier reliance on secret evidence by the AFP and the court that issued the interim control order.

This fact was observed by several members of the High Court in the 2007 case of *Thomas v Mowbray*. A control order had been issued over Jack Thomas soon after his successful appeal against his conviction for terrorism offences.[58] He launched a challenge to the scheme, arguing that the making of a control order was not an incidence of judicial power and therefore the legislation vesting federal courts with that capacity was unconstitutional. Although that argument was rejected 5:2, the judgments in the case nevertheless underscored the relative weakness, at least formally, of open justice as a constitutional value in the Australian system. Justice Kirby in dissent regarded the potential for secrecy throughout the process as an affront to the constitutional separation of

---

[56] *Lodhi v R* [2007] NSWCCA 360, [36], [72]–[73] (Spigelman CJ).

[57] See, for example, *Grollo v Palmer* (1995) 184 CLR 348, *Fardon v Attorney-General* (Qld) (2004) 223 CLR 575 and *Thomas v Mowbray* (2007) 233 CLR 307.

[58] *Jabbour v Thomas* [2006] FMCA 1286; for background and discussion, see, Andrew Lynch, *Thomas v Mowbray: Australia's 'War on Terror' Reaches the High Court*, 32 MELB. UNIV. L. REV. 1182 (2008).

judicial power by the orders.[59] The other members of the Court refused to discuss how the secrecy aspects of Division 104 would affect the validity of the power to issue interim control orders. In large part this was because they confined their decision to the interim orders without delving deeply into the restrictions on information as they extended through to the confirmation process. To the extent confirmation was addressed, the Court emphasized its positive, adversarial elements.[60] However, the Chief Justice acknowledged that 'particular issues as to procedural fairness ... could arise where, for example, particular information is not made available to the subject of a control order or his or her lawyers', but insisted deficits in procedural fairness did not go to constitutional validity of the scheme, but was to be 'decided in the light of the facts and circumstances of individual cases'.[61]

The majority joint judgment hinted at a different approach when it stated that 'there may remain a question whether in the terms used in the *Security Information Act* [the NSIA] the Parliament has sought to over-reach the bounds of the understanding of "national security"'.[62] However, the case itself presented facts that did not give rise to that question because the interim control order issued had not yet been confirmed. Therefore there was 'no challenge in this proceeding to the validity of the provisions of the Code which pick up the definitions in the *Security Information Act*'.[63] Justices Gummow and Crennan appeared to suggest that the potential extent of non-disclosure countenanced by the control order regime might have some deeper bearing on whether the control order legislation conferred upon federal courts a power that was either simply non-judicial, or one that was required to be exercised in a manner inconsistent with the essential character of a court or inconsistent with the nature of judicial power. Under Australia's strict separation of judicial power at the national level either outcome would result in constitutional invalidity. But this was a question for another day.

Following *Thomas v Mowbray*, a number of Australian States and Territories created new control order schemes, extending the reach of the preventive paradigm into the traditional ambit of the criminal law to deal

---

59 *Thomas v Mowbray* (2007) 233 CLR 307, [364] and [369] (Kirby J).
60 *Id.* [30].
61 *Id.* [31].
62 *Id.* [124].
63 *Id.* [125].

with serious organized crime and gangs.[64] In these jurisdictions, the tension between reliance upon criminal intelligence and fair trial principles has been resolved in favor of secrecy under the sole proviso that the courts retain the ability to independently assess the restricted classification of the evidence presented.[65] Two constitutional challenges to the control order schemes of the Australian States focused squarely on the executive's attempts to limit key aspects of the court's functions, demonstrating an ongoing tension between constitutional values and the control order regime. While both challenges succeeded, neither required the Court to revisit the high threshold of 'usurpation' reflected in *R v Lodhi* above.[66] Instead these cases suggest that maintaining the residual discretions of the court with respect to evidence, despite significant legislative curtailment or manipulation of the court's processes or the judge's decisional role, is generally sufficient to maintain an Act's constitutional validity.

5. CONCLUSION: TERROR CONTROL ORDERS AND CONSTITUTIONAL VALUES

This chapter has examined the means adopted in the UK and Australia to enable courts to use secret evidence in connection with the review and issuance of terrorism control orders. In the UK, the engagement of government-appointed special advocates has been pivotal to the use of

---

[64] See, e.g., Serious and Organised Crime (Control) Act 2008 (S. Austl.); Crimes (Criminal Organisations Control) Act 2009 (N.S.W.); Criminal Organisation Act 2009 (Queensl.); Serious Crime Control Act 2009 (N. Terr.).

[65] *Gypsy Jokers Motorcycle Club Inc v Commissioner of Police* (2008) 234 CLR 532, 560 (Gummow, Hayne, Heydon and Kiefel JJ); *K-Generation Pty Limited v Liquor Licensing Court* (2009) 237 CLR 501, 542–3 (Gummow, Hayne, Heydon, Crennan and Kiefel JJ), affirmed in the State control order cases: *South Australia v Totani* (2010) 242 CLR 1, [283] (Heydon J); *Wainohu v New South Wales* (2011) 243 CLR 181, [92] (Gummow, Hayne, Crennan and Bell JJ).

[66] In *South Australia v Totani* invalidity was limited to the provision rendering the issuing of a control order by the Supreme Court mandatory upon the Court finding an individual was a 'member' of an organization deemed to be a 'declared organisation' by the Attorney-General; in *Wainohu v New South Wales* invalidity rested on the removal of the obligation to give reasons for a judge's decision (exercised in a personal capacity but with the appearance of court proceedings) to 'declare' an organization, prior to the Supreme Court control order proceedings.

'closed material'. In Australia the NSIA has facilitated the use of summarized or redacted evidence through the issuing of a certificate by the Attorney-General and also, through its incorporation by reference in the control order provisions, the determination of the AFP or issuing court that full disclosure would be likely to prejudice national security within the meaning of the NSIA.

It is important to recognize that in the UK the starting assumption is that evidence will remain secret in the executive process for issuing TPIM notices, or non-derogating control orders under the prior regime, in contrast to the court-based Australian system which is necessarily predicated on a higher level of disclosure being made to the controlee, at least at the adversarial confirmation hearing. Australia's Chief Justice Gleeson consciously reflected on this dichotomy when upholding the validity of the federal courts' power to issue control orders, saying that 'the exercise of powers, independently, impartially and judicially, especially when such powers affect the liberty of the individual, would ordinarily be regarded as a good thing' in contrast to the same powers being 'exercised within the province of the executive branch of government'.[67] In this respect, the two schemes may, by adopting distinct processes and placing the primary responsibility for making an order with different arms of government, be viewed as not readily comparable – even on the sole criterion of disclosure and secrecy.

It is, however, certainly possible to look at the ways in which the constitutional values of a fair and open judicial process have operated in respect of the two schemes. Although, as the Green Paper states, 'protections to ensure procedural fairness and fair trials in the justice system have evolved gradually over the centuries',[68] the UK has benefitted in recent times from the articulation of constitutional values in the ECHR and the HRA, informed by a deeper body of transnational jurisprudence. This has enabled legal challenges through domestic and supranational courts, bringing about changes to the conditions imposed by the control orders to bring the scheme in line with human rights standards. The values that have driven litigation in the UK find no constitutional expression in Australia, where they instead exist merely as an incident of a broad constitutional implication that judicial power is to be strictly separate from that wielded by the other arms of government. Perhaps as a result, constitutional values have played a deeply underwhelming, almost marginal, role.

---

67 *Thomas v Mowbray*, [17].

68 Ministry of Justice, *supra* note 37, 5.

Indeed the inherent vulnerability of those values in Australia was made perfectly clear by the courts' acceptance of legislative directions that they should give less weight to the fairness of the process afforded a defendant or controlee in terrorism proceedings than to the government's own view of whether disclosure should be allowed. This is quite distinct from how the UK courts have approached similar issues. The extent of the UK courts' capacity to give effect to the constitutional values of open justice was starkly demonstrated in a different context where, unlike control orders and TPIM notices, an individual's liberty was not at stake. In 2010, the UK Court of Appeal ordered the publication of redacted paragraphs of shared intelligence sought by Binyan Mohammed in pursuit of his claim for compensation for his detention in Guantanamo Bay.[69] Had this same issue arisen under Australian law, the provisions of the NSIA would have compelled the courts to accord the government's stance a greater weight over whether release of the information would have a 'substantial adverse effect' upon the applicant's case. The need to maintain faith with important allies with whom intelligence is shared may have proved an insurmountable consideration in Australia while it did not do so in the UK decision.

Even so, it may be that the Australian process, in practice, offers better actual protections to an individual, but this is clearly not due to the existence of constitutional values in a readily helpful form. This statement is not to suggest support for the argument that the UK's HRA has played a negligible role in protecting liberties in the wake of September 11.[70] On the contrary, we accept the view that the HRA has made a substantial difference, even if the change has not been as rapid or extensive as some might have hoped.[71] Our point is simply that the constitutionalization of values in the UK gave them significance in the development of control orders and their replacement, TPIMs. Those same values have not possessed similar significance in Australia, where they exist foremost as part of the fabric of the common law and have been subject to regulation by statute.

---

69 Mohamed, R (on the application of) v. Secretary of State for Foreign & Commonwealth Affairs, [2010] EWCA Civ. 65 (10 February 2010), [46].

70 Keith Ewing and Joo-Cheong Tham, *The Continuing Futility of the Human Rights Act*, P.L. 668 [2008].

71 See, in particular: DAVID BONNER, EXECUTIVE MEASURES, TERRORISM AND NATIONAL SECURITY: HAVE THE RULES OF THE GAME CHANGED? 276 (Ashgate, 2008); Tomkins, *supra* note 27; Fenwick and Phillipson, *supra* note 27.

The way in which those values are represented in the constitutional framework of a polity is clearly significant for human rights protection. This chapter's focus on the similar control order regimes of the UK and Australia serves to illustrate more systemic issues in each jurisdiction's response to heightened national security objectives after September 11. The clear articulation of values as rights in the UK has provided a basis for the debate and review of control orders in both Parliament and by the courts, though this has been a complex process and one in which ultimately the role played by the ECtHR was significant. The depth of the changes wrought by the UK's enactment of the *Human Rights Act* is further demonstrated by the demise of control orders in that jurisdiction both through the process surrounding the introduction of TPIMs and in critique around the role of Special Advocates and CMPs in public and political responses to the recent Green Paper. In Australia, by contrast, the limited tools available in the protection of human rights values against legislative interference has stunted debate around the impact of control orders on fair process, and facilitated their legitimization and normalization throughout the federation.

Certainly neither jurisdiction has achieved an uncontroversial balance between fair process and national security concerns. Despite the close relationship between the UK and Australia and the transplantation of the control order device from one to the other, each jurisdiction's attempt to achieve this balance has played out very differently. While both approaches show constitutional values under pressure, it is difficult, and has not been our purpose, to conclude that one model of controlling terrorism suspects has manifest advantages over the other. Instead, this chapter has painted a picture of different methods of managing secret evidence in the use of an essentially similar preventative legal tool against terrorism. In the UK, the balance between security and justice has been the subject of recalibration due to ongoing judicial attention, and now has entered a different phase in which the political arms of government have not only done away with control orders but are attempting to put the use of secret evidence in courts more generally on a clearer footing. That has inevitably excited some serious controversy but is a conversation that has been long overdue. In Australia, in distinction from the UK experience, the very modest use made of control orders by the authorities has managed to avoid precipitating the collapse of that scheme. Control orders have been very marginal to the Australian legal system's role in national security over the last decade – with the result that the potential significance of non-disclosed material to sustain them has been hardly questioned.

While there is little sign that Australian control orders will be resorted to in future, that of course remains a possibility so long as the scheme remains on the statute books. Should the trend to prosecute individuals with terrorism offences subside and the ready availability of control orders be exploited, it may be that greater usage of the latter would drive the debate towards what has been happening in the UK in recent years – the emergence of an irreducible level of information that an individual must be provided with in order to assert their rights against the state. But it is positive that such a development in the policing of terrorists seems unlikely, especially since Australia's more ambiguous protection of the values in question offers no firm guarantee that the same result might follow for the protection of the individuals in question.

11. Comparative advantages: secret evidence and 'cleared counsel' in the United States, the United Kingdom and Canada

David Cole and Stephen I. Vladeck

Sometimes comparative constitutional law is not merely academic. In *Charkaoui v. Canada* ('*Charkaoui I*'),[1] the Canadian Supreme Court engaged in a kind of comparative constitutional analysis in assessing whether Canada's procedure for deporting foreign nationals on the basis of secret evidence was consistent with the guarantee of a fair hearing enshrined in the Canadian Charter of Rights and Freedoms.[2] Noting that the United Kingdom (UK) employed 'cleared counsel' to mitigate the unfairness of the process in similar circumstances, the Canadian Supreme Court held that Canada could, and therefore as a constitutional matter *must*, do more to ensure fairness. The Canadian Parliament then adopted a process, much like the UK's, that authorized lawyers with security clearances to see the otherwise secret evidence and to challenge it on behalf of the affected party in closed proceedings.[3]

In this instance, the Canadian Supreme Court looked to the practice of another nation to inform its judgment about whether Canada had done all it could to minimize its compromise of fair trial principles in the name of protecting national security. In this chapter, we propose to engage in

[1] 2007 SCC 9 [2007] 1 S.C.R. 350 (Can.). We refer to this decision as '*Charkaoui I*' to distinguish it from the Canadian Supreme Court's subsequent decision in the same case, *see* Charkaoui v. Canada, 2008 SCC 38 [2008] 2 S.C.R. 326 (Can.).

[2] Part I of the Constitution Act, 1982, being Schedule B to the Canada Act 1982, ch. 11, § 7 (UK).

[3] An Act to amend the Immigration and Refugee Protection Act (certificate and special advocate) and to make a consequential amendment to another Act, 2008, c. 3 (Can.).

comparative borrowing for a similar purpose by examining the use of 'cleared counsel' in the UK, Canada, and the United States (US). An analysis of the ways in which these three countries are using secret evidence and cleared counsel in roughly similar contexts sheds critical light on the practices of each. In the end, our analysis maintains that *none* of the three democracies is doing all that it can to mitigate the costs to a fair hearing of relying on secret evidence. Each country has chosen to employ 'cleared counsel'. But each nation has adopted distinct practices with respect to the limits on and powers of these cleared counsel. No one approach is necessarily the best. But the record suggests, at a minimum, that each of the three countries could do more – and therefore as a constitutional matter *must* do more – to improve fairness without undermining legitimate secrecy concerns.

All three countries have long recognized that the right to confront the evidence used to deprive one of his liberty is essential to fundamental (and indeed, constitutional) notions of fairness. In all three countries, however, the legislature and/or the courts have recently concluded that in limited situations involving national security, individuals may be deprived of their liberty on the basis of secret evidence that is not disclosed *to* the affected individual. All three systems have sought to address the tension between fundamental fairness and secrecy by letting *lawyers* see the secret evidence, but not the affected parties themselves. The lawyers must be approved by the government for security clearances, and are obligated not to reveal the secret evidence to anyone else, including the affected party. All three systems have concluded that this 'cleared counsel' compromise can be effectuated without violating fundamental fairness guarantees.

Despite these structural similarities, however, there are many salient differences in the ways each legal system has chosen to address the issue. A comparative analysis helps to illustrate the range of measures available to mitigate the grave fairness concerns raised by reliance on secret evidence. If, as *Charkaoui I* and comparable principles in American constitutional law and in the European Convention on Human Rights (ECHR) suggest, the state is obligated to adopt means that are minimally intrusive on the right to a fair hearing, each state should be required to introduce into its own system aspects that improve the fairness of the process without jeopardizing security and could use comparative constitutional law to learn from the experience of other systems. At the same time, considering all three models together illustrates some core common problems that may well be irreducible once a legal system abandons the fundamental principle that all evidence used to justify the deprivation of a person's liberty must be disclosed to him.

Thus, comparative borrowing in this context is not just a descriptive undertaking, but a normative project. It seizes upon the fact that each of these countries recognizes, as a constitutional principle, the idea that measures that increase procedural fairness without measurable cost to the government should generally be pursued where substantial liberty or property interests are at stake. Put another way, our thesis is not merely that each of these three countries *could* learn from each other when it comes to striking the right balance between secrecy and fairness in national security litigation, but that, because of their constitutional traditions, they *must* incorporate these lessons – as the Canadian Supreme Court concluded in *Charkaoui I*. To that end, Section 1 provides a brief overview of the different contexts in which each of these three legal systems considers secret evidence. Section 2 recounts the legal principles governing the admissibility of – and access to – such evidence in each system. Section 3 identifies 'best practices' that emerge upon such comparative assessment (and that should therefore be obligatory in each of these three legal systems). Section 4 considers whether, to the extent the comparative analysis provided in this chapter identifies challenges common to each of these legal systems, those problems underscore structural – and insurmountable – flaws in the use of secret evidence by democratic governments to deprive individuals of their liberty.

1. THE PROCESSES EXPLAINED

1.1 US Process

Although the US began detaining non-citizen terrorism suspects at Guantánamo Bay in January 2002, it was not until after the US Supreme Court's 2004 decision in *Rasul v. Bush*[4] that the detainees were first allowed to meet with counsel, and courts first began considering the merits of the detainees' challenges to their confinement. The convoluted and at times circuitous litigation that followed has produced a series of court orders governing a detainee's ability to contest evidence the government seeks simultaneously to use to justify his detention and to keep secret – including from the detainee.[5]

---

4 542 US 466 (2004) (holding that the US courts have the power to hear habeas petitions filed by non-citizens detained at Guantánamo).

5 *See generally* ROBERT TIMOTHY REAGAN, FED. JUD. CTR., NATIONAL SECURITY CASE STUDIES: SPECIAL CASE-MANAGEMENT CHALLENGES 118–212

It was settled early on in the habeas litigation that the US government may rely on classified information as part (or even all) of its legal justification for the detention.[6] In light of that determination, one of the most significant steps undertaken by the district court hearing the Guantánamo habeas petitions was the entry of a protective order to govern the use of classified information in the habeas proceedings.[7]

At the core of the rules fashioned by the courts dealing with the Guantánamo litigation is a cleared counsel model, pursuant to which the detainees' lawyers obtain security clearances, and then have access to information to which their clients – lacking such clearances – do not. However, unless the detainee has some independent right to examine the evidence – either because it is being used against him or because it is exculpatory – the detainee's counsel will not see it. Even in cases where such a right exists, the government may keep the evidence from the cleared counsel upon an individualized showing made *ex parte* and *in camera* that the classified information at issue either (1) is highly sensitive; (2) pertains to a highly sensitive source; or (3) pertains to someone other than the detainee.[8] The government can also avoid disclosure of classified evidence to the detainee's counsel if it can provide alternative, unclassified disclosures that are an effective substitute for the information that is properly classified.[9] But it is worth

(2011), available at www.fjc.gov/public/pdf.nsf/lookup/TS111114.pdf/$file/TS111114.pdf.

[6] *See, e.g.* Anam v. Obama, 696 F. Supp. 2d 1 (D.D.C. 2010) (denying a habeas petition based largely on classified evidence), aff'd sub nom. Al-Madhwani v. Obama, 642 F.3d 1071 (D.C. Cir. 2011); Al Odah v. United States, 346 F. Supp. 2d 1, 8–9 (D.D.C. 2004); *cf.* Al Odah v. United States, 608 F. Supp. 2d 42, 45–46 (D.D.C. 2009).

[7] *See* In re Guantanamo Bay Detainee Cases, 344 F. Supp. 2d 174 (D.D.C. 2004). These rules were superseded in their entirety after the Supreme Court's decision in Boumediene v. Bush, 553 US 723 (2008). *See* In re Guantanamo Bay Detainee Litig., 577 F. Supp. 2d 143 (D.D.C. 2008).

[8] *See* Bismullah v. Gates, 501 F.3d 178, 187–88 (D.C. Cir. 2007); *see also* In re Guantanamo Bay Detainee Litig., 787 F. Supp. 2d 5 (D.D.C. 2011).

[9] *See* Al Odah v. United States, 559 F.3d 539, 547 (D.C. Cir. 2009). In one decision, a D.C. district judge allowed the government to use Top Secret evidence affirmatively against a detainee without disclosing to the detainee's counsel either the evidence itself or an adequate summary thereof. (Detainee's counsel possessed only a 'Secret' clearance and therefore could not see 'Top Secret' material.) Mousovi v. Obama, No. 05-1124 (D.D.C. Jan. 9, 2013). The court emphasized that the Top Secret information concerned only the source, and was 'marginal, at best', in part because the government had disclosed the substance of what the source said, and the substance had already lent itself to an

emphasizing that the disclosures in these instances, even with respect to summaries, are generally to the attorneys only, and not to the detainee himself.

Counsel for the detainees are allowed to conduct their own investigations and communicate with their clients after they have become privy to the classified information relevant to the government's case. They are permitted to formulate questions that may be *informed* by the secret evidence to which they had access so long as the nature of the question does not disclose either the existence or content of the classified information. At the same time, however, counsel are not allowed to disclose any of the confidential evidence to their clients or to third parties.[10] One important exception, however, is that detainees' counsel are presumptively permitted to share classified information with other cleared counsel in other Guantánamo habeas cases.[11] Since many cases involve similar or even the same evidence and witnesses, this is a particularly important exception. Yet, in cases involving 'Top Secret' or 'Secure Compartmentalized Information' – mostly cases involving high-value detainees first held at CIA secret prisons – no presumption operates in this regard, and disclosures to counsel in other cases can be made only by establishing a 'need to know' on a case-by-case basis.[12]

There has been substantial wrangling over the secrecy of statements made *by* the detainees themselves, whether to government interrogators, the detainees' own counsel, or others. The government has argued that all such statements made by the detainees were at least presumptively classified, meaning that transcripts of them could not be shown back to the detainees who made them – and that the government's reliance upon those statements in its responsive filing to a detainee's habeas petition could itself be kept from the detainee.[13] Although the district court ultimately rejected this argument as a categorical matter, it allowed the government to argue on a case-by-case basis that certain detainees' statements were not material, and therefore *could* properly be withheld

---

attack based on credibility. This is the only Guantánamo habeas case of which we are aware in which the government has been permitted to rely on evidence without disclosing it or an adequate substitute to detainee's counsel.

[10] *See* In re Guantanamo Bay Detainee Litig., 577 F. Supp. 2d at 149–50.

[11] *See id.*; see also Bismullah, 501 F.3d at 187–8.

[12] *See* In re Guantanamo Bay Detainee Litig., No. 08-442, 2009 WL 50155, at *1 (D.D.C. Jan. 9, 2009).

[13] *See* In re Guantanamo Bay Detainee Litig., 630 F. Supp. 2d 1 (D.D.C. 2009); In re Guantanamo Bay Detainee Litig., 624 F. Supp. 2d 27 (D.D.C. 2009).

from them.[14] The same rules govern situations in which counsel for a detainee wishes to share statements made by the detainee with an outside expert.

1.2 Canadian Process

Canadian law permits the government to certify certain foreign nationals as 'inadmissible' as threats to the national security, on the basis of undisclosed evidence, and then to deport individuals so certified.[15] The government's action is subject to judicial review, but in that review the executive is permitted to present evidence *in camera* to the judge without having to disclose it to the individual sought to be deported. Moreover, while the deportation proceedings are pending, or if there are delays in effectuating deportation (often because of difficulty in identifying a country to which the individual can be deported without facing a risk of torture), the foreign national may be detained. Thus, Canadian law authorizes both deportation and detention on the basis of evidence the affected individual cannot see or confront.

The Canadian Supreme Court in *Charkaoui I* reasoned that an individual's right to have an opportunity to meet the case against him is an essential element of the fair hearing required by § 7 of the Canadian Charter of Rights and Freedoms, which forbids deprivations of liberty and property 'except in accordance with the principles of fundamental justice' and safeguards the individual's right to know the case against him and to respond to it.[16] The Court found it insufficient to rely on the judge in such circumstances to defend the affected individual's interests.[17] Accordingly, it concluded that the statute infringed § 7, but then turned to the government's contention that the infringement was justified, under § 1 of the Charter, by national security concerns.[18]

In making this assessment, the Court noted that Canada, in other circumstances, and the UK in very similar circumstances, used 'special advocates' or 'cleared counsel' to improve the adversarial testing of

---

[14] *See* In re Guantanamo Bay Detainee Litig., 634 F. Supp. 2d 17 (D.D.C. 2009).

[15] Immigration and Refugee Protection Act, S.C. 2001, c. 27 (Can.).

[16] *See* 2007 SCC 9 [2007] 1 S.C.R. 350 (Can.).

[17] *Id.* at para. 63.

[18] Section 1 of the Canadian Charter provides: 'The Canadian Charter of Rights and Freedoms guarantees the rights and freedoms set out in it subject only to such reasonable limits prescribed by law as can be demonstrably justified in a free and democratic society.'

undisclosed evidence.[19] Since this option had been utilized in other settings without any apparent endangerment of security interests, the Court concluded that a procedure that lacked that safeguard did not meet the test of 'minimally impair[ing]' the foreign national's rights.[20]

Canada then modified its process to provide for 'cleared counsel'.[21] The cleared counsel are separate lawyers selected and appointed by the state. They are not the affected individual's principal lawyer, and they are sharply limited in their ability to communicate with either the affected individual or his principal lawyer once they have seen the secret evidence. The 'cleared counsel' process in Canada essentially consists of two steps: First, the cleared counsel – who have access to the entire file – argues for as much disclosure of the undisclosed evidence as possible. Under Canadian law the decision on disclosure is the judge's, not the executive's, to make. Once the judge has ordered disclosure of as much as he decides can be disclosed, the cleared counsel and the open counsel each offer a response on the merits to the charges, to the best of their ability. The open counsel, however, is privy only to the evidence that has been disclosed, and the cleared counsel generally cannot consult with the open counsel once he has seen the secret evidence.

If cleared counsel seeks to communicate with open counsel, or with the affected individual, he or she must seek judicial approval. Approval is rarely sought, in part out of concern that seeking such approval might tip off the government and/or the judge to defense strategy. However, there is available a process by which cleared counsel can move to have such a request considered by a separate judge from the one deciding the appeal.

In the Canadian system, cleared counsel are given access not only to all the evidence the government affirmatively uses against the affected individual, but to the government's entire case file. This is an important feature of the defense, because it means counsel do not have to rely on the state to decide what it will disclose, and counsel not infrequently find evidence in the file that can be used to undermine the government's case.[22]

---

19 *Charkaoui I*, 2007 SCC 9 [2007] 1 S.C.R. 350 (Can.), at paras. 70–84.

20 *Id.* at para. 85.

21 An Act to amend the Immigration and Refugee Protection Act (certificate and special advocate) and to make a consequential amendment to another Act, 2008, c. 3 (Can.).

22 *See, e.g.* Kent Roach, *Must We Trade Rights for Security?: The Choice Between Smart, Harsh, or Proportionate Security Strategies in Canada and Britain*, 27 CARDOZO L. REV., 2151, 2178 n.118 (2006).

1.3 UK Process

In the UK, 'special advocates' have been used in a variety of settings in which the government is authorized to rely on undisclosed evidence to take action against an individual, including immigration proceedings, hearings on detention and 'control orders', and judicial review of decisions to freeze assets of individuals or groups designated as 'terrorist'.[23] As in Canada, the 'special advocates' in the UK are a distinct body of lawyers, and are barred from speaking with the affected individual or his counsel after seeing the secret evidence, absent special approval from a court.

'Special advocates' are given access to any evidence the government seeks to use affirmatively against an individual, and any potentially exculpatory information in the government's possession. Much as in Canada, they then first argue for greater disclosure to the affected individual, both on the ground that the relevant information is not properly secret, and on the ground, discussed below, that the affected individual must be given a more detailed summary, or 'gist', to enable him to instruct his open counsel regarding his defense. Once the judge resolves the disclosure issues, the special advocate and the open counsel then defend the individual on the merits, in separate closed and open proceedings.

According to 'special advocates' that we interviewed, British judges tend not to second-guess the executive on its determination that information is properly secret, but are more willing to rule that disclosures are required in order to satisfy the requirement that the individual be afforded sufficient information to meaningfully instruct his attorney. Judges understandably feel more competent assessing how much information an individual must have in order to have a fair opportunity to respond, a determination squarely within their expertise, than second-guessing the executive on its determination about national security risks.

The summary or 'gist' requirement stems from decisions of the European Court of Human Rights (ECtHR), and subsequently, the UK Supreme Court, both of which have recognized that at a bare minimum, the individual must be apprised of the case against him in sufficient detail to allow him to participate in his own defense. In reaching that result in a case reviewing procedures for preventive detention hearings, the ECtHR rejected the UK's argument that as long as the evidence was

---

[23] *See, e.g.* John Ip, *Al Rawi, Tariq, and the Future of Closed Material Procedures and Special Advocates*, 75 Modern L. Rev. 606 (2012).

disclosed to the 'special advocate' and the advocate did an effective job defending the individual, fairness could be satisfied, even if the individual himself was not informed of the evidence.[24] The Court held that the right at issue belongs to the individual whose liberty is being deprived, and therefore he himself – and not merely a proxy counsel acting on his behalf – must be afforded a meaningful opportunity to participate. The UK Supreme Court has applied that same principle to review of 'control orders', which involve restrictions on liberty, short of full-scale detention but nonetheless often very onerous, and the freezing of assets pursuant to 'terrorist' designations.[25] This 'gisting' requirement has led the government to withdraw evidence that it refuses to disclose even in summary form, and has led to the lifting of control orders in several cases.[26] There have been no reported incidents of terrorist activity by individuals who have been released as a result.

Special advocates in the UK are critical of the limitations on their ability to assist the affected individual. In December 2011, they filed a joint response to a government proposal to expand reliance on special advocates to any civil litigation in which evidence the government sought not to disclose might be relevant.[27] The special advocates strongly opposed the proposal, in large part because in their experience the limitations imposed on them have made the existing proceedings in which secret evidence is permitted 'fundamentally unfair'.[28] These restrictions include the fact that they cannot even ask the affected individual or his open counsel a question without seeking specific approval from the court, with notice to the government. This can be strategically dangerous, because if the individual does not have a good answer, the government and the court will know that he has been asked the question and may deduce that he has nothing helpful to his case to say on the subject. And special advocates cannot even consult with the

---

[24] A and Others v. UK (2009) 49 EHRR 29.

[25] Sec'y of State v. AF (No. 3), [2009] UKHL 28; Her Majesty's Treasury v. Ahmed, [2010] UKSC 2.

[26] *See* Daphne Barak-Erez & Matthew C. Waxman, *Secret Evidence and the Due Process of Terrorist Detentions*, 48 COLUM. J. TRANSNAT'L L. 3, 17 n.53 (2009).

[27] Justice and Security Green Paper, Response to Consultation from Special Advocates, Dec. 16, 2011, *available at* http://reprieve.org.uk/media/downloads/2011_12_16_Justice__Security_Special_Advocates_Response.pdf.

[28] *Id.* at para. 2; *see also* Joint Committee on Human Rights, The Justice and Security Green Paper, 24th Report of Session 2010–12, at paras. 81–6 (also concluding that closed material proceedings with special advocates are fundamentally unfair).

controlee's lawyer regarding this tactical decision without seeking judicial leave, again with notice to the government. As a result, special advocates feel that they must be very conservative about any efforts at communicating with the affected individual or his counsel, and are therefore often limited to raising questions that can be gleaned from the face of the documents they see. Indeed, they take the view that they cannot even do much independent investigation, because doing so might reveal knowledge they have obtained from the closed material. In practice, special advocates told us, they are limited to internet searches – and even those must be done on secure government computers, lest the searches they conduct reveal something about the content of what they have seen. (Internet searches have sometimes proved useful in demonstrating that information the government claims must be secret is actually already publicly available.[29])

2. APPLICABLE PRINCIPLES

Each jurisdiction studied here is subject to fundamental legal obligations to provide a fair hearing to persons whose liberty or property is being deprived. As noted in the introduction, the Canadian Charter recognizes a right to a fundamentally fair hearing, and requires that any intrusion on that right be minimal. Thus, if fairness can be improved without undermining security, the existing procedure is not 'minimally intrusive', and necessarily violates the Charter.

The UK is governed by the ECHR, which also guarantees a fundamentally fair hearing. And as noted above, that requires the state to provide individuals with fair notice and a meaningful opportunity to participate in their own defense where they are being deprived of their liberty. Again, under the ECHR, if fairness can be improved without jeopardizing the state's interests in security, the improvement would be required.[30]

In addition, English common law has long recognized the 'principle of natural justice' that individuals are entitled to know the case against them. As the Law Lords put it, this right provides that:

---

29 *See, e.g.* Scott Shane, *Documents in Plain Sight, but Still Classified*, N.Y. TIMES, July 24, 2012, at A13.

30 This development may best be seen as part of the transnational movement toward 'least restrictive means' analysis – or 'proportionality balancing' – as one of the dominant modes of rights adjudication. *See* Alec Stone Sweet & Jud Mathews, *Proportionality Balancing and Global Constitutionalism*, 47 COLUM. J. TRANSNAT'L L. 72 (2008).

> A person or other properly interested party must have the right to see all the information put before the judge, to comment on it, to challenge it and if needs be to combat it, and to try to establish by contrary evidence that it is wrong. It cannot be withheld from him in whole or in part.[31]

A similar principle governs in the US, both as a general matter under the Due Process Clause of the Fifth Amendment and specifically in habeas cases pursuant to the Constitution's Suspension Clause, which prohibits formal or effective suspensions of the writ of habeas corpus absent extraordinary and carefully circumscribed circumstances. In particular, the US Supreme Court has held that in due process analysis courts must balance the interest of the individual in more process, the likelihood of error from the process employed, and the costs to the state's interests from providing greater process.[32] If a specific procedural reform would further the individual's interest in fairness and reduce the likelihood of error *without* jeopardizing the government's security interests, the constitutional balance would require that procedure to be implemented.[33]

The US Supreme Court has not yet ruled on whether the detainees at Guantánamo, as foreign nationals outside US borders, have constitutional due process rights. It has, however, ruled that they are constitutionally entitled to habeas corpus.[34] Habeas corpus, the Court ruled, has its own constitutionally guaranteed minimal requirements: detained individuals must be afforded a meaningful opportunity to challenge the legality of their detention.[35] The guarantees of habeas corpus and due process may be interrelated, such that the less process that is afforded at the

---

[31] Official Solicitor v. K, [1963] Ch 381, per Upjohn LJ at 405. More recently, the UK Supreme Court recognized the principle again, stating: 'If the right to be heard is to be a real right which is worth anything, it must carry with it a right in the accused man to know the case which is made against him. He must know what evidence has been given and what statements have been made affecting him: and then he must be given a fair opportunity to correct or contradict them.' Al Rawi v. Security Service, [2011] UKSC 34, at para. 12 (quoting Kanda v. Government of Malaya [1962] AC 322, 337).

[32] Mathews v. Eldridge, 424 US 319 (1976); *see also* Hamdi v. Rumsfeld, 542 US 507 (2004) (applying the *Mathews* test to ascertain the amount of process to which a citizen is entitled to challenge his military detention without trial as a terrorism suspect).

[33] Wilkinson v. Austin, 545 US 209 (2005).

[34] Boumediene v. Bush, 553 US 723 (2008).

[35] *Id.* at 779.

administrative level, the more process is necessary at the judicial review stage to ensure meaningful habeas review, and vice versa.[36]

Where secret evidence is employed to justify detention, the Suspension Clause should compel any additional process necessary to ensure a meaningful opportunity to challenge the underlying detention, especially where such additional process does not materially interfere with the government's security interests. Whatever else the Supreme Court meant by a 'meaningful' opportunity to challenge detention, it appears to incorporate comparable principles to those articulated in the British and Canadian contexts.

3. IDENTIFYING 'BEST PRACTICES'

All three countries considered in this chapter have sought to mediate the tension between fairness and secrecy by granting 'cleared' lawyers access to the evidence, and then imposing on those lawyers restrictions on their ability to share that evidence with others, including, most significantly, their clients. Beyond that similarity, however, there are many differences in the ways each nation has structured this compromise. Each system has some distinct advantages and disadvantages. At a minimum, therefore, a comparative analysis might help to identify 'best practices', namely, those features that maximize the ability to test the closed evidence in a meaningful way and maximize fairness to the affected individual without unduly jeopardizing security concerns.[37] But identifying such 'best practices' ought not to be of merely practical interest. Because the use of secret evidence so directly compromises the fundamental principle that individuals should be able to see and confront all the evidence used against them, those compromises should be, as the Court in *Charkaoui I* put it, 'minimally intrusive' on the individual's right to a fair process. Thus, where one nation has demonstrated that practices more conducive to fairness can be undertaken without unduly compromising security, the other nations should be *required*, by domestic constitutional or ECHR

---

[36] *See* Brandon Garrett, *Habeas Corpus and Due Process*, 98 CORNELL L. REV. 47 (2012); *see also* Joshua Alexander Geltzer, *Of Suspension, Due Process, and Guantanamo: The Reach of the Fifth Amendment After* Boumediene *and the Relationship Between Habeas Corpus and Due Process*, 14 U. PA. J. CONST'L L. 719 (2012). *See generally Boumediene*, 553 US at 782–3.

[37] *See, e.g.* David Jenkins, *There and Back Again: The Strange Journey of Special Advocates and Comparative Law Methodology*, 42 COLUM. HUM. RTS. L. REV. 279 (2011).

law, respectively, to adopt those measures as well – or at least to meet a heavy burden of justifying why such a procedure would not be practicable or otherwise acceptable in their jurisdiction.

3.1 Advantages of US System

The principal advantages of the US system are two-fold: first, the client's attorneys *themselves* are given security clearances, and are permitted to continue consulting with their clients after seeing the secret evidence – subject to rules barring disclosure of the evidence to clients or others. Second, an individual detainee's lawyer is allowed to coordinate with cleared counsel for other detainees in most cases. By contrast, the inability of UK and Canadian cleared counsel to consult with the client is perhaps the single biggest obstacle to mounting an effective defense in those jurisdictions. The fact that hundreds of American attorneys have been afforded security clearances and been permitted to maintain their attorney-client contacts in connection with the Guantánamo habeas litigation suggests that the barrier erected in the UK and Canada is unnecessary, and that justifications for insisting upon separate 'cleared' counsel and open counsel are ultimately unavailing.

This is not to say that Guantánamo counsel are unhindered. They repeatedly challenge the legal, practical, and logistical limitations on their representation. An ordinary attorney-client relationship requires candor and trust, and it is often difficult to mount an effective response to government allegations or evidence without being able to ask one's client about it directly – let alone in an environment that the Guantánamo counsel have suggested is designed to foster mistrust between attorney and client. And no amount of access by cleared counsel can make up for the *client's* inability to confront the evidence himself. Still, it is certainly better to start with the presumption that one can communicate with one's client than to start with the opposite presumption. And the Guantánamo lawyers have learned that their questioning can often be guided usefully by the closed evidence without actually disclosing the evidence itself. For example, if the closed evidence includes an allegation that in March 2002 the client was in a terrorist training camp, the lawyer cannot ask his client, 'were you in a terrorist training camp in March 2002?' But he can get the information in a less direct way by asking the client, 'where were you in 2000? 2001? 2002?' To be sure, this is not always a solution. If the veracity of a particular informant is at issue, for example, it's not clear how counsel could ask his client what he knows about the informant without revealing the informant's identity. But it is certainly a fairer process than the presumptive barriers imposed by appointing separate lawyers as 'cleared counsel' and isolating them both practically and legally from the client and his open counsel, as Canada and the UK do.

Cleared lawyers in the Guantánamo habeas cases have also been able to share information among themselves and across individual cases, so long as that sharing takes place in a secure facility. This has proved to be very useful, because it means that lawyers can share notes about common allegations, informants, or sources of information. The lawyers are not, of course, allowed to share this information beyond their circle of security cleared counsel, but our interviews suggest that this ability to share information across cases has often substantially assisted in the investigation and presentation of specific detainees' defenses – to say nothing of the ability to identify problems encountered by all of the counsel collectively. This may be of particular value in the Guantánamo situation, where many of the detainees' cases involve common factual issues, but of less value in countries where evidence is less likely to be relevant across a number of cases. And yet, given the relatively small number of cleared counsel in the UK and Canada, it would seem that there should be a presumption that they can at least communicate with each other about potentially common factual issues – especially if, unlike in the US, they are prohibited from consulting with the individual in question or their open counsel.

3.2 Advantages of UK and Canadian Systems

The first and most important advantage of the UK and Canadian systems over the US system is the requirement that the client himself be apprised of the charges and evidence against him in sufficient detail to permit him to 'instruct' his lawyer, that is, to participate meaningfully in his defense. This is a critically important principle that is thus far lacking in the Guantánamo habeas litigation. Under the rules governing habeas review, a detainee could face imprisonment for the rest of his life without ever being informed of the factual basis for the case against him. There is no requirement that the detainee be afforded access to *any* of the secret evidence. As the ECtHR recognized in *A*, the right to a fair hearing encompasses the right of the affected individual *himself* to meet the 'gist' of the case against him; thus, if information is provided exclusively to an attorney who is then barred from sharing that information with the client, the client has not been afforded either notice or a meaningful opportunity to respond.

Second, the courts in both the UK and Canada have unquestioned authority to review classification decisions, and can order information disclosed if they determine that its disclosure will not undermine the public interest or national security. In Canada, cleared counsel report that over time, and likely because of the involvement of cleared counsel in advocating for disclosure, courts have become more demanding in their review of – and have increasingly overturned – government classification decisions. In the UK, the special advocates report that while the courts in theory can overrule the executive on whether disclosure would undermine national security, many judges are reluctant to exercise this authority in practice. However, courts have, again girded by arguments of the special advocates, proved more willing to insist that the executive disclose more to meet its 'gisting' obligations under the ECHR.

In the US, by contrast, judges frequently treat executive classification decisions as either formally or practically immune from judicial review. They consider themselves ill-equipped to assess an executive determination that information must be kept secret, and as yet they have not imposed a requirement that information be disclosed in the Guantánamo habeas cases in order to provide the detainee an adequate opportunity to participate in his own defense.[38] Although US law does recognize a comparable right on the part of an individual to confront evidence against him to that articulated under the Canadian Charter and the ECHR, such a right has thus far been traced solely to the Sixth Amendment's Confrontation Clause, which does not apply in civil proceedings such as the Guantánamo habeas cases.[39]

Third, in Canada, but not in the US or the UK, special advocates are automatically afforded access to the full intelligence file on the affected individual, and not just to the evidence the government seeks to use and exculpatory evidence, as is the case in the UK and the US. US cleared counsel have expended inordinate effort fighting for access to information that the government seeks to withhold, and even when they have clearances, much of the evidence they obtain is heavily redacted, on grounds that the government will not be using the redacted information, and it is not exculpatory, and therefore defense counsel do not have a right to see the information. The Canadian approach provides an important advantage, as it puts the special advocate and the government on the same footing regarding the government's evidence, and permits the advocate to make arguments based on contradictions, inconsistencies, or holes in the government's own files. In theory, the requirement to disclose exculpatory evidence should achieve similar ends, but battles

---

[38] *See, e.g.* ACLU v. Dep't of Justice, 681 F.3d 61, 70–71 (2d Cir. 2012).

[39] *See, e.g.* Turner v. Rogers, 131 S. Ct. 2507, 2516 (2011).

over what is exculpatory are legion, with prosecutors almost invariably taking a much narrower view of what is exculpatory than the defense. Given the constraints on the individual participating in his own defense, and on the ability of cleared counsel to conduct investigations, it seems particularly apt to require the government to disclose its full intelligence file to lawyers who already have the requisite clearances.

In conclusion, each system could learn from the experiences of the other systems, and could increase the overall fairness to the affected individuals by adopting practical solutions employed elsewhere without unduly undermining security. None of the countries considered has reported any significant security breaches under any of these procedures, so in terms of preserving security interests, there seems to be little reason not to derive best practices for fairness from the three different approaches. As each country's fundamental laws require that intrusions on the individual's right to know the case against him be as 'minimal' as possible, these practices are relevant not only as descriptive, policy-oriented guides about how to construct the best 'special advocate' system, but also as evidence supporting a normative legal argument, grounded in the Canadian Charter, the ECHR, or the US Constitution, respectively, that more process is due than is currently being afforded by any of these three countries.

4. SHARED PROBLEMS

A comparative analysis of the use of secret evidence also reveals a raft of shared problems that raise fundamental questions about whether the 'cleared counsel' model is an inherently flawed approach even with adoption of the best practices identified above.

The first problem is that there is inadequate checking of the executive branch's authority to declare that certain information must remain confidential.[40] While courts in the UK and Canada have the authority to review such assessments, the reviews tend to be quite deferential on the question of whether disclosure would implicate national security. In the US, for all intents and purposes, the executive exercises *carte blanche* in making these determinations. Almost everyone who comes into contact with the classification systems complains that they are skewed toward

---

[40] *See, e.g.* Special Advocates' Response at para. 37 (complaining about the 'inability effectively to challenge non-disclosure').

overclassification.[41] It is much easier, and less risky, to declare information secret than to declare that it can be disclosed. And there is little incentive to disclose if there is no meaningful oversight, no penalty for wrongful classification, and if nondisclosure gives the executive a litigation advantage. This problem exists with or without 'cleared counsel' procedures, of course, but the existence of a 'cleared counsel' option may have the perverse effect of reducing incentives to declassify, because it lends legitimacy to a system that relies heavily on undisclosed evidence.

Second, at bottom any 'cleared counsel' procedure denies to the affected individual the right to notice of the evidence against him and an opportunity to meet it. This has inescapable fairness costs to the affected individual, and also may undermine the accuracy of the outcome by permitting decisions to be predicated on evidence that is not subject to full adversarial testing. The affected individual is often in the best position to know how to respond to evidence that implicates him in some wrongdoing, so walling him off may undermine the accuracy of the outcome to the extent that it prevents his full participation. In addition, there is an intrinsic value to knowing the grounds upon which one's liberty or property have been deprived, even if one has nothing to say in response; it is an essential element of fairness wholly apart from its instrumental function in revealing the truth. The 'cleared counsel' systems attempt to offset these fairness costs in some measure, but at the end of the day they are predicated on an acceptance of a least-worst alternative in which individuals can be deprived of their liberty or property without being fully apprised of the case against them. The 'gisting' requirement imposed by the ECtHR is a critical check on this compromise, by requiring that the individual be afforded notice not of all the evidence against him, but of sufficient evidence, and in sufficient detail, to permit him to participate in his own defense. The meaning of that guarantee in practice, however, remains to be seen.

Third, all of the 'cleared counsel' models undermine the principle that justice should be open and transparent, particularly when the state is imposing onerous coercive burdens on individuals. The principle that justice should be public, known as the 'open justice' principle, is a fundamental principle of the common law.[42] In its absence, there is sharply limited public awareness of what is actually going on in closed

---

[41] *See generally* Steven Aftergood, *Reducing Government Secrecy: Finding What Works*, 27 YALE L. & POL'Y REV. 399, 401–407 (2009).

[42] Al Rawi, *supra* note 23 at paras. 10–11.

cases. Whatever happens behind closed doors remains there. The public will often have limited or no access to the determinative facts and issues in a case. For example, the opinions issued by the US federal courts reviewing Guantánamo detentions are often heavily redacted (if they are publicly released at all), and almost impossible for an outside reader to assess.[43] The public interest in open justice is not mitigated by providing lawyers security clearances to increase the fairness of closed-door justice. The proceeding still takes place behind closed doors, and to that extent, undermines the legitimacy of the result and the ability of the public to assess it.

Fourth, 'cleared counsel' procedures may make courts more willing to accept evidence that would not be accepted in a public proceeding. When the UK special advocates delineated problems with closed proceedings and cleared counsel, they expressly noted the 'lack of any formal rules of evidence, so allowing second or third hand hearsay to be admitted or even more remote evidence'.[44] To similar effect, one of the district judges in the Guantánamo habeas cases concluded a heavily redacted opinion upholding the government's detention of a particular individual with the observation that the (not publicly accessible) evidence was itself 'gossamer thin', 'of a kind fit only for these unique proceedings [redacted] and [with] very little weight'.[45] There is no necessary relation, of course, between the quality of the evidence accepted by a judge and the public nature of the proceedings, but it appears that in all three countries, much of the evidence adduced is in fact intelligence that often is second- or third-hand, and frequently does not identify its source, much less whether the source is credible or obtained its information in a reliable way. In each setting in which cleared counsel have been used, such hearsay and intelligence have proven admissible, albeit with different judges placing varying degrees of weight upon them. In a closed proceeding, jurists may be more inclined to grant such evidence weight than in a public proceeding in which issues of admissibility and weight could be assessed

---

[43] In one case, for example, the redacted opinion ultimately released by the district court granting a detainee's habeas petition was far less skeptical of the government's position than the opinion initially released, only to be withdrawn for security reasons. *See* Dafna Linzer, *In Gitmo Opinion, Two Versions of Reality*, PROPUBLICA, Oct. 8, 2010, www.propublica.org/article/in-gitmo-opinion-two-versions-of-reality; see also Uthman v. Obama, 637 F.3d 400 (D.C. Cir. 2011).

[44] Special Advocates' Response, *supra* at para. 17.

[45] Awad v. Obama, 646 F. Supp. 2d 20, 27 (D.D.C. 2009), aff'd, 608 F.3d 1 (D.C. Cir. 2010), cert. denied, 131 S. Ct. 1814 (2011).

not only by the immediate participants, but by the public at large. At present, the public has virtually no ability to assess the quality of the evidence relied upon in cleared counsel proceedings, to say nothing of other lawyers, legal observers, or jurists in future cases seeking to ascertain what their predecessors actually decided.

5. CONCLUSION

The comparative analysis we have sketched here suggests not just that each of the three nations *could* do more to improve fairness without undermining legitimate secrecy concerns, but that, to the extent they can, their constitutional and human rights traditions demand that they must. Canada and the UK could give clearances to the affected party's lawyers, not just to independent special advocates, and could allow much more communication and investigation after cleared counsel have seen closed evidence – subject to protective orders barring disclosure of such evidence. Canada and the UK could also allow cleared counsel in separate cases to share information among each other when material to the defense. The US and the UK could give cleared counsel automatic access to the entire intelligence file, as Canada does, rather than making lawyers fight for access to the information. And US and UK courts could subject the government's decisions that information cannot be disclosed to more rigorous judicial oversight in order to minimize the problem of overclassification. Finally, the US could require that the detainee be afforded a sufficient unclassified summary of the charges and evidence against him to enable him to participate in his own defense and to know the case against him.

The experience thus far suggests that all of these changes could be implemented without unduly jeopardizing national security. Moreover, because the Canadian Charter, the US Constitution, and the ECHR all require that intrusions on fair process be narrowly tailored, there is a good argument under each country's fundamental law that these changes are not just wise policy, but legally obligatory. That is not to say that the lessons surveyed herein are only relevant for these three countries. But for the reasons surveyed above, there are specific similarities between the existing processes for judicial consideration of secret evidence – and between the constitutional traditions of these three countries – to make the case for comparative 'borrowing' that much more compelling here.

At the end of the day, however, the common problems that all three systems have confronted with secret evidence suggest that perhaps we ought never to have gone down this road in the first place. In all three systems, much could be done to improve a fundamentally compromised system. But the real question is whether the decision to compromise on perhaps the most elemental feature of fundamental fairness – the right of an individual to confront the evidence against him when the government seeks to deprive him of liberty – is fatally flawed. As the UK special advocates argued recently, closed procedures 'are fundamentally unfair; they do *not* work effectively; nor do they deliver real procedural fairness'.[46]

[46] Response of the Special Advocates, at para. 15.

PART 4

Secrecy and criminal trials

12. The normalization of anonymous testimony

Jason Mazzone and Tobias Fischer

INTRODUCTION

In recent years a remarkable development has occurred in criminal justice systems around the world: an increase in the use of testimony from witnesses whose identities are kept secret. Most strikingly, use of anonymous testimony has expanded vastly in adversarial systems despite the long-recognized right of an accused to confront his or her accusers. Once confined to trials of war criminals before international tribunals, terrorists and other extraordinary defendants, anonymous testimony has become a normal part of criminal justice throughout much of the world. In the United States, by contrast, shielding a witness's identity in criminal cases is almost unheard of. In fact, during the period in which other adversarial systems have embraced anonymous testimony, the US Supreme Court has issued a series of rulings strengthening the right of criminal defendants to confront their accusers in open court.[1] Anonymous witnesses have been permitted to testify in US courts in cases involving terrorism and gang-related murders, for example, but they truly remain the exception.[2]

1 See, e.g. Crawford v. Washington, 541 U.S. 36, 57, 68 (2004) (holding that testimonial out-of-court statements are inadmissible under the Confrontation Clause of the Sixth Amendment unless the declarant is unavailable at trial and the defendant had a previous opportunity to cross-examine the declarant).

2 See, e.g. United States v. Ramos-Cruz, 667 F.3d 487, 500–501 (4th Cir. 2012) (affirming convictions on murder and other charges related to gang activity following a jury trial in which two El Salvadorian police officers testified under pseudonyms and without revealing their dates and places of birth, or home and work addresses, where the witnesses 'proffered no evidence directly involving Ramos-Cruz or his activities' but 'merely provided background information about the internal workings of … [the gang] generally'); Wadie E. Said, Material Support Prosecution and Foreign Policy, 86 Ind. L.J. 543, 585–7 (2011)

At first blush, it might appear that if there is to be anonymous testimony it should be – as it is in the United States – a rare occurrence because of both the resulting limitations on the rights of defendants and the increased risk of erroneous convictions. However there is a viable argument that normalizing anonymous testimony, as has occurred in the three countries surveyed here – the United Kingdom, Australia and New Zealand – better protects the interests of defendants. Normalization is arguably preferable because judges and lawyers may develop better safeguards for routine, rather than rare, practices and because the public is likely to be more vigilant about rules to which they themselves might one day be subject. Nonetheless, firm conclusions at this point about the benefits and risks of normalization would be premature. Making such an assessment requires future comparative research focused on the experiences of criminal justice systems that have embraced anonymity during the past decade or so. For present purposes the task is to set out the changes that have occurred and to identify their possible implications in order to provide a guide for future research.

This chapter begins in Section 1 with a brief introduction to the right of confrontation and the nature of anonymous testimony. Section 2 discusses the recent increased acceptance of anonymous testimony by focusing on developments in the United Kingdom, Australia and New Zealand. Section 3 identifies some possible risks and benefits of normalizing anonymity in order to lay the groundwork for future study.

1. CONFRONTATION AND ANONYMITY

The individual right to confront and cross-examine one's accusers has roots in Roman law. In England the right accompanied the emergence of

---

(discussing the use of a government expert witness, an Israeli intelligence officer, whose identity was not disclosed to the defense, in the successful criminal prosecution of leaders of the Holy Land Foundation for Relief and Development on charges that included providing material support to a terrorist organization). Beyond civilian courts, anonymous witnesses have also been used in military tribunals at Guantánamo. Serrin Turner and Stephen J. Schulhofer, The Secrecy Problem in Terrorism Trials 66 (Report of Brennan Center for Justice at NYU School of Law) (2005); William Glaberson, Witness Names to Be Withheld From Detainee, N.Y. Times, Dec. 1, 2007, at A1 (discussing use of an anonymous government witnesses in a military trial at Guantánamo).

jury trials in the twelfth century and was protected in treason prosecutions by statute in 1552.[3] Beginning in the early eighteenth century, a robust common-law right of confrontation developed, with one English court in 1720 declaring it 'the most effectual method for discovering the truth'[4] and Blackstone endorsing the truth-seeking function of confrontation in his 1765 *Commentaries on the Laws of England*.[5] The Sixth Amendment to the Constitution of the United States, adopted in 1791, gave a defendant in a federal criminal trial the right 'to be confronted with the witnesses against him',[6] and provisions in early American state constitutions secured a similar right in state court prosecutions.[7] The 1950 European Convention on Human Rights (ECHR) also guarantees that a defendant has the right 'to examine or have examined witnesses against him',[8] with the passive language preserving the practices of inquisitorial systems in which judges perform examinations.

Testimony by anonymous witnesses can threaten the truth-seeking function of a criminal trial, yet the extent of the threat depends on the specific circumstances in which anonymity occurs. Two issues are particularly relevant. One is the type of anonymity in question. Anonymity can mean different things. It can mean that a witness testifies in open court, but that the name of the witness is withheld. It can mean that the name of the witness is supplied, but other identifying information – such as the witness's address, place of work or family ties – is not disclosed. Anonymity can mean that a witness's physical appearance is kept hidden, such as by use of a wig, sunglasses or other disguise. Anonymity might mean that the witness testifies behind a screen so that the witness is heard but not seen. Anonymity also can entail testimony given from a

---

3 An Act for the Punishment of Diverse Treasons, 1552, 5 & 6 Edw. 6, c. 11, § 9 (Eng.) (requiring that accusers 'if they be then living, shall be brought in person before the party so accused, and avow and maintain that that they have to say against the said party to prove him guilty').

4 Duke of Dorset v. Girdler, (1720) 24 Eng. Rep. 238 (Ch.).

5 3 William Blackstone, Commentaries on the Laws of England 372–3 (1768) ('This open examination of witnesses *viva voce*, in the presence of all mankind, is much more conducive to the clearing up of truth than [a] private and secret examination. ... [A] witness may frequently depose that in private, which he will be shamed to testify in a public and solemn tribunal.').

6 U.S. Const. amend. VI.

7 See, e.g. Mass. Const. pt. I, art. 12 (1780) ('[E]very subject shall have a right ... to meet the witnesses against him face to face').

8 European Convention for the Protection of Human Rights and Fundamental Freedoms, art. 6, Nov. 4, 1950, 213 U.N.T.S. 221.

different room via closed-circuit television with technological distortion of the witness's image or voice or both.

Different types of anonymity measures should be expected to have different effects. For example, keeping the identity of a witness hidden will affect the ability of the defendant to offer evidence about a witness's character, motive to lie, incapacity, past contradictory statements and other factors that may undermine the witness's credibility. On the other hand, hiding the witness behind a screen might hinder the ability of the defense lawyer to conduct a thorough cross-examination because the lawyer will not see facial expressions that would ordinarily trigger follow-up questions. Certain kinds of anonymity can affect the behavior of the witness. For example, a witness who can testify out of the view of the defendant might find it easier to lie.[9]

The second issue relevant to the impact upon the truth-seeking function of a trial is the question of to whom the witness is anonymous. The identity of the witness might be withheld solely from the defendant (and the general public) but made available to the judge and jury. On the other hand, a witness's identity might remain known only to the prosecutor. So too, a witness who testifies behind a screen or on video monitors might be obscured from the defendant's view but remain visible to the judge and the jury. When a witness's voice is distorted to the courtroom, the judge and jury might nonetheless hear via headphones the witness's natural speech.

The impact anonymity has on a trial will depend upon the target of the anonymity measure. For example, there is likely to be a difference between shielding a witness only from the defendant and shielding the witness from the judge and jury as well. The latter case is more likely to undermine the reliability of a criminal trial than is the former because fact-finders often depend upon direct observation of a witness's demeanor in order to assess the reliability of the witness's testimony.

Although anonymity can undermine the truth-seeking function of trials, it might also, in some circumstances, enhance it. Just as there are reasons for allowing defendants to confront witnesses, there may be countervailing reasons for permitting witnesses to remain anonymous. Anonymity can protect the safety of witnesses; this benefit might be

---

9 See Ohio v. Roberts, 448 U.S. 56, 64 n.6 (1980) ('The requirement of personal presence … undoubtedly makes it more difficult to lie against someone, particularly if that person is an accused and present at trial.') (alterations in original) (quoting 4 J. WEINSTEIN AND M. BERGER, WEINSTEIN'S EVIDENCE ¶ 800 (1979)).

especially important in prosecutions involving organized crime or terrorism. A witness might refuse to testify at all unless the testimony can be anonymous; allowing anonymous testimony could be the only way to proceed with a prosecution. Special characteristics of witnesses may also justify anonymity. For example, anonymity can prevent disclosure of the identity of a confidential informant or undercover agent, which could undermine other investigations. Anonymity can safeguard witnesses from public hostility or embarrassment that might otherwise prevent witnesses from coming forward. Some form of anonymity – such as testimony behind a screen or via closed-circuit television – may be required to ensure accurate testimony from child victims and other especially vulnerable witnesses whose testimony can be affected by the mere presence of the accused.[10] For each of these reasons, anonymity might serve rather than inhibit the function of the trial in establishing the truth. To consider more closely whether and when anonymity is generally consistent with constitutional values requires first a discussion of the rise of anonymous testimony in adversarial systems, the subject of the next part.

2. THE RISE OF ANONYMITY

Three national case studies demonstrate the increased acceptance in recent years of testimony by anonymous witnesses: the United Kingdom, Australia and New Zealand.

2.1 The United Kingdom

Testimony by anonymous witnesses in courtrooms in the United Kingdom has sharply increased as a result of recent statutory developments. By way of background, in 2003, Parliament sharply limited the common law right of confrontation by enacting the Criminal Justice Act (CJA). The CJA expanded the power of courts to admit hearsay evidence where 'the court is satisfied that it is in the interests of justice for [the

---

[10] See, e.g. Maryland v. Craig, 497 U.S. 836, 857 (1990) ('[W]here necessary to protect a child witness from trauma that would be caused by testifying in the physical presence of the defendant, at least where such trauma would impair the child's ability to communicate, the Confrontation Clause does not prohibit use of a procedure that, despite the absence of face-to-face confrontation, ensures the reliability of the evidence by subjecting it to rigorous adversarial testing and thereby preserves the essence of effective confrontation').

out-of-court statement] to be admissible'.[11] Under the CJA, hearsay, which by definition undermines the right of confrontation because the declarant is not present, may be admitted when the declarant is unavailable and the court finds the evidence 'cogent and reliable'.[12] Among other circumstances, the unavailability condition is satisfied if 'through fear the relevant person does not [testify] in the proceedings'.[13]

It took just five years after enactment of the CJA for Parliament to implement additional safeguards against witness intimidation by permitting witnesses to testify anonymously. In the summer of 2008, in response to the decision of the House of Lords in *R. v. Davis*,[14] which overturned a criminal conviction following a trial at which prosecution witnesses had testified using pseudonyms, behind screens, and with their voices electronically disguised, Parliament enacted the Criminal Evidence (Witness Anonymity) Act (WAA). The WAA empowered trial courts to grant a 'witness anonymity order' permitting the use of various protective measures that the court deemed 'appropriate'.[15] Possible measures included: withholding witnesses' names and other identifying information; allowing witnesses to use pseudonyms; prohibiting questions tending to identify anonymous witnesses; using screens to hide witnesses; and using technology to conceal a witness's face or voice.[16] Before issuing an anonymity order under the WAA, the statute required the trial court to find that (a) 'the measures are necessary ... to protect the safety of the witness or another person or to prevent any serious damage to property, or ... to prevent real harm to the public interest'; (b) the measures 'would be consistent with the defendant receiving a fair trial'; and (c) 'it is important that the witness should testify' and 'the witness would not testify if the order were not made'.[17] The Act identified six factors for courts to consider in evaluating whether these conditions were present.[18] The WAA was designed as a temporary measure in specific response to the *Davis* decision and by its terms the statute expired at the end of 2009.[19] However, in that same year,

[11] Criminal Justice Act, 2003, c. 44, § 114(1)(d) (UK).
[12] Id. at § 114, n.396 (1)(d).
[13] Id. at § 116(2).
[14] R. v. Davis, (2008) UKHL 36, 1 A.C. 1128 (HL) (overturning conviction following a trial involving anonymous testimony).
[15] Criminal Evidence (Witness Anonymity) Act, 2008, c. 15, § 2(1) (UK).
[16] Id. at § 2(2).
[17] Id. at § 4(3–5).
[18] Id. at § 5.
[19] Id. at § 14.

Parliament enacted the Coroners and Justice Act, which incorporated the anonymity provisions of the WAA, and those provisions therefore remain in effect.[20] From July 2008 to December 2009 alone, courts issued at least 343 anonymity orders.[21]

The Human Rights Act of 1998 requires domestic courts to account for the decisions of the European Court of Human Rights (ECtHR)[22] and directs that parliamentary legislation 'be read and given effect in a way which is compatible with the Convention rights'.[23] Article 6 of the ECHR provides that criminal defendants are entitled to 'fair and public hear-ing[s]'[24] and 'to examine or have examined witnesses against [them]'.[25] Applying these provisions, the ECtHR has struck a balance among the rights of the accused, the interests of witnesses and the interests of contracting states.[26] Toward this end, the ECtHR has found that witness anonymity may be used only (1) when 'strictly necessary', (2) when the testimony from such witnesses does not constitute the 'sole or decisive basis for a conviction', and (3) when 'sufficient counter-balancing measures' are implemented to protect the accused's rights.[27]

UK domestic courts, however, have allowed more liberal use of anonymous testimony than that which the ECtHR has deemed consistent with Article 6 rights. For example, in *R. v. Mayers,* consolidated cases involving anonymous eye witnesses in prosecutions for murder and drug trafficking, the Court of Appeal adopted a broad view of the circumstances under which anonymity orders are appropriate.[28] The *Mayers* court recognized that the WAA provides that anonymous testimony may not be the 'sole or decisive' source of evidence against the accused. Yet the *Mayers* court read this limitation to apply where there is only one anonymous witness, noting that '[b]y definition where two or more anonymous witnesses give important incriminating evidence against the

---

[20] Coroners and Justice Act, 2009, c. 25 (UK).

[21] David Omerod, Guest Lecture at Middle Temple: Fair Trials – The Anonymous Witness Saga 1 (Mar. 22, 2010), available at www.middletemple.org.uk/Downloads/David%20Ormerod%20Guest%20Lecture%2022%2003%202010.pdf.

[22] Human Rights Act, 1998, c. 42, § 2(1) (UK).

[23] Id. at § 3(1).

[24] ECHR art. 6(1).

[25] ECHR art. 6(3)(d).

[26] See, e.g. Van Mechelen v. Netherlands, 1997-III Eur. Ct. H.R. (1998); Doorson v. Netherlands, 1996-II Eur. Ct. H.R.; Kostovski v. Netherlands, 166 Eur. Ct. H.R. (ser. A) (1989).

[27] Van Mechelen, 1997-III Eur. Ct. H.R. at ¶ 46.

[28] R. v. Mayers, (2009) 1 Cr App R 30, (2009) WLR 1915 (EWCA).

defendant, the evidence of one would not provide either the sole evidence or indeed the decisive evidence against him'.[29] The *Mayers* court also construed broadly the necessity provision of the WAA, holding that it does not require finding that the risk to the witness's safety is attributable to the defendant's actions; instead, 'the threat may come from any source'.[30] As striking as was the *Mayers* court's willingness to construe anonymity measures broadly, even more dramatic is the Supreme Court's recent suggestion in *R. v. Horncastle* (a case involving absent witnesses) that in light of statutory safeguards for defendants built into UK law,[31] domestic courts are simply free to ignore the ECtHR's sole or decisive rule with respect to anonymous witnesses.[32] The full impact of the *Horncastle* decision remains to be seen but the case gives UK courts a green light to adopt even more expansive anonymity measures than those that have been implemented to date.

2.2 Australia

In Australia, as in the United Kingdom, a defendant's right to confront a witness is not protected by a codified right but exists at common law.[33] Recent statutory measures have allowed witnesses to testify anonymously in criminal trials in certain circumstances. In 2000 Queensland extended existing protections for undercover law enforcement officers who testify anonymously[34] to apply also to participants in the state's witness protection program.[35] Witnesses who qualify for an anonymity order may testify under a pseudonym and cannot be required to answer questions 'that may lead to the disclosure of the protected witness's protected

---

[29] Id. ¶ 25.

[30] Id. ¶ 28.

[31] R. v. Horncastle, (2009) UKSC 14, ¶¶ 87–90, (2010) 2 W.L.R. 47 (SC) (quoting Criminal Evidence (Witness Anonymity) Act 2008, § 5(2) (UK)). In particular, the court cited section 5 of the WAA, which instructs judges to consider, among other factors, 'the extent to which the credibility of the witness ... would be a relevant factor when the weight of his or her evidence comes to be assessed' and 'whether there is any reason to believe that the witness ... has a tendency to be dishonest, or ... has any motive to be dishonest in the circumstances of the case'. Id. at ¶ 55.

[32] Id. at ¶¶ 50, 56, 92.

[33] David Lusty, Anonymous Accusers: An Historical and Comparative Analysis of Secret Witnesses in Criminal Trials, 24 Sydney L. Rev. 361, 409 (2002).

[34] Evidence Act 1977, (Qld) ss 21F–L (Austl.).

[35] Witness Protection Act 2000, (Qld) s 6 (Austl.).

identity or where the protected witness lives'.[36] Queensland law also provides for measures to protect vulnerable witnesses, including the use of a screen or a one-way mirror, the removal of the defendant or of the witness from the courtroom and the use of audio-visual links to transmit the testimony.[37] In other states, including New South Wales and Western Australia, participants in witness protection programs may testify under their new identities and the government is not required to disclose, even to the court, such a witness's true identity or background.[38] At the federal level, the Evidence Act of 1995 permits courts to exclude evidence when 'the public interest in admitting into evidence information or a document that relates to matters of state is outweighed by the public interest in preserving secrecy or confidentiality in relation to the information or document'.[39] The Act defines 'matters of state' to include instances where the evidence would 'disclose, or enable a person to ascertain, the existence or identity of a confidential source of information in relation to the enforcement or administration of a law'.[40]

2.3 New Zealand

The rise of anonymous testimony in New Zealand follows the trajectory that occurred in the United Kingdom of statutory liberalization in response to judicial rulings. In a 1986 decision the New Zealand Court of Appeal rejected the government's request that undercover police officers be permitted to testify without revealing their identities.[41] In response to that ruling, the New Zealand Parliament amended that country's 1908 Evidence Act to permit undercover officers to testify under an assumed name if the Police Commissioner certifies to the trial court that the officer has no criminal convictions and provides to the court notice of any incidents casting doubt on the officer's credibility.[42] In 1997, in a case involving an anonymous eyewitness in a gang violence prosecution, the Court of Appeal rejected the government's argument that under the common law, and based upon English authorities, civilian witnesses

---

[36] Witness Protection Act 2000, (Qld) ss 27(1) and 27(2)(a)–(b) (Austl.); Evidence Act 1977, (Qld) ss 21I(2)(a), 21I(2)(b)(i)–(ii) (Austl.).

[37] See Evidence Act 1977, (Qld) s 21AQ (Austl.).

[38] See Witness Protection Act 1995, (NSW) s 24; Witness Protection Act 1996, (WA) s 28 (Austl.).

[39] Evidence Act 1995, (Cth) s 130(1) (Austl.).

[40] Id. at s 130(4)(e).

[41] See R. v. Hughes, (1986) 2 NZLR 129.

[42] Evidence Act, 1908, cl. 13A (NZ).

could also be permitted to testify anonymously in the interests of justice.[43] Parliament again responded, enacting a broad new statutory provision giving trial courts authority to permit *any* witness to testify anonymously. That provision permits anonymous testimony if the court is satisfied that:

(a) the safety of the witness or of any other person is likely to be endangered, or there is likely to be serious damage to property, if the witness's identity is disclosed; and
(b) either –
  (i) there is no reason to believe that the witness has a motive or tendency to be dishonest, having regard (where applicable) to the witness's previous convictions or the witness's relationship with the accused or any associates of the accused; or
  (ii) the witness's credibility can be tested properly without disclosure of the witness's identity; and
(c) the making of the order would not deprive the accused of a fair trial.[44]

New Zealand judges have made broad use of this new statutory provision, allowing testimony by anonymous witnesses in a variety of trials. For example, in one murder case in 2008 involving a drive-by gang shooting, twenty-two witnesses gave evidence anonymously.[45] Some of those witnesses testified via closed-circuit television, with the witness's image on the screen blurred and the voice of the witness distorted; others testified in court behind a screen.[46]

3. NORMALIZATION: RISKS AND BENEFITS

Nations that permit anonymous testimony face a choice between two paths. They can limit the use of anonymous testimony to truly exceptional cases, for example to prosecutions of war criminals or terrorists, and require the government to show that circumstances are so extraordinary that anonymity is essential. Alternatively, nations can permit anonymous testimony to become a regular part of the criminal justice

---

[43] See R. v. Hines, (1997) 3 NZLR 529.

[44] Evidence Act 2006, cl. 112(4) (NZ).

[45] See 'Secret Witnesses "Crucial" to Jhia Trial' (Dec. 13, 2008), www.stuff.co.nz/national/crime/759647/Secret-witnesses-crucial-to-Jhia-trial.

[46] Id.

system, available in a wide range of cases, with looser standards that the government must satisfy in any particular case for anonymity to be granted.

Under the first approach anonymous testimony remains an exceptional departure from procedures thought to be generally necessary to protect defendants' rights and ensure fundamental fairness. In these circumstances, anonymity is accepted but never embraced as desirable. Its very use is noticed and provokes criticism. It is condemned for its irregularity and, because it carries political risks, the government must work to quell public opposition to it.

The second approach deems anonymous testimony, subject to appropriate safeguards, to be consistent with basic principles of fairness. Anonymity is considered a normal part of the criminal justice system, not aberrational. Anonymity is thus no different than any other trial procedure. While anonymous testimony may limit what defendants are able to do or achieve, so do many other procedures that govern how trials are conducted and, like them, anonymity cannot be condemned merely on this basis. The government may be required to make some showing that anonymity is necessary in a particular prosecution but it need not explain why anonymity in general is available. As a regular part of the criminal justice system, anonymity properly balances governmental interests, and those of the public more generally, with the interests of the defendant in receiving a fair trial. Anonymity is deemed consistent with protections for the right of confrontation, which is understood not to require that witnesses' identities be known but to be adequately secured by other means.[47]

There are some obvious risks to normalizing anonymity. Viewed from the perspective of the defendant, anonymity may present substantial dangers. A defendant who does not know a witness's identity cannot gather information about the witness before trial to argue that the witness is not credible because, for example, the witness has a flawed character or a grudge against the particular defendant, or because there are facts that show the witness has an incomplete memory of events or is simply mistaken. Witnesses who need not identify themselves have reduced incentives to testify accurately: other things being equal, it is normally

---

[47] See, e.g. United States v. Owens, 484 U.S. 554, 562 (1988) (defining 'subject to cross-examination' as 'when [a witness] is placed on the stand, under oath, and responds willingly to questions'); Kentucky v. Stincer, 482 U.S. 730, 739 (1987) ('[T]he Confrontation Clause guarantees only an opportunity for effective cross-examination, not cross-examination that is effective in whatever way, and to whatever extent, the defense might wish.').

more costly to be identified publicly with a lie than to tell one when few people will ever know the source. It may often be harder to challenge a witness who testifies from a different room, from behind a screen, or as a blurred image and whose voice has been altered. These mechanisms can mute bodily and vocal cues that the cross-examining lawyer would ordinarily take into account to identify the witness's weakness and to determine which lines of questioning to pursue in greater depth. For the defendant, the hazards may be greatest if, as in some jurisdictions, the judge or jury charged with assessing the testimony are themselves able to see the witness and hear the witness's natural voice. In such circumstances the fact-finder may see a defense lawyer seemingly ignore bodily and vocal cues and thus assume that any doubts suggested by those cues are unwarranted. Given these factors, defendants, guilty or not, may face an increased likelihood of conviction.

More generally the government's ability to offer anonymity to witnesses greatly increases its power of prosecution. Witnesses otherwise unwilling to come forward may be more inclined to testify if the government can promise that their identities will be kept secret. A case that would not otherwise be brought because the witnesses have backgrounds that cast doubt on their credibility, could be advanced if those backgrounds need not be revealed. Negative aspects of witnesses' demeanors can be reduced through testimony given behind a screen (or sunglasses) or as a blurred image on a television monitor. Witnesses with nervous courtroom voices can become more credible once their voices are distorted technologically. As anonymity renders prosecution easier, more people can be prosecuted and more convictions obtained. Fixed prosecutorial resources need not set significant caps because, in an age of plea-bargaining, these governmental benefits can be obtained without trial. The mere proffer of an anonymous witness may be enough to force a guilty plea.

A constitutional democracy that generally prohibits anonymous testimony and tolerates it only in truly exceptional cases acts in recognition of these risks. It deems the danger of false testimony, the increase in governmental power and the threat to defendants' rights to be too high for generalized anonymity to be consistent with constitutional principles of fair process. Such a system recognizes that without the general availability of anonymity some, perhaps many, criminals will not suffer judgment but this price is willingly paid given the costs of the alternative. Limiting anonymity to exceptional cases is, short of abolishing it entirely, the best means to minimize the associated dangers. Across the system as a whole very few individuals will be prosecuted in a manner that gives rise to the dangers of anonymity. There will therefore be few convictions obtained in which witnesses felt free to lie because their identities were unknown. The increase in governmental power that accompanies anonymity will, on the whole, be slight. The number of defendants whose rights are jeopardized or infringed as a result of anonymity will be few. Assessed as a whole this system of criminal justice comports with constitutional norms because the rate of departure from those norms is miniscule. True enough for individual defendants subject to those departures, the individual costs are enormous. But it may be far better for a few defendants to bear these costs than for them to be borne by many.

Although there are strong arguments for limiting anonymous testimony to exceptional cases, there may also be good reasons to think that allowing anonymous testimony to become a normal part of a criminal justice system is, in the end, more consistent with constitutional norms of fair process. Fact-finders may be better equipped to assess anonymous testimony when it is a routine part of criminal trials. Judges (and juries if they serve repeatedly) will gain experience hearing testimony from witnesses whose identities are hidden and, as a result, will develop new and tailored techniques for assessing their credibility. Just as the loss of one sense heightens other senses, fact-finders who regularly encounter anonymous testimony may focus their attention in different ways upon that evidence. If a witness's voice is distorted, the fact-finder may pay closer attention to the content of the statements rather than inflections in the witness's voice. If the witness wears sunglasses and heavy make-up, the fact-finder's eye may shift to hand movements and posture. Likewise in a system in which anonymity is routine, defense lawyers may develop new skills to confront anonymous witnesses. Resources once directed to investigating a witness's background can be used to probe more deeply other aspects of the government's case, such as the physical evidence. Over time, as defense lawyers become proficient in questioning anonymous witnesses and fact-finders become skilled in assessing their credibility, the strength of a prosecution's case may come to depend more on the reliability of other kinds of evidence.

In a system in which anonymous testimony is normal, judges may be more likely to develop procedural mechanisms to promote reliability and to protect defendants' interests than in a system in which there is little experience with witnesses whose identities are not revealed. Judges who encounter many cases in which the government seeks anonymity orders may do a better job assessing whether the basis for the government's request is sound. The judge will have experienced a range of methods to protect anonymity and will know which among the choices are necessary in any particular case and which go too far. The judge may also develop better instructions for the jury about anonymity measures. Similarly, to promote reliability, the experienced jurist can allow lines of questioning that might not be allowed with respect to non-anonymous witnesses. A judge experienced with anonymity also can ensure fairness through other aspects of a trial. Where anonymity is ordered, the judge could permit the defense greater leeway with respect to challenging other kinds of evidence that form part of the government's case or permit the defense to call additional witnesses or other evidence to rebut the prosecution's case.

When anonymity is normalized its effects may be measured and examined more easily. Over time studies can be expected to emerge that show when anonymous testimony is reliable and when it entails a high risk of error. Information of this nature will permeate the system as a whole and can be brought to the attention of the fact-finder in particular cases. Normalization can also enhance accountability. When the public understands that any individual can be subject to prosecution involving anonymous testimony – and that this technique is not reserved for war criminals, terrorists or others with whom the general public does not identify – there likely will be stronger public monitoring of the practice. The government itself therefore may face pressure to implement measures that enhance the reliability of anonymous witnesses.

CONCLUSION

The rise of anonymous testimony presents a challenge to adversarial systems that traditionally protect the right of the criminal defendant to confront witnesses. Yet anonymity need not undermine the truth-seeking function of the criminal trial. Accompanying the recent increase in anonymous testimony there might well emerge robust mechanisms that protect the interests of the defendant and promote the accuracy of the trial. As a result, making anonymous testimony a normal part of the criminal justice system may prove more consistent with constitutional values than allowing for anonymity in only exceptional circumstances.

This chapter represents the beginning of an investigation of an issue of increasing importance in criminal justice systems around the world. The purpose here has been to identify the recent rise in anonymous testimony and to outline some possible implications of this phenomenon. Additional research is now needed to provide the basis for properly weighing the risks that anonymity presents against its benefits. In addition to studies of how anonymity plays out in specific jurisdictions, comparative work will allow for a broader assessment of whether and when anonymous testimony comports with or undermines constitutional democracy.

13. Terrorists on trial: an open or closed case?

Clive Walker

INTRODUCTION

Consistent with his 'war on terror' paradigm, President George W. Bush asserted that 'it is not enough to serve our enemies with legal papers'.[1] The resonant primary United Kingdom legal focus in the immediate aftermath of 9/11 was similarly weighted more towards executive intervention through detention without trial rather than court-based criminal prosecution. This vying between executive action and criminal prosecution in the UK never pitched as decisively in favour of executive action as in the US, and is now fading in British domestic law.[2] Yet, the key question remains whether the traditions of openness, orality, and adversarial justice which are so revered by the common law world[3] can be preserved within criminal litigation which heavily impinges on national security interests.[4]

The first section of this chapter will examine the foundations for the reinvigoration of the criminal justice paradigm in the years following the fading of executive interventions. This aspect posits that regular models of criminal justice should predominate in counter-terrorism. The second section will explore the salient implications for British criminal justice, particularly by probing the extent to which the delivery of criminal justice has remained 'normal' or whether elements of exceptionality have

[1] State of the Union Address 20 January 2004 (http://georgewbush-whitehouse.archives.gov/news/releases/2004/01/20040120-7.html).

[2] For details see CLIVE WALKER, TERRORISM AND THE LAW (2011).

[3] For a survey of these principles in other exceptional circumstances, see LOUISE ELLISON, THE ADVERSARIAL PROCESS AND THE VULNERABLE WITNESS (2002).

[4] See further MARY L VOLCANSEK AND JOHN F STACK JR., COURTS AND TERRORISM (2011) p 8.

insinuated themselves into the criminal law or criminal processes, including, in particular, the role of undisclosed or secret evidence. The third section will reflect upon the future trends and implications.

1. THE PRIMACY OF CRIMINAL PROSECUTION

The then Home Officer Minister, Tony McNulty, stated in 2008 that 'prosecution is – first, second and third – the Government's preferred approach when dealing with suspected terrorists'.[5] The British Government might further assert that the primacy of criminal prosecution has been pursued ever since the Diplock Report[6] plotted in 1972 a path out of internment without trial in Northern Ireland. Implementation commenced in 1976, when internment was suspended and non-jury trials came to the fore.

Yet state practices between 2001 and 2005 appeared to amount to a reversal of this prosecution-based strategy. Detention without trial re-appeared under the Anti-terrorism, Crime and Security Act 2001, succeeded by the Prevention of Terrorism Act 2005 (setting up 'control orders') and the Terrorism Prevention and Investigation Measures Act 2011 (replacing control orders with 'TPIMs'). These orders and measures amount to further instances of 'executive intervention', allowing a government minister to impose obligations (such as curfews and restrictions on association and communication) on terrorism suspects without criminal trial.[7] The London bombings of 7 July 2005 aggravated the hostility to criminal justice. The warning of the then Prime Minister, Tony Blair – that 'the rules of the game are changing'[8] – attained traction against foreign suspects, who were subjected to new tactics under the immigration and nationality powers.[9] However, the trend of home-grown 'neighbour terrorism'[10] – the recognition that most terrorists now are

---

[5] Hansard (HC) vol.472 col.561 (21 February 2008).

[6] *Report of the Commission to consider legal procedures to deal with terrorist activities in Northern Ireland* (Cmnd 5185, 1972).

[7] See Clive Walker and Alexander Horne, The Terrorism Prevention and Investigation Measures Act 2011: One Thing But Not Much the Other? CRIMINAL LAW REVIEW 421 (2012).

[8] webarchive.nationalarchives.gov.uk/ and www.number10.gov.uk/Page 8041.

[9] See Clive Walker, The treatment of foreign terror suspects 70 MODERN LAW REVIEW 427 (2007).

[10] Clive Walker, 'Know thine enemy as thyself: Discerning friend from foe under anti-terrorism laws' 32 MELBOURNE LAW REVIEW 275 (2008).

British citizen 'neighbours' and not aliens – has paradoxically encouraged a reversion to criminal prosecution. This domestic trend towards criminal prosecution is evidenced by three indicators.

One is that recent accretions to anti-terrorism legislation have avoided primary reliance upon executive measures. Thus, the Terrorism Act 2006 created new criminal offences, such as incitement of terrorism and preparation of terrorism, and new police investigative powers. The Counter-Terrorism Act 2008 authorised new administrative measures of notification and foreign travel restriction and enhanced sentencing powers, but only for those with criminal convictions. Sections 22 to 27 of that Act allow post-charge questioning.[11] The ongoing march of this policy shift may be illustrated by the replacement of control orders by the Terrorism Prevention and Investigation Measures Act 2011. Though TPIMs remain firmly situated in the genus of 'executive intervention', the extent of restrictive obligations is reduced so as to encourage evidence-gathering for the purpose of prosecution.

The second indicator is the dearth of executive orders. Despite the apocalyptic analysis in 2007 of Jonathan Evans, the Director of the Security Service (MI5), that 2,000 suspects pose a threat to national security,[12] there were just 9 control orders in force when the system closed and no more than 52 ever issued.[13] This reticent usage is not for a want of customers but likely reflects the perception that these executive measures are less cost effective, legally certain, or legitimate compared to criminal prosecution.

The third indicator is a statistical upsurge in criminal terrorist prosecutions, evidenced by returns after 2004/5. Compared to the period in the aftermath of 9/11, there have been relatively high rates of criminal charges and low rates of 'other [executive] action'.

Moving from factual analysis to ethical evaluation, is the prioritisation of regular criminal prosecution preferable to executive measures? There are many arguments in favour of criminal prosecution. That option prizes individual responsibility and equality through the requirement of *mens rea*, whereas collective risk to public or state security predominates in executive measures. There are also gains for system legitimacy through involvement of victims, an open affirmation of public accountability, and the public observance of due process. There may also be some beneficial

---

[11] See Clive Walker, Post-charge questioning of suspects CRIMINAL LAW REVIEW 509 (2008).

[12] www.mi5.gov.uk/output/intelligence-counter-terrorism-and-trust.html.

[13] David Anderson, *Control Orders in 2011* (Home Office, 2012).

Table 13.1 Terrorist-related arrests, charges, convictions and other disposals

Date	Terrorism arrests			Charged (% of arrests)	Convictions (% of charged)	Other action: e.g. deport or control (% of arrests)
	s 41	Other	Total			
2001/02	95	14	109	38 (35%)	12 (32%)	13 (12%)
2002/03	236	38	274	94 (34%)	34 (36%)	40 (15%)
2003/04	178	13	191	90 (47%)	21 (23%)	20 (10%)
2004/05	156	12	168	47 (28%)	21 (45%)	11 (7%)
2005/06	273	12	285	78 (27%)	39 (50%)	15 (5%)
2006/07	191	22	213	102 (48%)	47 (46%)	17 (8%)
2007/08	156	75	231	76 (54%)	27 (36%)	19 (8%)
2008/09	123	67	190	73 (38%)	16 (22%)	18 (9%)
2009/10	76	98	174	58 (33%)	12 (21%)	37 (21%)
Total	1484	351	1835	566 (31%)	229 (40%)	190 (10%)

Source: Home Office, Statistics on Terrorism Arrests and Outcomes Great Britain 11 September 2001 to 31 March 2008 (04/09, 2009); Home Office Statistical Bulletin, Operation of police powers under the Terrorism Act 2000 and subsequent legislation: Arrests, outcomes and stop & searches Quarterly update to September 2010 (04/11, 2010).

impacts via the refinement of laws through their expert application and reapplication.[14]

Amongst the downsides of a criminal justice approach is the reduced capacity of the prosecution to incapacitate in anticipation of a terrorism event. Thus, the scale of the terrorist threat to life and political stability may justify a more pre-emptive strike than, say, in the case of 'normal' murders, most of which arise from a narrow domestic conflict between individuals and pose no political or broader social threat. As the then Director of the Security Service, Dame Eliza Manningham-Buller, warned in 2005:[15]

> We may be confident that an individual or group is planning an attack but that confidence comes from the sort of intelligence I described earlier, patchy and fragmentary and uncertain, to be interpreted and assessed. All too often it falls

[14] See Helen Duffy, Human rights litigation and the 'war on terror' 871 INTERNATIONAL REVIEW OF THE RED CROSS 573, 595 (2007).

[15] www.mi5.gov.uk/output/director-generals-speech-to-the-aivd-2005.html.

short of evidence to support criminal charges to bring an individual before the courts, the best solution if achievable.

The next problem of criminal prosecution arises from the necessity to disclose secret sources, techniques and data, if that evidence is to be used against the accused or may be exculpatory. The beauty of executive procedures is that they can handle 'intelligence information, whose disclosure may involve unacceptable risks'.[16] By contrast, the Government has recently highlighted the drawbacks of formal litigation, and though these comments were sparked by civil litigation, the same problems beset criminal trials. Thus:[17]

> the lack of an effective framework in which the courts can securely consider sensitive material presents a very real challenge in proceedings in which sensitive material is centrally relevant. The Government has strained key international relationships and risked compromise of vital sources and techniques.

The final disadvantage relates to the negative consequences of the courts being perceived as too allied with the interests of the state. The danger is that minority communities, upon whom the effects of anti-terrorism legislation unevenly impact, will feel distrust and a lesser inclination to cooperate with security authorities.[18] Authentication of that phenomenon is, however, disputed.[19]

2. THE CHALLENGES FACED IN CRIMINAL PROSECUTION

While a priority for criminal prosecution is warranted overall, account must still be taken of attendant costs and problems. Aside from the costs of physical security and prolonged imprisonment,[20] both criminal

---

[16] *Review of the Operation of the Prevention of Terrorism Acts 1974 and 1976* (Cmnd.7324, 1978) para 52.

[17] Ministry of Justice, *Justice & Security Green Paper* (Cm. 8194, 2011) para 1.18.

[18] See House of Commons Home Affairs Committee, *Terrorism and Community Relations* (2003–04 HC 165).

[19] Defence Science and Technology Laboratory, *What Perceptions do the UK Public have Concerning the Impact of Counter-terrorism Legislation Implemented since 2000?* (Home Office Occasional Paper 88, 2010).

[20] See CLIVE WALKER, TERRORISM AND THE LAW (2011) chap 6.

offences and criminal processes might be manipulated by the precautionary logic of neutralising imputed risk rather than punishing specific sustained misdeeds, incurring damage to system legitimacy.

2.1 Challenges in Criminal Processes

The enduring compromises within criminal justice process caused by coping with terrorism are illustrated above all by the juryless 'Diplock' courts in Northern Ireland, as already mentioned.[21] The Government's view is that 'there is nothing to show that the system has produced perverse judgments or that it has lowered standards'.[22] Some defendants may even prefer the more detailed and reasoned verdict of a judge to that of the Delphic jury verdict.[23] However, Diplock courts are generally viewed as, at best, second class justice and, at worst, devices to secure convictions through case-hardened judges.[24] Moreover, many quashed verdicts have emerged after peacetime reviews of convictions,[25] and more than 200 cases are reportedly pending.[26] The special criminal justice system to deal with terrorism in Northern Ireland[27] is set to endure, but the lessons from Northern Ireland are applied with great caution to England and Wales, contrary to the more general claims of the 'normalisation' of special powers or the 'contamination' of 'normal' laws.[28]

The drive to criminalise terrorism has entailed some modifications to criminal justice processes in England and Wales. Section 16 of the Terrorism Act 2006 provides that preparatory hearings are mandatory in terrorism cases, to ensure that enhanced and experienced judicial management is applied to every terrorism case upon indictment. This change has been underlined by the Protocol on the Management of Terrorism Cases issued by the President of the Queen's Bench Division.[29] The Protocol requires all indictable only[30] 'terrorism cases' to be managed via the 'terrorism cases list' by the Presiding Judges of the South Eastern Circuit and other nominated judges of the High Court and to be tried

---

21 See now Justice and Security (Northern Ireland) Act 2007.

22 Hansard HC vol 301 col 173 (18 November 1997), Adam Ingram.

23 See Taxquet v. Belgium, App no 926/05, 13 January 2009, para 48.

24 See Clive WALKER, TERRORISM AND THE LAW (2011) chap 11.

25 See LAURIE ELKS, RIGHTING MISCARRIAGES OF JUSTICE (2008) chap 13.

26 See THE GUARDIAN 12 October 2010 at 12.

27 It was extended for two years in 2011: SI 2011/1720.

28 See Paddy Hillyard, The normalisation of special powers in LAW, ORDER AND THE AUTHORITARIAN STATE (Phil Scraton ed, 1987).

29 2nd ed., Courts Service, 2007.

30 As defined by the Crime and Disorder Act 1998, ss 51, 52.

by a nominated judge of the High Court. This attention to detail and the imposition of senior judicial active involvement is generally to be welcomed as assigning the most experienced trial judges to demanding cases. But it potentially dilutes the principle of trial by local peers and could threaten further if the band of selected judges is small (risking the 'case-hardening' that allegedly occurred in Northern Ireland) and if those few judges allow their managerial concerns about cost and delay to become overweening. In *R v. Omar Khyam*,[31] the grievance was that the judges appeared so concerned about delays and costs that that they should have recused themselves from trial duties.

Next, there are pressures on the equality of arms because defence resources do not match those of the police and prosecution, such as for the employment of experts.[32] Another resource issue is that the payment of lawyers in 'Very High Cost (Crime) Cases' (which include major terrorism trials) is under pressure because of austerity measures.[33] Fees will be reduced by 13.5 percent over the next three years.[34] In addition, the construction of the defence case may be hampered by high security conditions.[35] Defendants also face media prejudice, which is encouraged by loose talk from police and politicians.[36]

Pressure also applies to the hallowed principle of 'open justice'.[37] First, there is the proliferation of special advocates. These legal counsellors perform a key role in executive-based processes such as control order and TPIM proceedings.[38] Their role is to 'represent the interests' of a relevant party in control order proceedings where that party and his legal representative are excluded from the proceedings because of the sensitivity of the information. Their function will comprise not only testing the Government's case to the full (though without client instructions in regard to the secret evidence) but also testing the very need for closed

---

31 [2008] EWCA Crim 1612.

32 See Ali N Bajwa, Learn by trial and terror 151 SOLICITORS' JOURNAL 7 (2007).

33 See Access to Justice Act 1999, s 15(5); Criminal Defence Service (Very High Cost Cases) Regulations 2008 SI 2008/40.

34 www.legalservices.gov.uk/criminal/very_high_cost_criminal_cases.asp.

35 For an extreme example, see R v. Benbrika [2008] VSC 80.

36 See R v. McCann and others [1991] 92 Cr App Rep 239; Lord Carlile, *Operation Pathway* (Home Office, 2009) para 40.

37 Scott v. Scott [1913] AC 417; A-G v. Leveller Magazine Ltd [1979] AC 440; R v. Felixstowe Justices, ex p Leigh [1987] QB 582.

38 See Prevention of Terrorism Act 2005, Sch; TPIM Act 2011, Sch 4.

sessions and closed evidence.[39] Their impact remains controversial. Lord Steyn declared that 'the special advocate procedure undermines the very essence of elementary justice',[40] though the European Court of Human Rights has expressed cautious approbation.[41] The House of Lords has ventured that special advocates would be unobjectionable in principle within criminal proceedings.[42] But the later precedents of *R v. Davis*[43] and *Al Rawi v. Security Service*[44] indicate that the courts will block any function creep in the absence of clear statutory approval.

The next unwelcome aspect of the trend towards secrecy in process is the suppression of judgments, even those of the criminal courts. Parts of the judgment regarding the fertiliser bomb plot in *R v. Omar Khyam* were redacted.[45] Virtually all of the judgment in the acquittal on appeal of Danny Morrison has been suppressed.[46] Morrison, a leader of Sinn Féin, had been convicted of being an accomplice in the kidnap of a police informant. On appeal, the prosecution conceded that non-disclosure undermined the conviction but would not reveal further facts.

The rules of evidence have not been altered substantially in recent terrorism prosecutions in England and Wales, in contrast to past experience in Northern Ireland.[47] Critics might argue that the damage has already been done and that changes to the right to silence and hearsay have been sustained in 'normal' laws rather than being confined to counter-terrorism laws.[48] Problems with admission and disclosure do, however, persist. The suppression of evidence through 'public interest

---

39 See Constitutional Affairs Committee, *The Operation of the Special Immigration Appeals Commission (SIAC) and the Use of Special Advocates* (2004–05 HC 323-I) para 61.

40 R v. Roberts [2005] UKHL 45, para 88. See further JUSTICE, SECRET EVIDENCE (2009) Pt IV; Mark Chamberlain, Update on procedural fairness in closed proceedings 28 CIVIL JUSTICE QUARTERLY 448 (2009); Gus van Harten, Weaknesses of adjudication in the face of secret evidence 13 INTERNATIONAL JOURNAL OF EVIDENCE AND PROOF 1, 15–17 (2009).

41 A v. United Kingdom App no 3455/05, 19 February 2009, paras 219, 220.

42 R v. H [2004] UKHL 3, para 22.

43 [2008] UKHL 36.

44 [2011] UKSC 34.

45 See on appeal [2008] EWCA Crim 1612.

46 [2009] NICA 1.

47 See especially Terrorism Act 2000, s 76 (which was ended by SI 2002/2141).

48 See Criminal Justice and Public Order Act 1994, ss 34–39; Criminal Justice Act 2003, Pt XI.

immunity' claims[49] has been handled tolerably well in criminal cases (though the Government is dissatisfied with this protection, as shall be discussed later). An exception is that it is envisaged that the future admissibility of intercept data as evidence pursuant to the *Chilcot Report* will require special rules to nullify any 'quixotic' judge who creates a 'material risk' to security.[50]

Another category of potential evidence which causes discomfort in terrorism cases concerns the admissibility of evidence obtained from torture.[51] The Law Lords rejected the use of such evidence in *A v. Secretary of State for the Home Department (No.2)*,[52] but the decision embodied important limits. Its emphasis upon torture belies an indulgence towards inhuman and degrading treatment, thereby ignoring the evil design of regimes such as Guantánamo.[53] Furthermore, while the victim need only advance some plausible evidence to raise the issue of torture and then it is for the prosecution or tribunal to inquire; where the tribunal is left in a state of suspicion about whether torture was used, the evidence can be admitted, which could be seen as giving the benefit of the doubt to torturers.[54] Another grey area where the courts have not been sufficiently strict concerns a continuum in joint operations with foreign states (notably Pakistan), whereby 'collaboration' might arise from briefings or even regular relations with unwholesome regimes.[55]

---

49 These are claims by the state or state agencies that the public interest in secrecy outweighs the normal rules of disclosure: Crown Prosecution Service, Disclosure Manual (www.cps.gov.uk/legal/d_to_g/disclosure_manual/index.html) chap 13.

50 *Privy Council Review of intercept as evidence* (Cm.7324, 2008) para 63; *The Home Office's Response to Terrorist Attacks* (Cm 7788, 2010) pp 10–13.

51 See R v. Khyam [2008] EWCA Crim 1612; R v. Ahmed [2010] EWCA Crim 1551.

52 [2005] UKHL 71.

53 For current UK military policy, see Ministry of Defence, Joint Doctrine Publication 1-10: Captured Persons (CPERS) (2nd ed., 2011).

54 Compare Selmouni v. France, App no 25803/94, 1999-V (1999) para 101.

55 This more expansive notion of 'collaboration' was rejected in R v. Ahmed and Ahmed [2011] EWCA Crim 184. See further Cabinet Office, *Consolidated Guidance to Intelligence Officers and Service Personnel on the Detention and Interviewing of Detainees Overseas, and on the Passing and Receipt of Intelligence Relating to Detainees* (2010); Equality and Human Rights Commission v. The Prime Minister [2011] EWHC 2401 (Admin); Foreign & Commonwealth Office, *Torture and Mistreatment Reporting Guidance and Overseas Justice and Security Guide* (2011).

The next problematic source of evidence concerns agents and informants. The handling of agents and informants to combat state crimes is a recurrent problem in the Irish context.[56] Recent examples have included the convictions of O'Farrell, Rafferty and McDonald, in May 2002 for attempting to acquire weaponry for the Real IRA.[57] The defendants were the objects of 'luring' and 'skilful manipulation' by British Security Service agents, pretending to be Iraqi Government representatives, who met them in Slovakia.[58] The Regulation of Investigatory Powers Act 2000, section 29, which imposes more formal administrative controls over 'covert human intelligence sources', may curtail some excesses but does not impose regular independent oversight. The fact that the informants against *jihadi* terrorism may be run by overseas agencies, such as the CIA, is a further twist that hampers judicial accountability.

Despite the manifold challenges outlined in this section, Lord Diplock's policy of criminal prosecution by processes that satisfy the due process demands of Article 6 of the European Convention on Human Rights remains valid and compelling. Nevertheless, the criminal processes in terrorist cases bear extra pressure to be speedy and to produce the 'right' result. Each failure to convict will bring calls for compromise. For example, acquittals on the principal charges in Operation Overt following the first 'Airline Liquid Bomb' trial in September 2008 caused Assistant Metropolitan Chief Commissioner Peter Clarke to complain about the jury's failure to sustain convictions 'despite strong evidence', though he also conceded that there is 'no need for military commissions or the juryless Diplock courts of Northern Ireland'.[59] Still, the very mention of that agenda shows that 'normal' trials are themselves constantly on trial.[60]

2.2 Challenges in Criminal Offences

The design of criminal offences within anti-terrorism legislation evinces several signs of adaptation to the precautionary dynamic of risk aversion.

---

[56] See McKevitt v. DPP [2003] IESC9/03; Breslin v. McKenna [2005] NIQB 18; R v. Stewart [2010] NICC 8; R v. McCaugherty [2011] NICA 45; Case of MC, (Vilnius Regional Court, 21 October 2011).

[57] [2005] EWCA Crim 1945, [2005] EWCA Crim 1970.

[58] *Ibid.*, para 19.

[59] The Times 9 September 2008 p 7.

[60] See N. Morris, Reid attacks judges who hamper 'life and death' terrorism battle, The Independent 10 August 2006 p 4.

Three consequent problems can be identified: net-widening; guilt by association; and reverse burdens of proof.

Net-widening first arises through the utilisation of the term 'terrorism', as very broadly defined by section 1 of the Terrorism Act 2000. Without analysing in full the meaning of that term, the point here is that there is no offence of terrorism *per se* and section 1 deliberately exceeds by some way the bounds of any single offence, though overall it remains sufficiently grounded within the notion of criminality to satisfy the precepts of Article 5 of the European Convention on Human Rights as a ground for arrest.[61] However, as well as special policing powers, the foremost special offences embody the blurred concept of 'terrorism', including membership offences under the Terrorism Act 2000, Part II, and offences of the possession of preparatory materials or information under sections 57 and 58 of the Terrorism Act 2000.[62]

A second aspect of net-widening is the criminalisation of foreign terrorism committed overseas and aimed against foreign regimes, sometimes without regard to the legitimacy of those regimes or whether any threat is posed within the United Kingdom or for British citizens abroad.[63] The Terrorism Act 2000 extends the proscription of terrorist organisations beyond the Irish context; most of the newly listed organisations relate to *jihadi* terrorism.[64] The Terrorism Act 2000 also reformulated the definition of 'terrorism' in section 1(4)(d) expressly to encompass actions directed against foreign governments. In addition, there is a growing trend of according extra-territorial effect to terrorism offences, such as by the Terrorism Act 2006, section 17, so that prosecutions become viable even when 'terrorism' is plotted against foreign tyrannies.[65] One response has been to impose the filter of consent by a Law Officer for prosecutions with a foreign element,[66] though this filter does not reverse the chilling effect on the political activities of émigré groups.

---

61 Brogan v. United Kingdom, App nos 11209, 11234, 11266/84, 11386/85, Ser. A 145-B (1988) para 50.

62 See CLIVE WALKER, TERRORISM AND THE LAW (2011) chap 5. Defences under s 58 were held to be sufficiently certain in Jobe v. United Kingdom, App no 48278/09, 14 June 2011.

63 See DAVID ANDERSON, *The Terrorism Acts in 2011* (Home Office, 2012) paras 4.38–40.

64 See CLIVE WALKER, TERRORISM AND THE LAW (2011) chap 8.

65 See R v. F [2007] EWCA Crim 243; R v. Gul [2012] EWCA Crim 280.

66 Terrorism Act 2000, s 117; Terrorism Act 2006, s 37; Counter-Terrorism Act 2008, s 29.

Guilt by association through offences of membership of proscribed organisations (such as the Irish Republican Army and Al-Qa'ida) is the next problem engendered by the criminalisation of terrorism. As operated in Britain at least, the main answer to the danger of guilt by association has again been a very low rate of prosecutions: there were no convictions from 1990 to 2001 and just 55 charges between 2001 and 2007. Consequently, the membership offence largely serves a symbolic purpose. Again, however, the chilling effect remains considerable.

The third development that has tainted criminal law concerns the deployment of 'reverse burdens' in special precursor offences by which specified factual presumptions are sustained unless the defendant meets at least an evidential burden of proof of an exculpatory matter (such as a statutory defence). The problem is relevant to membership offences just described,[67] but it has become acute and recurrent in connection with offences of possession contrary to sections 57 (possession of articles relevant to terrorism, subject to statutory defences related to lack of knowledge of presence or lack of relevant purpose) and 58 (possession of information relevant to terrorism, subject to proof of reasonable excuse) of the Terrorism Act 2000.[68] The judicial responses to these reverse burdens have been complex, but, mindful of Article 6(2) of the European Convention on Human Rights, the courts have ensured that the switch in burden of proof is interpreted as 'evidential' and not 'legal', in other words that the defendant must simply introduce enough evidence to question the issue rather than proving innocence beyond doubt.[69] Various other interpretive efforts have imposed curtailments.[70] But these judicial restraints are evaded in the later special offence, section 5 of the Terrorism Act 2006, by which an offence arises if, with the intention of (a) committing acts of terrorism; or (b) assisting another to commit such acts, a person engages in any conduct in preparation for giving effect to that intention.[71] This wording is designed to intervene beyond the normal limits of the criminal law concept of an 'attempt', which is defined as activity which is 'more than merely preparatory'.[72] The concern is that

---

67 See Attorney General's Reference (No. 4 of 2002) [2004] UKHL 43.

68 See Clive Walker, Terrorism and the Law (2011) chap 5.

69 R v. Director of Public Prosecutions, ex parte Kebilene [2000] 2 AC 326; Sheldrake v. Director of Public Prosecutions; Attorney General's Reference (No. 4 of 2002) [2004] UKHL 43.

70 See especially R v. G [2009] UKHL 13; R v. AY [2010] EWCA Crim 762.

71 See R v. Roddis [2009] EWCA 585.

72 Criminal Attempts Act 1981, s 1(1).

equivocal or foolish dabbling in the fringes of extremism by individuals with neither the intention nor resolve to go further can be criminalised.

The overall impact is that more drastic alterations have been sustained with respect to criminal offences than with respect to criminal processes. Two questions thereby arise. The first is why the government and legislature should feel more confident about intervention into the first area than the second? Perhaps a reason is that the judiciary has been more hostile to procedural changes, as they concern matters where the judges claim expertise and control.[73] Judges may be more relaxed about criminal offences since their signal is as much directed to the police as to the courts. There may also appear to be less threat from very specialist offences which are rarely used compared to procedural changes which can affect more cases. In addition, international law, such as the Council of Europe's Convention on the Prevention of Terrorism 2005 (the basis for section 5 above), has sanctioned some of these developments. The second question concerns the overall impact in terms of the spectrum between normal and exceptional justice. These criminal offences have not created exceptional criminal justice, since Article 6 of the European Convention on Human Rights is still observed. Besides, similar trends have occurred in other areas of criminal justice, affecting fraudsters, sex offenders, drug traffickers, and gangsters.[74]

3. FUTURE MANIPULATION IN TERRORISM CRIMINALISATION

This final section will speculate about potential future reforms that might be pressed in the name of criminalisation as the prime counter-terrorism response.

3.1 Future Criminal Offences

As for offences, pressures might in future build in three directions.

The first is to persist with the extension of jurisdictional coverage, so as to prosecute foreign attacks. Here, however, much has already been achieved, and more pressing problems relate to the effectiveness and

---

[73] See International Transport Roth GmbH v. Secretary of State for the Home Department [2002] EWCA Civ 158 at paras 85, 86 *per* Laws LJ.

[74] See Criminal Justice Act 1987, Youth Justice and Criminal Evidence Act 1999, Pt II, Drug Trafficking Act 1994, Serious Organised Crime and Police Act 2005.

probity of international police cooperation in investigations. In addition, the transformation of United Kingdom terrorism offences into offences of universal jurisdiction would lack legitimacy and respect in so far as they are not backed by international law.[75]

The second pressure might be to create ever-wider precursor offences. One precedent, actively raised by the Home Office in 2007,[76] is offered by the French Penal Code, article 421.2.1 – the charge of *association de malfaiteurs en relation avec une entreprise terroriste*. However, critics argue that such charges permit convictions based on 'a minimum of objective, independent evidence and a maximum of speculation, innuendo and inference, some of which is supplied by sources of questionable impartiality and integrity'.[77]

The third pressure might be to revive offences against the state, such as treason, in order to impart a more ringing form of denunciation. But much of the drive behind this idea dissipated once the death penalty was removed as a punishment for treason in 1998.[78] The woeful British experiences of miscarriages of justice in terrorism cases[79] as well as the technicalities surrounding this ancient crime[80] have muted enthusiasm for revival.

3.2 Future Criminal Process – The Admission and Disclosure of Evidence

Turning to criminal processes, pressures are being felt to migrate to the lowest common denominator of the due process standards. In response, the courts have asserted that even someone subject to executive measures 'must be given sufficient information about the allegations against him to enable him to give effective instructions in relation to those allegations'.[81] The frequent judicial interventions flowing from this bottom line

---

75 Hansard (HC) vol.438 col.1045 (3 November 2005), Dominic Grieve.

76 See Home Office, *Terrorist Investigations and the French Examining Magistrates System* (2007) p 4.

77 MICHAEL MCCOLGAN AND ALESSANDRO ATTANASIO, FRANCE: PAVING THE WAY FOR ARBITRARY JUSTICE (1999) p 35.

78 Crime and Disorder Act 1998, s 36. Sedition was abolished by the Coroners and Justice Act 2009, s 73.

79 See CLIVE WALKER AND KEIR STARMER, MISCARRIAGES OF JUSTICE (1999) chap 2.

80 See Graham S McBain, Abolishing the crimes of treason 81 AUSTRALIAN LAW JOURNAL 94 (2007).

81 Re AF (No. 3) [2009] UKHL 28 at para 59.

make the executive orders less attractive and encourage prosecutions and surveillance instead.

The systemic rules for control orders and TPIMs include several radical changes, such as that the court may 'receive evidence that would not, but for this rule, be admissible'[82] and that evidence may be heard in the absence of the controlled person or his legal representative subject to the appointment of vetted lawyers as 'special advocates'.[83] By contrast, no such adaptations have been made to regular criminal proceedings, and none is immediately on the horizon with the one exception (highlighted previously) of the potential admission of communications intercept evidence.[84]

The notion that some 'rebalancing' of interests in litigation might be necessary has been encouraged in official discourse because of the experience of civil claimants who have alleged British complicity in abusive treatment abroad. The most notable suit, brought by Binyam Mohamed, also involved the further delicate problem of his demand for the disclosure of information held by the United Kingdom Government which had been provided by the US Department of State,[85] the disclosure of which left Secretary Hillary Clinton 'deeply disappointed'.[86] The Court of Appeal's judgment was also notable for the comment by Lord Neuberger that 'some SyS officials appear to have a dubious record when it comes to human rights and coercive techniques, and indeed when it comes to frankness about the United Kingdom's involvement with the mistreatment of Mr Mohamed by US officials'.[87] The United Kingdom Government thereafter settled the cases of 16 former detainees, allegedly at a cost of £10m[88] and also established an inquiry into the events (since

---

[82] Civil Procedure Rules (CPR) 76.26, 80.22.

[83] Prevention of Terrorism Act 2005, Sch. and CPR 76.24; TPIM Act 2011, Sch 4 and CPR 80.19.

[84] See *Privy Council Review of intercept as evidence* (Cm 7324, 2008) paras 53, 58; Advisory Group of Privy Counsellors, *Intercept as Evidence* (Cm 7760, 2009); Lord Carlile, *Third Report of the Independent Reviewer pursuant to Section 14(3) of the Prevention of Terrorism Act 2005* (2008) para 38.

[85] R (Binyam Mohamed) v. Secretary of State for the Foreign & Commonwealth Office [2008] EWHC 2048, 2100, 2519, 2549, 2973 (Admin), [2009] EWHC 152 (Admin), [2010] EWCA Civ 65. See further Joint Committee on Human Rights, *Allegations of UK complicity in torture* (2008–09 HL 152/HC 230) and Government Reply (Cm 7714, 2009).

[86] http://news.bbc.co.uk/1/hi/uk/8509787.stm.

[87] [2010] EWCA Civ 158 at para 17.

[88] THE TIMES 17 November 2010 at 18.

abandoned because of superseding criminal investigations)[89] and into the legal rules.

The results of the latter inquiry were published as the *Justice & Security Green Paper* in November 2011.[90] The acute mischief, which the Government feels keenly, is that the growing reliance on intelligence activity in the protection of the public, allied with the greater activism of the judiciary (as encouraged by the Human Rights Act 1998), means that more and more cases involve 'evidence of a genuinely sensitive nature' and 'have a disproportionately high impact, including in terms of the strain that they place on our crucial relationships with international partners'.[91] The particular downside for the Government is that when it appears as a defendant, it may be able to convince a judge to suppress sensitive evidence under the doctrine of public interest immunity, but this option incurs important drawbacks:[92]

> judgments in these cases risk being reached based only on a partial and potentially misleading picture of the overall facts ... [or] the case is struck out for a lack of a mechanism with which to hear it.

The detriments include not only the frustration of the Government as a litigant but also a diminished opportunity for the courts to scrutinise the security agencies and for the public to be better informed. The Government wants to be able to contest fully court claims and to adduce sensitive evidence in pursuance of its defence but not to reveal that evidence as a normal consequence of open justice. This stance might be said to be equivalent to wanting to have one's cake and to eat it, too, while the benefits to other stakeholders (including the public who are unlikely to be educated by secret evidence) are not evident.

The primary route by which the *Green Paper* seeks to secure an adjustment is by extrapolating from the special procedures in executive counter-terrorism measures (and from the Special Immigration Appeals Commission Act 1997) and applying them to all civil proceedings potentially involving national security. These are summarised as 'Closed Material Procedures (CMPs)'.[93] CMPs are claimed to be 'capable of

---

89 Hansard (HC) vol. 538 col.751 (18 January 2012), Kenneth Clarke.
90 (Cm 8194, 2011).
91 *Ibid.*, para 1.51.
92 *Ibid.,* para 1.52.
93 *Ibid.*, para 1.28.

satisfying the requirements of the ECHR',[94] a rightly hesitant claim in the light of the examination of control orders under Article 6.

The Government has determined to proceed with a Bill before Parliament for the session 2012–13,[95] but there might be several reasons for rejecting its key proposal.[96] Foremost is that the *Green Paper* offers no reflection on whether procedures in the executive measures jurisdictions represent in some sense 'special' categories. Thus, it might be argued that they involve processes where rights claims may be attenuated because the claimants are foreigners or because the obligations (such as TPIMs) involve no more than a temporary status. In this light, it is misleading for the *Green Paper* to claim simply that 'CMPs have been a part of the framework of the courts of the UK since 1997'.[97] The *Green Paper* is advocating the undesirable 'normalisation' of special powers or the 'contamination' of 'normal' laws.

Finally, consideration should be given to whether the solutions in the *Green Paper* for civil process represent an apt pathway for the problems caused by the ventilation of security information in criminal process. At the outset, it must be recognised that the *Green Paper* emphatically disclaims any seepage into criminal proceedings:[98]

> Civil and criminal proceedings in England and Wales are fundamentally different. In civil cases, the courts adjudicate on disputes between parties under the civil law. In criminal cases, it is usually the state which prosecutes individuals for the commission of criminal offences; where defendants are convicted, they face criminal sanctions including imprisonment. Due to the understandably more onerous requirements of the right to a fair trial in criminal cases, the rules concerning the use and protection of sensitive evidence are different to those in civil cases.

Yet, given that CMPs already represent a decisive phase of seepage from special process into normal process, who can guarantee that there will not be another bout of seepage from civil to criminal, especially since the

---

94 *Ibid.*, para 1.29.

95 Justice and Security Bill 2012–13 HL 27. See also Ministry of Justice, *Government Response to the public consultation on Justice and Security* (Cm 8364, 2012).

96 See further Joint Committee on Human Rights, *The Justice and Security Green Paper* (2010–12 HL 286 / HC 1777) and Government Reply (Cm. 8365, 2012; Tim Otty, The slow creep of complacency and the soul of justice EUROPEAN HUMAN RIGHTS LAW REVIEW 267 (2012).

97 *Ibid.*, para 2.3.

98 (Cm. 8194, 2011) p 7.

judicial House of Lords has declared elements of CMPs to be unobjectionable in principle and since a recent declaration of the Parliamentary Assembly of the Council of Europe makes no distinction between civil and criminal process?[99]

3.3 Future Criminal Process – The Appropriate Tribunal

'National security courts' are not on the United Kingdom Government's counter-terrorism agenda. Juries largely survive in Britain, aside from the judge-only criminal trials (not confined to terrorism) when there is proof of jury intimidation under the Criminal Justice Act 2003, section 44,[100] and aside from the unique non-jury Scottish trial (in the Netherlands) of those accused of the Lockerbie bombing.[101] Further incursions into jury trial have been mooted for coroners' inquests[102] but were finally defeated in the context of the Coroners and Justice Bill 2008–09, clause 11, though the tensions of handling sensitive evidence have recently resulted in the setting up of the Holland Inquiry as a prelude to an inquest into the police shooting of an alleged gangster.[103] Even the Ministry of Justice's *Justice & Security Green Paper* shows little enthusiasm for a specialist national security court:[104]

> proposals to establish a specialist court carry significant risks and unclear benefits. Establishing such a structure would represent a significant cultural upheaval for many members of the judiciary and would unnecessarily distinguish cases involving sensitive material from other types of proceedings, against the usual case management practices of our courts.

An ultimate concern is whether the regular criminal trial system can measure up to the multiple difficulties of the rehearsal of extensive and complex evidence and the protection of security identities and methods when there are multiple offences, activities, and confederates, as can arise in the trials of the most notorious and egregious terrorists? Three arguments might be offered in favour of the fitness of criminal trials.

---

[99] Resolution 1838, 6 October 2011, para 2. See also Recommendation 1983, 6 October 2011, para 2.3.

[100] See R v. Twomey [2009] EWCA 1035.

[101] See High Court of Justiciary (Proceedings in the Netherlands) Order 1998, SI 1998/2251.

[102] For the use of juries in inquests see Coroners Act 1988, s 8(3), which will be replaced by the Coroners and Justice Act 2009, s 7.

[103] See http://azellerodneyinquiry.independent.gov.uk.

[104] (Cm. 8194, 2011) para 2.60.

First, it is telling that US Attorney General Eric Holder selected the five most notorious prisoners (including Khalid Sheikh Mohammed) to be transferred from indefinite detention at Guantánamo Bay and to be slated for trial in the Federal criminal courts in Manhattan.[105] True enough, this policy was later blocked by Congressional legislation,[106] and so the Military Commissions have resumed operation.[107] However, this episode does demonstrate that when legal, rather than political, considerations prevail, the criminal trial of the most notorious terrorists of all remains the favoured option of lawyers.[108]

The second argument is that it is precisely in cases of greatest notoriety that efforts should be made to accentuate normality in order to maximise legitimacy.

The third argument is that if a special trial process is determined to be the most appropriate, then perhaps internationalisation rather than militarisation might offer a more promising model to avoid the charge of 'victor's justice'.[109] The compromises to the Lockerbie trial processes,[110] allied to doubts about the verdicts,[111] demonstrate some of the downsides to nationalistic approaches to criminal process. Nevertheless, the Nuremberg trials demonstrate that it is possible to frame criminal charges and processes for defendants, who are accused not just of 3,000 murders but of millions, and the establishment of international criminal tribunals and the International Criminal Court underlines the faith in judicial trial processes.

---

105 www.justice.gov/ag/speeches/2009/ag-speech-091113.html, 13 November 2009.

106 National Defense Authorization Act for Fiscal Year 2011, s 1032 ('Prohibition on the use of funds for the transfer or release of individuals detained at United States Naval Station, Guantanamo Bay, Cuba').

107 See www.mc.mil/CASES/MilitaryCommissions.aspx.

108 See www.justice.gov/iso/opa/ag/speeches/2011/ag-speech-110404.html.

109 See Geoffrey Robertson, Fair trial for terrorists? in HUMAN RIGHTS IN THE 'WAR ON TERROR' (Richard A Wilson ed, 2005) 169.

110 See *Agreement between the Government of the United Kingdom of Great Britain and Northern Ireland and the Government of the Kingdom of the Netherlands concerning a Scottish Trial in the Netherlands 1998* (Cm 4378, 1999).

111 See Megrahi v. HM Advocate [2008] HCJAC 15, [2008] HCJAC 58.

CONCLUSIONS

The resurgence of criminal justice solutions to terrorism in the United Kingdom and their partial displacement of executive interventions are welcome trends. Nevertheless, the fundamental paradox of public proof beyond doubt in a climate of precautionary and often secretive risk management has fostered a slide towards minimum standards of due process. The British struggle with this paradox suggests that a willingness to engage in reflection and reform (ranging from the Diplock Report on special courts to the Macdonald Report in 2011 on the reform of control orders)[112] can produce positive counter-terrorism legal developments all of which affirm the primacy of prosecution.

The British experience also underlines the elasticity of 'normal' and 'special' in criminal justice. Thus, the 'normal' criminal justice system is able to recalibrate what is 'normal', illustrated by sweeping changes to the right to silence in the Criminal Justice and Public Order Act 1994. Equally, elasticity applies in the realm of the 'special', ranging from a 'Diplock' system in Northern Ireland through to the more piecemeal features in Britain. As a result, the vital questions regarding the criminalisation of terrorism are not so much about 'exceptionalism' or specialism. Rather, the legal system must assess, first, whether the new format addresses the problem of terrorism effectively and, second, whether it does so in a way that affirms legitimacy. Secrecy is unlikely to assist such claim to legitimacy.

---

[112] Lord Macdonald, *Review of Counter Terrorism and Security Powers* (Cm. 8003, 2011).

14. In/visible courts: military tribunals as other spaces

Ori Aronson*

INTRODUCTION

Liberal democracy's insistence on open, visible, and publicly accessible courts as an institutional staple of the ideal of the rule of law has faced a substantial challenge in the era of the legal fight against terrorism. As terrorist-suspects are apprehended and as detaining countries seek to 'bring them to justice', the requirements of security and secrecy as well as the politics of wartime sentiment have led democracies to devise an institutional alternative to regular civilian courts in the form of military tribunals. These forums, such as US military commissions, have been criticized as closed, secret, and inaccessible courts, and as such as affronts to the ideal of the rule of law and to the moral commitments of liberal democracy more generally.[1]

This chapter seeks to qualify these plausible critiques to military adjudication. I would like to suggest that in some contexts and in some respects, creating separate judicial forums for terrorism-related criminal adjudication might in fact enhance the visibility of the political and moral stakes involved in such exercises of state power; namely legal-judicial power employed as part of a conflict that retains essential qualities of ongoing war. I use Foucault's concept of *heterotopia* in order to capture the unique qualities of military tribunals – spaces that societies establish in order to distinguish among the 'normal' elements of moral and political life (civilian adjudication) and those which are their essential *others* (military tribunals).

* The author thanks Hila Gafni for research assistance.

[1] See, e.g. Harold Hongju Koh, *The Case Against Military Commissions*. 96 A.J.I.L. 337, 338–42 (2002); Jordan J. Paust, *Still Unlawful: The Obama Military Commissions, Supreme Court Holdings, and Deviant Dicta in the D.C. Circuit*, 45 CORNELL INT'L L.J. 367 (2012).

Military tribunals are revealed in this analysis as sites that draw attention – and in this sense are constantly visible – precisely because of the normative challenges they pose to mainstream democratic institutions. Secrecy turns out to enhance visibility – if not to all aspects of the trial, then to its exceptional existence. While this understanding does not ensure in itself that military tribunals are not used to violate individuals' rights, it does call upon us to consider whether certain kinds of trials are better left in a status of otherness, rather than being incorporated in the normal processes of civilian adjudication, and thus losing much of their unique nature.

I proceed in comparative fashion, discussing both the US experience with military commissions in the past decade, and the military courts system used by Israel in the Palestinian West Bank for more than four decades. While the two systems are different in many ways, they also share some fundamental institutional similarities – especially with respect to visibility and accessibility – which I believe make a comparative analysis worthwhile.

In the latter part of the chapter I focus on two specific, high-profile prosecutions undertaken by the US and Israel in the past decade – of Khalid Sheikh Mohammed by the US and of Marwan Barghouthi by Israel. Both cases involved strategic choices of forums for prosecution: Mohammed was about to be tried in federal civilian court, only to remain eventually under the jurisdiction of the military commission in Guantánamo Bay; Barghouthi was made an exception and prosecuted in Israeli civilian court, unlike most Palestinian terrorist-suspects. Both ordeals involved calculations of public image and democratic accountability, and have exemplified the equivocal nature of jurisdictional choices in trying terrorism-suspects.[2]

The chapter does not offer a definite resolution to the question of the most appropriate forum for holding terrorism-related trials. Rather, it seeks to define and reveal some costs and benefits involved in such choices, ones that are often drowned out by vocal partisan preferences to one kind of jurisdictional solution or another. Secrecy is recast as a political *strategy*, rather than as a political ideology. As such it can be employed in the furtherance of multiple, even conflicting, visions of legality and adjudication in time of war.

---

[2] While not all legal systems allow for executive discretion with regard to the forum of prosecution, the very creation of multiple jurisdictions requires designers to strategically devise allocation mechanisms among competing forums. In this respect the discussion of the US and Israeli examples may be instructive to other systems as well.

1. FIGHTING BY PROSECUTING

1.1 Choice of Forum in Terrorism Trials

One of the recurrent challenges facing democracies that seek to employ legal means in the struggle against terrorism is the institutional setting for trying terrorist suspects. The challenge emerges once the suspect is apprehended and removed from the 'battlefield', and ceases to be an immediate threat. These detainees, who are not treated as prisoners of war, are presumed to have engaged in illegal acts of violence, stripping them of the status of 'privileged belligerent' under international humanitarian law. Seeking means to 'bring to justice' such persons in a manner compatible with notions of the rule of law, capturing countries have therefore resorted to various modes of criminal adjudication.

Once prosecution is sought, a jurisdictional choice ensues. In various countries around the world – the US and Israel will serve as examples – multiple forums have become available for trying terrorist suspects. The familiar choice, highlighted in the post-9/11 era, is between the country's civilian court system, which would normally have criminal jurisdiction over acts of terrorism perpetrated against the state or its citizens, and a military forum for trying belligerents, which would derive its jurisdiction from a combination of national laws and international norms.

Perhaps the most familiar debate waged in this respect in the past decade has concerned the military commissions, re-instituted by the US as part of its post-9/11 operations. A more consistent military tribunal system of comparative character – the military courts system – has been implemented by Israel in the Palestinian Territories, under belligerent occupation since 1967. To a large extent, both systems – American military commissions and Israeli military courts – exercise concurrent jurisdiction along with the countries' civilian courts over many terrorism-related prosecutions. Both systems have also garnered their fair measures of criticism and detraction for failing to comply with common baselines of procedural justice and defendants' rights protection, including specifically the requirements of visibility and publicity of the judicial process. In both cases the choice of forum therefore implicates rule-of-law concerns of secrecy in adjudication. Following is a brief exposition of the normative and institutional foundations of these two forums, with a focus on their secrecy-enabling elements. In the next section I assess the secrecy-related critiques of their design.

1.2 United States: Military Commissions

The history of the military commission as the American mechanism of choice for dealing with wartime acts dates back to the eighteenth century. Military tribunals were used by the US over the centuries primarily in two kinds of circumstances: as an *ad-hoc*, sometimes secret, mechanism for dealing with detainees that posed a challenge to the regular civilian court system; and as part of a temporary occupation regime in wartime or post-war contexts.[3] With the enactment of the Uniform Code of Military Justice in 1950, the President was granted a general authority to establish military commissions when necessary, and instructed that such commissions would, as far as 'practicable', follow the rules of procedure and evidence applied in US district courts and courts-martial.[4]

Then came September 11, 2001, and pursuant wars, which presented the new challenge of treating terrorist suspects within a rule of law system. Some two months after the attacks, President Bush ordered the creation of military commissions to try terrorist suspects that would be apprehended in the evolving anti-terror campaign.[5] The decade since has witnessed an ongoing inter-branch process of recalibration of the procedural, institutional, and constitutional elements of the reinvented military commissions system, including several rounds of legislation,[6] judicial review,[7] and executive policy adjustments.[8]

While much has happened in the law and politics of military commissions over the past decade, some fundamental institutional elements have remained fixed, weathering judicial interventions as well as electoral and policymaking shifts. The commissions are still located at Guantánamo Bay, on a distant island within a heavily guarded military facility, and essentially away from the public eye: to know how justice is meted out in those tribunals one has to invest considerable effort and resources. While these are not secret courts in the formal sense – civilian attorneys can be

---

[3] See Neal K. Katyall and Laurence H. Tribe, *Waging War, Deciding Guilt: Trying the Military Tribunals*, 111 YALE L.J. 1259, 1277–95 (2002); David Glazier, *Kangaroo Court or Competent Tribunal?: Judging the 21st Century Military Commission*, 89 VA. L. REV. 2005, 2023–73 (2003).

[4] 10 U.S.C. § 836 (2006).

[5] Military Order of November 13, 2001: Detention, Treatment, and Trial of Certain Non-Citizens in the War Against Terrorism, 3 C.F.R. 918 (2002).

[6] Military Commissions Act of 2006; Military Commissions Act of 2009.

[7] Hamdan v. Rumsfeld, 548 U.S. 557 (2006); Boumediene v. Bush, 553 U.S. 723 (2008).

[8] E.g., Evan Perez, *U.S. Reverses on 9/11 Trials*, W.S.J., April 5, 2011.

commissioned to represent defendants,[9] and media is allowed regulated coverage of the proceedings – the judge can close the proceeding to the public after finding, based on a party's presentation that could be made *ex parte*, that holding open court would harm national security or the safety of an individual.[10]

The Obama administration's latest attempt to introduce yet another reform in the way military commissions exercise their jurisdiction – namely, to shut down the Guantánamo facility and resume military commission adjudication on US soil, was foiled by Congress and effectively abandoned by the President in early 2011. At the same time, however, federal district courts still regularly try defendants not held in Guantánamo for terrorism-related offenses.[11]

1.3 Israel: Military Courts

Military courts – not to be confused with courts martial which try Israeli service members – have been employed in one form or another by Israel since its very inception, primarily for the criminal prosecution of Palestinians living under Israeli military control both within Israel proper and in areas it occupied. Currently however Israel's military court system applies almost exclusively to the Palestinian subjects of the Israeli 46-year occupation of the West Bank.[12]

The jurisdiction of these military courts was established in the immediate aftermath of the 1967 occupation of the West Bank, as the Israeli military commander issued a series of orders establishing the legal control of the area by the Israeli occupation forces. These orders, which roughly followed the directives of the Hague and Geneva Conventions regarding the treatment of civilians during war and under belligerent occupation, expressed the normative continuity principle, but at the same time authorized the military commander to enact new legislation and to

---

9 10 U.S.C. § 949c(b)(3). However civilian attorneys are permitted only under special security clearances, and their access to their clients and the information they hold is strictly regulated. See David Luban, *Lawfare and Legal Ethics in Guantanamo*, 60 STAN. L.REV. 1981, 1989–92 (2008).

10 10 U.S.C. § 949d(c).

11 See Owen Fiss, *Aberrations No More*, 2010 UTAH L. REV. 1085, 1087, 1096.

12 The Gaza Strip, also occupied in 1967, was subject to the same legal regime until Israel's withdrawal from the Strip in 2005. Military courts also have formal jurisdiction over Israelis in the West Bank, however it is very rarely exercised.

establish mechanisms of governance for its enforcement.[13] Military courts for the occupied territories were therefore soon instituted, their jurisdiction encompassing, *inter alia*, the adjudication of Palestinian residents accused of offenses according to a criminal code enacted for the Territories – mainly offenses relating to the security of the area and its occupying forces.[14]

Military courts are currently located at two venues in the West Bank, housed within Israeli military facilities near Ramallah and Nablus. They have additional makeshift locations in detention facilities within Israel, where many Palestinian suspects are held. The military courts system has tried scores of Palestinians since 1967. During this period it underwent substantial structural reforms, reflecting an ongoing normalization of its activities and a gradual enhancement of its judicial independence. This process included the introduction in 1989 of an appellate level[15] and later a juvenile court;[16] the revocation in 1990 of the authority of the region's military commander to review court decisions;[17] and the replacement by 2001 of all officer lay-judges with professional military judges.[18]

Notwithstanding these reforms, Israeli military courts – like US military commissions – still retain a nagging measure of inaccessibility and invisibility. Court sessions are formally public, and at least two members of a defendant's family are allowed to be present at trial. However since the courts are located within military bases in the West Bank, they are far from sight for the average Israeli, and access to Palestinians is subject to stringent security limitations. And since courtrooms are small and cramped, those allowed into the base are not always capable of attending the sessions. In addition, like her American counterpart, the military judge can order that hearings be held behind closed

---

13 See Pamphlet on Procedures of Government and Law (West Bank) (No. 2), 1967, §§ 2–3.

14 See Order on Security Instructions (Judea and Samaria) (No. 378), 1970.

15 See Order on Security Instructions (Amendment No. 58) (Judea and Samaria) (No. 1265), 1989.

16 See Order on Security Instructions (Amendment No. 109) (Judea and Samaria) (No. 1644), 2009.

17 See Order on Security Instructions (Amendment No. 62) (Judea and Samaria) (No.1309), 1990.

18 See YESH DIN, BACKYARD PROCEEDINGS: THE IMPLEMENTATION OF DUE PROCESS RIGHTS IN THE MILITARY COURTS IN THE OCCUPIED TERRITORIES 50–51 (report prepared by Lior Yavne, 2007), available at http://tinyurl.com/93skl4k (March 6, 2013).

doors for diverse reasons, including general security considerations.[19] Court opinions are formally available but are officially published only sporadically. While defendants have the right to examine the evidence presented against them and to cross-examine witnesses, the military commander may order certain pieces of evidence confidential and inadmissible.

While military courts have tried the lion's share of Palestinian defendants in terrorism-related prosecutions over the decades, Israeli civilian courts have retained concurrent jurisdiction and have been used from time to time for the adjudication of Palestinian terrorist-suspects.

2. IN/VISIBLE COURTS

2.1 The Vanishing Court: A Liberal Charge

While military courts were established by Israel partly in fulfillment of its obligations under international law as a belligerent occupier, military commissions resulted from the combination of two independent choices by the US – to bring terrorist-suspects to trial, and to do so away from the already-available civilian federal courts. Both tribunal systems, however, were designed in a way that diminishes their transparency and publicity, as well as the assurance of full accessibility to evidence relevant to a defendant's defense. As such, they pose a significant challenge to the democratic and often constitutional norm of trial in open court.

The creation of such semi-secret courts has garnered significant criticism, both from within the countries involved as well as from the international community. The physical and legal inaccessibility of the adjudication process has been perceived as an infringement upon several staples of procedural justice, notably the right to be tried in open court – a guarantee against abuse of defendants' rights; as well as a public interest in assuring governmental accountability in the use of official violence, and the potential of turning court proceedings into means of public education and civic participation.[20] Indeed, secrecy in the practices of court systems is understandably seen as an affront to the liberal foundations of democratic governance.

---

[19] See Order on Security Instructions (Judea and Samaria) (No. 378), 1970, §§ 11–11A.

[20] See David Luban, *The Publicity Principle*, in THE THEORY OF INSTITUTIONAL DESIGN 154 (Robert Goodin ed., 1998).

A useful articulation of this critique was offered of late by Judith Resnik. In a series of articles condemning the demise of the open court as a foundation of democratic adjudication, Resnik has warned against the relegation of adjudication to private, administrative, international, and indeed military forums – all reflecting an ongoing process of distancing adjudication from the publicly accessible courthouse, and on the way relaxing our commitments to procedural justice and human dignity. Public processes, Resnik states, make us accord 'individuals of all kinds – including "suspected terrorists" – ... the respect and fairness due to all persons'.[21]

Trying these suspects in semi-secret courts, Resnik argues, undermines their central function – to serve as stylized loci for engaging in equality-ensuring democratic agency. Creating separate forums 'aimed at controlling access and information as well as limiting the rights of detainees by augmenting the powers of the state', Resnik states, reflects a deliberate effort to avoid '[t]he function of [open] courts as potentially egalitarian political venues'.[22] Tracking the institutional phenomenon that may be termed *the vanishing court*,[23] Resnik decries the circumvention of procedural rights-guarantees and the erosion of unique institutional conditions for participatory deliberation on public values. She questions the idea that a secret court may be considered a 'court' at all, denoting as an essential oxymoron the notion of a 'closed military court'.[24]

Notions of openness, visibility, publicity, and accessibility of court proceedings are thus understood in mainstream liberal thought as essentials of dignified treatment of those subject to a just legal order, as well as instruments for ensuring fair, legitimate and accountable use of judicial power more generally. Indeed some have questioned whether a normative order that flouts the guarantees of open court may at all be worthy of the title 'legal'.[25] This understanding of the legitimate adjudicatory process stands in contrast to the elements of invisibility engrained

---

[21] Judith Resnik, *Bring Back Bentham: 'Open Courts,' 'Terror Trials,' and Public Sphere(s)*, 5 L. & ETHICS HUM. RTS. 2, 6 (2011).

[22] Judith Resnik, *Courts: In and Out of Sight, Site, and Cite*, 53 VILL. L. REV. 771, 807–08 (2008).

[23] *Cf.* Marc Galanter, *The Vanishing Trial: An Examination of Trials and Related Matters in Federal and State Courts*, 1 J. EMP. LEGAL STUD. 459 (2004).

[24] Resnik, *supra* note 21, at 4.

[25] See Jeremy Waldron, *The Rule of Law and the Importance of Procedure*, pp. 13–14 (NYU School of Law Public Law Research Paper No. 10-73, 2010), *available at* http://ssrn.com/abstract=1688491 (March 6, 2013) (suggesting that basic elements of procedural fairness in the judicial process, including trial in open court, are essential to any viable concept of 'law').

in the practice of US military commissions and Israeli military courts. But the story can perhaps be told from a broader perspective that would highlight some unique qualities of these tribunals – qualities that might complicate our understanding of what we see when we look at an institution designed to be invisible.

2.2 Visibility Recast: Of Other Spaces

In a famous lecture given in 1967, Michel Foucault coined the term *heterotopia*, as a signifier of spaces and places – geographical, architectural, institutional, and sometimes even purely symbolic – in which society defines, locates, and confines that which is its *other*; the spheres of social life that challenge its utopias and exemplify their unattainability.[26] Heterotopias familiarly materialize in closeted institutions that appear in any modernized political society – the hospital, the nursing home, the prison, the psychiatric ward; spaces in which 'individuals whose behavior is deviant in relation to the required mean or norm are placed'.[27] Heterotopias are 'outside of all places', and are 'absolutely different from all the sites that they reflect and speak about'.[28] They are locations that accommodate contradictions and incompatibilities, and reside under a constant regime of 'opening and closing that both isolates them and makes them penetrable'.[29]

What distinguishes heterotopias, however, is that they exist at all times *in relation to* the normal institutions and social realities of our daily lives.[30] Societies create these other spaces to instill order, meaning, and purpose in social and political structures; and in order to clarify and solidify, by manner of juxtaposition, the institutional ideals to which society strives. These spaces are off limits, but at the same time draw our constant attention because of their function as comparative sources for self-assessment and self-congratulation (among his many metaphors, Foucault also speaks of the mirror as a heterotopic device).[31] Like social taboos, they are designed to be invisible and unmentionable, but by differentiating them from our regular lives we make sure that we know

---

[26] Michel Foucault, *On Other Spaces*, 16 DIACRITICS 22 (Jay Miskowiec trans., Spring 1986).

[27] *Id.* at 25.

[28] *Id.* at 24.

[29] *Id.* at 26.

[30] See *id.* at 27.

[31] See *id.*, at 24 (the mirror is a heterotopia 'in so far as the mirror does exist in reality, where it exerts a sort of counteraction on the position that I occupy').

where they are, and in what ways they are distinct from that which is 'normal'.

The notion of heterotopia can be usefully employed in our thinking about military tribunals in the age of terrorism. These forums too are secluded facilities with complex systems regulating entry and exit. They accommodate essentially contradictory missions, as they engage in summarily ordered indefinite detentions of some individuals, while at the same time trying others under elaborate due process safeguards. They reside in distant locations and behind walls and fences, handling some of society's most feared adversaries, but are managed by men and women in uniform, in an ironic cohabitation of the reviled and the glorious. They are designed to be invisible, defying our normal democratic assumptions of the open court and the public proceeding, but by the same token are singled out as the *other* kind of forum by which to measure and test a political community's constitutional convictions and political inhibitions.

Guantánamo Bay is no doubt as heterotopic a site as could be imagined: an island subject to multiple sovereignties, long considered – at least until the US Supreme Court implied otherwise[32] – a constitutional no-man's land,[33] in which resides a prison that is also a court that is also a fort in the service of a war that is also a law-enforcement mission that is also a retributive campaign. Israel's military bases in the heart of the Palestinian West Bank, though not as richly symbolic, lag not far behind, as heterotopias that have already settled into a generation-old, distinct institutional normalcy. These judicial facilities are not as visible and as accessible as civilian courts, but their very *otherness* provides a different kind of visibility that should be recognized and strategically employed. I turn now to discuss this potential with a little more detail.

2.3 Military Tribunals and the Visibility of Invisible Courts

Choices to conduct terrorism-related trials in civilian courts often involve procedural, evidentiary, political, and security challenges that render them exceptional judicial events, for better or worse.[34] To the extent that

[32] See Boumediene v. Bush, 553 U.S. 723 (2008) (due to its complete effective control over Guantánamo Bay, individuals the US detains there are entitled to the writ of habeas corpus).

[33] See Gerald Neuman, *Anomalous Zones*, 48 STAN. L. REV. 1197, 1197–1201, 1228–33 (1996).

[34] See, e.g. Samuel Issacharoff, *Judging in the Time of the Extraordinary*, 47 HOUS. L. REV. 533, 546–51 (2010); Stephen I. Vladeck, *Terrorism Trials and the Article III Courts after* Abu Ali, 88 Tex. L. Rev. 1501, 1502–04, 1531–32 (2010).

this is the case, there are arguable benefits – in terms of visibility! – to conducting this exceptional treatment in a separate tribunal rather than through existing generalist civilian courts. In this way, the few trials of these defendants are not drowned out by the masses of cases managed by civilian courts as part of their regular dockets. These cases have a dedicated judicial forum that can draw the separate attention of lawyers, activists, politicians, and scholars. While it is often more difficult to know what happens in military tribunals than in regular courts – their heterotopic nature calls for seclusion and concealment – the very existence of these black boxes makes them at the same time more noticeable and thus more readily subject to review and critique.

If indeed the best place to hide a politically charged activity is in plain sight – for example, on the loaded dockets of civilian courts – then establishing special military tribunals does make this practice somewhat harder to conceal and ignore. Observers of the judicial system are made to realize that it includes a unique class of cases, to which a political determination has been made not to afford the full rights of detainees and defendants currently available in civilian courts. This determination is taken away from the discretion of generalist courts, which have at their disposal multiple doctrinal strategies, some more latent than others, for discriminating among classes of cases,[35] and presented as an overt political choice.

Military tribunals thus help to expose the special nature of terrorism-related trials, and make visible the institutional innovations and the moral concessions democracies resort to in the face of the legal challenges posed by an opponent that defies the normal distinctions between criminal and enemy. While the available alternative – criminal proceedings in civilian courts – might fall 'below the radar' of international, political, and scholarly focus, a separate institutional setting for trying terrorism suspects necessarily invokes special awareness and scrutiny, as it likely should. Like other heterotopic sites, by the act of institutional and procedural individuation we are made aware of the existence and persistence of these separate forums for trying terrorist-suspects, and in

---

See also Ori Aronson, *Out of Many: Military Commissions, Religious Tribunals, and the Democratic Virtues of Court Specialization*, 51 VA. J. INT'L L. 231, 278–9 (2011) (reviewing proposals for establishing a special civilian forum for terrorist affairs).

[35] Consider, for example, the regulation of briefing and of evidence and witness examination, decisions concerning appointed counsel, or presence of a disturbing defendant in the courtroom, or even the discretion of court security personnel.

that way we get to question the limits of our convictions as to what war entails and what the ideal of the rule of law means.[36]

Further, trying terrorism suspects in a military forum keeps visible the state of hostility that persists between the state and the defendant. While the defendant enjoys no political membership in the institutions that try him – the notion of member participation in democratic deliberation, often attached to the open court principle, does not apply here – he is kept in the status of a belligerent in an international conflict, rather than being rendered an alien criminal offender under the purview of internal law enforcement jurisdiction. Trial by a jury of one's own peers is inherently irrelevant to the alien belligerent prosecuted by his enemy country, but among the alternatives, trial by military service members may be somewhat closer to a notion of peer adjudication than trial by foreign civilians.

This view may not present the legal order in the best possible light;[37] indeed, it seeks to demystify the judicial function by linking it to the political context of its invocation and the types of agents with whom it interacts and among whom it allocates power. A particularized concept of adjudication thus undermines the ideal-type 'court' as a locus of generalist knowledge and methodology that is detached from, and is independent of, the subject matter that it faces. Instead it perceives the court forum as an institutional vehicle for pursuing diverse social and political goals.

From a normative point of view, the understanding that military adjudication can actually enhance the visibility of the moral stakes it involves does not necessarily win the day. Traditional instrumental open-court concerns still have force and gravity. But this kind of analysis does enable a more questioning exploration of the politics of jurisdictional choices in this constitutional minefield of terrorism-related adjudication. It calls upon us to realize that societies engage in complex trade-offs when they resort to heterotopic jurisdictions like military commissions or military courts; and that normative liberal evaluations might vary according to circumstance. The examination that follows of the prosecutions of two high-level terrorist suspects by the US and Israel will seek to demonstrate this complexity.

---

[36] Of course, some civilian trials – including terrorism-related ones – manage to garner much public attention. What is unique about trial in a separate forum, however, is that it can draw attention to the uniqueness *of the forum*, with its cultural and political contexts, rather than merely to the case at hand.

[37] Compare Ronald Dworkin, Law's Empire 52, 231 (1986) (describing one of the constraints of interpretation in showing the law in its best possible light).

3 TRYING LEADERS

3.1 Khalid Sheikh Mohammed

In January 2011, President Obama signed into law an appropriations provision enacted by Congress, prohibiting the use of federal funds 'to transfer, release, or assist in the transfer or release to or within the United States, its territories, or possessions of Khalid Sheikh Mohammed'.[38] This peculiar act of legislation, tending to the fate of a single individual, was the culmination of another phase in the ongoing American endeavor to deal in a manner that would be both effective and just with persons involved in the 9/11 attacks and their wartime aftermath.

Among other elements of this complex story, the Congressional enactment signaled the by-then obvious failure of the Obama administration to live up to its plan of shutting down the Guantánamo detention facility, and transferring its detainees to either trial or detention on US soil. Mohammed, the alleged mastermind of the 9/11 attacks, remains in detention in Guantánamo, and his trial resumed there before military commission.[39]

The law prohibiting the transfer of Mohammed into the US for trial, and the decision it compelled by US Attorney General Eric Holder to renew prosecution of Mohammed in military commission, followed a heated political debate on the appropriate forum for trying terrorism suspects. While Holder intended to try Mohammed and his main accomplices as criminal defendants in federal district court in New York City, a diverse opposition galvanized against the plan, calling instead for keeping Mohammed off US shores and bringing him to trial, if at all, before the military commission that had originally begun to handle his prosecution. Security concerns and prohibitive costs were cited, as well as the mental and emotional strain that would be involved in deliberating guilt and punishment regarding the 9/11 plot near the site of its execution.[40] A populist frenzy ensued, stoked by a rejection of the symbolic image of Mohammed enjoying the constitutional rights of a normal criminal defendant. Mohammed was deemed to warrant a *different* kind of legal

---

[38] National Defense Authorization Act for Fiscal Year 2011, § 1032.

[39] See Charlie Savage, *At a Hearing, 9/11 Detainees Show Defiance*, N.Y. TIMES, May 6, 2012, at A1.

[40] See, e.g. Jane Mayer, *The Trial; Eric Holder and the battle over Khalid Sheikh Mohammed*, THE NEW YORKER, vol. 86(1) p. 52 (February 15, 2010). See *also* Vladeck, *supra* note 34, at 1501–2.

treatment, one that would maintain his unique terrorist status among mass-murderers.

That the opposition prevailed and Mohammed was left to be tried by military commission in Guantánamo has been perceived by many as a failure of the liberal promise of the Obama administration to transform the treatment of terrorism-related detainees into a system of civilian enforcement and democratic accountability.[41] That may be so, although it is worth noting that alien belligerents are not members of the political community whose courts are in question, and in that sense might not have the same moral interest in accessing an open forum of normative deliberation – as courts are portrayed in accounts such as Resnik's. Instead, they are treated as what they perhaps perceive themselves to be – soldiers in a war against the US, engaged in hostilities against their enemy. Prosecuting authorities, like courts, are not used to taking into account the preferences of defendants regarding the forum that would try them, and we don't really know Mohammed's side of the story. But there is a possibility that military adjudication in fact expresses with greater fidelity than its civilian alternative the relationship between the parties to this case.

Further, from the point of view of the US constituency, it would be difficult to say today that Americans are unaware of the fact that Mohammed is being tried before a military tribunal on a distant island – they sent him there, employing the full force of their political agency in face of an executive plan to have him prosecuted in civilian court. This does not mean that he is awarded the same procedural rights he would have had in a federal district court,[42] nor that it will be easy for us to know what exactly goes on in his island-based trial. But from the perspective of visibility of the political and moral implications of Mohammed's prosecution, it seems that the stakes could hardly be made clearer. By insisting on the exceptionality of the treatment of Mohammed and his cohorts – by maintaining the heterotopic jurisdiction of military commissions – Americans have engaged in a process of delimitation of their own sense of legality.

---

[41] See, e.g. Fiss, *supra* note 11, at 1096–97; Tung Yin, *'Anything But Bush?': The Obama Administration and Guantanamo Bay*, 34 HARV. J.L. & PUB. POL'Y 453, 471–3 (2011); Paust, *supra* note 1.

[42] Although it was difficult to have fathomed a possibility of acquittal: 'Khalid Sheikh Mohammed is going to meet justice, and he's going to meet his maker', assured then-White House press secretary Robert Gibbs on CNN in January 2010, when a civilian federal prosecution of Mohammed was still on the table. See, e.g. http://tinyurl.com/d6sejuz (March 6, 2013).

3.2 Marwan Barghouthi[43]

While Khalid Sheikh Mohammed was being pursued and finally captured, in early 2003, Marwan Barghouthi was already subject to a criminal prosecution in the Tel-Aviv district court. Barghouthi, a veteran *Fatah* leader in the West Bank, was one of the central leaders of the second *Intifadah* (2000–04) during which Israelis and Palestinians clashed recurrently with scores of armed and civilian casualties on both sides. While Israel was targeting terrorism activists in violent manner, it also sought to capture and indict the leaders of the uprising, who were thought to tread the military/political line. One of the most intensely sought targets of this effort, Barghouthi was apprehended by Israeli military forces in April 2002, and after a prolonged period of detention and interrogation under military custody, was to be indicted for his involvement in the orchestration of several attacks that led to the death of civilians.

Barghouthi, of course, was not the only Palestinian detained by Israel during that period. Thousands of Palestinians were arrested and detained by the Israeli military in the wake of the second *Intifadah* – for acts ranging from stone throwing to suicide bombing – and almost all were processed by the military courts system. While civilian courts had formal jurisdiction over most offenses (based on extra-territorial and protectionist foundations), and while the State Attorney's official choice-of-forum policy cited the 'majority of links' test, prosecutions were filed wholesale in military courts, which were institutionally more adept at coping with the spiking case volumes: the military court system could expand its workforce (judges, prosecutors, defenders) at short notice by enlisting officers in reserve duty, and in that way provide immediate response to shifting needs.

Barghouthi, however, was a special case. Because of his high rank and the political interest in him – he is regularly tapped as the next leader of the Palestinian nation – prosecutorial authorities in Israel decided to bring him to trial in civilian court, and thus ostensibly make his trial a showcase of Israeli legal fairness in the treatment of its topmost adversaries. As public and international awareness was sure to be drawn to Barghouthi's trial, officials also preferred to keep his case away from military courts and thus leave that exceptional forum beyond the limelight of journalistic and political coverage and review. The concern for

---

[43] I am indebted to Adv. Dvorah Chen, the leading prosecutor in the Barghouthi trial, for much background information that has infused this section.

visibility therefore led to an interesting twist: had Barghouthi's trial been conducted in military court, that forum would have likely gained unprecedented publicity, which was deflected from it by the very choice to prosecute him in the assumedly more visible civilian court. While his own trial may have become more visible, the forum that had tried most of his peers was left in shadow.

At the start of the trial, Barghouthi – clad in brown prison uniform like any other criminal defendant – attempted to challenge the court's jurisdiction to try him as political persecution in contravention of international law. His threshold claims denied, Barghouthi declined to pursue a defense on the merits of the accusations against him, all of which were located in the plainly criminal sections of the penal code; the prosecutor made a calculated choice not to charge him with political offenses against Israel's national security. While he was nominally represented by a public defense attorney, he did not actively participate in the trial, and was convicted based on undisputed evidence on five counts of murder.[44] He was sentenced to multiple terms of life imprisonment, which he currently serves. He did not appeal.

Exempt from the political forces that had such an impact in the US on the attempt to try Khalid Sheikh Mohammed in New York, Israel's Attorney General – a civil servant – was effectively free to make his own choice of forum in the prosecution of Barghouthi. Later reflecting on his choice, then-Attorney General Elyakim Rubinstein explained that Barghouthi may have been a political leader, but he was also a leader of murderous groups, and as such was justified in standing to trial in civilian court.[45] The choice to prosecute Barghouthi in civilian court, and the prosecutorial strategies employed by the state attorneys during the trial, were therefore clearly intended to downplay as much as possible the political elements of the judicial process, and to portray it as a 'normal' criminal prosecution. The genuine stakes of the trial – a prominent Palestinian leader tried by his occupier for acts which he determinedly claimed were measures in a national freedom fight – were sought to be blurred, to be rendered invisible, through the choice of the ostensibly more visible civilian forum and penal decorum.

---

[44] S.C.C. (Dist. Ct., Tel-Aviv) 1158/02 State of Israel v. Barghouthi (May 20, 2004).

[45] See Elyakim Rubinstein, *On Security and Human Rights during the Fight against Terrorism*, 16 LAW & MILITARY 765, 784 (2003) (Heb.).

3.3 Lessons Learned

In both cases, of Mohammed and of Barghouthi, an initial attempt was made to deviate from what had become in the past decade the usual method for wartime prosecution of terrorist suspects – to make a special case of the leaders by trying them in civilian courts, rather than in the more readily available military tribunals. The US attempt fell through; the Israeli succeeded, with exceptional ease. And while Mohammed's trial is still ongoing, some comparable lessons can already be drawn.

The choice to try Marwan Barghouthi in civilian court, and the manner in which his prosecution was handled, reflected a deliberate Israeli effort to conceal the political and the international characteristics of the trial, and indeed of the troubled era which it signified. Israel's choice of forum sought to de-contextualize its relationship with Barghouthi, by constructing it as a run-of-the-mill criminal trial, rather than a clash of national narratives. Its interests in opting for this strategy are of course understandable, but they certainly had little to do with transparency of context or meaning; in fact they were mostly concerned with *obscuring* the political elements of a highly political event.

The plan to prosecute Khalid Sheikh Mohammed in civilian court, on the other hand, was apparently envisioned as a purifying spectacle of American justice, seen and done; Attorney General Eric Holder was famously cited predicting that the proceeding in New York's federal court would be 'the trial of the century'.[46] Visibility was clearly a matter of concern in the choice of forum, but it would seem that it was not the kind of visibility the liberal ideal of the open court envisions. In a curious coalescence of interests, the US polity turned out to be determined to give up on the assured excitement of trial in the city square. Americans wanted to *see* Mohammed tried by military commission; they sought the knowledge of Mohammed being treated in a way that distinguishes him from criminal defendants. In that sense at least, the choice of the less visible forum has rendered the political stakes, and the moral costs, more noticeable.

In the Israeli case, then, the military court served as the forum to be avoided, lest it reveal to Israelis and to the world the antithetical essence of its parallel existence alongside Israel's civilian, rule-of-law-abiding legal system. In the US case, the military commission was the forum to be reached, lest the war that underlies the prosecution be obscured by the niceties of democratic civilian adjudication. Both played an essential heterotopic role in the jurisdictional strategies that were employed; they

---

46 See Mayer, *supra* note 40.

were the *other* jurisdictions, against which both political communities had an opportunity to test and evaluate their commitments to the ideal of the rule of law.

This does not mean that the military forums could have, or will have, assured either defendant sufficiently fair procedures under which to be tried. But their availability might engender heightened awareness to what we are willing to give up when we subject our enemies to adjudication in general, and in such forums in particular. In this sense, at least, they have made something that is latent, somewhat more visible.

CONCLUSION

Exploring the choice of forum strategies involved in the prosecution of high-profile terrorist-suspects risks missing the full picture. Most detainees/defendants bear unfamiliar names and faces, and focusing on the leaders might fail to tell the whole institutional story. But the Mohammed and Barghouthi cases are in a sense all about visibility. Through them political and legal agents have engaged the public with the considerations and the tradeoffs invoked by picking forums; and through these cases the heterotopic challenge of the military tribunal is posed in full view for civilian decision-makers and constituents to acknowledge and measure up against.

Because the alternative of military adjudication *is* out there, we are able to take genuine account of the unique status and experience of the alien enemies whom we choose to put to trial. We have created literal, physical, and institutional spaces for the accommodation of the special role legality plays during wartime. Having seen these places – even under the obscurity that terrorism-related adjudication compels – we may well conclude that civilian adjudication is superior after all, in given circumstances or for certain kinds of trials, or regardless of context whatsoever. But these will be civilian trials, and the terror that invoked them will become civilian strife. Indeed, we might see more of what happens *in* those trials, but less of what they actually *are*.

Secrecy, it turns out, is not an ideology, rather it is a *strategy*. It is not so much a moral vice as it is a political *device*, grounded in social practices of exclusion, distinction, and taboo; in our tendency to delineate 'other' spaces in the process of self-definition. Realizing its normative elasticity should enable us to think more critically, as well as more imaginatively, on the ways it has been employed, and on the ways it could be employed, in the design of terrorism-related adjudication.

PART 5

Secrecy and administrative measures

15. Administrative counter-terrorism measures – a strategy to circumvent human rights in the fight against terrorism?

Tuomas Ojanen

1. INTRODUCTION

This chapter takes stock of the use of administrative measures in the name of countering terrorism. After a short introduction to administrative counter-terrorism measures, the focus is on the following questions: What explains the increased use of administrative measures, either as an addition to or as an alternative to criminal law, to counter terrorism? What are the main objectives of these administrative measures? What are the major consequences of the 'administrative approach'; especially what are the constitutional repercussions for the protection of human rights?

The chapter is intended to be illustrative rather than comprehensive. Therefore, the focus is on human rights concerns originating in the nexus of administrative counter-terrorism measures and intelligence, that is secret information provided by intelligence services about individuals or groups who are believed to be potential perpetrators of terrorist acts or other threats to national security. Human rights concerns pertaining to the use of intelligence are illustrated by Finnish immigration proceedings in which intelligence has been used to justify the rejection of applications for citizenship or a residence permit. It is hoped that this discussion will bring some added value as human rights concerns originating in the use of secret intelligence have so far largely, if not exclusively, been discussed with reference to such 'high-profile' cases as detention proceedings at Guantanamo, the targeted sanctions regime initiated by the UN Security Council under Security Council Resolution 1267 and the EU listing regime. Besides, Finland is one of those EU Member States who have traditionally favored access to documents and transparency and who also played an important role in bringing transparency to the EU agenda in the 1990s. Therefore, Finland is not necessarily the first country with whom human rights concerns stemming from the use of such 'secret evidence' as intelligence is associated.

2. ADMINISTRATIVE COUNTER-TERRORISM MEASURES: MANIFESTATIONS AND RATIONALES

Post-9/11, administrative counter-terrorism measures have become a widespread and significant component of counter-terrorism activities at the national, regional and global levels. Administrative authorities have increasingly been called upon to contribute to the fight against terrorism either as an addition or, increasingly, as an alternative to the more traditional criminal law approach.[1] The repertoire of administrative counter-terrorism measures is multiform. While new measures specifically designed to counter terrorism have been created, such as asset freezing, travel bans, arms embargoes and other forms of so-called smart (or targeted) sanctions,[2] existing and more traditional measures under administrative law, such as the rejection of various licenses, including applications for citizenship and residence permits, have also been used for the purpose of countering terrorism. Various forms of administrative detention and control order proceedings offer further examples of using administrative law as an instrument for counter-terrorism activities.[3]

---

[1] The use of administrative measures is not confined to counter-terrorism activities but extends to cover organized crime and crime control in general. See e.g. Wim Huisman and Monique Koemans, Administrative measures in crime control, Erasmus Law Review, Vol 1 (2008), 121–44.

[2] The system of sanctions provided for under Article 41 of the UN Charter was originally designed to act against States but the use of comprehensive sanctions against States gave rise to serious humanitarian concerns. Therefore, smart or targeted sanctions that only target specific individuals or organizations were introduced under UN Security Council Resolution 1267 (1999), S/RES/1267, clause 14(b). Through Resolution 1267, the UN Security Council imposed financial sanctions on the Taliban and established the 1267 Committee to maintain the Consolidated List of proscribed organizations and individuals. The targeted sanctions regime was extended to Al Qaida by Resolution 1333 (2000). Any Member State may submit a name to the 1267 Committee, and if consensus is reached within the Committee, the name is added to the list. Where a person or group appears on the list, all UN Member States are obligated to freeze their assets, as well as bar the individuals from travelling and prevent the supply of arms to such groups or individuals.

[3] For administrative detention, see Ken Roach's contribution in this volume.

The details of administrative counter-terrorism measures have already been discussed elsewhere, especially insofar as smart sanctions are concerned. Therefore, instead of going into the details of various forms of administrative counter-terrorism measures, it is more fruitful to ponder the following questions: Why has 'the administrative approach' become such a significant tool for counter-terrorism activities at national, regional and global levels in recent years? What are the constitutional implications of this trend, particularly insofar as the protection of human rights is concerned?

The major explanation for the popularity of the administrative approach seems to be quite evident: administrative measures are predominantly *proactive* and *preventive* in nature although they may also have a punitive and a repressive dimension. Therefore, the application of administrative measures allows serviceable means for *preventing terrorism* – one of the cornerstones around which both the EU with its Member States and the UN currently organize their counter-terrorism strategies.[4] One of the major theoretical assumptions underpinning the administrative approach also appears to be that the level of terrorism is determined by the presence of facilitating factors and, accordingly, administrative authorities are mobilized to limit the opportunities for terrorist activities through various measures available under administrative law.

The preventive and proactive nature of administrative counter-terrorism measures is most apparent in the context of such smart sanctions as the freezing of assets which, according to the UN Security Council Sanctions Committee, aims at denying 'listed individuals, groups, undertakings and entities the means to support terrorism', and ensuring 'that no funds, financial assets or economic resources of any kind are available to them for so long as they remain subject to the sanctions measures'.[5] In other

---

4 The four pillars of the EU's counter-terrorism strategy are prevention, protection, pursuit and response. The European Union Counter-Terrorism Strategy. The Council of the European Union, Brussels, 30 November 2005, 14469/4/05 REV 4. The UN global counter-terrorism strategy, in turn, is based on four pillars: tackling the conditions conducive to the spread of terrorism; preventing and combating terrorism; building States' capacity to prevent and combat terrorism and to strengthen the role of the UN system in that regard; ensuring respect for human rights for all and the rule of law as the fundamental basis for the fight against terrorism. See the United Nations Global Counter-Terrorism Strategy, adopted by General Assembly resolution 60/288 in 2006.

5 Security Council Committee pursuant to resolutions 1267 (1999) and 1989 (2011) concerning Al-Qaida and associated individuals and entities, ASSETS FREEZE: EXPLANATION OF TERMS (Updated in Oct 2011 and approved by the Committee on 30 December 2011), paragraph 4. 14 June 2012, available at www.un.org/sc/committees/1267/usefulpapers.shtml.

words, therefore, the goal of the asset freezing measures is to limit opportunities for terrorist activities and to remove incentives for them. However, the aim of prevention is also realized on occasions on which applications for a residence permit or citizenship are rejected by the competent administrative agency on the ground that the applicant is considered a threat to national security.

That measures under administrative law quite nicely lend themselves to the prevention of terrorism becomes even more apparent by focusing on some idiosyncrasies of administrative proceedings. In particular, the following four characteristics are particularly worthy of elaboration. First authorities can take advantage of administrative measures at a much earlier stage than is ever possible in the context of the criminal justice system. As a rule, administrative authorities do not have to initiate court proceedings to obtain approval to impose a certain administrative measure, nor do they need to suspect a crime or wait for the starting of a criminal procedure against the individual or entity.[6] Instead, only a few indications that certain individuals or groups may have a propensity for terrorism, or that there may be links to suspected terrorist groups or individual terrorists, can be sufficient to justify the adoption of an administrative measure, such as putting individuals or groups on a blacklist and having their assets frozen.

Second, the standard of proof and the assessment of evidence in administrative proceedings differ from those applied in criminal trials. Similarly, the burden of proof is lower in administrative law proceedings than in criminal trials. For instance, the concept of evidence is practically unknown in Finnish administrative procedure law which instead speaks of information on which administrative measures may be based.[7] As a result, administrative measures can usually be imposed on the basis of lesser 'evidence' than criminal convictions. Furthermore, such basic principles of criminal law as the presumption of innocence do not usually apply to administrative procedures. The EU General Court (formerly the Court of First Instance), for example, has explicitly held that the

[6] The lack of the requirement of a criminal trial as a precondition for the adoption of administrative counterterrorism measures is emphasized by the UN Al-Qaida and Taliban Sanctions Committee in its updated guidelines of 2007 pertaining to the blacklisting process as follows: 'A criminal charge or conviction is not necessary for inclusion on the Consolidated List as the sanctions are intended to be preventive in nature.' Al-Qaida and Taliban Sanctions Committee, Guidelines of the Committee for the Conduct of its Work, updated as of 12 February 2007, p. 3.

[7] Olli Mäenpää, Hallintoprosessioikeus, Helsinki 2007, 374–5.

presumption of innocence does not prevent the imposition of such a precautionary measure with a preventive aim as asset freezing because such measures do not constitute criminal sanctions and do not imply any accusation of a criminal nature.[8]

Third, a distinct feature of administrative procedures is that there is usually an absence of a clear 'two-party procedure' in the same sense as in criminal or civil law procedures – a feature that in turn has effects on procedural equality and the distribution of the burden of proof in administrative procedures. Indeed, there typically exists such an asymmetry between the parties in administrative procedures due to the procedural setting of an individual vs. a public authority that one cannot speak about 'equality of arms' in the same sense as in the context of criminal procedure.[9] In such administrative procedures as in immigration law procedures this asymmetry is often increased by factors such as culture and language to the detriment of the applicant.

Fourth and finally, the scope and the intensity of judicial scrutiny of administrative measures may be limited, and some dimensions of administrative decision-making can even be immune to judicial review as courts often embrace a minimalist approach and allow administrative authorities a broad discretion as to what to take into consideration for the purpose of adopting various measures under administrative law. Moreover, courts usually cannot replace administrative decisions, but can only annul or quash the decisions of the administrative authorities. In addition, the judicial review of administrative measures typically comes into play *after* the adoption of the administrative measure, as well as only if the person involved challenges the measure. Actually, the administrative approach to counter terrorism includes a kind of 'staying out of court' dimension, and the fact that court proceedings, not to speak of a criminal charge or conviction, are not needed at all to issue administrative counter-terrorism measures is probably one of the major reasons why the administrative approach has been favored in the fight against terrorism at both national, regional and global levels in recent years.

---

[8] See Joined Cases T-37/07 and T-323/07 *El Morabit v Council* [2009], nyr, para 43; and Case T-49/07 *Fahas v Council* [2010] nyr, para 64.

[9] The equality of arms, that is the procedural equality of the parties to the case, is one of the key elements of 'fair trial' in the institutional framework of criminal procedure. In addition, fair trial includes the right that criminal proceedings should be adversarial. See e.g. the judgment of the ECtHR in the case of *Brandstetter*, judgment of 28 August 1991, Series A, No. 211, para 68.

3. REPERCUSSIONS OF THE ADMINISTRATIVE APPROACH ON CONSTITUTIONAL AND CRIMINAL LAW

The administrative approach to terrorism has several significant repercussions. The first one has to do with the relationship between administrative law and criminal law.[10] As the administrative approach seeks to counter terrorism without bringing criminal law into play, the scope of the administrative law system has expanded at the expense of the criminal justice system. At the same time, however, the use of administrative counter-terrorism measures has blurred the distinction between administrative law and criminal law because many administrative counter-terrorism measures bear resemblance to criminal sanctions. Although administrative counter-measures are primarily presented – or, perhaps more to the point, sold out – as being preventive rather than punitive in nature, the impact of many administrative measures is often very severe on the affected individuals and even their family members. To be sure, their consequences may often go far beyond the effects of traditional criminal sanctions. Asset freezing, for instance, causes severe economic disruption and financial hardship on the individuals and their families, and at worst may even amount to a kind of 'civil death'.[11]

For these reasons, some legal scholars have argued that asset freezing should actually be qualified as a 'criminal charge' under Article 6(1) of

---

[10] For the consequences of the administrative approach to crime control in general regarding the division between administrative law and criminal law, see Huisman and Koemans, supra note 1.

[11] See also the judgment of the General Court in Case T-85/09: *Yassin Abdullah Kadi v European Commission*, [2010] ECR II-5177, para 149 in which the court made the following observations on the nature and effects of fund-freezing measures: 'Such measures are particularly draconian for those who are subject to them. All the applicant's funds and other assets have been indefinitely frozen for nearly 10 years now and he cannot gain access to them without first obtaining an exemption from the Sanctions Committee. At paragraph 358 of its judgment in *Kadi*, the Court of Justice had already noted that the measure freezing his funds entailed a restriction of the exercise of the applicant's right to property that had to be classified as considerable, having regard to the general application of the measure and the fact that it had been applied to him since 20 October 2001. In *Ahmed and Others* (paragraphs 60 and 192), the UK Supreme Court took the view that it was no exaggeration to say that persons designated in this way are effectively "prisoners" of the State: their freedom of movement is severely restricted without access to their funds and the effect of the freeze on both them and their families can be devastating.'

the ECHR with the outcome that the targeted individuals would enjoy the full range of fair trial rights available to a criminal defendant under that Article.[12] If this is not the case, it has been argued that blacklisting and, *a fortiori*, asset freezing fits into the ECHR framework of disputes over 'civil rights' under Article 6(1), that is the rights to property and to reputation.[13] However, the EU courts have denied the criminal character of administrative sanctions, including asset freezing,[14] and it is likely that asset freezing is not seen as a criminal charge under the ECHR, either.[15]

---

[12] See, e.g. Melissa van den Broek, Monique Hazelhorst and Wouter de Zanger, Asset Freezing: Smart Sanction or Criminal Charge? Merkourios 2010, 18–27.

[13] For this argumentation, see especially Iain Cameron, The European Convention on Human Rights, Due Process and UN Security Council Counter-Terrorism Sanctions, Report prepared for the Council of Europe, 6 Feb. 2006. The ECtHR will shortly be pronouncing on the question of targeted sanctions in the case of *Nada v. Swizerland*. Application No. 10593/08. It concerns an Italian national resident in the Italian enclave of Campione in Switzerland, who was placed at Switzerland's request on a terrorist suspect list by the UNSCR 1267 Committee, and subjected to targeted sanctions. Among these sanctions is a travel ban that Switzerland implemented through its domestic legal mechanisms. Mr Nada complains that the Swiss travel ban violates his rights under Arts. 5 (liberty of person) and 8 (private life) of the ECHR.

[14] For judgments by the ECJ denying the criminal character of administrative sanctions, see e.g. Case C-137/85 *Maizena and Others* [1987] ECR 4587, para 13; Case C-240/90 *Germany v Commission* [1992] ECR I-5383, para 25; and Case C-210/00 *Käserei Champignon Hofmeister* [2002] ECR I-6453, para 43. On the legal character of asset freezing, see especially Joined Cases T-37/07 and T-323/07 *El Morabit v Council* [2009], nyr, para 43; and Case T-49/07 *Fahas v Council* [2010] nyr, para 64.

[15] See also the decision by the UN Human Rights Committee *Nabil Sayadi and Patricia Vinck v. Belgium* (Communication No. 1472/2006), Final Views by the Human Rights Committee, 22 October 2008, para 10.11, where the Committee takes view that 'the assets freeze was not a penalty imposed in connection with a criminal procedure or conviction' and that 'this regime does not concern a "criminal charge" in the meaning of article 14, para 1'. For criticism of this view, see *Report of the Special Rapporteur on the promotion and protection of human rights and fundamental freedoms while countering terrorism*, Martin Scheinin, A/61/267 (2006), para 35, where it is emphasized that 'it is generally accepted that the determination of whether the charges are criminal or civil depend on the seriousness of the sanction or punishment. If the sanctions linked to inclusion on the list are permanent, then no matter how they are qualified, they may fall within the scope of criminal sanctions for the purposes of international human rights law.'

The other major repercussions of the administrative approach are constitutional in nature. On the one hand, this trend has entailed a re-location of authority as there has been a shift from the law enforcement organs and the judiciary to the administrative authorities and the executive in general. Because of the great reliance on intelligence, however, the 'beneficiaries' of the relocation of authority also include intelligence services. This, of course, accentuates the importance of the existence of such legal and institutional frameworks and measures that ensure respect for human rights and the rule of law by intelligence agencies while countering terrorism, including their effective and comprehensive oversight. However, one of the many concerns pertaining to the use of administrative counter-terrorism measures is that there are shortcomings insofar as effective oversight and the protection of human rights by intelligence agencies are concerned.[16] On the other hand, the use of administrative measures has significantly shaped the protection of human rights in the fight against terrorism. Human rights problems originating in the EU and UN smart sanctions regimes have already been discussed in great detail elsewhere[17] Therefore, it suffices here to note that the most significant shortcomings of administrative counter-terrorism measures have to do with procedural rights. The affected individuals usually fail to enjoy similar protection as suspects in criminal trials. In particular, the use of administrative measures weakens (and in some cases even reverses) the burden of proof; limits (or even overrides) the presumption of innocence; modifies evidentiary rules to permit various types of evidence that would at least largely, if not exclusively, be regarded as inadmissible in criminal trials; and lowers the standards for

---

[16] For compilation of good practices on legal and institutional frameworks and measures that ensure respect for human rights by intelligence agencies while countering terrorism, including on their oversight, see Report of the Special Rapporteur on the promotion and protection of human rights and fundamental freedoms while countering terrorism, Martin Scheinin. United Nations, 17 May 2010, A/HRC/14/46.

[17] The ECJ ruling in *Kadi* lists a whole range of shortcomings in the UN listing and delisting procedures under the 1267 sanctions regime. See Joined Cases C-402/05 P and C-415/05 P *Kadi and Al Barakaat International Foundation v Council and Commission* [2008] ECR I-6351. See also judgment of the Court of First Instance in Case T-256/07 *People's Mojahedin Organization of Iran v Council* [2008] ECR II-3019. For legal literature over smart sanctions and their implications on the protection of fundamental human rights, see e.g. papers included in the collection of Marise Cremona, Francesco Francioni and Sara Poli, Challenging the EU Counter-Terrorism Measures through the Courts, EUI Working Papers, Academy of European Law 2009/10.

determining guilt. In addition, there may be shortcomings of right to an effective remedy and to a fair trial.

In short, the effects of administrative counter-terrorism measures are often much more far-reaching than those of criminal sanctions, but safeguards for human rights tend to be considerably less so. Of course, these explanations for the success of the administrative approach are speculative. It should be emphasized that administrative counter-terrorism measures have a valid legal basis and a proper scope of application. Yet, it is also well-known that many governments have resorted to a wide range of constructions to justify their unilateral exceptions to fundamental human rights in the name of countering terrorism. As the administrative approach seems to offer room for manoeuvre for counter-terrorism activities by governments without arduous court proceedings and strong safeguards of due process, the increased use of administrative counter-terrorism measures inevitably appears to feature as one of those many strategies through which governments seek to carve out more leeway for action in the name of countering terrorism to the detriment of human rights.[18]

4. RELIANCE ON INTELLIGENCE AS THE BASIS FOR ADMINISTRATIVE COUNTER-TERRORISM MEASURES

Intelligence, that is information collected, analyzed and disseminated by intelligence agencies to provide assistance to policymakers and administrative authorities in taking measures relevant to the protection of national security, plays a crucial role in the context of administrative counter-terrorism measures, particularly those pertaining to immigration law and detention proceedings and processes of blacklisting. Indeed, it is usually intelligence concerning the person involved that has been decisive in determining whether there have been sufficient reasons to put persons on the blacklist and have their assets frozen or to reject their applications for a residence permit or citizenship.

---

[18] For a critical legal analysis of a range of constructions by governments to justify, under international law, their unilateral exceptions to human rights in the name of countering terrorism, see Martin Scheinin and Mathias Vermeulen, Unilateral Exceptions to International Law: Systematic Legal Analysis and Critique of Doctrines that Seek to Deny or Reduce the Applicability of Human Rights Norms in the Fight against Terrorism, EUI Working Papers Law No. 2010/08.

While some dimensions of intelligence may be public and accessible, the essence of intelligence usually remains behind a veil of secrecy. Secrecy of intelligence is related to the need to protect the sources and methods used to collect intelligence from disclosure which can threaten the continued collection of intelligence. In addition, the non-disclosure of intelligence relates to protection of the public interest as regards international relations because intelligence increasingly originates in intelligence sharing and cooperation between States. Therefore, intelligence provided by other agencies under the third party rule cannot be disclosed without the consent of the agency that provided the intelligence.

Due to its secrecy, the use of intelligence as the basis for administrative counter-terrorism measures poses a special challenge to the rights to a fair hearing and a fair trial.[19] It is quite typical that neither the targeted individuals nor their lawyers have access to secret intelligence although it may be decisive in imposing a certain administrative measure on the individual. Even though the entitlement to disclosure of relevant evidence is not an absolute right but may be limited in some cases so as to preserve the human rights of another individual or to safeguard an important public interest,[20] reliance on secret intelligence inevitably hinders the ability of the individuals, including their lawyers, to contest administrative counter-terrorism measures and have them reviewed on substantive grounds before independent courts or tribunals. Similarly, administrative authorities are often unable to check the origin and reliability of intelligence although they are bound to act on the basis of it. There may also be significant limitations for the courts to review intelligence.

---

19 For a detailed discussion of legal and political controversies surrounding the use of secret evidence, see Kent Roach's contribution in this volume.

20 See, e.g. the judgment by the ECtHR in *Edwards and Lewis v. the United Kingdom*, judgment of 27 October 2004, Applications No. 39647/98, 40461/98, at para 46: 'The entitlement to disclosure of relevant evidence is not, however, an absolute right. In any criminal proceedings there may be competing interests, such as national security or the need to protect witnesses at risk of reprisals or keep secret police methods of investigation of crime, which must be weighed against the rights of the accused. In some cases it may be necessary to withhold certain evidence from the defence so as to preserve the fundamental rights of another individual or to safeguard an important public interest. Nonetheless, only such measures restricting the rights of the defence which are strictly necessary are permissible under Article 6(1). Furthermore, in order to ensure that the accused receives a fair trial, any difficulties caused to the defence by a limitation on its rights must be sufficiently counterbalanced by the procedures followed by the judicial authorities.'

Furthermore, the use of intelligence as the basis for administrative counter-terrorism measures may raise the issue of illegally obtained evidence. As the use of intelligence has increasingly been accompanied by international co-operation between intelligence agencies in different States, the risk that sources and methods used to collect intelligence can be unlawful has increased significantly. At worst, intelligence may include information obtained through torture or other forms of ill-treatment. However, there already exist significant variations between the EU Member States, let alone other countries, regarding the use of illegally obtained evidence in criminal proceedings.[21] It is likely that these variations are even greater insofar as the use of illegally obtained intelligence in administrative proceedings is concerned. In addition, the methods for collecting intelligence are not directed by the same evidentiary standards and the standard of proof than the collection of evidence for criminal proceedings. These features can only intensify the human rights concerns pertaining to the use of intelligence in making decisions regarding various administrative counter-terrorism measures.

5. EXCURSION: THE USE OF OPINIONS BY THE FINNISH SECURITY INTELLIGENCE SERVICE IN FINNISH IMMIGRATION LAW PROCEEDINGS

The use of opinions by the Finnish Security Intelligence Service in immigration law proceedings neatly illustrates human rights concerns pertaining to the use of intelligence. Annually, the Finnish Security Intelligence Service issues ca. 200–300 so-called security opinions on applications for a residence permit[22] and citizenship. In addition, it may conduct an asylum interview, if Finland's national security or international relations so require.[23]

Up until the mid-2000s, the administrative practice was that if the Finnish Security Intelligence Service had not supported the application

---

[21] See EU network of independent experts on fundamental rights, Opinion on the status of illegally obtained evidence in criminal procedures in the Member States of the European Union. 30 November 2003, CFR-CDF.opinion 3-2003.

[22] According to section 116, subsection 2, of the Aliens Act (*ulkomaalaislaki*, Act No 301 of 2004) the Finnish Immigration Service (Maahanmuuttovirasto) decides on applications for a first residence permit on the basis of refugee status or subsidiary protection to an alien admitted to Finland under the refugee quota after receiving the opinion of the Finnish Security Intelligence Service.

[23] Section 97, subsection 3 of the Aliens Act.

for a residence permit or citizenship on the view that the applicant was considered a threat to State security, the competent administrative authority rejected the application on a routine basis. Similarly, the administrative courts, including the Supreme Administrative Court, invariably endorsed the finding of the Intelligence Service that the applicant was a threat to State security. Moreover, courts routinely dismissed requests for oral hearings so that the Intelligence Service could be heard and its views could be challenged and reviewed on substantive grounds. Likewise, courts dismissed requests for disclosure of documents containing intelligence used as evidence in support of the view that the applicant is a threat to State security. Usually, the reasoning adopted by the court in favor of non-disclosure was that the Intelligence Service's opinion was based on information received through international intelligence and concerned the applicant's previous activity and background. In conclusion, both the competent administrative authority and the administrative courts reviewing administrative decisions showed great deference to assessment by the Intelligence Service, both in respect of the issue whether there was credible evidence on which its views were based and in respect of recognizing potential restrictions on access to intelligence on grounds of public security or the maintenance of international relations. Indeed, not only the role of administrative authority but also the role of the courts was subdued regarding intelligence in immigration procedures.

Over the years, this way of using intelligence in Finnish administrative procedures involving applications for a residence permit or citizenship was criticized by human rights activists and NGOs but the practice continued essentially intact. The practice also attracted some publicity as an individual whose citizenship application had been rejected succeeded in gaining attention for this in the domestic press and television, even to the extent that he started featuring as a kind of fairness martyr in Finland.[24]

---

[24] In 2004, an application against Finland was lodged before the ECtHR. Among others, the applicant complained that there had been a violation of Article 13 of the ECHR because he had not been informed why he was considered a threat to national security by the prevention of terrorism branch of the Finnish Security Intelligence Service with the outcome that his application for a residence permit had been rejected on that ground by the administrative authority and the administrative courts. The applicant claimed that he had been unable to produce counter-evidence with a view to dispelling the unfounded suspicions against him. He also relied on Articles 6(1) and 8 of the ECHR. However, the matter giving rise to the complaint was resolved when the complaint was pending before the ECtHR. Therefore, the ECtHR decided to

In summer 2007, the Supreme Administrative Court of Finland eventually handed down two judgments that were intended to feature as precedents for cases involving the use of intelligence in immigration proceedings.[25] These judgments were supposed to reconcile better the competing demands of secrecy of intelligence and procedural fairness. The starting point of this new approach is that the administrative authority cannot reject applications for a residence permit or citizenship with reference solely to the opinion by the Intelligence Service that the applicant is a threat to State security. Instead, the matter must be appropriately clarified and the administrative authority ought to state adequate reasons for its decision.

Furthermore, the relation between the disclosure of intelligence and the use of intelligence to make decisions on applications for a residence permit and citizenship was revised as follows. On the one hand, the Supreme Administrative Court acknowledged that overriding security concerns may continue to preclude the communication of certain information to a party, thereby recognizing the need for keeping secret information derived from intelligence sources. Drawing on the case law of the ECtHR, the Court also concluded that the non-disclosure of confidential material to a party on national security grounds is not as such in violation of the ECHR, either. On the other hand, however, the Court emphasized that non-disclosure did not mean that this confidential material would be immune from judicial review. The Court inferred from the case law of the ECtHR that courts must have the opportunity to review the material in order to assess whether it can be deemed confidential and whether it truly constitutes sufficient ground to conclude that the applicant is a threat to national security. For this purpose, the Court adopted the practice that judicial review of intelligence should be carried out by administrative courts in *closed oral hearings* in which the

---

strike the application out of its list of cases. Insofar as the applicant had complained that he had been refused information underlying the Intelligence Service opinion, the ECtHR took the view that the complaint was premature since this issue was still pending before the Supreme Administrative Court. The ECtHR therefore declared the complaint manifestly ill-founded and rejected it in accordance with Article 35(3) and (4) of the ECHR. See *Q v. Finland*, Application no. 42640/04, Decision 22 May 2007 of the European Court of Human Rights (Fourth Section).

[25] Supreme Administrative Court KHO 2007:48, judgment of 12.7.2007, Report no. 1830; 2752/3/06; and KHO 2007:49, judgment of 12.7.2007, Report no. 1831; 757/3/07.

representatives of the Intelligence Service are heard but which remain inaccessible to the applicant.

The current position of the Finnish administrative courts is neatly illustrated by the judgment of the Supreme Administrative Court of Finland in the case of KHO 2007:49.[26] In that case, the Finnish Immigration Service had rejected X's application for a residence permit on the basis of a family tie. As grounds for its decision the Immigration Service stated that the Security Police was not in favor of granting X a residence permit. On X's appeal, the administrative court ruled that the Immigration Service could not reject X's application with reference solely to the opinion of the Security Police. In the court's view, the matter had not been appropriately clarified and the Immigration Service had failed to state adequate reasons for its decision. The court referred the matter back to the Immigration Service which then appealed to the Supreme Administrative Court.

The Supreme Administrative Court found apparent from the case law of the ECtHR that confidential material which is not disclosed to a party on national security grounds is not as such in violation of the ECHR.[27] However, in such a case a competent court must have the opportunity to review the material to which the party has not had access in order to assess whether it can be deemed confidential and whether it can ground the decision of the administrative authority. The Court continued that, in order to meet the requirements for effective remedy stipulated in Article 13 of the ECHR and section 21 of the Finnish Constitution Act, an administrative court has a duty to consider whether there is a just balance between individual rights, on the one hand, and public order and national security, on the other. The Court then ruled that, in view of the exceptions to the parties' right of access to documents, as laid down by law, and the duty of authorities to to state reasons for their decisions in cases in which national security is involved, the administrative court should not have referred the matter back to the Immigration Service. Instead, it should

---

[26] Supreme Administrative Court KHO 2007:48, judgment of 12.7.2007, Report no. 1830; 2752/3/06.

[27] The Court made explicit reference to the cases of *Chahal v. the United Kingdom*, judgment of 15 November 1996, Reports of Judgments and Decisions 1996-V; *Al-Nashif v. Bulgaria*, judgment of 20 June 2002; *Brinks v. the Netherlands*, judgment of 5 April 2005; *Segerstedt-Wiberg and Others v. Sweden*, judgment of 6 June 2006, Reports of Judgments and Decisions 2006-VII; *Lupsa v. Romania*, judgment of 8 June 2006, Reports of Judgments and Decisions 2006-VII; *Kaya v. Romania*, judgment of 12 October 2006; *and Jasper v. the United Kingdom*, judgment of 16 February 2000.

have reviewed the confidential material in order to assess whether there were sufficient grounds to deny X's residence permit with reference to reasons of public interest, public safety and national security. In order to avoid any further delay, the Supreme Administrative Court did not return the case to the lower administrative court, but considered X's appeal instead. It heard the representatives of the Security Police in a closed oral hearing and concluded that the material upon which the opinion of the Security Police was based could be classified as secret documents to which a party had no right of access.[28] The Court found that the reasons presented by the Security Police were as such worth noticing. However, in the Court's view, the reasons were not weighty enough for denying X a residence permit when the right to the protection of family life was balanced against the security interests of the State in this case. The Court quashed the decisions of the administrative court and the Immigration Service and referred the matter back to the Immigration Service.[29]

The new Court practice can be welcomed as a modest first step in the right direction. The first improvement relates to the reason-giving requirement that serves both an instrumental and a rule of law-based rationale as it enables those affected by an administrative measure to defend their rights, as well as facilitates the exercise of judicial review. Given limitations on the right to be heard and the disclosure of such confidential material as intelligence, the requirement to state adequate reasons actually becomes one of the key aspects of due process. However, the significance of the reason-giving requirement cannot be overplayed. It must also be acknowledged that this requirement may be subject to similar limitations as those applicable to the right to a hearing and disclosure of confidential material. Security considerations or the need to protect the sources and methods used to collect intelligence from disclosure may thus limit or even preclude the statement of specific and complete reasons for the decision to reject the application for a residence permit or citizenship.

The second and clearly the most significant improvement relates to judicial review. The new approach put at rest the previous practice that had effectively curtailed the ability of the courts to review intelligence for the purpose of determining whether it really constitutes a sufficient ground for rejecting an application for a residence permit or citizenship. Judicial review of intelligence is all the more important as it is actually

---

[28] Under the Act No 621 of 1999 on the Openness of Government Activities.

[29] See also KHO 2007:49, judgment of 12.7.2007, Report no. 1831; 757/3/07.

the only procedural safeguard ensuring that a fair balance is struck between security concerns and the protection of human rights. After all, the current Court practice also stems from the premise that overriding security concerns or considerations relating to the conduct of the international relations may continue to preclude the communication of certain information to the parties concerned, including the hearing of those parties with regard to such information. Therefore, it is crucial that (at least) administrative courts are able to review, on a case-by-case basis, whether intelligence needs to be disclosed to the accused in the interests of trial fairness and whether it really constitutes sufficient grounds to deny a residence permit or citizenship with reference to reasons of State security.

Despite these improvements, however, the new approach leaves much to be desired. In particular, the right to a fair hearing remains problematic as the applicants, including their lawyers, are still left in a position where the key 'evidence' against them is set out in *closed oral hearings* on the basis of information not made available to them. Although the right to a fair hearing does not necessarily entitle a person to a formal hearing, it nonetheless requires that the person concerned has been put into a position where they can make their views effectively known to the authorities. This puts emphasis on the decision-maker's duty to give an adequate statement of the reasons for its decision but, given the potential limitations of the reason-giving requirement, it is questionable whether the current practice fully succeeds in meeting this minimum requirement. In addition, the non-disclosure of relevant information to the applicant and his lawyer easily gives an appearance of unfair proceeding and, accordingly, can turn the (rejected) applicants into fairness martyrs even if, at least in some cases, the secret information may be wholly accurate and the applicant can really be considered a threat to State security. It is indicative that one of the applicants started gaining even wider publicity for his (allegedly) unfair treatment after the Supreme Administrative Court, having heard the representatives of the Security Police in a closed oral hearing, had ruled that the reasons were weighty enough for denying his application for citizenship.[30]

Obviously, therefore, the new approach cannot dispel all doubts of unfair secret proceedings when intelligence is used in immigration procedures in Finland. It is also safe to argue that the new approach by

---

[30] KHO 2007:49, judgment of 12.7.2007, Report no. 1831; 757/3/07. See, e.g. television progamme http://yle.fi/vintti/ohjelmat.yle.fi/harkaa_sarvista/jaksot/supon_vankina.html.

the Supreme Administrative Court opts for rather a minimalist approach as regards finding a decent balance between, on the one hand, the overriding interests of public security and, on the other hand, the rights of the individual. The balance scale still tilts towards the interests of public security and the non-disclosure of secret intelligence at the expense of adjudicative fairness. Among various means to manage the use of intelligence, the new approach is clearly closer to that end of the secrecy–disclosure spectrum where intelligence is used as secret evidence that is not disclosed to the persons concerned. Therefore, the new approach should be understood as marking the beginning rather than the end of the process of elaborating further on the scope of procedural rights and the appropriate level of judicial scrutiny of administrative decisions involving the use of intelligence.

Exactly how to reconcile the tension between the demands of disclosure and secrecy of intelligence is a multifaceted issue that cannot be resolved here. A general reference should just be made to a range of less rights-intrusive alternatives to the use of intelligence, such as those revolving around the use of special advocates or security-cleared advocates who are allowed to see and challenge secret evidence. There may also be active and expert judges or Ombudspersons to challenge the use of secret intelligence.[31]

However, these kinds of solutions do not necessarily suit all legal systems, such as the Finnish one. At least, the introduction of special advocates or security cleared counsels would require a thorough rethinking of the role of advocates in Finnish court proceedings in general. Besides, there is not necessarily much call for them because the path chosen by the Finnish Supreme Administrative Court, resting on a case-by-case judicial review of whether intelligence needs to be disclosed and whether it is sufficient for denying the application, is quite feasible. It is only that the court's new approach is far from perfect and needs to be elaborated. Aside from involving a questionable practice of hearing the representatives of the Security Police in a closed oral hearing, the main weakness of the current approach appears to be that the interest of secrecy of intelligence is emphasized too much at the expense of adjudicative fairness and transparency. Therefore, further improvements should be premised on *a priori* acceptance that some intelligence will have to be disclosed for the sake of procedural fairness and overall

[31] For a detailed analysis of alternatives to the use of secret evidence, see Kent Roach's contribution to this volume.

legitimacy of immigration procedures. This approach should be accompanied by a more critical scrutiny of the various categories to which the secrecy of intelligence may be related (i.e. origins of intelligence, methods of collecting intelligence, content and nature of information, information of other individuals, etc.). By also emphasizing the need to understand the right of access to documents in a broad sense so that it actually entails the right of access to *information,* the starting point of judicial scrutiny would then be that all exceptions to right of access to information must be interpreted strictly, and in the light of the principle of the right to information and the principle of proportionality. In the final analysis, judicial deliberation would involve the process of balancing and weighing, in accordance with the principle of proportionality, between the right of access to documents, on the one hand, and secrecy of intelligence information, on the other hand. Total refusal of access to all categories of intelligence may often be unwarranted because it may be possible to grant *partial* access to a document (or, perhaps more to the point, some categories of intelligence), while at the same time sufficiently taking into account the demand of secrecy of (some other categories of) intelligence.

Finally, the context-dependency of determining between the demands of disclosure and secrecy of intelligence must be emphasized. It is not appropriate to regard the secrecy of intelligence as a static quality, covering all instances of using intelligence irrespective of the context. Instead, the matter is ultimately a dynamic moment-to-moment construction. As the context in question changes, intelligence that was previously perceived as claiming secrecy may need disclosure – and *vice versa.*

6. CONCLUDING OBSERVATIONS

Administrative measures have increasingly been introduced as instruments for countering terrorism. These measures seek to prevent terrorism by limiting the opportunities for terrorist activities and by removing incentives for them. However, while administrative counter-terrorism measures primarily function as preventive tools for combating terrorism they also have a repressive, punitive side. Actually, their consequences can often be more severe and far-reaching than those of traditional criminal sanctions.

Administrative counter-terrorism measures also engage a range of human rights but the protection of fundamental human rights often leaves much to be desired. Problems relating to human rights protection have already been discussed in great detail regarding the UN and the EU sanctions regimes, but human rights concerns can also be detected in other forms of administrative counter-terrorism measures – and also in such democracies as Finland, which is renowned for respecting and promoting human rights and favoring transparency and openness of administrative proceedings.

Human rights concerns surrounding administrative counter-terrorism measures are intensified by the extensive use of secret intelligence. While intelligence plays an important role in countering terrorism and enables States to fulfill their positive obligation to safeguard the human rights of all individuals under their jurisdiction, the use of intelligence represents a serious challenge to the norms of adjudicative fairness. Intelligence is usually kept secret and, accordingly, not disclosed to the affected persons and their lawyers. Intelligence may also limit the ability of the court to review whether intelligence is factually accurate and reliable and whether it is really capable of substantiating the conclusions drawn from it.

The use of administrative counter-terrorism measures without adequate protection of fundamental human rights is liable to undermine the credibility and effectiveness of these measures. As effective counter-terrorism measures and the protection of fundamental human rights are complementary and mutually reinforcing, this calls for a better balance between, on the one hand, the overriding interests of public security and, on the other hand, the rights of the individuals. Although a series of incremental improvements has already been made at domestic, regional and global levels,[32] there is still urgent need to elaborate further the protection of human rights, including the demands of openness and transparency, in the context of administrative counter-terrorism measures. After all, it cannot just be that measures under administrative law, often building essentially on such secret evidence as intelligence, are harnessed to the purpose of countering terrorism without simultaneously reinventing and rethinking various means for protecting appropriately human rights.

---

[32] As noted by the ECJ in *Kadi*, the UN listing and delisting procedures have been subject to piecemeal reforms by the Security Council itself, including through incremental improvements in the status of the affected individual. Furthermore, Security Council Resolution 1822 (2008) introduced new improvements, such as the notification of listed individuals and the mandatory review of all entries on the list by June 2010.

16. Secret evidence in EU security law: special advocates before the Court of Justice?

Cian C. Murphy*

INTRODUCTION

The aftermath of the *Kadi* judgment from the European Court of Justice (ECJ) has left jurists unpicking the many implications of the judgment for EU law.[1] In its judgment the Court refused to defer to the UN Security Council's decision to designate Mr. Kadi as an individual 'associated with' Osama bin Laden and Al-Qaeda. Instead, it held that the failure to respect Mr. Kadi's due process rights rendered unlawful the EU implementation of the sanctions against him. This decision has been reinforced by the judgment of the General Court in *Kadi II* which dismissed the brief statement of reasons given to Mr. Kadi as insufficient to allow him to challenge the case against him. One of the more difficult questions the Court of Justice's review of the asset-freezing sanctions raises is how, if at all, the Court might review the any evidence presented to it.

This question will become more and more important in the coming years. At present the EU operates two systems of targeted sanctions against terrorism.[2] Both systems rely on designations taken outside of the

---

* The author is grateful to Sofia Marques da Silva for comments on a previous draft and to Maya Lester for conversations on upcoming sanctions litigation before the EU courts.

[1] Joined Cases C-402/05 P and C-415/05 P *Kadi and Al Barakaat International Foundation v Council and Commission* [2008] ECR I-6351. See, in general, CIAN C MURPHY, EU COUNTER-TERRORISM LAW: PRE-EMPTION AND THE RULE OF LAW (2012) ch. 5.

[2] See CHRISTINA ECKES, EU COUNTER-TERRORIST POLICIES AND FUNDAMENTAL RIGHTS: THE CASE OF INDIVIDUAL SANCTIONS (2009).

EU institutions. EU Regulation 881/2002 establishes a system of designation of those suspected of involvement with Al-Qaeda and the Taliban. Designation on this list effectively happens at UN level with the EU system merely implementing decisions of the UN 1267 Committee (a subcommittee of the UN Security Council).[3] EU Regulation 2580/2001 establishes a separate system of designation wherein the EU lists individuals and entities based on decisions taken by 'competent national authorities'. In these cases the EU acts when a Member State has identified an individual or entity linked to terrorism and it wishes to have the target designated across the EU. Two sets of cases, *Kadi* in respect of the UN list, and *OMPI/PMOI* in respect of the EU list, have afforded the EU courts the opportunity to consider the lawfulness of the designations and the processes by which individuals and entities are listed.[4] The courts have been robust in their review of EU action in this field – though the question to date has largely been limited to whether or not review should be undertaken. As no evidence has yet been presented to the EU institutions the ECJ has not yet dealt with the question of how to treat any secret evidence that forms the basis of the case against the targets.

Nevertheless, it is clear that EU law will soon have to grapple in a very real way with the question. It arises not only in the context of counter-terrorism sanctions, but also in sanctions in relation to a wide range of situations in international law (e.g. nuclear non-proliferation in Iran).[5] This chapter gives an exposition of the problem and a critical evaluation of one proposed solution – the UK system of special advocates. It cautions against the transplant of the flawed UK model into the EU system where, to date, the courts have robustly upheld the rule of law.

1. THE ONGOING *KADI* SAGA

Following the decision of the ECJ in *Kadi I*, Mr. Kadi was provided with a one-page 'narrative summary' that purported to explain to him his

---

[3] There are now several UN Security Council resolutions governing this system of sanctions. For a collection of the relevant resolutions see www.un.org/sc/committees/1267/.

[4] See, most recently, Case T-85/09 *Kadi v Commission* [2010] ECR 0000 (hereafter '*Kadi II*'; Case T-284/08 *People's Mojahedin Organization of Iran v Council* [2008] ECR II-3487.

[5] Although the ECJ does not have a general competence in the field of the common foreign and security policy under Article 275 TFEU it may review measures adopted to target specific individuals and may also review regulations adopted to implement common foreign and security policy instruments.

designation under the UN Security Council system of sanctions. After (a brief) consideration of Mr. Kadi's response to this letter the European Commission took the decision to maintain Mr. Kadi's listing. The EU General Court gave short shrift to the European Commission's argument that this was sufficient to allow Mr. Kadi to vindicate his due process rights – noting that the Commission itself did not have any evidence before it when it made the decision to maintain Mr. Kadi on the sanctions list.[6] Several questions arise as a result of the *Kadi II* decision. First, does the UN Security Council possess the evidence that formed the basis for the listing of Mr. Kadi? Ginsborg and Scheinin suggest that this may well not be the case – noting that the US and Libya have, in recent years, both been members of the UN Security Council and that it is highly unlikely that the former would be willing to share any evidence or intelligence with the latter.[7] Second, regardless of whether or not the Security Council possesses the evidence that is the basis for Mr. Kadi's listing, would the designating state – the US – be willing to release that information to the ECJ? Although such release might seem unlikely, there has been some discussion of the possibility within the US Government.[8] Third, if the US was willing to release the information, under what circumstances would it do so and what disclosure of the information would it permit to the litigants in *Kadi II*? The EU courts have indicated that it is unlikely to be enough for the EU institutions themselves to consider the evidence – they must also present the evidence for the court's assessment. Fourth, as a consequence, how should the ECJ address the question of evidence that is security-sensitive but which nonetheless forms the basis for restrictive measures against individuals? This evidence, referred to here as 'secret

[6] *Kadi II*, para 95.

[7] Lisa Ginsborg and Martin Scheinin, Judicial Powers, Due Process and Evidence in the Security Council 1267 Terrorist Sanctions Regime: The *Kadi II* Conundrum, EUI Working Papers RSCAS 2011/44, fn 72.

[8] Several of the WikiLeaks US Diplomatic Cables hint in this direction. See cable reference 09BRUSSELS41 (13 January 2009 – copy with author): 'We must confront the possibility that working with the Council on designations may entail enabling the EU court to access unclassified or even classified information to review the legality of the EU listing … Assuming the U.S. classified material necessary to support an EU designation decision is not amenable to declassification, the agreement could perhaps be used to facilitate information sharing and the provision of evidence in the event of anticipated EU judicial challenges. However, the Council itself does not yet have a consensus view on whether its own classified information can be shared with the EU courts.'

evidence', is the subject of a lively debate in Anglo-American constitutional, administrative and criminal procedural law.[9] However, it has not yet been considered in detail in EU security law. In her Opinion in the case of *French Republic v OMPI* Advocate General Sharpston sought to do just that.[10] The case arose as the appellant Member States sought to have the ECJ rule on certain points of law raised in the litigation before the EU General Court. As a legal dispute the case had become moot – the Council had delisted the People's Mujahedin Organization of Iran (OMPI) after the General Court ruling.[11] The French Republic, however, was concerned about the implications for Member State national security practices if the only way to maintain a listing was to disclose the evidence that was the basis for the listing to the EU courts and therefore to the litigants before it.

2. ADVOCATE GENERAL SHARPSTON OPINION IN *FRENCH REPUBLIC V OMPI*

In her Opinion Advocate General Sharpston notes that 'both the General Court and the Court of Justice have anticipated that the need may arise for specific procedures governing confidential evidence to be introduced'.[12] In *OMPI* the General Court held that it was unlawful to designate an organisation as 'terrorist' if that designation was based on secret evidence that was not disclosed. On appeal, the French Republic argued that the evidence in question was classified and therefore could not be disclosed to the General Court. As the General Court may only take into account materials that have been disclosed to the parties to the case the French Republic argued it could not disclose the material to the General Court without disclosing it to OMPI and therefore compromising French national security.[13] In light of this problem the Advocate General argued that amending the General Court's Rules of Procedure merited

---

[9] See the other contributions to this volume, but also, Kent Roach, The Eroding Distinction between Intelligence and Evidence in Terrorism Investigations, in COUNTER-TERRORISM AND BEYOND: THE CULTURE OF LAW AND JUSTICE AFTER 9/11 (Andrew Lynch, Nicola McGarrity and George Williams eds., 2010).

[10] C-27/09 P *French Republic v People's Mojahedin Organization of Iran*, Opinion of Advocate General Sharpston of 14 July 2011 (hereafter 'Sharpston Opinion').

[11] Case T-284/08 *People's Mojahedin Organization of Iran v Council* [2008] ECR II-3487.

[12] Sharpston Opinion para 178–80.

[13] Ibid para 171.

'serious consideration'.[14] The amendments should 'make provision for the production of evidence that is truly confidential for consideration by that Court in a way that is compatible with its character' without causing 'unacceptable violence' to due process rights.[15]

Is it appropriate, therefore, for the EU to consider the use of special advocates or some similar system of approaching secret evidence? The General Court judgment in *OMPI* already highlighted the first problem with such a system: the evidence is likely to be held by national law enforcement and security agencies. Even if it is disclosed to the Council, the Member State holding the evidence may not be willing to risk disclosure to the target of EU action through judicial review. However, the Advocate General makes the minimum requirement at the administrative stage in the EU listing process clear. She regards 'the availability of a non-confidential summary as an irreducible minimum guarantee in a Union governed by the rule of law'. Without such a summary 'it is impossible for the rights of the defence to be safeguarded'.[16] The Advocate General acknowledges that the national authorities involved in designation may vary from Member State to Member State and that in some instances open evidence may be used whereas in others the evidence may be closed. She holds that if there was not a judicial authority involved in designation at national level, or if the evidence at national level was not disclosed, then the Council should be more cautious in its decision-making as to whether or not to designate the individual or entity at EU level.[17]

When it comes to the review by the General Court and the Court of Justice of any designation based on secret evidence the Advocate General turns to the decision of the European Court of Human Rights in *A. v United Kingdom*.[18] According to the Advocate General's summary:

> in order for the requirements of the Convention to be satisfied, it is necessary that as much information about the allegations and evidence against each applicant be disclosed as is possible without compromising national security or the safety of others, that the party concerned be 'provided with sufficient information about the allegations against him to enable him to give effective instructions to the special advocate' and that 'any difficulties caused to the

---

[14] Ibid para 186.
[15] Ibid.
[16] Ibid para 216.
[17] Ibid para 220–21.
[18] *A. v United Kingdom* [2009] 49 EHRR 695.

> defendant by a limitation on his rights [be] sufficiently counterbalanced by the procedures followed by the judicial authorities'.[19]

Sharpston once again uses the term 'irreducible minimum requirement' in respect of the above principles.[20] This is the high point of the Opinion as it confirms that – at the very least – the 'gist' of the evidence should be disclosed to the subject of the proceedings.

What is not clear from the Opinion is whether or not the Advocate General is endorsing a system of special advocates, as used in the UK, for EU courts. The only reference to special advocates is in a footnote to the Opinion. However, she appears to be cautiously accepting of the use of a special advocate system. The footnote sets out the operation of the system before observing that although 'the system has been adapted since its introduction in order to meet objections made, that does not mean that it is now without its critics'. While the Advocate General does acknowledge a report of the UK Parliament's Joint Committee on Human Rights that is highly critical of special advocates she emphasises that the criticisms 'relate essentially to the operation of the system rather than its core structure'.[21] Given that the system of special advocates has been in place since 1997 and is still, as recently as November 2011, the subject of severe criticism it is difficult to accept it as a model for the EU.[22] A brief exposition of the problems with special advocates in closed hearings (called closed material proceedings in the UK) serves to demonstrate the reasons for caution.

3. THE PROBLEM WITH SPECIAL ADVOCATES

In the UK, the use of special advocates in closed material proceedings has been the subject of rigorous judicial examination, academic critique and review by civil society. The range of views varies from endorsement (UK Government) through cautious acceptance (European Court of Human Rights and some members of the UK judiciary) to denunciation (other members of the UK judiciary, parliamentarians, and civil society

---

19 Sharpston Opinion para 244.

20 Ibid para 245.

21 Ibid, fn 89.

22 JOINT COMMITTEE ON HUMAN RIGHTS, JUSTICE AND SECURITY GREEN PAPER: LETTER TO THE SECRETARY OF STATE FOR JUSTICE, 9 November 2011.

groups).[23] It is clear that despite their proliferation there remain problems with special advocates as a remedy for the due process restrictions in closed material proceedings. The fundamental flaw was put rather eloquently by a 2009 JUSTICE report. It drew on Euripides' *Medea*: 'he who decides on something without hearing the other side is not just, even if he makes a just decision'.[24] This is the central problem with the operation of special advocates and closed material proceedings. At precisely the point at which the accused's participation is most important, both to ensure the legitimacy of the process and the effectiveness of counter-terrorism, he is excluded from the process. At that point, no matter how skilled or conscientious the special advocate is, he has become part of a system to which the accused is subject rather than in which the accused participates.

One reason for this is that special advocates cannot be held accountable to those whose interests they seek to represent. This restriction was introduced by the Special Immigration Appeals Commission (SIAC) Act 1997, which introduced special advocates into UK law, and has been replicated in other statutes. Section 6(4) of the SIAC legislation states that the special advocate 'shall not be responsible to the person whose interests he is appointed to represent'.[25] This is a fundamental change to the role of a lawyer with implications not just for the legitimacy and effectiveness of the system but also for questions of professional ethics.[26] Notwithstanding the lack of accountability special advocates tend to be highly qualified and diligent professionals. The former Independent Reviewer of Terrorism Legislation, Lord Carlile, reported that he received no complaints about the use of special advocates whom he described as 'skilled and conscientious, and certainly useful'.[27] The system did encounter something of a crisis in 2004–2005 when a mass resignation of special advocates was threatened over their use in cases of

---

23 For a summary see CLIVE WALKER, TERRORISM AND THE LAW 267–9 (2011).

24 ERIC METCALFE, SECRET EVIDENCE 7 (2009).

25 See also s 7 of the Schedule to the Prevention of Terrorism Act 2005; s 68(2) Counter-Terrorism Act 2008.

26 Andrew Boon and Susan Nash, Special Advocacy: Political Expediency and Legal Roles in Modern Judicial Systems, 9 LEGAL ETHICS 101 (2006).

27 LORD CARLILE, SECOND REPORT OF THE INDEPENDENT REVIEWER OF TERRORISM LEGISLATION PURSUANT TO SECTION 14(3) OF THE PREVENTION OF TERRORISM ACT 2005, para 49 (2007).

preventive detention where personal liberty was at stake. Although two special advocates did resign the mass resignation was averted.[28]

Special advocates have therefore been said to 'occupy an interstitial space somewhere between an amicus curiae and an ordinary legal representative'.[29] This is problematic. If the special advocate is closer to an *amicus curiae* then the subject of the state action goes effectively unrepresented in the closed material proceedings. It is clear from those special advocates who have spoken publicly about their role that they do not see themselves as amici curiae.[30] However, because of the restrictions on their role, special advocates are not an ordinary legal representative. As a result the relationship is not easily defined – which is a concern given the severity of the interference with the rights of those subject to the proceedings. Although the legal culture amongst special advocates may be respectful of the rule of law, that culture faces significant resistance from the UK Government. As it is the latter that ultimately decides on the rules of the closed material proceedings (through legislation) attempts by special advocates to uphold the rule of law have been hampered on several fronts.

First, special advocates cannot, except in certain very limited circumstances, communicate with the subject of the proceedings after they have seen the closed evidence. The only communication that is permitted is with the permission of the court, which must notify the Secretary of State, who then has the opportunity to object to the communication. As any disclosure to the court or the Secretary of State may indicate case strategy, special advocates have rarely sought permission to communicate with those being represented. The individual may write to the special advocate but the latter is not permitted to reply except to acknowledge receipt. The Green Paper, *Justice & Security*, has proposed to encourage special advocates to communicate with those they represent by putting in place a 'Chinese wall' between the Government counsel in the case and

---

[28] SIAC itself had to survive the resignation in 2002 of Brian Barder, one of the first lay members to be appointed, following decisions of both the Court of Appeal and House of Lords to overturn the decision of SIAC in *Rehman* [2001] UKHL 47. Brian Barder, On SIAC 26 LONDON REVIEW OF BOOKS, 18 March 2004, at 40–41.

[29] John Ip, The Rise and Spread of the Special Advocate, PUBLIC LAW 717, 735 (2008).

[30] See discussion in HOUSE OF COMMONS CONSTITUTIONAL AFFAIRS COMMITTEE, REPORT ON THE OPERATION OF THE SPECIAL IMMIGRATION APPEALS COMMISSION (SIAC) AND THE USE OF SPECIAL ADVOCATES, HC PAPER NO 323-I (2004–2005).

those appointed to clear communication between the special advocate and the person they represent.[31] It is difficult to see how such a Chinese wall could operate in practice and the proposal does not remedy the concern that the special advocate may have to disclose strategy to the judge who will ultimately decide the case. An incidental restriction is that special advocates cannot act in subsequent proceedings if closed materials they have seen in one case might give rise to a leak of information to an individual in a subsequent one. The measures taken to avoid leaking or 'tainting' are therefore quite extensive.

Second, in a similar vein, courts in closed materials proceedings may hand down closed judgments. Closed judgments contain the reasoning of the court but exclude material which the court has considered if the publication of such material would be prejudicial to national security. Of course, special advocates might derive benefit from reading closed judgments of relevance to their case. However, without knowing what is in a particular closed judgment it is difficult for special advocates to identify relevant precedents. To remedy this the Home Office is exploring the possibility of developing closed head notes for such judgments with searchable keywords.[32] Nevertheless, there remains the problem of the absence of any academic discourse on such judgments. If the academy plays a role in upholding the rule of law and cultivating a culture of legality it is in subjecting case law to critical appraisal so as to highlight problems with the law both as a system of rules and as it operates in broader context. The veil of secrecy over closed judgments makes such appraisal impossible and impoverishes the culture of legality as a result.

Third, special advocates do not have instructing solicitors in the usual manner. This places an onerous burden on the special advocate in preparing the case – in particular when they can no longer communicate with the individual that is the subject of the proceedings or his ordinary legal representatives. The problem has in part been resolved by the introduction of the Special Advocates Support Office. The Government has proposed that special advocates be offered 'sufficient resources in terms of independent junior legal support' in light of the likely extension of their use to more complex proceedings.[33] The difficulty in addressing the closed materials may be exacerbated by the late delivery of those materials – though the Government denies there is a systemic problem in

---

[31] HM Government, Justice and Security: Green Paper (2011), para 2.33.

[32] Ibid, Appendix F.

[33] Ibid, para 2.27.

this respect.[34] In addition, much of the time special advocates spend in closed proceedings is aimed at attempting to make more material openly available. This is a valuable role but it means that the material is not being challenged on substance – rather the special advocate is performing a form of meta-advocacy that may leave the case against the individual standing.

Fourth, on a related point, there are limits on the ability of a special advocate to challenge the national security evidence presented against those whose interests they are representing. In the past special advocates were unable to call expert witnesses to challenge the state's evidence. While special advocates may now call expert witnesses they may not call current or former members of security agencies. There are further restrictions (security vetting) that would appear to limit the effectiveness of such witnesses for the special advocate.[35] The *Justice & Security* Green Paper proposes to offer additional training for special advocates on intelligence analysis and assessment. This proposal seeks to improve the rigour of the special advocate's examination of closed material.[36] However, it does not address the fundamental imbalance in the use of expert evidence in closed material proceedings. A further problem in this respect is the lack of clear rules on the probative value and the rules of evidence to be used in relation to closed materials.[37]

These restrictions indicate that no matter how skilled the special advocate he or she will face significant disadvantages in their effort to ensure that rule of law principles are upheld. The difficult choice faced by those who operate the legal system is whether or not to co-operate with a system that is ultimately contrary to the rule of law. Despite its problems the system of special advocates will be available in all civil litigation in the UK if the Justice and Security Bill 2012 becomes law.[38] However, the above problems remain, and Advocate General Sharpston's

---

34 Ibid, Appendix F.

35 Ibid, Appendix F.

36 Ibid, para 2.24.

37 SPECIAL ADVOCATES, JUSTICE AND SECURITY GREEN PAPER: RESPONSE TO CONSULTATION FROM SPECIAL ADVOCATES (2011), para 17.

38 In the UK legal system it is typical for the Government to consult on major legislative proposals prior to introducing a bill into Parliament. A Green Paper is an exploratory document seeking engagement with the subject of the paper. A Green Paper is sometimes followed by a White Paper that sets out the Government's proposals in more detail for further consultation before publication of a bill. In the case of the *Justice and Security* Green Paper no White Paper was produced and the Government instead proceeded directly to introducing a legislative proposal.

musings on exporting the system to Europe does not suggest how they might be resolved.

4. EXPORTING THE PROBLEMS TO EUROPE?

In many respects the problems for the EU in relation to special advocates may be even greater than the problems for the UK. All of the flaws of closed material proceedings at national level are writ large when transposed to the supranational legal order of the EU. An initial problem with the solution proposed by the Advocate General is that the multi-level nature of governance in the EU system of targeted sanctions may render the Advocate General's proposed rules of review rather arcane (one hesitates to use the hackneyed 'Kafkaesque'). The Opinion sets out in detail a system of review that varies depending on the decision-making process at national level. Asking first the Council, and then the General Court, to ascertain if the national proceedings are judicial or non-judicial, and based on open or closed evidence, is likely to complicate already complex litigation. Although complexity in this matter may be unavoidable it nonetheless impairs transparency and increases the difficulty of challenging a listing for the individuals and entities targeted. The Opinion did not address whether such a system of review should also operate in relation to EU sanctions that seek to implement decisions of the UN Security Council – though there are obvious analogies.

A further potential problem is the ability of courts to make appropriate assessments about evidence. SIAC, for example, includes an intelligence expert and an immigration expert as well as a High Court judge. Appeals to the Court of Appeal are limited to points of law. The Commission is therefore a specialised tribunal with the appropriate competence to assess the claims made by intelligence services. It is difficult to see how the European judiciary, acting in the best possible faith, could be said to have these skills. Although the EU courts have expertise in dealing with complex, specialised, data – such as in anti-trust litigation – they do not have a history of addressing intelligence data or criminal evidence. While the criticism that courts 'are in no position to act as risk assessors'[39] goes too far there is certainly a difficulty in requiring a *de facto* constitutional judiciary to assess evidence based on intelligence. The differences in the

---

[39] Thomas Poole, Courts and Conditions of Uncertainty in Times of Crisis, PUBLIC LAW 234, 247 (2008).

legal profession across the EU may also pose challenges.[40] There is no reason to believe that lawyers in the UK legal system are more skilled or more diligent in their pursuit of justice than lawyers in other legal systems.[41] Nonetheless, experience may play a role. Because of the zealous pursuit of counter-terrorism policies by successive UK governments there are many advocates in that Member State with experience of dealing with secret evidence. The same may not be true of advocates in other Member States. It is therefore difficult to conceive of EU special advocates that could perform an equivalent role to special advocates in the UK.[42]

As a result of these limitations the proposal that the EU would adopt the UK model, even if the problems with that model could be solved, is not convincing. Thus, while some alteration to the Rules of Procedure for the General Court and the Court of Justice might be advisable, the use of special advocates does not seem advisable.[43] A further question posed by the Sharpston Opinion relates to the current absence of *any* system for dealing with secret evidence. If the Advocate General endorses the principle in *A. v United Kingdom*, then not only is she explicitly requiring disclosure of a gist of the evidence to the target of the sanctions, she may be implicitly requiring disclosure of the whole case to someone acting on his behalf (i.e. the special advocate). This system would likely cause the Council, or at least some of its members, such as France, much consternation. As it is the Council itself that must approve any amendments to the Rules of Procedure there is the distinct possibility

---

40 For a discussion of some differences in the legal profession across the EU see the Opinion of Advocate General Maduro and the judgment of the ECJ in C-305/05 *Ordre de barreaux francophones et germanophone, Ordre francais des avocats du barreau de Bruxelles, Ordre dex barreaux flamands, Ordre néerlandais des avocats du barreau de Bruxelles v Conseil des Ministres* [2007] ECR I-5305.

41 David Dyzenhaus, The state of emergency in legal theory, in GLOBAL ANTI-TERRORISM LAW AND POLICY 88 (Victor V. Ramraj, Michael Hor and Kent Roach eds., 2006).

42 Indeed, anecdotal evidence suggests that much of the sanctions litigation in the EU is being run from London law firms and chambers, such as Brick Court Chambers, which has provided counsel for Mr. Kadi, for OMPI, and for applicants challenging several other sanctions systems (www.brickcourt.co.uk).

43 It seems unlikely that the 'judicial management model', discussed elsewhere in this volume, is suitable either – the same problems of expertise would arise – and such a system would arguably require an even more radical rethink of the Rules of Procedure.

that a system could be adopted that is not favourable to applicants.[44] Any derogation from the ordinary Rules of Procedure should be approached with caution – both at the stage of devising the rules and applying them. However, it is difficult to disagree with the Advocate General's assessment that some action will have to be taken on this matter before too long.

5. SECRET EVIDENCE IN EUROPE

It is clear that although *Kadi* remains the leading case it is by no means the whole story on sanctions in the EU. The proliferation of sanctions litigation is apparent from the case-list before the EU courts. The *Kadi* reasoning is being applied in these new areas – extending the courts' counter-terrorism reasoning into the wider field of security law. Thus *Kadi I* has been confirmed by the ECJ in the Iranian sanctions case of *Bank Melli Iran*.[45] The decision of the General Court in *Fulmen*, concerning sanctions against an Iranian electrical engineering company, also involved a high degree of scrutiny following the *Kadi* logic.[46] Indeed, the list of cases concerning the Iranian sanctions is rather a long one.[47] Furthermore, the sanctions litigation is broader than both counter-terrorism and nuclear non-proliferation. There are, at present, cases pending before the EU courts concerning sanctions against Belarus, Côte d'Ivoire, Egypt, Syria, Tunisia, and Zimbabwe.[48] There is therefore an emerging EU security jurisprudence being developed by the EU courts.

---

[44] See Article 281 TFEU and Protocol (No 3) to the Treaty on the Functioning of the European Union on the Statute of the Court of Justice of the European Union.

[45] Case C-548/09 P *Bank Melli of Iran v Council* Judgment 16 November 2011, nyr.

[46] Case C-280/12 P *Council v Fulmen* (application lodged 6 June 2012).

[47] See, e.g., Case T-57/12 *Good Luck Shipping v Council* OJ C 109 14.04.2012, p 23; T-58/12 *Nabipour & Others v Council* OJ C 109 14.04.2012, p 23; T-63/12 *Oil Turbo Compressor v Council* OJ C 98 31.03.2012, p 27; T-56/12 *IRISL Maritime Training Institute and Others v Council* OJ C 109 14.04.2012, p 22; T-53/12 *CF Sharp Shipping Agencies Pte v Council* OJ C 89 24.03.2012, p 29; T-42/12 *Bateni v Council* OJ C 98 31.03.2012, p 23; T-656/11 *Morison Menon Chartered Accountants and Others v Council* OJ C 58 25.02.2012, p 14. For a full list see the ECJ website (fn 48 below).

[48] The cases are too numerous to list in full here. A search of the Curia database on 30 June 2012 for cases pending before the Court of Justice and the General Court related to the common foreign and security policy returned 85 results – almost all of which were challenges to sanctions systems.

These cases will raise questions as to the standard of judicial review and, in time, the role of secret evidence and how the courts address it. The ECJ declined to follow Advocate General Sharpston's lead in its judgment in the *French Republic v OMPI*.[49] However it may be required to at least comment on the UK model when a reference from the UK Court of Appeal reaches it. The question referred in *ZZ v Secretary of State for the Home Department* is simple but of great significance in this area. The Court of Appeal has asked whether, in a case concerning the exclusion of an EU citizen from a Member State on national security grounds, EU law requires that the individual

> is informed of the essence of the grounds against him, notwithstanding the fact that the authorities of the Member State and the relevant domestic court, after consideration of the totality of the evidence against the European Union citizen relied upon by the authorities of the Member State, conclude that the disclosure of the essence of the grounds against him would be contrary to the interests of state security?[50]

Resolution of the reference in *ZZ* may therefore have broader implications for the EU rule of law. The Opinion and Judgment in *Kadi I* still tower over EU law in the field of counter-terrorism. The invocation by Advocate General Maduro of the words of Israeli Supreme Court Justice Aahron Barak is prescient in the current context: 'it is when the cannons roar that we especially need the laws ... There is always law which the state must comply with. There are no "black holes".'[51] The *Kadi I* Opinion and Judgment represent a high watermark in the development of judicial protection. On the other hand, the UK system of special advocates was born from a desire to comply in the barest possible way with a decision of the European Court of Human Rights and has been corrosive for the culture of legality in that Member State. It would be a retrograde step, in a post-'war on terror' world,[52] for the EU to adopt a system that has been the subject of such criticism within its home Member State.

---

[49] The ECJ declined to discuss the matter in its judgment following Advocate General Sharpston's Opinion C-27/09 P *French Republic v People's Mojahedin Organization of Iran* Judgment of 21 December 2011, nyr.

[50] Case C-300/11 *ZZ v Secretary of State for the Home Department* OJ C 252/20 27.8.2011.

[51] Opinion AG Maduro in C-402/05 P, *Kadi* [2008] ECR I-6351.

[52] Murphy, *supra* fn 1, 260.

CONCLUSION: 'FORCE YIELDS PLACE TO LAW'

How then should the EU courts deal with secret evidence? The former UN Special Rapporteur, Martin Scheinin, has advocated reform along the lines of 'best practice'.[53] This has been described as 'legal and institutional frameworks that serve to promote and to protect human rights and the rule of law in all aspects of counter-terrorism'.[54] Best practice is not just about complying with the 'irreducible minimum requirement' of human rights law but also about developing 'principles that go beyond these legally binding obligations'.[55] In respect of the evidence used as the basis of designation for suspected terrorists best practice is said to require that sanctions are used where there are 'reasonable grounds' for belief that the individual or group has been involved in terrorism.[56] In relation to judicial review best practice requires that the target has the right to judicial review 'with due process rights applying to such review *including disclosure of the case against him, her or it*, and such rules concerning the burden of proof that are commensurate with the severity of the sanctions'.[57] The analysis in this chapter suggests that the UK system of special advocates does not fulfil the requirements of best practice but that the EU system of judicial review may be developing in this direction – *if* the strong position taken to date endures. So long as the prevailing culture is one of control, or security, then formal rules will only ever serve to check but not eliminate threats to the rule of law. EU counter-terrorism is by no means above reproach.[58] However, the EU rule of law remains robust in the field of targeted sanctions. In the EU, in this field, 'force yields place to law'.[59]

Any consideration of EU law in the field of national security must recall that the EU is hardly a typical security actor. It has no army, navy, air force or police force. Nevertheless EU counter-terrorism law is a vibrant area of European law that is proving to be the focal point for the development of broader EU security law. The idea of European security

---

[53] Martin Scheinin, Ten Areas of Best Practice in Countering Terrorism: Report of the Special Rapporteur on the Promotion and Protection of Human Rights and Fundamental Freedoms While Countering Terrorism, A/HRC/16/51.

[54] Ibid, para 10.

[55] Ibid.

[56] Ibid, para 34.

[57] Ibid, para 35.

[58] On the contrary – it demonstrates many of the traits of the pre-emptive shift. See MURPHY, *supra* fn 1, ch. 8.

[59] Euripides *Medea* [525–62].

is 'a complex constellation' which can be said to involve 'national cultures, institutional norms, political agendas, local perceptions and global needs'. At the heart of the project is 'an attempt to standardize and create a systematic juridical, institutional and technical approach to the threats that Europe faces today'.[60] This description by Burgess is an apt snapshot of the difficulty of describing European security or, as he puts it, European securities. The heterogeneity of the different EU systems and the different perceptions of security within Europe should caution against any attempt to crudely transplant a counter-terrorism power or safeguard from one Member State into another or, through the EU, into all other Member States. Unless the special advocate system is proven to operate satisfactorily in its home Member State the EU courts should seek another solution to the challenge of secret evidence.

---

60 J Peter Burgess, There is No European Security, Only European Securities, 44 COOPERATION AND CONFLICT 309, 310 (2009).

17. Global sanctions, state secrets and supranational review: seeking due process in an interconnected world

Federico Fabbrini

INTRODUCTION

In the twenty-first century, the fight against terrorism has increasingly acquired a global dimension. States and international organizations have developed cooperative instruments to tackle the terrorist threat, notably through the adoption of administrative measures for freezing the assets of individuals and entities suspected of financing terrorism. The sanctions adopted at the global level have a profound impact on fundamental rights and not surprisingly courts in multiple jurisdictions – including in the supranational framework of the European Union (EU) – have been called upon to review their legality. In recent years, courts, especially in the EU, have begun taking seriously their task to protect core due process rights and have demanded that natural and legal persons subjected to global financial sanctions be provided with the evidence that assertedly justifies the restrictive measures against them. Despite their solicitude, however, EU courts have been confronted with a new challenge. Supranational and international institutions often do not have access to the evidence, which is possessed, and secretly held, mainly by the United States (US) – the country with the most sophisticated intelligence apparatus worldwide and that has been at the forefront of the global fight against terrorism.

The purpose of this chapter is to explore the intricacies that arise from *supranational* review of *global* sanctions based on *state* secrets and to suggest ways in which due process for designated individuals and entities could be sought in our interconnected world. The chapter takes stock of the recent decision of the EU General Court (GC) in *Kadi II*[1] that the petitioner must have access to the gist of the evidence against him and

1 Case T-85/09, *Kadi v. Commission (Kadi II)* [2010] ECR II-5177.

explains why this holding raises serious practical difficulties for EU and international institutions alike. As the chapter claims, because the US often has the evidence on which sanctions are based, a possibility for listed individuals and entities might be to challenge their designation by seeking review in US courts. The US runs a financial sanctions regime that is the equivalent of (and has, in fact, been the model for) the global one. US federal courts have in some cases ruled that the executive must disclose the gist of the classified information to a designated person (or the classified information itself to his lawyer, subject to a security clearance) in order to give him a fair opportunity to respond to the domestic allegations against him. Because EU courts cannot compel international institutions to disclose evidence which only the US holds, the chapter discusses how US courts could provide relief to targeted persons. Nevertheless, the chapter also highlights the difficulties that this avenue presents.

The chapter is structured as follows. Section 1 outlines the main contours of the global administrative regime created in the aftermath of 9/11 to fight terrorism financing. Section 2 surveys the recent developments in the case law of the EU courts and the judicial pressure to secure a meaningful degree of due process to the individuals and entities subject to the global sanctions. Section 3 summarizes the pervasive request of the GC in *Kadi II* to disclose the evidence against Mr. Kadi and explains the problems that this holding faces given the lack of access to the evidence by both the EU and the global institutions. Section 4 underlines the central role of the US in managing classified information that is often the basis for global sanctions and examines how listed persons could turn to US courts to obtain disclosure of the evidence against them. Section 5, finally, discusses the case law of US courts on the designation of targeted entities and cautions about the role of the federal judiciary in protecting the constitutional rights of foreigners and embracing an expansive conception of due process. In the end, the chapter suggests that while EU courts may be willing but unable to disclose secret evidence to targeted persons, US courts may be able but unwilling to do so. If a global counter-terrorism regime is to be maintained, therefore, the protection of core due process values requires US courts to become more aware of their systemic position in a tightly interconnected legal world.

1. THE GLOBAL ADMINISTRATIVE FRAMEWORK AGAINST TERRORISM

Given the global nature of the threat posed by contemporary terrorism, in the late 1990s states began to develop forms of international cooperation to fight terrorism within the framework of the United Nations (UN).[2] An important pillar of the global fight against terrorism is the adoption of administrative measures aimed at preventing financing of terrorism networks through the freezing of the economic resources of individuals and entities suspected of being engaged in or supporting terrorism.[3] In particular, with Resolution 1267 (1999), the UN Security Council established an auxiliary Committee (where all the members of the UN Security Council are represented) charged to adopt financial sanctions against the Taliban and later expanded the powers of the Committee to maintain a 'blacklist' of natural and legal persons suspected of being involved in terrorist activities.[4]

The Committee directly identifies the individuals and entities it regards as terrorists and subjects them to a temporary, precautionary sanction of the freeze of all their financial resources.[5] Although the administrative procedures by which the Committee functions have been amended several times since 1999, the Committee essentially operates as a diplomatic body.[6] Representatives of the members of the Security Council identify the persons who are to be targeted. The listing procedure is governed by consensus and based on the often limited and confidential information gathered by the security services of the member states of the Security Council or by other UN countries. At the same time, while the Sanctions Committee attempted to set up a procedure by which listed

---

[2] Peter Fitzgerald, Responding to Rogue Regimes: from Smart Bombs to Smart Sanctions. Managing 'Smart Sanctions' Against Terrorism Wisely, 36 NEW ENG. L. REV. 957 (2002).

[3] On the UN global counter-terrorism strategy see: A/RES/60/228 (2006); A/RES/62/272 (2008).

[4] See ERIKA DE WET, THE CHAPTER VII POWERS OF THE UNITED NATIONS SECURITY COUNCIL (2004).

[5] Enzo Cannizzaro, The Machiavellian Moment? The UN Security Council and the Rule of Law, 13 INT'L ORG. L.REV. 195 (2006).

[6] For an overview of the administrative procedure that governs the functioning of the Sanctions Committee see Clemens Feinaugle, The UN Security Council Al-Qaida and Taliban Sanctions Committee: Emerging Principles of International Institutional Law for the Protection of the Individuals?, 9 GERMAN L.J. 1513 (2008).

persons could seek delisting, no independent mechanism is available to challenge its political determinations.[7]

Once an individual or an entity is placed on the UN sanctions list, all UN member states are required to implement the determinations of the Sanctions Committee in their domestic legal systems, materially freezing the financial assets of listed individuals and entities. Since the counter-terrorism framework established by the Security Council is based on Chapter VII of the UN Charter, which grants the Security Council the power to take all measures necessary for the maintenance of international peace and security,[8] its resolutions are binding on all states of the UN and must be faithfully executed in their domestic legal systems.[9]

In the context of the EU, states decided to implement the UN sanctions regime through legislative measures adopted at the supranational level.[10] This was accomplished through a complex, three-step, procedure. First, member states adopted an act in the area of the Common Foreign and Security Policy.[11] Second, because of the economic implications of the UN sanctions, the EU institutions enacted a regulation in the framework of the European Community (EC). The regulation ordered the freezing of the assets of all natural and legal persons listed in the Annex to the

---

7 The most significant improvements in this regard have been brought about by resolutions S/RES/1904 (2009), S/RES/1988 (2011) and S/RES/1989 (2011). In particular, an independent Ombudsperson can now hear individual requests for delisting and take a decision which becomes final unless within 60 days the Sanctions Committee decides by consensus to retain the suspected individual and entity on the 'black-list'. Absent consensus, however, member states can refer the matter to the Security Council where usual rules (including veto rules by permanent members) apply.

8 See Jochen Frowein and Nico Krisch, Chapter VII: Action with Respect to Threats to Peace, Breaches of Peace and Acts of Aggression, in THE CHARTER OF THE UNITED NATIONS. A COMMENTARY. VOLUME 1 701 (Bruno Simma et al eds, 2002).

9 Article 25 UN Charter. See also Jost Delbrück, Article 25 in THE CHARTER OF THE UNITED NATIONS. A COMMENTARY. VOLUME 1 452 (Bruno Simma et al eds, 2002).

10 See Martin Nettesheim, UN Sanctions Against Individuals: a Challenge to the Architecture of the EU Governance, 44 COMMON MKT L.REV. 567, 571 (2007).

11 See, e.g. Council Common Position 1999/727/CFSP OJ 1999 L 294/01; Council Common Position 2001/154/CFSP OJ 2001 L 57/01; Council Common Position 2002/402/CFSP OJ 2002 L 139/04.

regulation, and empowered the EU Commission to update the Annex.[12] Finally, each EU member state gave effect to the regulation at the national level, with administrative acts that froze the financial assets of the listed individuals and entities.[13]

2. THE PROMISE OF JUDICIAL REVIEW OF GLOBAL SANCTIONS IN EU COURTS

The administrative sanctions adopted by the UN Security Council have a significant impact on the fundamental rights of targeted individuals and entities.[14] Listed persons experience an almost total limitation on their right to property, with adverse consequences also on their right to travel and the right to respect for private and family life. Given the effects of the sanctions, due process principles would require, at a minimum, that before the adoption of the sanctions or in its immediate aftermath, interested persons be informed of the reasons that justify the restrictive measure taken against them and have the right to defend their position by accessing a neutral and independent decision-maker.[15] Wide consensus exists nonetheless about the deficiencies of the procedure by which the auxiliary Committee of the UN Security Council identifies the persons whose funds ought to be frozen: because of the political mechanisms by which the listing takes place, significant violations of fundamental rights have been identified.[16]

---

[12] See, e.g., Council Regulation 337/2000/EC OJ 2000 L 43/01; Council Regulation 881/2002/EC OJ 2002 L 139/09; Council Regulation 561/2003/EC OJ 2003 L 082/01.

[13] See on the state disciplines of assets freezing, e.g. Mario Savino, La disciplina italiana della lotta al finanziamento del terrorismo, GIORNALE DI DIRITTO AMMINISTRATIVO 497 (2008) (on Italy); Torbjörn Andersson et al, EU Blacklisting: The Renaissance of Imperial Power, but on a Global Scale, 14 EUR. BUS. L.REV. 111 (2003) (on Sweden).

[14] See Frederic Mégret and Florian Hoffman, The UN as a Human Rights Violator? Some Reflections on the United Nations Changing Human Rights Responsibilities, 25 HUM. R. QUART. 314 (2003).

[15] See August Reinish, Developing Human Rights and Humanitarian Law Accountability of the Security Council for the Imposition of Economic Sanctions, 95 AM. J. INT'L L. 851 (2001).

[16] See Bardo Fassbender, Targeted Sanctions Imposed by the UN Security Council and Due Process Rights, 13 INT'L ORG. L.REV. 437 (2006); Iain Cameron, UN Targeted Sanctions, Legal Safeguards and the European Convention on Human Rights, 72 NORDIC J. INT'L L. 159 (2003).

In light of the serious consequences produced by the economic sanctions, black-listed individuals and entities soon began to challenge these UN counter-terrorism measures in court.[17] Because of the impossibility of commencing judicial proceedings at the UN level,[18] targeted persons sought due process and judicial redress before domestic courts, challenging the measures adopted by states and supranational organizations to implement the UN sanctions. The EU courts emerged as a rather responsive forum in this regard.[19] In the *Kadi* case,[20] the Court of First Instance (CFI) initially refused to address the dispute maintaining that the contested EU regulation was implementing a UN resolution, necessary 'as the world now stands'[21] to fight international terrorism, and was therefore immune from judicial review, except for compatibility with *jus cogens*. The decision of the CFI, however, was overruled on appeal by the European Court of Justice (ECJ).

In *Kadi*,[22] the ECJ, as the 'constitutional court of the municipal order that is the EU',[23] took seriously its duty to protect fundamental rights.[24] The ECJ excluded that an EU regulation could escape judicial review because it 'concern[ed] national security and terrorism'[25] and reaffirmed the need to respect due process rights in the listing process. The ECJ annulled the regulation listing the petitioner on the ground that it denied him due process, and instructed the Commission to provide Mr. Kadi

---

17 John Dugard, Judicial Review of Sanctions in UNITED NATIONS SANCTIONS AND INTERNATIONAL LAW 83 (Vera Gowlland-Debbas et al eds, 2005).

18 Giacinto Della Cananea, Global Security and Procedural Due Process of Law Between the United Nations and the European Union: *Kadi v. Council*, 15 COLUMBIA J. EUR. L. 519, 523 (2009) (explaining how individuals lack *locus standi* before the International Court of Justice, 'traditionally conceived as a judge between states').

19 Daniel Halberstam and Eric Stein, The United Nations, the European Union and the King of Sweden: Economic Sanctions and Individual Rights in a Plural World Order, 46 COMMON MKT L.REV. 13 (2009).

20 Case T-351/01 *Yassin A. Kadi v. Council of the EU and Commission of the EC* [2005] ECR II-3649.

21 Id par 133.

22 Joined Cases C-402/05 P and C-415/05 P *Yassin A. Kadi and Al Barakaat International Foundation v. EU Council and Commission* [2008] ECR I-6351.

23 Id Opinion of AG Maduro, par 37.

24 The literature on the decision of the ECJ is copious. For an assessment in a transatlantic perspective see Federico Fabbrini, The Role of the Judiciary in Times of Emergency: Judicial Review of Counter-Terrorism Measures in the United States Supreme Court and the European Court of Justice, 28 YBK EUR. L. 664 (2009).

25 *Kadi* par 343.

with sufficient procedural guarantees to challenge his listing on the merits. Pursuant to the ECJ's request, the Commission communicated to Mr. Kadi a short statement of reasons justifying his listing and re-designated him in the EU assets freezing regime.[26] Mr. Kadi, however, claimed that the process used to re-list him was still incompatible with EU due process standards and challenged the new regulation before the CFI (which, in the meanwhile, had been renamed as the GC by the Lisbon Treaty).

In September 2010, the GC delivered its *Kadi II* judgment, holding that the new regulation also violated EU fundamental rights. The GC surprisingly insisted that it was 'not bound … by the points of law decided by the [ECJ] in its judgment in *Kadi*'.[27] In addition, with an unprecedented step for a lower court, the GC remarked that 'certain doubts may have been voiced in legal circles as to whether the judgment of the [ECJ] in *Kadi* is wholly consistent with, on the one hand, international law and, more particularly, … the Charter of the [UN] and, on the other hand, the EC and EU Treaties'[28] and, indicating rulings of UK[29] and Swiss[30] courts in support, stated 'that those criticisms are not entirely without foundation'.[31] However, the GC recognized that 'the appellate principle itself and the hierarchical judicial structure which is its corollary generally advise[d] against the [GC] revisiting points of law which have been decided by the [ECJ]'[32] and set out to apply a 'strict review'[33] of the contested regulation.

On the merits, the GC noted that the counter-terrorism sanctions were 'particularly draconian. All the applicant's funds and other assets have been indefinitely frozen for nearly 10 years now and he cannot gain access to them without first obtaining an exemption from the [UN] Sanctions Committee.'[34] With respect to the procedure followed to re-list Mr. Kadi, the GC remarked how 'the applicant's rights of defence ha[d]

---

26 Commission Regulation 1190/2008/EC OJ 2008 L 322.

27 *Kadi II* par 112.

28 Id par 115.

29 See *R (on the Application of Al-Jedda) v. Secretary of State* [2007] UKHL 58.

30 See *Youssef Nada v. SECO* 1A.45/2007/daa judgment of 14 November 2007.

31 *Kadi II* par 121.

32 Id.

33 Armin Cuyvers, The *Kadi II* Judgment of the General Court: the ECJ's Predicament and the Consequences for the Member States, 7 EUR. CON. L.REV. 494 (2011).

34 *Kadi II* par 149.

been "observed" only in the most formal and superficial sense'.[35] As the GC made clear, 'the procedure followed by the Commission, in response to the applicant's request, did not grant him even the most minimal access to the evidence against him'.[36] Moreover, because the EU institutions had not produced any evidence in court, the GC itself was 'not able to undertake a review of the lawfulness of the contested regulation, with the result that [also] the applicant's fundamental right to effective judicial review ha[d] not ... been observed'.[37] The GC, finally, held that 'the imposition on the applicant of the restrictive measures ... constitute[d] an unjustified restriction of [his] right to property'[38] and entailed also a violation of the principle of proportionality. The GC, thus, annulled the regulation in so far as it concerned the applicant. The decision of the GC has been appealed and is now pending before the ECJ.[39]

3. THE PROBLEM OF SECRET EVIDENCE

Scholars have praised the decision of the GC in *Kadi II* for confirming the role of the EU judiciary in providing '*complete legal protection* by fully reviewing and safeguarding fundamental rights'.[40] In defining the standard of review, in fact, the GC explained that it 'must not only establish whether the evidence relied on is factually accurate, reliable and consistent, but must also ascertain whether that evidence contains all the relevant information to be taken into account in order to assess the situation and whether it is capable of substantiating the conclusions drawn from it'.[41] In addition, recalling its precedent in the *OMPI* case,[42] the GC clarified that 'the [EU] judicature must be able to review the lawfulness and merits of [EC] measures to freeze funds without its being possible to raise objections that the evidence and information used by the competent [EU] institution is secret or confidential'.[43]

---

[35] Id par 171.
[36] Id par 173.
[37] Id par 183.
[38] Id par 193.
[39] Joined Cases C-584/10 P, C-593/10 P and C-595/10 P, *Commission, Council and UK v. Kadi* pending.
[40] Cuyvers, *supra* note 33, 493 (emphasis in the original).
[41] *Kadi II*, par 142.
[42] Case T-228/02 *Organisation des Modjahedines du peuple d'Iran (OMPI) v. Council of the EU*, [2006] ECR II-4665.
[43] *Kadi II* par 144.

At the same time, in assessing the procedural complaint raised by Mr. Kadi, the GC invoked the reasoning of the European Court of Human Rights in *A. v. United Kingdom*[44] to affirm that the principle of due process required that a person 'be given an opportunity effectively to challenge the allegations made against him, which as a general rule requires that all the evidence against him be disclosed'.[45] While the GC recognized that limitations 'may be placed on the right to disclosure of all material evidence where an important public interest militates in favour of secrecy',[46] it insisted that a fair balance had to be struck between the interest of the individual to access the evidence against him and the need to protect the confidential nature of the information.[47] Yet, as the GC remarked, these basic criteria had not been respected in the present case, since the 'few pieces of information and the imprecise allegations in the summary of reasons appear clearly insufficient to enable the applicant to launch an effective challenge to the allegations against him so far as his alleged participation in terrorist activities is concerned'.[48]

As such, the GC in *Kadi II* framed a demanding standard of scrutiny requiring that any person subject to sanctions be provided with the 'gist' of the classified evidence against him.[49] The holding of the GC, however, faces two major problems that threaten to make the judicial victory of Mr. Kadi purely illusory.[50] To begin with, it is uncertain whether the EU

---

[44] *A. v. United Kingdom* [2009] 49 EHRR 695.

[45] *Kadi II* par 176.

[46] Id.

[47] Id par 173.

[48] Id par 174.

[49] On the notion of 'gist of evidence' see Daphne Barak-Erez and Matthew Waxman, Secret Evidence and the Due Process of Terrorist Detention, 48 COLUMBIA J. TRANS. L. 3 (2009).

[50] The decision of the GC annulling the regulation listing Mr. Kadi has been suspended pending appeal before the ECJ. Technically speaking, the ECJ can remove an individual from the EU sanctions list, so that if the EU institutions do not comply with the requirement to provide more due process to Mr. Kadi, his name can be deleted from the EU sanctions list. Nevertheless, because of the importance that international law plays in the EU legal order, EU courts appear reluctant to go down this road. Were the EU courts to annul *tout court* a EU freezing measure that implements the UN sanctions list, in fact, this would put the EU and its member states in violation of international law (i.e. their obligation to give faithful execution to the determinations of the UN Security Council). As the decision of the ECJ in *Kadi* confirms, EU courts are extremely concerned about this possibility. In that case, the ECJ annulled the regulation listing Mr. Kadi for violating his due process rights but suspended for three

institutions will be able to comply with the request of the EU judiciary. EU institutions have a consistent pattern of obeying the decisions of the EU courts. Nevertheless, in the case at hand, they may be unable to meet the high procedural threshold set by the GC. In this case, EU counter-terrorism sanctions simply implement measures decided at the UN, and the EU institutions may not have access to the information relied upon by the auxiliary Committee of the UN Security Council that decided the listing in the first place.[51] As such, disclosure of evidence would have to be accorded by the UN Security Council, rather than by the EU institutions.[52]

Furthermore, even if the EU political and judicial branches could secure the cooperation of the UN Sanctions Committee to allow the sharing of the classified information that was the basis for the sanctions, a second difficulty would emerge.[53] As Martin Scheinin and Lisa

---

months the effects of the decision in order to give the EU institutions time to send Mr. Kadi a new summary of reasons. In this way, the ECJ was able to avoid any violation of the UN Charter which, as explained *supra* at note 9, requires members of the international community to carry out the decision of the UN Security Council (including, in this case, the listing of Mr. Kadi). See Joris Larik, Two Ships in the Night or in the Same Boat Together: How the ECJ Squared the Circle and Foreshadowed Lisbon in its *Kadi* Judgment, 13 YBK POLISH EUR. STUDIES 149, 165 (2010). In conclusion, because the ECJ does not seem eager to strike down *tout court* the EU sanctions regime, the only alternative option is that EU institutions provide Mr. Kadi with more due process. Yet, for the reasons that will be explained, this does not seem a feasible possibility either.

[51] This problem does not arise in the context of the 'purely internal' sanctions list that the EU also manages. In this case, in fact, EU institutions designated several individuals and entities as suspected terrorists with an autonomous decision, and not in application of a UN mandate. EU institutions are therefore in possession of the information that led to the designation and if they are unwilling to comply with the procedural requirement of disclosure, EU courts can strike down the sanctions without affecting any violation of international law. See Case T-284/08, *OMPI v. Council* [2008] ECR II-334 (striking down the listing of an organization given the unwillingness of the EU institutions and the member states to communicate to the court the reasons justifying the designation).

[52] Erika de Wet, Human Rights Considerations and Enforcement of Targeted Sanctions in Europe, in THE UNITED NATIONS SECURITY COUNCIL AND HUMAN RIGHTS 37 (Bardo Fassbender ed., 2012).

[53] Principles of jurisdictional limits exclude EU courts from ordering UN institutions to provide information (including classified evidence) needed in a pending trial. At the maximum, EU courts could order EU institutions to do all that is in their power to obtain information from the UN. See also Case T- 253/02 *Ayadi v. Council* [2006] ECR II-2139 (holding that listed individuals have an EU

Ginsborg have explained, 'practice indicate[s] that the Sanctions Committee itself does not have access to the evidence and the listing of individuals on the basis of undisclosed intelligence. Such intelligence may be discussed bilaterally between concerned Member States of the Security Council in advance of reaching consensus on a particular listing but is actually not presented collectively to the … Committee.'[54] Most of the intelligence, in particular, seems to be possessed by the US, which is unwilling to share it with the whole Committee.[55] In light of this, it is hard to see how the GC's demands of disclosure could ever be met, and alternative options need to be discussed in order to get out of the '*Kadi II* conundrum'.[56]

4. THE ROOTS OF THE PROBLEM

The global administrative framework for the fight against terrorism has to a large extent been *crafted* by the US. As Kim Lane Scheppele has emphasized, after 9/11 the US government 'promot[ed] a new body of international law to sustain the [US] anti-terror project' and crucially resorted to UN Security Council resolutions to set up a new global security law coordinating the diverse efforts of states around the world in a common campaign against terrorism.[57] The US played a leading role in establishing within the Security Council a legal framework to target persons suspected of financing terrorism.[58] Moreover, because the US has the most sophisticated intelligence apparatus world-wide, most of the information needed to identify suspected terrorist financiers is provided by the US and, in fact, most of the individuals and entities subject to the UN sanctions regime have been listed at the request of the US.[59] At the

---

right to begin proceedings in state courts against national authorities who have failed to act before the UN Sanctions Committee).

54 Lisa Ginsborg and Martin Scheinin, You Can't Always Get What you Want. The *Kadi II* Conundrum and the Security Council 1267 Terrorist Sanctions Regime, ESSEX HUM. R. REV. 7, 18 (2011).

55 Id 18, fn. 78 (explaining the unwillingness of the US to share evidence by recalling how in 2008–2009 also Libya was a member of the Security Council).

56 Id 19.

57 Kim Lane Scheppele, Global Security Law and the Challenge to Constitutionalism after 9/11, PUBLIC L. 352, 354–5 (2011).

58 Id 358.

59 Andrew Hudson, Not A Great Asset: the UN Security Council's Counter Terrorism Regime: Violating Human Rights, 25 BERKELEY J. INT'L L. 101, 105 (2007).

same time, the global administrative framework for the fight against terrorism appears to be *modelled* on the US domestic anti-terrorism framework. The sanctions regime that is administered by the auxiliary Committee of the UN Security Council, in particular, mirrors the assets freezing regime in force in the US under the International Emergency Economic Powers Act (IEEPA).[60]

The IEEPA gives to the US President the power to declare a national emergency and adopt action, notably economic sanctions, to deal with the threat.[61] In the aftermath of 9/11 the Bush Administration resorted to its power under IEEPA to authorize a special Office of Foreign Assets Control (OFAC) within the Department of the Treasury to freeze the financial assets of individuals and entities, foreigners or nationals, suspected of financing terrorism.[62] OFAC manages and updates a list of natural or legal persons who are suspected of being involved in the financing of terrorism.[63] Once a person is designated by OFAC as a 'specially designated global terrorist' all their assets are frozen.[64] Since the enactment of the PATRIOT Act, moreover, OFAC can adopt a precautionary freeze against a suspected person even pending investigation.[65]

Given the similarities between the global and the US administrative regimes to fight terrorism financing, there is a wide overlap in the addressees of these financial sanctions. While the OFAC regime is designed to target individuals or entities which are subject to US jurisdiction, the UN system operates to expand the reach of the US sanctions regime overseas by imposing on all the members of the international community the duty to block the financial assets of the listed individuals and entities.[66] As such, it comes as no surprise that the natural or legal persons that are designated as global terrorist organizations by OFAC are also blacklisted by the auxiliary Committee

---

60 Pub. L. No. 95-223 (1977) codified as 50 U.S.C. §§ 1701–7.

61 Peter Fitzgerald, 'If Property Rights Were Treated Like Human Rights They Could Never Get Away with This': Blacklisting and Due Process in the U.S. Economic Sanctions Program, 51 HASTINGS L.J. 73 (1999).

62 Exec. Order 13, 224, 3 C.F.R. 785 (2001).

63 James Savage, Executive Use of International Emergency Powers Act – Evolution Through the Terrorist and Taliban Sanctions, 10 CURRENTS: INT'L TRADE L.J. 28 (2001).

64 Nicole Nice Petersen, Justice for the 'Designated': The Process that Is Due to Alleged U.S. Financiers of Terrorism, 93 GEO. L.J. 1387, 1390–91 (2005).

65 Pub. L. No. 107-56 (2001) § 106 amending 50 U.S.C. § 1702.

66 See Joseph Mayers, Disrupting Terrorist Networks: the New US and International Regime for Halting Terrorist Fundings, 34 LAW & POL'Y INT'L BUS. 17 (2002).

of the UN Security Council.[67] Taking this symmetry into account, it would seem that the conundrum left open by the GC in *Kadi II* might be bypassed by challenging in US courts the measures adopted domestically by OFAC. Given the impossibility of obtaining full relief in EU courts, because of the impossibility of obtaining evidence from the UN, individuals and entities listed by the Security Council Sanctions Committee might seek remedies before US courts.

This solution would most likely tackle the real source of the difficulties highlighted in the previous section. Because it is the US that possesses the classified evidence used by the UN auxiliary Committee, and considering that the UN sanctions regime mirrors the US one, affected persons could seek a domestic avenue of recourse by challenging their designation before a US court. If a party could succeed in obtaining the disclosure of the evidence that sustains its listing in the US and successfully challenge it, the reasons for its listing at the UN would fall. Indeed, because the domestic and the global freezing measures pursue the same goal to prevent a suspected person from financing terrorism and are based on the same supporting evidence, once the validity and credibility of the information is successfully challenged at the domestic level, the same information cannot reasonably operate as the ground for the maintenance of sanctions at the global level. As such, challenging the designation by OFAC might provide an indirect avenue for obtaining due process *vis-à-vis* the UN Sanctions Committee.

5. THE DIFFICULTIES OF JUDICIAL REVIEW OF DOMESTIC SANCTIONS IN US COURTS

The prospect of seeking due process and judicial relief against sanctions before US courts meets however with its fair share of difficulties. First, it is uncertain to what extent US courts are willing to provide due process to foreign listed individuals and entities. US courts generally extend

---

67 The OFAC list (www.treasury.gov/ofac/downloads/t11sdn.pdf) is broader than the UN Sanctions Committee list (www.un.org/sc/committees/1267/pdf/AQList.pdf). While the latter is targeted only on Al-Qaida, the Taliban and other terrorist organizations, the former includes also other groups of individuals and entities. Nevertheless, there seems to be a striking correspondence between the names of the specially designated global terrorists in the OFAC list and the terrorist individuals and organizations in the UN list. Mr. Kadi, for example, is listed both in the consolidated list of the UN Sanctions Committee and as a 'specially designated global terrorist' in the list of OFAC.

constitutional rights only to persons residing in the US or with substantial connections to the US.[68] In the context of the US anti-terrorism sanctions regime, possession of property in the US has been consistently regarded by federal courts as a proof that a targeted person has substantial connections to the US, entitling him to due process rights.[69] Nevertheless, it is plausible to argue that the substantial connections test should be interpreted more broadly, and that federal courts should extend due process guarantees to foreign nationals when it is the US that is imposing restrictions on them at the roots. Given the severe implications of the OFAC designation, it appears that foreign persons should enjoy the same procedural protections that US persons have.[70]

Some interesting insights on the capacity of US courts to provide due process rights to foreign nationals have been recently offered by the case of *Kadi v. Geithner*.[71] Mr. Kadi, in fact, brought proceedings in the District Court for the District of Columbia challenging his designation by OFAC as a specially designated terrorist and seeking disclosure of the evidence assertedly justifying his designation.[72] As the court explained, there was 'arguably a factual dispute whether Kadi d[id], indeed have sufficient connection to the US … Kadi's complaint d[id] not clearly indicate where his assets ha[d] been frozen, and if any of those assets were located in the US'.[73] Yet, the court *de facto* sidelined the question of whether Mr. Kadi had a sufficient connection with the US and moved to consider his constitutional complaints on the merits, eventually rejecting them.[74] While the court did not conclusively address the question of

---

68 See *United States v. Verdugo-Urquidez*, 494 U.S. 259 (1990).

69 See *National Council of Resistance of Iran v. Department of State*, 251 F.3d 192 (D.C. Cir. 2001) (holding that a foreign entity designated by the Department of State as a foreign terrorist organization has due process rights when it has come within the territory of the US and developed substantial connections with it).

70 See generally, DAVID COLE, ENEMY ALIENS 218 (2003) (arguing that constitutional due process rights, as human rights, should apply equally to citizens and non-citizens).

71 *Kadi v. Geithner*, 2012 U.S. Dist. LEXIS 36053 (D.D.C., March 19, 2012).

72 It may be interesting to underline that Mr. Kadi began proceedings in US courts on 16 January 2009, i.e. after the ECJ had formally ruled in his favour, only to suspend the effect of its decision, *de facto* keeping him on the EU sanctions list.

73 *Kadi v. Geithner*, *41–2.

74 Id *43–68.

standing, it treated Mr. Kadi as being entitled to due process rights, offering him a forum in which to make his claims.

Second, it is uncertain whether US courts are able to exercise a searching judicial review on the OFAC designation process. As Nicole Nice-Petersen has explained, OFAC operates behind closed doors, on the basis of the often confidential information shared by other executive agencies and through a one-sided process shrouded in secrecy.[75] Because of this, the administrative process for the designation of individuals and entities under the IEEPA has given rise to the same human rights concerns surrounding the listing regime at the UN level.[76] Despite the severe impact that OFAC designation and freezing orders have on the rights of targeted individuals and entities, US courts have been rather deferential *vis-à-vis* the executive branch. In their early decisions, in particular, federal courts shied away from enforcing a vigorous understanding of due process, adopting a very limited standard of review under the 'arbitrary and capricious' test of the Administrative Procedure Act[77] and allowing the government to use undisclosed classified evidence to make its case.[78]

Nevertheless, some reasons of optimism on the capacity of US federal courts to provide a meaningful judicial forum in which listed persons can challenge the sanctions against them, are left open by more recent cases. In particular, in *KindHearts v. Geithner*,[79] the District Court of the Northern District of Ohio refused to adopt a deferential approach and concluded that OFAC had violated the petitioner's 'fundamental right to be told on what basis and for what reasons the government deprived it of all access to its assets'.[80] In a separate opinion addressing the issue of

---

75 Nice Petersen, *supra* note 64, 1394.

76 See Laura Donohue, Constitutional and Legal Challenges to the Anti-Terrorist Finance Regime, 43 WAKE FOREST L. REV. 643 (2008).

77 Pub. L. 79-404 (1946) codified as 5 U.S.C. § 706(2)(a).

78 See *Holy Land Foundations for Relief and Development v. Ashcroft*, 333 F.3d 156, 164 (D.C. Cir. 2003) (upholding the OFAC's listing of a US corporation and rejecting its due process claims arguing that its considerations of classified evidence were justified by the executive compelling interest in withholding national security information); *Islamic Am. Relief Agency v. Gonzales*, 477 F.3d 728, 734 (D.C. Cir. 2007) (rejected the petitioner's claim stating that, although the unclassified evidence for the designation was not overwhelming, its 'review – in an area at the intersection of national security, foreign policy and administrative law – is extremely deferential').

79 *KindHearts for Charitable Humanitarian Developments v. Geithner*, 647 F Supp 2d 857 (N.D. Ohio 2009).

80 Id 906.

remedy, in addition, the court clearly stated that OFAC had to disclose to the petitioner '*each* legal basis for the [freezing of its assets]'[81] and convened an *ex parte, in camera* hearing with the government to determine what classified information would have to be made available to the petitioner, while recognizing that, if the declassification of some secret evidence would be impossible, the petitioner's counsel might obtain an adequate security clearance to view the necessary documents *in camera* under protective order.[82]

So far, the US Supreme Court has not solved the divergences that persist between lower federal courts both on whether foreign nationals enjoy due process to challenge their designation and on what standard of judicial scrutiny is due in reviewing OFAC's decisions.[83] The traditional deference that the Supreme Court has given to the executive branch on matters of national security and state secrecy does not augur well for the protection of due process rights of designated persons.[84] Yet, for the reasons explained above, the fact remains that the only opportunity for targeted individuals and entities (or for their special advocates) to have access to the 'gist' of the secret evidence justifying their listing might be by challenging their designation in US courts. Federal courts, if willing to open their doors to foreign nationals and to exercise their role 'to ensure the protection of fundamental rights',[85] can mandate disclosure of classified information to the US executive and thus provide petitioners

---

[81] *KindHearts for Charitable Humanitarian Developments v. Geithner (No. 2)*, 710 F. Supp. 2d 637, 660 fn. 17 (N.D. Ohio 2010) (emphasis in the original).

[82] Jeffrey Davenport, Freezing Terrorist Finance in its Tracks: the Fourth Amendment, Due Process and the Office of Foreign Assets Control after *KindHearts v. Geithner*, 61 SYRACUSE L.REV. 173, 191 (2011).

[83] Another open question among lower federal courts is also whether due process requires that the individual be entitled to see the classified evidence (in summary or other form, or pursuant to security clearances) or whether he is only entitled to see the unclassified administrative record. Compare *Holy Land Foundations*, 333 F.3d 164 (stating that there is no right to access classified evidence) with *Al Haramain Islamic Foundation v. Dept. of the Treasury*, 660 F.3d 1019, 1054 (9th Cir. 2011) (holding that that OFAC had violated the petitioner's 'Fifth Amendment right to due process by failing to provide constitutionally adequate notice and a meaningful opportunity to respond and by failing to mitigate the use of classified information by, for example, preparing and disclosing an unclassified summary' but concluding that the procedural due process violation was harmless).

[84] See Sudha Setty, Litigating Secrets: Comparative Perspectives on the State Secrets Privilege, 75 BROOKLYN L.REV. 201 (2009).

[85] *KindHearts No. 2* 658.

with the means to effectively seek delisting.[86] At the same time, if the executive is unwilling to disclose enough to provide due process, federal courts can remove a designated person from the list with final effect.[87] In the end, however, seeking due process against financial sanctions in US courts is not an easy ride. Contrary to EU courts – which appear *willing* but *unable* to ensure due process – US courts may be *able* but *unwilling* to do so, unless they become aware of their central role in securing transnational respect for fundamental fairness principles.

CONCLUSION

This chapter has described the intricacies that arise from supranational review of global sanctions based on state secrets and explored the challenges and the opportunities that an interconnected world offers in seeking due process and procedural justice for individuals and entities targeted by anti-terrorism sanctions. While in the last decade the threat of international terrorism has been broadly addressed through a global administrative framework, EU courts have increasingly asserted their role in reviewing UN anti-terrorism sanctions at the supranational level. Yet, sanctions are often based on evidence that is classified, and not shared, by states: notably by the US. In this context, the chapter has discussed how US courts could potentially turn out to be a forum to secure disclosure of secret evidence and provide listed individuals and entities with the information to challenge the restrictive measures against them. However, given the uncertainties about the extent to which foreigners enjoy due process rights and the still diffuse practice of judicial deference *vis-à-vis* the executive, it is very hard to predict whether US courts will

---

[86] For the reasons explained *supra* at note 53, the ECJ can not order disclosure of information to the UN or the US, as this is beyond its jurisdictional reach. On the contrary, this problem clearly does not arise in the context of judicial review of domestic sanctions by US courts. The federal judiciary has full jurisdiction in domestic matters and can address specific orders to the executive branch.

[87] For the reasons explained *supra* at note 50, the ECJ seems reluctant to autonomously remove the name of a designated individual from the EU sanctions list (which gives effect to the UN list), because this would put the EU and its member states in violation of international law. On the contrary, this problem clearly does not arise in the context of judicial review of domestic sanctions by US courts. If the US executive is unwilling to provide a designated person with more information to challenge his domestic designation, a court can remove his name from the OFAC list without triggering any question of international law.

be willing to provide an effective remedy for designated persons. Recent cases such as *Kadi v. Geithner* and *KindHearts v. Geithner* open some interesting scenarios.[88] Securing due process for suspected terrorist financiers nevertheless requires US courts to become more aware of their role and responsibility in an ever more complex, interdependent, trans-systemic legal world.

---

[88] It may be noticed that the District Court ruling in *KindHearts v. Geithner* has not been appealed and the same is now true of *Kadi v. Geithner*. See *Kadi v. Geithner*, 2012 U.S. App. LEXIS 17174 (D.C. Cir., July 31, 2012) (accepting the request for dismissal on appeal).

18. Secrecy regulation by the European Union inside out

Deirdre Curtin

1. TRANSPARENCY AND SECRECY: MIRROR IMAGES

The normative concept of *transparency* tends to promise the sun, the moon and the stars. The aim of opening up government is to create a democratic and accountable state as well as an efficient one. In the European Union (EU) it is no different – indeed, if anything the expectations are higher. Transparency – most frequently used as a short hand for access to documents, although this is arguably too limited a view as to its scope[1] – has for the past twenty years (since the run up to the ratification of the Maastricht Treaty) been presented as a type of holistic medicine designed to remedy many of the ailments the EU is perceived to have.[2] A central ailment is its limited legitimacy and transparency have been propagated as a means to boost the legitimacy of the EU. The aim of achieving more transparency in the functioning of the various EU institutions is lauded by almost everyone: the European institutions, the politicians and bureaucrats, the members of parliament, the judges and civil society.[3] All these actors proclaim and expect beneficial effect from the implementation of transparency in the EU.

Yet it seems we may have to learn to live, rather counter-intuitively, with the opposite: *less* and not more transparency and access to documents. Since 2008 the effort to revise the Access Regulation (from

---

[1] Albert Meijer, Deirdre Curtin and Maarten Hillebrandt, Open Government. Connecting Vision and Voice, 78 INT REV ADM SCI 1, 10–29 (2012).

[2] Deirdre Curtin and Albert Meijer, Does Transparency Strengthen Legitimacy?, 11(2) INFORMATION POLITY, 109–122 (2006).

[3] See further ibid.

2001)[4] has been seriously held up because of inter-institutional disagreement as to procedure and content as well as among the Member States themselves. The Danish Presidency, attempting to break a deadlock of several years, circulated in 2012 a draft deal for agreement among the Member States that included a number of compromise provisions that are arguably (much) more restrictive than the *status quo* on the public access to documents.[5] This is in line with various debates and discussions over the years on the substance of the revisions with both the Commission and the Council wishing to restrict in seemingly new ways the right of access to documents and the manner in which it has been implemented.[6] These efforts seem to mirror *secret* administrative and legislative practices that the EU executive power[7] wishes to be able to maintain and there is some evidence of trying to limit the effects of some Court judgments that displease them (effectively by legislative over-rule).

At the same time, and as a partially separate development, the law and practices of secrecy, and in particular the classification of documents, are a growth area in EU law, although often taking place below the radar and without external 'publicity'. The 'real world' of the secretive exercise of administrative/executive power may remove whole areas and activities from the possibility of any meaningful public accountability structures. A growing number of actors in the EU and outside it share classified information and adopt their own rules on the basis of their internal organisation power as well as those of other systems (e.g. NATO, US etc). In addition the rules governing the principle of 'originator control' are reinforced and applied extensively within the context of the EU often barring access to documents by third parties and Member States in practice.

---

[4] Regulation (EC) No. 1049/2001 of the European Parliament and of the Council of the 30 May 2001 regarding public access to European Parliament, Council and Commission documents, Official Journal of the European Union L 145/43 (31 May 2001).

[5] Steven Peers, Article-by-Article commentary, 'Red Lines' for the negotiations, and the undemocratic recast procedure, STATEWATCH (May 2012), www.statewatch.org/analyses/no-177-access-to-docs.pdf.

[6] Francesco Maini, Jean-Patrick Villeneuve and Martial Pasquier, 'Less is more'? Les propositions de la commission sur l'accès aux documents de l'Union européenne, 137–138 REVUE FRANCAISE D'ADMINISTRATION PUBLIQUE 1, 155–70 (2011).

[7] See further, Deirdre Curtin, Executive Power in the European Union. Law, Practices and the Living Constitution (OUP, 2009). The supranational executive power of the EU is non-unitary and includes the European Council, Council of Ministers, the Commission and various agencies.

The manner in which the classification of documents is being regulated in the context of the EU is linked to the way the EU has more generally developed over the course of the past decade as a political and economic union, both in law and in practice. Since the Treaty of Lisbon of 2009 in particular there can be no doubt that the Union exercises far-reaching legislative, executive and judicial powers including over economic and monetary issues, justice and home affairs and defence and security. Its role as a security actor globally has triggered numerous international agreements with third states and other international agreements in areas that affect the rights and interests of individuals.[8] At the same time, the EU is in the process of implementing an *area of internal security* that mirrors legislative and executive developments more globally.[9] And it does so by a variety of actors all using information in the security field that is classified either at the supranational level or by the Member States and used in the context of EU decision-making.

This chapter aims to put the issue of secrecy and the EU squarely on the map in and of itself at a salient moment in its development towards a 'political' union – that of increasingly dense cooperation constructing and reinforcing a European area of 'internal security'.[10] The fact that there is a growing number of actors both internally and externally sharing (classified) information and adopting their own rules on the basis of their internal organisation power is seen as problematic and as *de facto* undermining parallel constitutional level developments, such as the drive for ever more open decision-making as laid down in Article 1 of the Treaty of the EU. Secrecy as the flip side of transparency is understudied both normatively and empirically, both in general and in relation to the EU in particular and this chapter aims to explore the way in which it is regulated at present and in its historical context (section 2). The chapter highlights the problem of overclassification of documents and some techniques of classification that may foster a culture of secrecy (section 3). It raises (section 4) the issue of parliamentary oversight in the context

[8] Wyn Rees, Cooperation on Counter-Terrorism and the Internationalisation of Law Enforcement, in THE EXTERNAL DIMENSION OF THE EUROPEAN UNION'S AREA OF FREEDOM, SECURITY AND JUSTICE (Marise Cremona, Jörg Monar and Sara Poli, eds., 2011), 389–405.

[9] Deirdre Curtin, 'Top Secret Europe', INAUGURAL LECTURE DELIVERED AT THE UNIVERSITY OF AMSTERDAM, 20 October 2011. Available at http://www.oratiereeks.nl/upload/pdf/PDF-5066weboratie_Curtin.pdf (last visited 17 January 2013).

[10] Marieke de Goede, The SWIFT affair and the global politics of European security, 50(2) JOURNAL OF COMMON MARKET STUDIES, 214–30 (2012).

of the EU by way of the specific example of international negotiations (in particular with the US). The constitutional context of parliamentary oversight over EU executive actors is only beginning to be explored in the context where information is classified but shared with various actors both at the European level, internationally and nationally.[11] The role of the EU judiciary – beyond the scope of the current contribution – is more established but still rather uneven in terms of its constitutionalising role and oversight.[12] A brief conclusion follows (section 5).

2. THE FORMAL REGULATION OF SECRECY IN THE EU: A FIRST CUT

2.1 From 1958 to 1992: A Subterranean Classification System

Traditionally decision-making in the Council of Ministers was behind closed doors to allow the Member States to conduct diplomatic negotiations. This inevitably entailed some sharing of information, even from the very early days, and the creation of documents at the European level. The first rules on the classification of documents for security reasons already date from 1958 when the Council of the European Atomic Energy Community (Euratom)[13] gave the supranational Commission a classification and supervisory role over 'Euratom Classified Information' (hereafter: ECI) as well as establishing a security vetting infrastructure. The security gradings for ECI were from the very beginning *four*fold: Top Secret, Secret, Confidential and Restricted. The latter security level – Restricted – is an additional one compared to what was common in the US and many other democracies but reflects NATO rules. This lowest level of classification (for which no special authorisation for access is necessary) was required 'where unauthorised disclosure would *affect* the *defence interests of one or more Member States*'.[14] Once information is

---

[11] Aidan Will and Mathias Vermeulen, Parliamentary Oversight of Security and Intelligence Agencies in the European Union, EUROPEAN PARLIAMENT DIRECTORATE GENERAL FOR INTERNAL POLICIES (2011).

[12] Deirdre Curtin, The Role of Judge Made Law. A Bumpy Road from Secrecy to Translucence? in EMPOWERMENT AND DISEMPOWERMENT OF THE EU CITIZEN (Eleanor Spavanata, ed., 2012), 101–128.

[13] Regulation No. 3 implementing Article 24 of the Treaty establishing the European Atomic Energy Community, Official Journal of the European Union L 17, 1958, 406–16.

[14] Article 10(4) of Regulation No. 3 (emphasis added).

classified, it is marked accordingly and given various forms of protection – including restricting access to people with a security clearance at the appropriate level, physical protection and restrictions on how it may be transferred from one person to another.

ECI covers 'information acquired by the Community or communicated by the Member States which is covered by Articles 24 and 25 of the Treaty establishing the European Atomic Community',[15] EU classification rules applied from the very early days of European integration to both relevant Member State documents and other more autonomous Community level information. The link with Member State documents and the limit on national executive discretion to grant public access and/or declassify was reinforced – twenty-five years later – in the general Archives Regulation of the European Community (1983).[16] *Member States* could not release through national archives to the public on terms less strict than those in the Archives Regulation (i.e. 30 years) 'documents and records emanating from institutions and physically held in their public archives, which have been classified and have not been declassified'.[17] This rule also applied to such documents and records of the Member States that reproduce in full or in part the content of such classified documents. In this way, via the Archives Regulation, it became clear that what was initially only applied to specific Euratom documents had, in fact, a more general application.

It took almost forty years after the Euratom classification decision for the subject of classification of documents to re-emerge again, this time at the level of the EU as such. Just over two weeks after the Treaty of Maastricht was signed in 1992, the Commission proposed a Council Regulation on the security measures applicable to classified information produced or transmitted in connection with EEC or Euratom activities. This sought to widen the scope of the rather subterranean classification system that had operated since 1958 to the full width of Community activities and to regulate it openly in a legislative measure with an advisory role for the European Parliament (EP). The main objective was to afford protection to 'sensitive information whose unauthorised disclosure could be detrimental to the essential interests of the European

---

15 Article 1(1) of Regulation No. 3.

16 Council Regulation (EEC, Euratom) No. 354/83, February 1, 1983, concerning the opening to the public of the historical archives of the European Economic Community and the European Atomic Energy Community, Official Journal of the European Union L 43, 1983, 1–15 (hereafter the Archives Regulation).

17 See, Article 6(1) of the Archives Regulation.

Communities and of Member states'.[18] The EP was hostile to the draft Council Regulation both on grounds of the proposed legal basis which limited its own role as well as by the failure of the Commission to concurrently bring forward a directive on freedom of information.[19]

The proposal was eventually withdrawn for the surprising reason of 'subsidiarity'.[20] With the benefit of hindsight the shooting down of the proposal by the European Parliament is regrettable both for substantive and procedural reasons. The security gradings proposed by the Commission were only three and did not include the contested NATO-inspired fourth category 'restricted'. Moreover, some emphasis was put by the Commission on the fact that classification gradings should be necessary, temporary and take into account wider imperatives relating to access to information. Unfortunately for the European Parliament and in spite of the fact that its legislative and other roles have increased dramatically since 1992, its ability to actually openly debate the contents of the EU-wide secrecy regulation have not improved in a procedural sense since the Commission's 1992 proposal. Rather, its role has worsened considerably when the executive institutions (starting with the Council and the Commission) opted to treat the issue of security and classification rules purely as a matter of their own *internal* organisation. Even when the EP later acquired with the Lisbon Treaty a role in the negotiation processes of international agreements, the executive institutions continued to treat the issue of special access by members of the European Parliament as a matter of (secret) inter-institutional deliberation and agreement – a process which they dominate.[21]

2.2 New Rules (2001): 'Sensitive' Documents Ring-Fenced and Expanded

The reason for the Commission and the Council to adopt new internal rules on the security measures applicable to classified information

---

[18] Recital 6 of Proposal for a Council Regulation on the security measures applicable to classified information produced or transmitted in connection with European Economic Community or Euratom activities, COM (92) 56 final, submitted by the Commission on 26 February 1992.

[19] Resolution on the proposal for a Council Regulation (EEC) on the security measures applicable to classified information produced or transmitted in connection with EEC or Euratom activities, Official Journal of the European Union C 176, 1993, 60.

[20] Bulletin of the European Communities, November 1993, at point 1.7.3.

[21] See further below section 4.

produced or transmitted in connection with EU activities, was the fact that in the context of the new common foreign and security policy *sensitive documents* would be produced, shared and circulated. The thinking was that the EU's expansion into the field of defence policy would require the exchange of particularly sensitive information, and that this could be accomplished only if the originator of such information could be confident that no information put out by him will be disclosed against his will. Mind you, this was the case since the entry into force of the Treaty of Maastricht in 1993 and it took the Council until 2001 to adopt new security rules on the classification of documents although it had earlier adopted general rules on security clearances for Council officials in the General Secretariat.[22] The actual catalyst was presumably the planned adoption of new EU legislative rules on access to documents, the Access Regulation. The Council staged what was described as a 'summertime coup' by adopting its own new security rules just two months *prior* to the new and fundamental public access legislation.[23] At the same time the notion of 'sensitive documents' was successfully introduced into the Access Regulation itself.[24] These new security rules together with the exclusions on 'sensitive documents' contained in the EU Access Regulation meant that virtually all classified information was excluded from the scope of the law on public access to documents that

---

22 The Secretary-General of the Council adopted, for its part, a Council Decision on measures to protect classified information applicable to the General Secretariat of the Council Decision No. 24 of 30 January 1995. These rules have been supplemented by internal rules of the Council and Commission, adopted on the basis of Articles 151(3) and 162(2) EC, on security screening of persons authorised to have access to classified information. See, Council Decision 98/319/EC of 27 April 1998 relating to the procedures whereby officials and employees of the General Secretariat of the Council may be allowed access to classified information held by the Council, Official Journal of the European Union L 140, 1998, 12 and Commission Decision 99/218/EC of 25 February 1999 relating to the procedures whereby officials and employees of the European Commission may be allowed access to classified information held by the Commission (notified under document number C (1999) 423, Official Journal of the European Union L 80, 1999, 22.

23 See, Statewatch Bulletin, www.statewatch.org/subscriber/protected/sw10n34.pdf.

24 In the amendment to the rules dating from 2009 that still have not been adopted this category is included. See, Proposal for a regulation of the European Parliament and of the Council regarding public access to European Parliament, Council and Commission documents (recast) COM (2008)0229 – C6-0184/2008 – 2008/0090(COD), 11 March 2009, at 21.

was eventually adopted in 2001.[25] The span of the Council's new security regulations was moreover not limited to EU institutions: Member States were placed under an obligation to adopt 'appropriate national measures' to ensure that the Council's rules on the handling of classified information are respected within their governments.[26] This led in particular to a spate of new state secrets laws in newly joined Eastern European Member States.[27] In addition the EU Access Regulation provided in not so veiled terms that the principle of loyal cooperation governing relations between the institutions and the Member States required that Member States 'take care not to hamper the proper application of this Regulation and should respect the security rules of the institutions'.[28]

2.3 New Rules (2011): The Council and the Implementation of its Rules by Other Actors

In March 2011, almost a decade to the day after the controversial 2001 security rules, the Council adopted the next generation of its internal security rules and formally launched *EUCI* (EU Classified Information). These rules emerged at a moment when the planned revision of the access-to-documents law was stalled in what seemed a structural impasse despite the fact that the Lisbon Treaty had introduced a number of salient changes in the legal framework.[29] However, the full access revision process was re-ignited in September 2011.[30] The Council's new security rules emerged into the public realm only after adoption and subsequent publication in the Official Journal but they were worked on – in secret – for a period of at least two years in the Council's security committee and the Antici Group, responsible for preparing the meetings of the EU's ambassadors (COREPER), and then COREPER itself before final agreement at the ministerial level in early 2011. These new rules are much

---

[25] See, Article 9 of Regulation 1049/2001, *supra* note 4.

[26] Council Decision 2001/264/EC adopting Council's Security Regulations, Official Journal of the European Union, L 101 , 2001.1 Preamble and Art. 2

[27] Alasdair S. Roberts, Entangling Alliances: NATO's Security Policy and the Entrenchment of State Secrecy, 26 CORNELL INT'L L.J. 2, 329–60.

[28] Recital 15 of Regulation 1049/2001, *supra* note 4.

[29] See, Commission, Proposal for a Regulation of the European Parliament and of the Council amending Regulation (EC) No. 1049/2001 regarding public access to European Parliament, Council and Commission documents, COM (2011), www.statewatch.org/news/2011/mar/eu-com-access-reg-1049-proposal.pdf.

[30] See, European Parliament resolution of 14 September 2011 on public access to documents (Rule 104(7)) for the years 2009–2010 (2010/2294(INI)).

more far reaching in terms of scope and width of application than their 2001 counterpart and constitute an excellent illustration of the expanded scope of supranational executive activity in the EU context.[31]

This is not the place for a detailed analysis of the new security provisions but a selective number of points indicate how the domain of secrecy regulation has multiplied. The four (NATO) levels of security gradings are now applied well beyond the common foreign and defence realm. From 2011 the justifications for classifying documents includes *in general* terms 'the interests of the European Union' as well as those of 'one or more of the Member States'.[32] In other words, the EU now has clearly marked out a classification system that applies across the broad spectrum of its activities with no special mention or position given anymore to the Common Security and Defence Policy. This illustrates indeed how the nature of the EU polity has evolved in the decade since 2001 and how much matters of internal security have become intertwined with external security and the impossibility of separating the two into a separate 'pillar' as was still the case a decade earlier.

The Council no longer adopts rules based on its own rules of procedure only for its *own* internal organisation. Its explicit strategy, reflected in its decision, is to obtain the commitment by the Commission, by the Member States and by the other EU institutions, agencies, bodies and offices to comply with its own rules and standards 'necessary in order to protect the interests of the Union and its Member States'.[33] Several declarations appended to the decision make this perfectly clear.[34] In particular, 'the Council and the Commission consider that their respective security rules, and the Agreement between the Member States, meeting within the Council, regarding the protection of classified information exchanged in the interests of the European Union, together constitute a more comprehensive and coherent general framework within the European Union for the protection of classified information originating in the Member States, in institutions of the European Union or in EU agencies, bodies or offices, or received from third States or international

---

[31] See CURTIN, *supra* note 7.

[32] Council Decision of 31 March 2011 on the security rules for protecting EU classified information, Official Journal of the European Union L 141, 2011, 17–65.

[33] Recital 5 of the Council Decision, ibid.

[34] See, in particular a series of five declarations entered in the minutes of the Council session at which the Council Decision was formally adopted, www.statewatch.org/news/2011/mar/eu-council-classified-information-8054-add 1-11.pdf.

organisations'.[35] Thus the Council's strategy of achieving a comprehensive general framework for the protection of EUCI across the spectrum of the actors and the activities of the EU is spelt out in black and white.

One can refer to the less than upfront process as effectively a type of rule-making of secrecy in the shadows, with the Council as the central spider weaving an elaborate and often opaque web. Within its reach are various actors linked to its security system by various mechanisms, all negotiated and agreed in secret. Thus, the Member States signed a binding agreement less than two weeks after the Council adopted its new security rules, guaranteeing in a legally binding fashion that they would protect classified information originating in the 'European Union institutions, or in agencies, bodies or offices established by the latter and provided to or exchanged with the Member States' as well as their own documents provided to or exchanged with EU institutions etc.[36] In other words, this agreement made explicit what has been feared for a long time: not only does the EU adopt rules that bind its own institutions, agencies, etc., but even rules adopted as a matter of the internal organisation of the same institutions can in practice lead to the Member States being restricted under their own national law, constitutional or otherwise, and obliged to give primacy to the EU classification rules. The remarkable point about this process is above all the incremental and barely visible manner in which it occurs, never at any stage having been openly discussed and debated.

An example of how embedded even an institution such as the EP has become within the comprehensive secrecy rule-making of the Council is the decision by the Bureau of the EP[37] concerning the rules governing the treatment of 'confidential information' by the EP. In pursuance of inter-institutional agreement with the Council the implementing rules by the EP[38] are based on its own internal rule making power and relies on its

---

[35] Declaration by the Council and the Commission on the protection and handling of classified information, www.statewatch.org/news/2011/mar/eu-council-classified-information-8054-add1-11.pdf.

[36] Agreement between the Member States of the European Union, meeting within the Council, regarding the protection of classified information exchanged in the interests of the European Union, Official Journal of the European Union C 202, 2011, 13–23.

[37] The Bureau consists of the President and the 14 Vice-Presidents, representing six out of seven political groups in the EP.

[38] European Parliament, Decision of the Bureau of the European Parliament of 6 June 2011 concerning the rules governing the treatment of confidential information by the European Parliament, Official Journal of the European Union C 190, 2011, 2.

own rules of procedure as the legal basis.[39] This 'decision' by the bureaucracy of the EP takes over the Council rules on EUCI but at the same time explicitly covers what is termed 'other' confidential information. This term refers to non-classified confidential information and lays down the basic principles and minimum standards. Such 'other' confidential information is part of a whole new category of *sensitive but unclassified information* (in the US known as *Controlled Unclassified Information*, CUI)[40] that is difficult to pin down and define, in part because of the greatly varied rationales used to justify its protection.[41] Such information often receives the grading of 'limited' in the EU context, which is actually not referred to anywhere in the formal security rules but exists *outside* the formal classification system. The confusion about why 'limited' information is to be protected and how it is to be handled may lead to it being effectively mistaken for another classification level, causing unclassified information with this marking level to be treated like classified information.[42]

A further and expanding part of security regulation includes the *external* dimension. This includes a variety of agreements with third states and international organisations. For example, at the same time as the adoption of the 2001 security rules, the Secretary General of the Council had entered into an interim security agreement with NATO that incorporated the key elements of NATO security policy.[43] In March 2003, an EU–NATO agreement was concluded for permanent relations, which

---

39 The Council subsequently is adopting its own internal implementing rules of its part of the inter-institutional agreement. See, Working Party on General Affairs, Interinstitutional Agreement between the EP and the Council concerning the forwarding to and handling by the EP of classified information held by the Council on matters other than those in area of Common Foreign and Security Policy – Council implementing arrangements, 84361/12, 8 May 2012.

40 See further, in the US, CUI Archives, www.archives.gov/cui.

41 For the history of the evolution of the category sensitive but unclassified, see further, Genevieve J. Knezo, 'Sensitive but unclassified' and other federal security controls on scientific and technical information: history and current controversy, CONGRESSIONAL RESEARCH SERVICE (Library of Congress), www.fas.org/sgp/crs/RL31845.pdf.

42 See for the US, Report of the Commission on Protecting and Reducing Government Secrecy (hereafter: the Moynihan Committee Report), Washington: US Government Printing Office, 1997, at 29.

43 Roberts, *supra* note 27, at 356.

included the exchange of classified information.[44] This was the first of many 'security-of-information agreements' concluded by the Council as well as administrative arrangements for the lowest classification level. Article 12 of the new 2011 Council rules explicitly provides for this exchange of classified information with third states and international organisations and mandates that their classification levels are no less stringent than those laid down in the Council Decision.

Information sharing among a wide variety of internal and external actors thus takes place without it being clear how such non-legislative practices relate to the mandate of Article 1 of the EU Treaty that decision-making in the EU will be as open as possible. Information sharing can lead to structural opacity over what information is being shared and may make the issue of responsibility for classification and declassification fuzzy. Entanglement in the sense of a commingling of information that is so deep that it becomes difficult to separate information that was generated internally and information received externally is likely. When information sharing is combined with the two main tools that cause secrecy to multiply quasi-automatically, the principle of derivative classification and the principle of originator control, we can speak of a culture of secrecy. I will now explore the parameters of secrecy in this cultural sense and its relevance to the EU.

3. A CULTURE OF SECRECY?

Equally important to the formal rules adopted by the institutions themselves is whether a culture of secrecy prevails within the government institutions or agencies in question. This is often tied up with a phenomenon known as '*ORCON* creep'.[45] This is the acronym for the phenomenon of *originator control* that leads to the multiplication or accumulation of government secrecy.[46] Traditionally, governments have insisted on applying the rule of originator control before they share information with other governments or international organisations. This rule allows originating governments or agencies/institutions to retain

[44] Agreement between the European Union and the North Atlantic Treaty Organization on the Security of Information, Official Journal of the European Union L 080, 2003, 36–8.

[45] Alasdair S. Roberts, ORCON Creep: Networked Governance, Information Sharing and the Threat to Government Accountability, 21 GOVERNMENT INFORMATION QUARTERLY 3, 249 (2004).

[46] See, for example, Article 4(5) of Regulation 1049/2001, *supra* note 4.

control over the declassification of information (if it is classified) or its release to non-governmental parties (if it is not). Within the context of the EU this rule has been there since 1958[47] but it has mutated and expanded considerably since then. In a nutshell, it provides that if the information has been classified by State (or Agency) A, it cannot be reclassified or declassified by State B (or an international organisation), unless State A consents to the change. Similarly, no information provided by State A can be given by State B (or an international organisation) to a third party – such as another government, non-governmental organisation or citizen – without the consent of State A. The ORCON rule thus eliminates the ability of states/agencies/international organisations to make their own judgments about the wisdom of releasing shared information. The requirement to consult the author (the originator) before granting public access or declassifying is deeply embedded within the EU secrecy rules but also features in several places in the Access Regulation from 2001.[48]

The other tool that causes secrecy to multiply is the process known as *derivative* classification. This process effectively gives the power of secrecy classification to any persons who are cleared to see documents in the respective classification categories.[49] Thus, only the persons who, for example, have Top Secret classification clearances are empowered to create Top Secret documents. Whenever a person uses for example a Top Secret source in preparing a *new document* they are obliged to classify the new document according to the classification of the source of information. Since documents must carry the highest classification of their component parts any document which uses a Top Secret source must itself be classified Top Secret. However, since classification is typically both anonymous and nonspecific, a user of a Top Secret source has no way of knowing what particular piece of information led to it being classified Top Secret. As a result the derivative classifier may feel bound to apply a Top Secret Classification to his document if she has used any information whatsoever from a Top Secret source (although that

47 See, for example, Article 29(1) of Regulation No. 3 implementing Article 24 of the Treaty establishing the European Atomic Energy Community, Official Journal of the European Union L 17, 1958, 406–16.

48 See, Article 4(4) and Article 9(3) of Regulation 1049/2001, *supra* note 4.

49 Charles R. Nesson, Aspects of the Executive's Power over National Security Matters: Secrecy Classifications and Foreign Intelligence Wiretaps, 49 IND. L.J. 3 (1974), 399–421, 402; Moynihan Committee Report, *supra* note 42, at 31–2.

may not in fact be the 'Top Secret' bit). The principle of derivative classification applies to all levels of classification.

Derivative classification leads very simply and easily to the risk of *overclassification*. The problem of overclassification is not a new problem. Classifying too much is a lower risk strategy for public officials than classifying too little and there is often little incentive for them not to classify material as well as little control in practice over the substance of overclassification or unnecessary classification. During the course of the past sixty years in the US alone there have been no less than eight 'major reviews' of the security classification systems precisely because overclassification remains such a problem. It is also *not* a minor problem.[50] We do not have the equivalent figures for the EU nor has there ever been a review, major or minor, of the security classification system in the EU and its link with those of the Member States.

The WikiLeaks cables illustrate that although classification rules are designed to strictly limit who has access to the secret and how, such limitations may in practice be wholly illusory. This has to do with how many people knew, what sorts of people knew, how much they knew and the timing when they knew. WikiLeaks revealed huge security failings in the protection of classified material including the fact that an extremely substantial number of persons within the US administration had access to such 'secrets'. According to one report more than three *million* US military and civilian personnel had the security clearance necessary to access the US Defense Department *Secret Internet Router Network* (SIPRNet). How secret is a secret that three million people have access to? Benjamin Franklin already knew the answer to that. As he put it: 'Three may keep a secret if two of them are dead.'[51] The reality may well be, also in Europe, that thousands of soldiers, analysts and intelligence officers as well as sub-contractors among others get access to huge volumes of classified and sensitive (but unclassified) material.

---

[50] Experts' assessments estimate that between 50% to 90% of what is classified in the US is either overclassified or should not be classified at all. See, Statement of Carol A. Haave, Deputy Secretary of Defence for Counter-intelligence and Security, Too Many Secrets: Overclassification as a Barrier to Information Sharing, HEARING BEFORE THE SUBCOMMITTEE ON NATIONAL SECURITY, EMERGING THREATS, AND INTERNATIONAL RELATIONS OF THE COMMITTEE ON GOVERNMENT REFORM HOUSE OF REPRESENTATIVES, 108th Cong., at 82 (24 August 2004); Donald Rumsfeld, War of the Words, WALL ST. J., 18 July 2005, at A12 (acknowledging 'too much material is classified across the federal government as a general rule').

[51] Benjamin Franklin, quoted in the Moynihan Committee Report, *supra* note 42, at 4.

When a small group of similarly situated officials conceals from outsiders the fact that it is concealing something, the result is a *deep secret*.[52] Deep secrets may more often involve bad faith or fraud.[53] The targets cannot protect themselves against information they cannot imagine and so the secret keeper can always gain advantage at the expense of the target. The concepts of deep and shallow secrets can best be illustrated with metaphors of light. Whereas the deep secret's target is 'completely in the dark, never imagining that relevant information might be had', the shallow secret's target 'has at least some shadowy sense' that she is lacking relevant information.[54] Deep-secret keepers will generally be more concerned to conceal from the target the fact that they wish to conceal something than shallow-secret keepers.[55] When members of the general public or of oversight institutions (perhaps via a document register) understand that they are being denied particular items of information, the result is a *shallow secret*. Information which has been classified but the existence of which is not hidden (either in document registers or otherwise) is a shallow secret. A shallow secret may be challenged by procedural or other means and may be brought further to light in parliamentary oversight processes in particular. In the EU it is the supranational EP that can exercise some oversight over classified or sensitive but unclassified material and the manner of its regulation and application. It can do so in two ways: either by challenging denials to grant it information through the courts or by attempting to activate its own oversight powers. To date, there has been quite some use of the former option with the latter remaining as yet rather under-developed. I will now explore one specific area: EP access to classified and sensitive but unclassified information in the context of the negotiation of international agreements by the Council.

4. EUROPEAN PARLIAMENT OVERSIGHT OVER INTERNATIONAL AGREEMENTS: CAUGHT IN A TRAP?

The parliamentary oversight at the European level over institutional secrecy and the negotiation of international agreements (typically the executive prerogative within the EU) has undoubtedly improved in recent

---

52 David E. Pozen, Deep Secrecy, 62(2) STAN. L. REV. (2010), 257–339.
53 Moynihan Committee Report, *supra* note 42.
54 Pozen, *supra* note 52.
55 Ibid.

years thanks to a pro-active stance by the EP and helped by the new legal regime introduced by the Treaty of Lisbon. One of the most significant new powers given to the EP in the Lisbon Treaty is, in Articles 218(6) and (4) TFEU, the power to veto the conclusion of international agreements negotiated on behalf of the EU by the executive power (a combination of the Council and the Commission or in some cases the High Representative). Moreover, Article 281(10) explicitly provides that the EP is to be 'immediately and fully informed at all stages of the (negotiating) procedure'. In this way, some democratic oversight has been introduced over what was hitherto a matter purely of closed diplomatic negotiations at the European level.

Given the highly political type of issues that the EU is currently negotiating with third states or other international organisations,[56] this is a timely and much needed oversight. It is also the only parliamentary oversight possible where the agreements fall under the exclusive competence of the EU since national parliaments are then inevitably sidelined. But even with the new Treaty provisions the EP has experienced considerable difficulties in practice in getting timely access to classified documents. The executive institutions argue that strict secrecy is required because otherwise their negotiation strategies with the third country would be undermined. Moreover, by invoking NATO standards the Council and the Commission have opposed to the EP the principle of 'originator control'. As we have already seen this principle entails that the third country concerned can exert the right to oppose the diffusion to the EP of classified information.

The classification level of negotiation mandates is generally 'restricted', yet this level is not mentioned in the specific provisions in the Access Regulation from 2001. This classification level is introduced in the internal rules of the institutions themselves and is applied to 'information and material the unauthorised disclosure of which could be *disadvantageous* to the interests of the Union or of one or more of the Member States'.[57] It is not at all clear what would be 'disadvantageous to the interests of the Union' in making public the actual 'negotiation

---

[56] See for example, Council, 17434/11, Agreement between the USA and the EU on the use and transfer of Passenger Name Record data to the US Department of Homeland Security, http://register.consilium.europa.eu/pdf/en/11/st17/st17434.en11.pdf. See also, Council of Europe, Draft legal instruments on the accession of the European Union to the European Convention on Human Rights, 19 July 2011, www.statewatch.org/news/2011/jul/eu-coe-echr-final.pdf.

[57] Article 2(2) (d) of the Council Decision of 30 March 2011 on the security rules protecting EUCI, *supra* note 32.

mandate' other than it being disadvantageous to the interest of the institutions in having their own space to negotiate 'diplomatically' freed up from the constraints of publicity. The interest of the citizens of the EU who will see their rights and interests directly affected by the subject matter under negotiation does not seem to be factored into the notion of 'the interests of the Union'. This is the case even where what is being negotiated has a constitutional nature and could change the existing rules of the game.

The EP for its part is clearly keen to reassure the Council and the Commission that it is very serious about the measures it has taken to ensure the security of classified and unclassified but sensitive information which it receives from the executive institutions, as is evident in the new security rules adopted by its Bureau mid-2011. At the same time the executive institutions do seem to be intent on setting in place a *limited* exchange of classified information with the EP. This is witnessed in particular by the insistence first by the Commission in 2010 and later by the Council in 2011 that the principle of originator control fully applies, not only to documents produced by third states and other international organisations but also to documents by the more 'internal' EU actors: Member States, other institutions and bodies. This reinforcement of the ORCON principle in the context of the inter-institutional exchange of (classified) material does not augur well for the ability of the EP to carry out its oversight role effectively. The 'trap' was the enticing prospect of more information exchange but the reality was information with much of the 'meat' removed, at least in the context of international agreements being negotiated with third countries where they can insist on the EP not being given access to many classified documents. In the case of the US, given that all documents relating to foreign 'governments' are automatically classified, this automatically means that no access will be given to the EP unless the US agrees to declassify – a highly unsatisfactory position for the EP.

With regard to the controversial category of sensitive but unclassified documents, the EP is clearly staking a claim as is evident from its own internal rules adopted by its Bureau earlier in 2011. Yet there is a problem here that has to do with the attitude of the executive institutions to their own internal preparatory documents which they feel they must keep secret in the interests of their own decision making process.[58] A

---

[58] This is explicitly stated by the Council Security Committee in its 'Draft Policy on handling of documents internal to the Council', 7470/11, 8 March 2011.

good example of their secrecy reflex in this regard is provided by their refusal in 2009 to give a MEP, Sophie in 't Veld, a copy of a ('restricted') legal service opinion of the Council on the appropriate legal basis to negotiate and conclude a new SWIFT agreement with the US. She challenged their refusal to give full public access on grounds of international relations and court proceedings and legal advice before the courts and won the case before the General Court. The Court ruled that the principle of transparency applied to external relations and that in principle she should have been given access to the legal opinion in question.[59]

This raises the key issue whether executive institutions can claim, contrary to existing court case law,[60] the right to keep their internal opinion on the appropriate legal basis of international negotiations secret. This kind of reasoning refusing access is not so much based on a concern for the equivalent of 'national security' in the EU context but rather on a different rationale for secrecy already commented on by Max Weber – the inherent tendency of bureaucracies to want to keep their internal deliberations secret.[61] Officials typically view secrecy as the best protection against outside interference in their activities. Recent history in the US in particular has shown the extent to which keeping internal legal opinions secret can be perverted to facilitate wrongdoing and undermine legal accountability.[62]

---

[59] Case T-529/09, *Sophie in 't Veld v. Council*, Judgment of 4 May 2012, nyr. The case is currently pending appeal and it remains to be seen whether it will be upheld. See further, Deirdre Curtin, Official Secrets and the Negotiation of International Agreements: Is the EU Executive Unbound?, 50 CML REV. (2013), 1–36.

[60] Case C-39/05, *Sweden and Turco v. Council*, [2008] ECR I-4723. See also, Case C-506/08, *Sweden v. MyTravel and Commission*, Judgment of 21 July 2011, nyr. See further, Deirdre Curtin, Judging EU Secrecy, CAHIER DE DROIT EUROPÉEN (2012), 457–490.

[61] See, Max Weber, Bureaucracy, in ESSAYS IN SOCIOLOGY (Hans Heinrich Gerth and Charles Wright Mills, eds. 1946) ('Every bureaucracy seeks to increase the superiority of the professionally informed by keeping their knowledge and intentions secret').

[62] See, for example, the President's Office of Legal Counsel legal opinion (at the time secret) authorising torture. By limiting internal circulation of the legal opinion the Bush Administration was able to delay the leaking of its improper conduct and limit internal – and external – criticism, www.aclu.org/national-security/memo-regarding-torture-and-military-interrogation-alien-unlawful-combatants-held-o.

5. CONCLUDING REMARKS

Secrecy is much easier to define than *transparency* but surprisingly it is largely ignored as a subject and rarely mapped out in the context of the EU. Yet it provides fascinating empirical evidence for a much wider phenomenon of the growth of *executive power* both at the level of the EU itself and its intricate interaction with national executive power. The exercise of the power to limit the flow of information to the public is felt throughout the length and breadth of government today. But its impact is still sharpest in the areas of defence and security affairs where even nowadays public officials come closest to having monopoly power in the field of information. There is of course a serious case to be made for a limited sharing of properly classified information but the policy and limits should be upfront. The puzzle is how and why reliance on the different rationales for administrative secrecy is expanding both in law and as a matter of practice at precisely the time that the law and practice of transparency is more accepted and implemented.

At the same time the topic of secrecy brings to light what can be termed dilemmas of democracy and must also be understood in this wider context. After all, the topic is about the ability of executive power, however defined, to control a process vital to the health of modern democracy – the flow of information to the public. The growth of secrecy diminishes the people's information about government and thus people's participation in government. The growth of secrecy will affect the ability of the other two powers – legislative and judiciary – to provide countervailing checks and balances and thus affect the very values underlying the principle of separation or balance of powers. At the same time, one of the paradoxes is that there may well be considerable ambivalence by both the legislative power and the judicial power as to their own need to keep secret their own deliberations and/or documents. Finally, as Max Weber already pointed out, a preoccupation with secrecy is an inherent characteristic of administrative institutions and can be understood in good part as functional necessity. Administrative secrecy is still today often defended on grounds of *efficient* decision-making.

Oversight mechanisms are evolving in practice and in particular the role of the supranational EP as an accountability forum is salient – but the EP too is itself increasingly bound by the constraints of secrecy. It is too early to assess how effectively the EP is actually maintaining oversight over the negotiation and agreement process of international agreements in the new legal regime after entry into force of the Lisbon Treaty and no empirical research has been carried out yet. It is not clear to what extent the EP is fully being given access to classified information and to unclassified but sensitive information. The initial indicators however are that it is not.

The time is more than ripe to treat the issue of secrecy regulation in and of itself seriously. This means in my view that it must be regulated at the *legislative* level and across the spectrum of EU activities and no longer as a matter of internal executive prerogative. I believe that the contours of the classification system should ideally be laid out in a separate legislative measure and not as part of the public access legislation.[63] Its relationship with the public access law and other laws (such as data protection etc.) should then be explicitly discussed and openly regulated. This entails the normal legislative process with co-decision by the EP using a general legal basis for unenumerated powers using essentially the same legal basis the Commission proposed in 1992. Issues such as declassification processes, periodic classification review, classification oversight and extending declassification authority beyond the originator can then be systematically and structurally regulated in a manner that does justice both to the need for executive secrecy and for more openness as constitutionally prescribed. The best response to the dilemma of ensuring that secrecy is democratic is to make certain that there is proper *public* discussion of the rules that determine when secrets shall be kept.[64]

---

[63] See, contra, European Parliament, 'Draft Report on the proposal for a regulation of the European Parliament and of the Council regarding public access to European Parliament', Council and Commission documents (recast), Rapporteur M. Cashman, 1 September 2010, new Article 3a (Amendment 27) which proposes a novel 'procedure for the classification and declassification of documents'.

[64] See, Dennis F. Thompson, Democratic Secrecy, POLITICAL SCIENCE QUARTERLY 114(2), 181–93 (1999).

19. Concluding remarks

Justice (retired) Lech Garlicki

1. GENERAL OBSERVATIONS

This book debates the role of constitutional law in elaborating a fair balance between secrecy, understood as a necessary tool to protect the national security, and human rights. Three introductory questions may help to put this debate into a broader perspective:

- How new is the inclination to resort to secret measures when the society is in danger?
- If so, is there anything new in the present crisis that distinguishes it from earlier historical situations?
- Is the modern constitutional doctrine better equipped to respond to the emerging problems and risks?

1.1

In the twenty-first century, it cannot be denied that effective anti-terrorist measures require a fair amount of secrecy. But, at the same time, it may be useful to put this observation into a wider historical context.

Although it is true that balancing secrecy, national security and constitutional law is particularly pertinent to the modern world, similar problems have existed for centuries. There have always been evil forces, genuine or imagined, perceived as a threat to society, and there has always been a strong belief that secret measures are particularly efficient to protect those who deserve such protection. The Holy Inquisition operated this way for several centuries. It was no accident that as modern society became more organized, matters of state security were assigned to different 'secret' services and institutions. And it was not a coincidence that some of the most dreaded organizations of that kind, like the Nazi Gestapo, included the adjective 'secret' in their very names (Geheim Staatspolizei).

This combination of enemy threats and secret counter-measures produced another inclination, namely, to delegate powers to the executive branch to efficiently respond to crisis situations. In the institutional dimension, it usually led to an extension of executive power at the expense of both legislative assemblies and judicial bodies. On some occasions, that extension went as far as to transform the whole constitutional system into a regime characterized by 'executive dominance', as it was pointed out by Stephen Schulhofer in his contribution. In the political dimension, it often resulted in distortions and sometimes the resulting cure was worse than the disease.

The present days are far from being immune to those dangers.

1.2

This brings me to the second question, namely, whether the present crisis, as it has developed since 9/11, shows any difference in comparison to some of its historical predecessors. On the one hand, there has been a traumatic shift within the last decade. The world of 2012 seems to be less safe, less peaceful and less human rights-friendly than in 2000. On the other hand, terrorism has never been absent in post-WWII Europe: one can just mention the tragedy of Northern Ireland or the experience of Germany and Italy in the 1970s. Nevertheless, there are strong reasons to believe that the current situation is more complicated and, in many respects, quite different. Three developments seem to be of a particular importance: globalization; the technical sophistication of daily life; and the evolution of the legal (constitutional) context.

Globalization means that the whole planet is now confronted with a clear and present danger of terrorist attack that may disrupt the world order. Although it is not the first time our world has been put in jeopardy, earlier threats culminated in 'conventional' (cold or hot) wars, in which both sides were easily identifiable. Terrorism is an invisible enemy that escapes such identification and, by its very definition, it is a constant threat present everywhere in the world. The general process of globalization led not only to globalization of terrorist activity (we are thus far away from the 'old good times' when terrorism remained mostly confined to particular countries), but also to the need for a global response. Consequentially, the 'war on terror' became, to a considerable extent, detached from the national constitutional context.

Globalization has been accompanied by sophistication of both terrorist action and security responses. On one hand, technical progress in communication and information assists terrorist activities. Elimination of technical obstacles goes hand in hand with transformation of legal regulation: human capacities have been considerably enhanced by the reduction of the traditional limitations to foreign travel, global communication, access to information etc. Those opportunities have already been used, and surely will be used in the future, by those who are commonly characterized as 'terrorists'.

On the other hand, today's technical infrastructure allows permanent control of everybody's daily activities that goes far beyond Orwell's depiction of '1984'. We are no longer constantly watched by secret police, but this job was taken by someone else, in particular by the private sector. Almost everything today is registered and stored, including a person's internet usage, bank and credit card transactions, telephone calls, airline travel, and many other interactions. Street and industrial cameras replaced the 'Big Brother' eye, satellite navigation and mobile phones systems allow everyone to be located almost everywhere in the world. All of this privately-collected data is easily accessible by state security agencies and easily exchangeable all around the world.

At the same time, however, legal instruments are becoming more sophisticated, particularly on the constitutional level. Within the last four decades, the definition of antiterrorist responses has been, to a considerable extent, removed from the exclusive domain of executive regulation and subject to the limits of constitutional law (on the domestic level) and/or human rights law (on the supranational level).

In other words, in most of today's democracies, there is no alternative other than to place anti-terrorist measures into a more general framework of democratic constitutionalism, constitutional jurisdictions and human rights institutions. As a consequence, parliaments and courts – domestic as well as supranational – enter the area that used to be regarded as an exclusive province of the executive branch. Such a framework was absent in earlier times.

In the beginning of the twenty-first century, we no longer have only a group of committed but marginal scholars who are talking about vindication of constitutional law and human rights when addressing the terrorist threat. There are also countries and institutions that are ready to take seriously those modern values in the awareness that whenever the executive branch is given a blank check to act, human rights disappear first and terrorists are still around. This evolution can be seen, albeit in different forms, on both shores of the Atlantic. Constitutional jurisprudence on terrorism (and on responses to it) represents a developing branch of constitutional law. Special attention should be given here to the lessons coming from Israel, particularly to the case-law of its Supreme Court, reported in this book by Shiri Krebs and Ori Aronson.

1.3

My last general observation is that modern constitutional law doctrine seems to be better equipped than ever to respond to the emerging problems and to offer some guidance to both politicians and judges. This was well documented in practically all chapters of this book. Three conclusions may be submitted as a summary of those contributions.

First, even in academic discussions one cannot be blind: we are living in dangerous times and the public authorities are under a constitutionally-mandated obligation to protect us from terrorism, as well as to respond to other threats. Those responses have their price in the area of human rights; no constitution should be interpreted in a manner that would transform it into a suicide pact. Some trade-offs are, therefore, unavoidable, as observed by Lord Sedley: states may sometimes be required to constrict the rights of some in order to assure them for all. This leaves us with the question, which constitutional law is fit to answer, of how to delineate restrictions and what must be left untouched.

Second, it seems that proportionality analysis and the balancing of the competing interests represents the most common, and also the most natural, way of constitutional reasoning. Although we should be aware of dangers of constitutional relativism, relegating terms like 'compromise' or 'balancing' from the toolkit of modern constitutional law would be both impracticable and unwise. Few rights are absolute in nature and others may be restricted whenever there is a genuine necessity. Hence, proportionality analysis is becoming a common tool in the jurisprudence of many constitutional and supreme courts around the world. Their case-law has already transformed proportionality from an abstract and undetermined concept into a category of constitutional law which can be applied in a manner assuring both predictability and coherence. But, at the same time, the advantages of the proportionality approach, like flexibility to adjust to changing situations, call for particular skills in the process of its application. Proportionality is an attractive toy, but its use must be restricted to those who know how to play with it, that is courts and judges. This is the only branch that remains (or, at least, is expected to remain) sufficiently detached from daily politics and sufficiently impartial in the balancing process to decide what responses are in proportion to a given threat.

Finally, all attractiveness of the proportionality notwithstanding, there still are limits to flexible interpretations of individual rights. Thus, another mission of modern constitutional law is to delineate where the bottom-line is to any compromise and to any 'proportional' restriction on human rights.

Substantively, a particular prominence belongs to the concept of absolute rights, complemented by the concept of 'core-elements', 'gist', or 'essence' of each and every right. On the supranational (international) level, those concepts are placed within the framework of universalism, that is, of the recognition that certain rights cannot be divided and tailored according to national traditions or regional differences. Those prohibitions find their source in basic, universal values that are common to all civilizations and constitutional traditions. As was pointed out by Lord Sedley, we cannot defend basic values by sacrificing them.

Procedurally, it is now commonly accepted, as David Cole noted, that the survival of individual rights cannot be assured without the securing of appropriate procedural safeguards. Whenever there are imperative reasons to restrict a substantive right, such restrictions must be counterbalanced by the existence of a fair procedure which allows individuals to vindicate their rights before an independent body. Courts and judges are simply irreplaceable in this area. And once the judiciary is vested with appropriate powers of review, the executive branch loses its claim to uncontrolled dominance, even in matters of national security.

None of the previous observations seems to be particularly inventive or innovative, but the very fact that they may be regarded as trivia of modern constitutional law shows how advanced the law has become at the outset of the twenty-first century. Today's understanding of the role of constitutional law clearly differs from the situation after WWII when, in many European countries, the very notions of human rights, judicial review and supranational jurisdictions remained, at best, within the area of wishful thinking. Today's constitutional law has long departed from the realm of a pure politics and amounts to a genuine branch of law that is able to meet challenges arising upon executive responses to terrorism and, in particular, executive abuses of secrecy. It is our mission to develop that function of constitutional law and to contribute to the protection of basic values like the rule of law and democracy. We are here to vindicate rights and not, as we were reminded by Kent Roach, to supply arguments for the cold-war-secrecy mentality.

2. THE DIMENSIONS OF SECRECY

2.1

Secrecy seems to be an inevitable companion of both protection of national security and elaboration of anti-terrorist measures. Two aspects of the problem were discussed in this book. First, in the institutional setting, the book addressed the respective roles of the legislative assemblies and of the judicial bodies. Second, upon that institutional background, the book focused on areas where secrecy plays an important role, in particular detentions, criminal trials, and administrative measures. We were confronted with a sometimes frightening description of an omnipresence of secrecy in matters of national security.

2.2

Discussions on detentions, criminal trials and administrative measures cover most of the areas where secrecy plays a prominent role. At the same time, it should be kept in mind that the use of secrecy in detentions and criminal trials remains in collision with the general principles of penal investigation and judicial proceedings. Secret detentions and secret trials are incompatible with the present understanding of human rights. This does not mean that, in some instances, secrecy cannot be warranted by higher imperatives. But any departure from general human rights principles must be regarded as exceptional and allowed only upon sufficient and reasonable grounds. This is an area in which procedural safeguards should play a particularly prominent role and, as it was shown by Jason Mazzone and Clive Walker, this is the area in which there is a well-established framework of principles, norms and institutions.

What remain less defined and more scarcely regulated are so-called administrative measures; that is, all measures, other than detention and trial, taken by the public authorities in the fight against terrorism. Some of those measures appear very problematic when assessed in the perspective of human rights.

First, there is a phenomenon of secret information and intelligence, that is information secretly gathered about potential suspects but never used or revealed in any formalized procedure. This information often constitutes the secret basis to decide on application of other measures and only those subsequent measures are communicated to the affected persons and subject to some review. But the 'pre-information' remains entirely secret and, as no one except the security agencies knows about it, may be used in an arbitrary manner according to the whims of security officials. The globalization process significantly contributes to the lack of transparency. Quite often national security agencies use information gathered elsewhere and communicated to them for further action. Thus, even assuming that national authorities are acting in good faith, they may be unable to verify where and how particular information was acquired.

Another dimension of secrecy is related to secret regulations. While legislation is adopted through open parliamentary procedures and is accessible via publication, this is not the case with each and every executive regulation. Particularly in such fields as national security, there is a vast category of regulations that remain classified and inaccessible to those who may be affected by their application. Most modern constitutions require publication of regulatory instruments that may affect individual rights or liberties. But those published regulations are often accompanied by entirely secret sub-regulations and, as outlined by Deidre Curtin, by different intra-departmental directives, circulars and guidelines. While technically those regulations are not regarded as 'the law' (and may therefore remain secret), in practice they play a large role in organizing the use of 'administrative measures'. This process can be seen in immigration, deportation, surveillance, wire-tapping, or black-listing. Often officially published laws are either missing or, at best, reserve a vast margin of discretion for the executive authorities. And, even if nothing is officially known about other areas of secret regulation, one can easily imagine that they may also play a role in such human rights-sensitive situations as detention of aliens and targeted killing.

Finally, secrecy extends also to secret procedures and secret institutions. The former are often hidden behind different forms of international cooperation. Federico Fabbrini's chapter addressed one of the most shocking practices of our times. After the *Kadi* case,[1] we know that secret procedures apply to 'international black-listing' and freezing orders. We have no knowledge of what, if any, procedures are used to decide on targeted killings, but it cannot be excluded that there may be some kind of secret 'trial' before an actual elimination takes place. Equally terrifying may be the record of secret institutions, particularly in the context of 'secret jails', located outside the reach of national constitutions and national safeguards. This implies a good deal of international tolerance for and compliance with human rights abuses.

In brief, the necessities of the 'war on terror' encourage the creation of a parallel 'secret state' that gathers its own secret information, is ruled by its own secret regulations, and uses its own secret procedures and institutions. In consequence, secrecy takes a new dimension; we are not even supposed to know what is going on and we can only feel that 'something' is encroaching upon fundamental rights of some, or most, of us. The famous remark of Rumsfeld that the most dreadful secrets are those 'we don't know we don't know' seems to be particularly illustrative here.

---

[1] Joined Cases C-402/05 P and C-415/05 P *Kadi and Al Barakaat International Foundation v. Council and Commission* [2008] ECR I-6351.

2.3

These developments are not new. Security agencies have always been inclined to excessive secrecy. Historical experience provides us with a fair warning; on many occasions, executive dominance in matters of national security has degenerated into a dominance of the security apparatus over the executive branch and, in consequence, over the entire state.

At the same time, modern constitutional law is better equipped than ever, to offer at least some safeguards and remedies. Among them, the separation of powers may be regarded as one of the most important. Thus the trend of consolidating power in the executive when national security is at stake must be counterbalanced by reserving certain core competencies for both legislatures and courts.

The role of legislative assemblies has been extensively discussed in Part II of this book. While it is not possible to depict the full richness of all assessments and proposals, three main issues seem noteworthy.

First, the legislative branch must not neglect its basic mission, that is, it must not delegate too much regulatory power to the executive. Parliaments should be able and willing to adopt specific legislation that does not leave excessive space for secret administrative measures and instruments. In particular, parliaments should take seriously the requirement (known in the continental vocabulary as '*Gesetzesvorbehalt*' or '*matières réservées à la loi*') that certain matters must be regulated by legislation and that such regulation must be complete, that is, must not leave a blank check for those who are entrusted with its implementation. As clarified by Lord Sedley, legislative assemblies must retain 'the last word' in security matters and reject temptation to delegate regulation to the executive branch.

Second, legislatures must be able to constantly scrutinize the executive implementation of all national security measures. This requires, on the one hand, elaboration of an appropriate legislative framework (in particular, proper procedures) and, on the other hand, political readiness to use the existing procedures. Access to information and planning, especially before the administration has taken any measure of basic importance, constitutes one of the basic prerequisites of that scrutiny. While some legislatures are now scrutinizing executive action more closely than they did ten years ago, there is still considerable room for improvement.

Finally, information can be effective only if addressed to the correct persons and institutions. The choice of addressees is complicated due to the very structure of parliamentary assemblies, which are composed of a large number of members supported by different categories of their staffers. On the one hand, very sensitive information simply cannot be transmitted to all members of parliament (MPs); such generosity would destroy any chance of keeping it confidential. Maintaining confidentiality requires prudence and many parliaments have addressed the need for secrecy by categorizing MPs into several levels and revealing the most secret information to carefully selected subcommittees. On the other hand, the decision on which MPs should be permitted to receive classified information cannot be left to executive discretion. In some parliaments such information is sometimes transmitted to staffers with appropriate security clearances and it is the staff's role to keep the MPs informed. This may be necessary to prevent leaks, but, as rightly explained by Kathleen Clark, this may create a situation in which parliamentary staffers (who also may have previous experience within the executive branch) become principal partners of security services.

The courts constitute another counterbalancing mechanism, as emphasized in Part I of this book. Their role deserves a more developed comment, but let me start with two general observations.

First, it is a common mission of courts and legislatures, all structural and functional differences notwithstanding, to prevent any cancerous growth of the executive in matters of national security. This requires the two branches to develop a culture of cooperation when scrutinizing executive action. On the one hand, the courts may assist legislatures directly by enforcing the primacy of the legislation (under the continental model of judicial review, this is the mission of constitutional courts as Mindia Vashakmadze noted). On the other hand, courts must have the 'last word' regarding the legality (and, hence also the validity) of any executive measure which affects individual rights and liberties.

Second, the basic mission of the courts is to protect and to enforce individual rights. Here I have a problem accepting the citizenship (territorial) criterion that is based on the assumption that rights should be reserved only (or mostly) for those lucky persons who are nationals or, at least those who reside within the national territory. That assumption must not be interpreted in an *a contrario* manner. It would lead to the conclusion that the judicial protection need not be extended to non-nationals located outside of the national territory. There may be some rational core in such an approach because the situation of such persons is generally regulated by the international law of armed conflicts and/or international humanitarian law. At the same time, however, we should not forget that those who remain outside the national territory are also human beings and some basic rights are universal. Thus, in an era when military interventions are regularly used in the interest of national security, there may be some room for reconsidering or remodeling an approach to human rights that relies on territorial criteria.

3. DOMESTIC COURTS: THE FAIR TRIAL AND STATE SECRETS

3.1

The book's discussion on the judicial branch put particular emphasis on how courts make decisions regarding detention and conviction. This is the core area for both liberty and due process. The principle that whenever there is a detention there must also be a judge and a procedure is well-rooted in our legal culture.

This principle applies to detention following conviction as well as to detention on remand when imposed within the framework of a regular criminal procedure. More complicated situations arise when so-called administrative detentions are at issue, that is, when detentions are detached from any trial and are justified only by national security imperatives. Nevertheless, considerations of national security cannot justify the existence of 'black holes' that allow individuals to be detained indefinitely without charge at the unfettered discretion of administrative authorities. This conclusion was recently confirmed by the European Court of Human Rights in the 2009 judgment of *A. v. United Kingdom*.[2] Under the European standard, any detention must involve an independent judge, a defined charge and a fair procedure.

It cannot be denied that there are circumstances in which restrictions on individual rights may become unavoidable, even when a precious right, such as personal freedom, is affected. Those circumstances are often related to considerations of national security. The balancing approach may also be applied when courts are invited to assess different types of (pre- and post-trial) detention. Nevertheless, preservation of the procedural safeguards constitutes one of the basic 'counter-balances' that serve to protect individual rights. Such safeguards must, by definition, involve courts and judges and, consequentially, must be based on the logic of a fair trial. These principles seem to be the general message underlying the book. They may be supplemented by two more detailed observations.

---

[2] *A. et al. v. United Kingdom* [2009] 49 EHRR 695.

3.2

First of all, I would like to reiterate once more that whenever there is a detention there also must be a judge. A real one, that is, a judge placed in a position that vests him or her with the necessary degree of independence of and separation from the executive branch. The notion of a 'judge' cannot be validly applied to institutions and bodies (like military commissions) that remain within the control of the executive. A 'judge' must be vested with the ultimate power to decide the legality of a detention and that power cannot be exercised without access to all relevant information. As, in the context of national security, this information must often remain secret, a question arises regarding to whom and to what extent such information can nevertheless be disclosed.

Without question judges should be trusted. But, particularly in those judicial systems where judges number in the thousands, it may be counterproductive to share sensitive secrets with all of them. Therefore, some lines must drawn within the judicial branch.

The Israeli experience (the so-called 'judicial self-management' model) is attractive for this purpose. Because the Israeli Supreme Court decides on detention of alleged terrorists, there are no obstacles to supplying the justices with all information, even the most sensitive information. As Daphne Barak-Erez remarked such a system combines competence, power and trust. Nevertheless, Shiri Krebs underlined that this model also has practical limits and it seems to be impracticable for larger countries.

An alternative may be to establish a special court that has authority over all final decisions on detention and, perhaps, also conviction. This model would take most of the burden away from the Supreme Court and it would safely provide full access to information for all judges sitting in such court. This proposal, however, is not unproblematic as Stephen Schulhofer emphasized. The historical experience of many countries shows that special courts may have difficulties maintaining the necessary distance and impartiality to ensure fair procedures. While special courts guarantee trust as well as competence, they may sometimes become too inclined to identify with the 'cause'.

A mid-way solution is to organize special courts (or 'quasi-courts') at the lower levels of jurisdiction and to subject their decisions to final review by a 'regular' court. In such a system, the appellate court's review may concentrate on the questions of law and not on the establishment of facts. Therefore, the appellate court may not always need full access to information. The U.K. example of the S.I.A.C. tribunals demonstrates the attractiveness of such a two-tiered solution. There is, however, a danger of a 'sliding-scale' developing: once we accept that a special court need not meet all the characteristics of a 'regular' court, the next step may be to relax institutional and procedural safeguards and, as was the case in some countries, introduce a system of 'state security' courts or military jurisdictions.

Proposals to protect the exclusive jurisdiction of regular courts may ensure better impartiality, but, at the same time, concentrating decisions on national security matters at the higher levels and, perhaps, within specialized divisions, may best ensure secret information remains confidential.

3.3

Second, detention requires a fair procedure and one aspect of a fair procedure is the disclosure of evidence. This problem has been discussed with a particular intensity in the contributions by Jason Mazzone and Clive Walker and it is difficult to deny that full disclosure is not compatible with considerations of national security. Thus, even in 'regular' criminal trials, some limitations may be imposed on the disclosure requirement when, on balance, they are justified.

The same approach must be applied to trials involving matters of national security. This cannot, however, affect the position of a judge because judges cannot be required to refer to evidence they have never been able to examine. While the state may be entitled to invoke a 'state-secret privilege' (as explained by Sudha Setty), it must also be aware that withholding or failing to disclose some relevant evidence may result in an acquittal.

More flexibility applies to the position of the defense lawyer. On the one hand, the equality of arms constitutes one of the basic principles of a fair trial and any disadvantage imposed on the defense would unfairly strengthen the prosecution. On the other hand, defense lawyers may abuse their position and the experience of both terrorism and organized crime demonstrates that not every attorney may be given a full security clearance.

This dilemma may be addressed in many ways. Some countries restrict access to information only to lawyers with adequate security clearance. This method may protect the security of classified information, but it may also lead to 'political' selection and may affect the defendant's right to choose his or her lawyer. In other systems (including the U.K. and Canada) there is a special advocate. A special advocate may have full access to secret evidence, but – as explained by Cian Murphy – his contacts with the defendant may be limited considerably. Finally, as highlighted by Tuomas Ojanen, some procedures provide that, once a disclosure problem arises, a judge may intervene in place of the defense. While this method may remove security concerns, the role of the judge should not change the trial into an inquisition.

4. SUPRANATIONAL JURISDICTIONS: ANOTHER FACE OF THE GLOBALIZATION PROCESS?

4.1

Globalization has, by definition, global effects and, as mentioned earlier, affects terrorist networks as well as law-enforcement responses. The role of international and supranational jurisdictions must be understood in the context of a larger trend toward globalization.

As terrorism no longer remains limited to particular territories or situations, there is no alternative but to organize a global response. Yet, it is uncertain who has the legal and practical power to do this and how this should be done. Most modern states have already developed a legal framework that allows them not only to deal with emergencies, but also to put some checks on executive power in matters of national security. Parliamentary scrutiny, constitutional courts and other independent mechanisms of review are now present in the constitutional order of most democratic states.

Such a framework is still absent on the supranational level. The globalization of anti-terrorist responses is reflected, primarily, by the intensification of contacts between administrative and security agencies. In other words, there are global and regional networks of anti-terrorist responses, but those networks lie mostly within the executive branch. What is missing now is the supranational equivalent of the legislative branch. Even within integrated regional bodies like the European Union, the position of representative bodies remains quite limited. Consequentially, who is entitled to legislate and how such legislation should be carried forward is still unclear in the international context. This task is arrogated by different executive agencies and other, less defined, regulators. As Martin Scheinin rightly emphasized, the experience with so-called 'black-lists' is a particularly alarming example of undefined regulators limiting human rights internationally.

Similar problems arise in respect of the judicial branch. On the global level, there are very few independent mechanisms of a judicial or quasi-judicial nature, the Geneva Human Rights Committee being the most developed one. On the regional level, the situation appears to be more promising, at least in Europe with its two well-established supranational jurisdictions: the European Court of Human Rights and the Court of Justice of the European Union. Both have an extensive jurisdiction and both are entitled to implement supranational human rights instruments. The Inter-American system of human rights protection follows the European pattern. Its effectiveness is, however, limited by the fact that not all countries of the region are fully integrated into the jurisdiction of the San Jose Court.

4.2

The experience of the European Court of Human Rights may be of particular importance, as evidenced by references to its decisions in many chapters of this book.

First of all, the Strasbourg system has been in operation for several decades and it has gained a particular momentum since the new permanent Court was established in 1998. The European Court, as a quasi-constitutional court, acts in the European legal space and takes an active part in the elaboration of the European public order. Due to the scope and nature of its jurisdiction, the Court is able to address all sensitive matters of human rights, including matters of national security and state responses to terrorism. In fact, the very first judgment of the European Court of Human Rights was related exactly to those matters.[3]

Second, the Strasbourg Court can and should coordinate its actions with both the European Court of Justice and the domestic supreme and/or constitutional courts. This coordination creates a type of judicial triangle that has more capacity to resist executive abuses as suggested by Lord Sedley.

At the same time, however, the Strasbourg system is not free from weak points and some of them, like legitimacy, implementation and political support, are presently producing certain difficulties.

In the early years, the legitimacy argument was mostly raised by unsuccessful applicants who claimed that the Court, being composed of judges nominated by the respective Governments, may have problems maintaining its independence and impartiality. Later on, when the case law of the Strasbourg Court became more developed, this criticism was rephrased by some Governments who challenged the Court's legitimacy to impose (and to invent) supranational human rights standards not only

[3] *Lawless v. Ireland* [1961] 1 EHRR 15.

upon the 'new democracies', but also upon the founding members of the European Convention.

Additionally, implementation puts the Court in a particularly vulnerable position because its judgments, while binding, do not have any direct annulment or cassation effect. The enforcement process remains reserved to the member states and the only supervisory mechanism is placed within a political body: the Committee of Ministers. Thus, if there is a flat refusal to comply on the part of a state (as occurred recently in the cases of prisoners' voting rights in the U.K.),[4] the Court has very limited room for reaction.

Political support is the other side of the same coin. The Court cannot fulfill its functions without an umbrella of a benevolent acceptance from the major member-states, particularly of the 'old democracies'. It is regrettable that in some of those democracies politicians are unable to resist the temptation to attack the Court and its judgments. While political criticism of the Court will probably not cause any extensive damage to the level of human rights protection in such countries as the U.K., it may result in a 'tsunami-effect' elsewhere, encouraging the less stable democracies to follow. This may lead to the destruction of the whole system.

4.3

After more than a half of century, the record of the Strasbourg Court in 'national security' matters and terrorism has become quite rich. While, on several occasions, the Court displayed visible restraint (as in the cases of *Lawless*,[5] *Brogan*,[6] *Banković*,[7] *Behrami and Saramati*[8]), its recent jurisprudence demonstrates concern about the nature and impact of the executive action.

The present 'terrorism' case-law of the European Court of Human Rights is not mere rubber-stamping business. The Court has no hesitations in reminding, even the oldest democracies, that national security considerations cannot result in a blank check to restrict human rights. A

---

4 *Hirst v. United Kingdom*, application no. 74025/01, judgment of 5 October 2005.

5 See *supra* note 3.

6 *Brogan et al. v. United Kingdom* [1988] 11 EHRR 117.

7 *Banković et al. v. Belgium et al.*, application no. 52207/99, decision of 12 December 2001.

8 *Behrami et al. v. France* and *Saramati v. France et al.*, application nos. 71412/01, 78166/01, judgment of 2 May 2007.

good illustration of that trend can be found in reactions of the Strasbourg Court to some recent decisions taken by the U.K. authorities. In many judgments, including *Gillan and Quinton*,[9] *A. et al.*,[10] *Al-Saadoon and Mufhdi*,[11] *Al-Jedda*,[12] *Al-Skeini et al.*[13] and *Othman (Abu Quatada)*,[14] the Court found that the U.K. had violated the Convention. These decisions elaborated new standards in respect of detention and extradition of aliens and also in respect of the extraterritorial applicability of the Convention.

In brief, the European Court of Human Rights, and other supranational jurisdictions, are well placed to address the globalization challenges and to vindicate human rights standards in cases involving national security.

Three general conclusions may be drawn at the closure of this book:

1. Constitutional law of today is better-than-ever prepared to address the challenge of national security, including issues relating to how to handle secret information and intelligence. We, as scholars and judges, have an immense potential to contribute to developing checks on secret security measures taken within the realm of the executive branch.
2. The task of constitutional law remains, however, quite hazardous. It must address a situation that is genuinely dangerous for the world order. We cannot ignore the fact that there is a wide public support for secret security measures of different kinds.
3. Constitutional aspects of secrecy must be analyzed within the more general context of politics and economy. This not an optimistic context[15] and I am afraid that it does not make our future as bright as we would like it to be.

---

[9] *Gillan & Quinton v. United Kingdom*, application no. 4158/05, judgment of 12 January 2010.

[10] See *supra* note 2.

[11] *Al-Saadoon and Mufhdi v. United Kingdom*, application no. 61498/08, judgment of 2 March 2010.

[12] *Al-Jedda v. United Kingdom*, application no. 27021/08, judgment of 7 July 2011.

[13] *Al-Skeini v. United Kingdom*, application no. 55721/07, judgment of 7 July 2011.

[14] *Othman (Abu Qatada) v. United Kingdom*, application no. 8139/09, judgment of 17 January 2012.

[15] Let me just refer to BRUCE ACKERMAN, THE DECLINE AND FALL OF THE AMERICAN REPUBLIC (2010).

Index